NIEUWE ZIJDE
Pages 70–85

OUDE ZIJDE
Pages 56–69

Nieuwe Zijde

Oude Zijde

Plantage

Eastern Canal Ring

D0552816

EASTERN CANAL RING
Page 114–123

PLANTAGE
Pages 138–147

0 metres   500

0 yards   500

EYEWITNESS TRAVEL

AMSTERDAM

EYEWITNESS TRAVEL

AMSTERDAM

MAIN CONTRIBUTORS:
ROBIN PASCOE
CHRISTOPHER CATLING

DK

LONDON, NEW YORK,
MELBOURNE, MUNICH AND DELHI
www.dk.com

PROJECT EDITOR Heather Jones
ART EDITOR Vanessa Hamilton
EDITORS Peter Adams, Sasha Heseltine,
Fiona Morgan, Alice Peebles, Nichola Tyrrell
DESIGNERS Emma Hutton, Erika Lang Malcolm Parchment

CONTRIBUTORS
Paul Andrews, Hedda Archbold, Marlene Edmunds,
Pip Farquharson, Adam Hopkins, Fred Mawer, Alison Melvin,
Kim Renfrew, Catherine Stebbings, Richard Widdows

PHOTOGRAPHERS
Max Alexander, Rupert Horrox, Kim Sayer

ILLUSTRATORS
Nick Gibbard, Maltings Partnership,
Derrick Stone, Martin Woodward

Reproduced by Colourscan, Singapore
Printed and bound in China
by L. Rex Printing Company Limited

First published in Great Britain in 1995
by Dorling Kindersley Limited
80 Strand, London WC2R 0RL

Reprinted with revisions 1996, 1997, 1999, 2000, 2001,
2002, 2003, 2004, 2005, 2006, 2007

Copyright 1995, 2007 © Dorling Kindersley Limited, London
A Penguin Company

ISBN: 978 1 4053 1696 5

FLOORS ARE REFERRED TO THROUGHOUT IN ACCORDANCE WITH EUROPEAN
USAGE; IE THE "FIRST FLOOR" IS THE FLOOR ABOVE GROUND LEVEL.

*Front cover main image: Bridge lit up at night along Herengracht,
at the corner of Blauwburgwal*

**The information in this
Dorling Kindersley Travel Guide is checked regularly.**
Every effort has been made to ensure that this book is as up-to-date
as possible at the time of going to press. Some details, however, such
as telephone numbers, opening hours, prices, gallery hanging
arrangements and travel information are liable to change. The
publishers cannot accept responsibility for any consequences arising
from the use of this book, nor for any material on third party
websites, and cannot guarantee that any website address in this book
will be a suitable source of travel information. We value the views
and suggestions of our readers very highly. Please write to: Publisher,
DK Eyewitness Travel Guides, Dorling Kindersley,
80 Strand, London WC2R 0RL, Great Britain.

◁ **Boats lining Prinsengracht, with Westerkerk in the background**

CONTENTS

Model boat at Scheepvaart Museum

INTRODUCING
AMSTERDAM

AMSTERDAM AREA
BY AREA

Traditional lift bridge

Children in Dutch costume outside a church in the Zuiderzee Museum

Café terrace in Artis zoo

Façade of the Rijksmuseum

Wheels of Gouda cheese

Dutch Renaissance canal house and details of cornices and gables

HOW TO USE THIS GUIDE

This guide helps you get the most from your stay in Amsterdam. It provides expert recommendations as well as detailed practical information. *Introducing Amsterdam* maps the city and sets it in its historical and cultural context. *Amsterdam Area by Area* describes the important sights, with maps, pictures and illustrations. *Further Afield* looks at sights outside the city centre and *Beyond Amsterdam* explores other places near Amsterdam. Suggestions on food, drink, where to stay and what to do are made in *Travellers' Needs*, and *Survival Guide* has tips on everything from travel to Dutch telephones.

AMSTERDAM AREA BY AREA

The centre of the city has been divided into seven sightseeing areas. Each area has its own chapter, which opens with a list of the sights described. All the sights are numbered and plotted on an *Area Map*. The detailed information for each sight is presented in numerical order, making it easy to locate within the chapter.

Sights at a Glance lists the chapter's sights by category: Churches, Museums and Galleries, Historic Buildings, Streets and Canals.

Each area of central Amsterdam has colour-coded thumb tabs.

A locator map shows where you are in relation to other areas of the city centre.

1 Area Map
For easy reference, the sights are numbered and located on a map. The sights are also shown on the Amsterdam Street Finder on pages 280–87.

2 Street-by-Street Map
This gives a bird's-eye view of the heart of each sightseeing area.

A suggested route for a walk covers the more interesting streets in the area.

Stars indicate the sights that no visitor should miss.

3 Detailed information on each sight
All the sights in Amsterdam are described individually. Addresses and practical information are provided. The key to the symbols used in the information block is shown on the back flap.

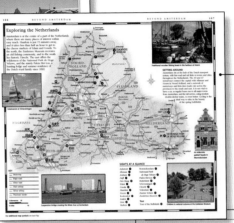

4 Introduction to Beyond Amsterdam

Beyond Amsterdam has its own introduction, which provides an overview of the history and character of the region around Amsterdam and outlines what the region has to offer the visitor today. The area covered by this section is highlighted on the map of the Netherlands shown on page 165. It covers important cities, such as Den Haag, as well as attractive towns and places of interest in the Dutch

5 Regional Map

This gives an illustrated overview of the whole region. All the sights covered in this section are numbered, and the network of major roads is marked. There are also useful tips on getting around the region by bus and train.

6 Detailed information on each sight

All the important cities, towns and other places to visit are described individually. They are listed in order, following the numbering given on the Regional Map. Within each town or city, there is detailed information on important buildings and other sights.

Stars indicate the best features and works of art.

The Visitors' Checklist

provides a summary of the practical information you will need to plan your visit.

7 The top sights

These are given two or more full pages. Historic buildings are dissected to reveal their interiors; museums and galleries have colour-coded floorplans to help you locate the most interesting exhibits.

INTRODUCING AMSTERDAM

FOUR GREAT DAYS IN AMSTERDAM

Despite its compact size, Amsterdam is a city with many different aspects and offers a range of attractions to suit all tastes and budgets. The city is home to some of the world's finest art galleries, there are bustling markets for those in search of street life and for kids, there is

Anne Frank statue, Westerkerk

also a great choice of things to see and do. Here are four themed days out to explore four different sides of the city. Many of the places have cross-references so you can look up more details and tailor the days to suit you. Price guides include transport, meals and admission charges.

Rembrandt's studio in the Rembrandthuis

TWO GREAT ARTISTS

• **At home with Rembrandt**
• **Lunch by the canal**
• **Van Gogh's greatest works**

TWO ADULTS allow at least 115

Morning

Of all the great painters that Amsterdam claims as its own, two stand head and shoulders above the rest: Rembrandt van Rijn and Vincent van Gogh. Rembrandt's home from 1639 to 1658 is now the **Museum Het Rembrandthuis** *(see pp62–3)* and has been restored to look as it might have when he lived here, at the height of his wealth and fame. The atmosphere is such that one can clearly imagine the great artist and his family roaming these rooms. The museum houses an exhibition of Rembrandt's etchings and sketches, as well as paintings by his contemporaries, notably his teacher Pieter Lastman.

Equally interesting is the recreation of the artist's studio, complete with chalks, charcoal, easels and brushes, and his wonderful "cabinet of curiosities" – a room cluttered with statues, stuffed birds and small beasts, arms and armour, all of which Rembrandt would have used as props in his portraits and still-lives. A great spot for lunch after the Rembranthuis is Dantzig, the café of the **Muziektheater** *(see p248)*, just a minute's walk away. In summer its sunny terrace has a fine view of the Amstel, while in winter there is a cosy indoor restaurant.

Afternoon

The **Van Gogh Museum** *(see pp134–5)* houses the world's largest collection of the Dutch painter's work, with almost 800 paintings and drawings along with the painter's own collection of glorious Japanese prints and an array of paintings by his contemporaries. It is a dazzling collection, and you should allow two to three hours to take it in at leisure.

HIDDEN HISTORIES

• **Explore life in hiding**
• **A vanished community**
• **Living history**
• **Secret churches**

TWO ADULTS allow at least 86

Morning

The **Anne Frank Huis** *(see pp90–91)* receives up to 1,000 visitors a day, so try to get there early. In a tiny secret apartment above Otto Frank's warehouse, the Jewish Frank and van Pels families hid from the Nazis from 1942 until 1944, when they were betrayed and deported to concentration camps. The 13-year-old Anne Frank began recording life in hiding in her diary in July 1942 and it was published in 1947, two years after her death in Bergen-Belsen. There is a touching statue of Anne outside the **Westerkerk** *(see p90)*. Completed in 1631, its tower is the tallest in the city at 85 m (278 ft) and the climb to the top offers a breathtaking view. The

View of Prinsengracht from the tower of the Westerkerk

◁ **The Dutch Fleet of the India Company, 1675, by Ludolf Backhuysen**

Waterlooplein area was the heart of a Jewish community who were drawn to the city in the 17th century because of its tolerance. The **Joods Historisch Museum** *(see pp64–5)* is housed in four former synagogues built in the 17th and 18th centuries and contains a collection of religious artifacts as well as documents relating to the Holocaust. The museum has a fine restaurant serving both Dutch and Jewish food.

Afternoon

A short walk away, the huge **Portugees-Israelitische Synagogue** *(see p66)*, with its candle-lit interiors, is still in use by the city's Sephardic Jews. Protestant Amsterdam in the 17th century, however, was less tolerant of Catholic worship. The **Museum Amstelkring** *(see pp84–5)* is a perfectly restored example of the "clandestine" churches built during this time.

A FAMILY DAY

- **Messing about in boats**
- **Ice cream, jugglers and fire-eaters**
- **Hi-tech hands-on fun**

FAMILY OF FOUR allow at least 130

Morning

Parental pedal-power provides the impetus for the first part of this day out. Amsterdam's **canal bikes** *(see p277)* are four-seater pedal boats that move at a gentle pace, passing old canalside houses, houseboats and nesting waterfowl. They can be rented in winter too, but for families this is really a summer activity. A good option is to pick up your vessel at the **Westerkerk** mooring and paddle around the picturesque Keizers-gracht, then drop it off at Leidsestraat. This should take no more than an hour. Then stroll down to **Leidseplein** *(see p108)* with its many outdoor cafés and street entertainers for well earned coffee and ice cream.

Hands-on exhibits at the Nemo Science Center Amsterdam

Afternoon

Take a tram to the **Nemo Science Center Amsterdam** *(see p150)*. This spectacular building looks like a giant futuristic ship and is full of hands-on, state-of-the-art interactive exhibits for children of all ages. Allow at least a couple of hours to explore the possibilities of the themed technology, energy, science and humanity zones before heading for the centre's pleasant waterside terrace café-restaurant.

COLOURFUL MARKETS

- **Antiques and collectables**
- **Ethnic eating**
- **Vibrant street life**
- **Legendary nightlife**

TWO ADULTS allow at least 50

Morning

You can buy just about anything in Amsterdam's markets. The **Waterlooplein** *(see p63)* open-air market still has the definite feel of the hippie era, with stalls selling tie-dyed clothing, exotic statuettes, vintage leather coats, army-surplus equipment and ceramics. Dive further into this open-air labyrinth to find 19th- and 20th-century collectables, from classic rock albums to psychedelic posters, pipes and cigarette holders, china, glassware, and more. A short walk and tram ride from Waterlooplein, the **Albert**

Cuypmarkt *(see p122)* is the heart and soul of de Pijp, the most cosmopolitan part of Amsterdam. It is an ideal place for lunch – there are many ethnic restaurants on and around Albert Cuyp-straat, including Moroccan, Surinamese and Turkish.

Afternoon

There are more than 100 shops and 300 street-stalls along Albert Cuypstraat, selling everything from exotic fruit and spices to Dutch cheese, chocolates, sausage and seafood, flowers, clothes and house-hold goods. This is authentic Amsterdam street life at its best. You could easily spend an afternoon here, before taking a 10-minute stroll back to the **Leidseplein** *(see p108)* and a night out at one of its top night-time venues.

Eclectic stalls lining the length of the Albert Cuypmarket

Putting Amsterdam on the Map

Although the Netherlands' seat of government is at
Den Haag, Amsterdam is the nominal capital. It is
the country's largest city, with a population of almost
750,000, and the most visited, receiving over 7.5 million
foreign visitors a year. It stands on precariously low-lying
ground at the confluence of the Amstel and IJ rivers near
the IJsselmeer and, like much of the Netherlands, would
flood frequently but for land reclamation and sea defences.
This position places Amsterdam at the heart of the Randstad, a term used to describe the crescent-shaped conur-
bation covering much of the provinces of Noord Holland,
Zuid Holland and Utrecht, and encompassing the cities
of Utrecht, Rotterdam, Den Haag, Leiden and Haarlem.

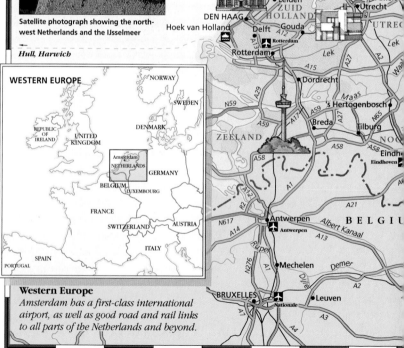

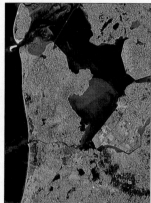

**Satellite photograph showing the north-
west Netherlands and the IJsselmeer**

Hull, Harwich

WESTERN EUROPE

Western Europe
*Amsterdam has a first-class international
airport, as well as good road and rail links
to all parts of the Netherlands and beyond.*

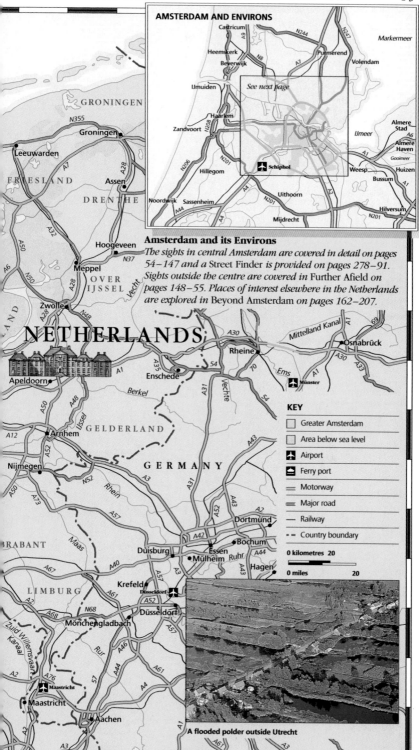

AMSTERDAM AND ENVIRONS

Castricum

N244

N247

Markermeer

Heemskerk

N8

A7

Purmerend

Volendam

Beverwijk

IJmuiden

See next page

Almere
Stad

A6

Haarlem

Zandvoort

N208

IJmeer

Almere
Haven

Gooimeer

A1

N206

N201

Weesp

Huizen

Schiphol

Bussum

A1

Hillegom

Noordwijk

Sassenheim

N201

Uithoorn

Hilversum

A44

Mijdrecht

N201

GRONINGEN

N355

Groningen

Leeuwarden

A7

A28

FRIESLAND

Assen

DRENTHE

A32

Hoogeveen

N37

A6

Meppel

OVER

A50

A28

IJSSEL

Vecht

Zwolle

N48

N50

Amsterdam and its Environs

*The sights in central Amsterdam are covered in detail on pages
54–147 and a* Street Finder *is provided on pages 278–91.
Sights outside the centre are covered in* Further Afield *on
pages 148–55. Places of interest elsewhere in the Netherlands
are explored in* Beyond Amsterdam *on pages 162–207.*

NETHERLANDS

A30

Mittelland Kanal

A1

69

Rheine

Osnabrück

Apeldoorn

A1

A35

54

70

Ems

A30

A33

Enschede

A31

Münster

Berkel

Vechte

54

A50

A48

IJssel

A12

A52

Arnhem

GELDERLAND

A43

Nijmegen

N52

GERMANY

A3

A31

A52

A43

A2

A50

A73

A57

Rhein

Dortmund

A42

KEY

Greater Amsterdam

Area below sea level

✈ Airport

⚓ Ferry port

═══ Motorway

▬▬ Major road

── Railway

- - Country boundary

0 kilometres 20

0 miles 20

BRABANT

Maas

Duisburg

Essen

A44

Bochum

A40

A3

Mülheim

Ruhr

Hagen

A67

A57

Krefeld

A43

LIMBURG

A61

Düsseldorf

A2

N68

A52

Zuid Willemsvaart

Mönchengladbach

Düsseldorf

A57

Rur

A46

A61

A2

A76

A44

57

Maastricht

A4

Maastricht

Aachen

A2

A3

A flooded polder outside Utrecht

Greater Amsterdam

Amsterdam retained its characteristic horseshoe shape within the Singelgracht until well into the 19th century. This pattern is still clearly visible in the network of streets and canals in the city centre. Since then the city has expanded dramatically in all directions. The whole of Greater Amsterdam enjoys first-class public transport *(see Transport Map on inside back cover).*

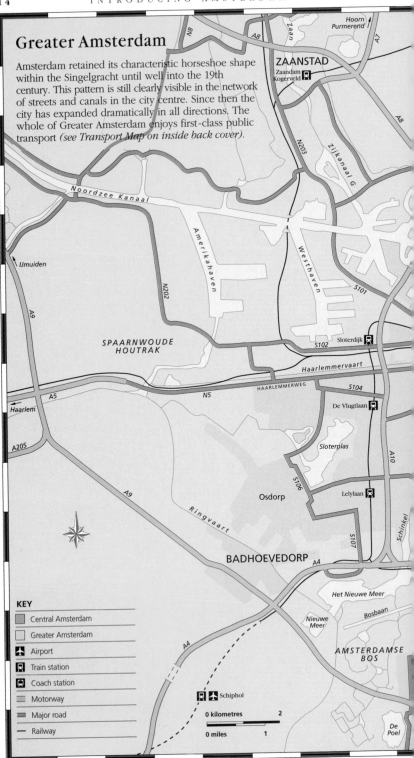

KEY

	Central Amsterdam
	Greater Amsterdam
	Airport
	Train station
	Coach station
	Motorway
	Major road
	Railway

ZAANSTAD
Zaandam
Kogerveld

Hoorn
Purmerend

Noordzee Kanaal

Amerikahaven

Westhaven

IJmuiden

SPAARNWOUDE
HOUTRAK

Sloterdijk

Haarlemmervaart

HAARLEMMERWEG

De Vlugtlaan

Haarlem

Sloterplas

Osdorp

Lelylaan

BADHOEVEDORP

Het Nieuwe Meer

Bosbaan

Nieuwe
Meer

AMSTERDAMSE
BOS

Schiphol

0 kilometres　　　2

0 miles　　1

De
Poel

Central Amsterdam

This guide divides central Amsterdam into seven distinct areas, each of which has its own chapter. Most city sights are contained in these areas. The Oude Zijde and Nieuwe Zijde make up the two halves of medieval Amsterdam,

A street musician on Waterlooplein

while the Museum Quarter was developed in the 19th century and has the three most important national museums. In between lies the Canal Ring, which retains many fine buildings from Amsterdam's Golden Age, while the Plantage *(see pp138–47)*, once an area of green space outside the city, is today best known for the zoological and botanical gardens.

Houses along the Singel
The Singel was the first concentric canal to be cut in Amsterdam. It forms the border between the medieval centre and the newer Western and Central Canal Rings (see pp86–113).

Vondelpark
This attractive park in the Museum Quarter (see pp124–37) is a good place to relax after a visit to one of Amsterdam's museums.

| 0 metres | 500 |
| 0 yards | 500 |

**Spires of Nieuwe Kerk
and the Magna Plaza**
*The Nieuwe Zijde's sky-
line* (see pp70–85) *is
pierced by the Neo-Gothic
spire of Magna Plaza
(the former Postkantoor),
the steeples of the Nieuwe
Kerk and the statues on
the Koninklijk Paleis.*

**House on the
Oudezijds Voorburgwal**
*This attractive residential canal,
which now runs through the
Red Light District, was first cut in
front of the ramparts protecting
the Oude Zijde* (see pp56–69).

Flowers at the Bloemenmarkt
*A fragrant, floating flower market,
the Bloemenmarkt is situated beside
the Munttoren on the Singel in the
Eastern Canal Ring* (see pp114–23).

KEY

▨	Major sight
🚉	Train station
M	Metro
P	Parking
ℹ	Tourist information
🚓	Police station
✝	Church
✡	Synagogue
C	Mosque

THE HISTORY OF AMSTERDAM

Amsterdam, the greatest planned city of northern Europe, is today one in which beauty and serenity co-exist happily with a slightly seamy underside. Both parts of this split personality continue to draw visitors. Most of the racier aspects of Amsterdam spring directly from the city's long tradition of religious and political tolerance. The notion of individual freedom of conscience was fought for, long and hard, during the struggles against Spanish domination in the 16th century. This belief stands firm today, with the caveat that no-one should be harmed by the actions of others – a factor that sparked off the riots involving squatters in the 1970s.

Amsterdam's coat of arms on the Munttoren

The city was founded as a small fishing village in an improbable position on marsh at the mouth of the Amstel river. The waters around the village were controlled by a system of dykes and polders, and the young township expanded prodigiously to become the chief trading city of northern Europe, and ultimately, in the 17th century, the centre of a massive empire stretching across the world. The construction of the canals and gabled houses in the 16th and 17th centuries coincided with a period of fine domestic architecture. The result is a city centre of unusually consistent visual beauty. By the 18th century, Amsterdam was a major financial centre, but internal unrest and restrictions imposed under Napoleonic rule led to a decline in her fortunes.

The city quietly slipped into a period of obscurity, and industrialization came late. In the 20th century, however, the city entered the mainstream again. Now, the start of a new millennium has marked a period of urban growth for Amsterdam: ambitious architectural projects have given a new lease of life to former derelict areas such as the Eastern Docklands, while Zuidas, the area south of the ring road, is fast becoming a major business hub, complemented by top-notch cultural facilities.

Plan of Amsterdam (c. 1725) showing the Grachtengordel and Plantage (*see pp138–47*)

◁ *The Maid of Amsterdam Receiving the Homage of her People (c. 1685) by Gérard de Lairesse*

The Origins of Amsterdam

Amsterdam emerged from the mists of the Low Countries in about 1200, on a watery site at the mouth of the Amstel river. It was a settlement of fisherfolk before turning to trade. The first permanent dwellings were built on terps,

Windmills drained the land

man-made mounds high enough to provide protection from flood water. As the settlement grew, it was fashioned by dynastic and religious combat, with feudal struggles between the Lords van Amstel and the counts of Holland, who had the backing of the all-powerful bishops of Utrecht *(see p202)*. This rivalry continued into the next century.

EXTENT OF THE CITY

1100	Today

Farming on polders outside the village walls

Dam

Cooking Pot
Sturdy earthenware pots were used for cooking communal meals over an open fire in the kitchen area of 13th-century houses.

Wooden defence walls

Lord Gijsbrecht
The 19th-century etching shows Gijsbrecht van Amstel IV being marched into Utrecht as a prisoner by Guy of Hainaut, brother of the Count of Holland, in 1298.

Livestock grazed on reclaimed land called polder.

THE VILLAGE OF AMSTERDAM IN 1300

This medieval artist's impression shows the first tiny settlement on polders along the Damrak. The village was protected by wooden walls, and it is thought that the castle of the Van Amstels may have been located in the area around today's Dam square *(see pp72–3)*.

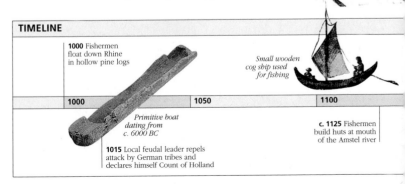

TIMELINE

1000 Fishermen float down Rhine in hollow pine logs

Small wooden cog ship used for fishing

1000	1050	1100

Primitive boat dating from c. 6000 BC

1015 Local feudal leader repels attack by German tribes and declares himself Count of Holland

c. 1125 Fishermen build huts at mouth of the Amstel river

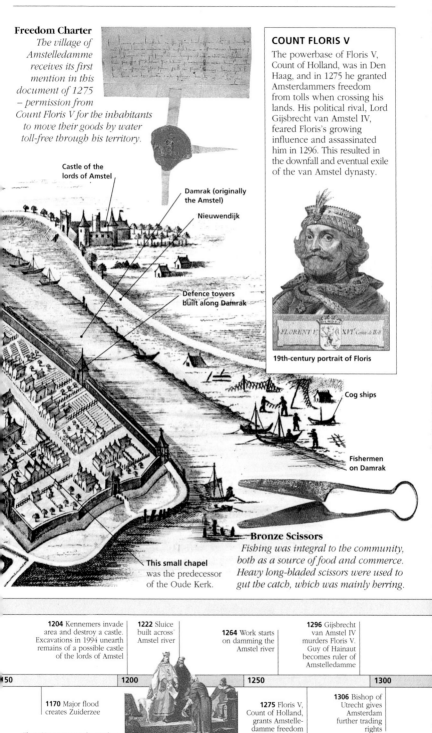

Freedom Charter
The village of Amstelledamme receives its first mention in this document of 1275 – permission from Count Floris V for the inhabitants to move their goods by water toll-free through his territory.

Castle of the lords of Amstel

Damrak (originally the Amstel)

Nieuwendijk

Defence towers built along Damrak

COUNT FLORIS V

The powerbase of Floris V, Count of Holland, was in Den Haag, and in 1275 he granted Amsterdammers freedom from tolls when crossing his lands. His political rival, Lord Gijsbrecht van Amstel IV, feared Floris's growing influence and assassinated him in 1296. This resulted in the downfall and eventual exile of the van Amstel dynasty.

FLORENT V XVI Comte de Holl

19th-century portrait of Floris

Cog ships

Fishermen on Damrak

Bronze Scissors
Fishing was integral to the community, both as a source of food and commerce. Heavy long-bladed scissors were used to gut the catch, which was mainly herring.

This small chapel was the predecessor of the Oude Kerk.

1204 Kennemers invade area and destroy a castle. Excavations in 1994 unearth remains of a possible castle of the lords of Amstel

1222 Sluice built across Amstel river

1264 Work starts on damming the Amstel river

1296 Gijsbrecht van Amstel IV murders Floris V. Guy of Hainaut becomes ruler of Amstelledamme

50 | 1200 | 1250 | 1300

1170 Major flood creates Zuiderzee

Floris V presents trade privilege to village of Amstelledamme

1275 Floris V, Count of Holland, grants Amstelledamme freedom from tolls

1306 Bishop of Utrecht gives Amsterdam further trading rights

Medieval Amsterdam

The little town at the mouth of the Amstel fortified itself against both its enemies and the surrounding water. Amsterdam grew rich quickly after the discovery of a method of curing herring in 1385, which preserved the fish longer, enabling it to be exported. The town became a port for handling beer from Hamburg. Elaborate waterside houses were used to service the trade. The Low Countries were under the rule of the Dukes of Burgundy, and control passed by marriage to the Austrian Habsburgs.

Medieval leather boot (c. 1500)

EXTENT OF THE CITY

☐ 1300   ☐ Today

Miracle of Amsterdam
This tapestry cushion depicts a miraculous event. A dying man was given the Sacrament which he regurgitated. Thrown on the fire, the Host would not burn.

CANALSIDE HOUSE

Early canal houses were simple structures, built of wood with a thatched roof. From a single-storey design with the front and back on different levels, the layouts grew more complex. At the front, side rooms became separated off from the main room, and the back house was similarly divided up. The family slept on the first floor and goods were stored under the roof.

The wooden façades had simple spout gables (*see pp96–7*).

Flour, beer and other foodstuffs were stored under the sloping roof.

Philip of Burgundy and Isabella of Portugal
Philip was the ruler of the Low Countries after 1419. He married Isabella of Portugal in 1430.

Timber structure

TIMELINE

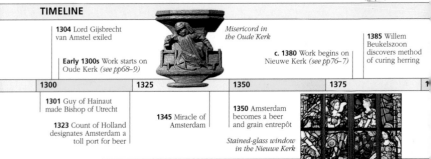

1304 Lord Gijsbrecht van Amstel exiled

Early 1300s Work starts on Oude Kerk (*see pp68–9*)

Misericord in the Oude Kerk

c. 1380 Work begins on Nieuwe Kerk (*see pp76–7*)

1385 Willem Beukelszoon discovers method of curing herring

| 1300 | 1325 | 1350 | 1375 | |

1301 Guy of Hainaut made Bishop of Utrecht

1323 Count of Holland designates Amsterdam a toll port for beer

1345 Miracle of Amsterdam

1350 Amsterdam becomes a beer and grain entrepôt

Stained-glass window in the Nieuwe Kerk

Making Beer

The brewing industry expanded after 1323, when the Count of Holland permitted Amsterdam to become a toll port for beer. Hops were introduced early in the century.

Thatched roof

The Great Fire of 1452

After Amsterdam's second devastating blaze, which destroyed the Nieuwe Kerk, legislation was passed preventing the use of wood as a building material.

Access to canal at rear

Stone side walls

Wooden support piles were driven into the first stable layer of sand.

Warehouse space

Amsterdam's Seal

The seal shows the diagonal crosses of St Andrew, the coat of arms of the Habsburgs and the cog ship that brought wealth through trade.

WHERE TO SEE MEDIEVAL AMSTERDAM

Few buildings remain from this period, as fire destroyed two-thirds of the city. The Oude Kerk *(see pp68–9)* dates from the early 14th century and the Nieuwe Kerk *(pp76–7)* from 1380. The Agnieten-kapel *(p61)* was built in 1470 and is one of very few Gothic chapels to survive the Alter-ation of 1578 *(pp24–5)*.

The Waag (p60)
Built in 1488, this was originally a gateway in the city wall.

No. 34 Begijnhof (p75)
The oldest wooden house in the city, it dates from about 1420.

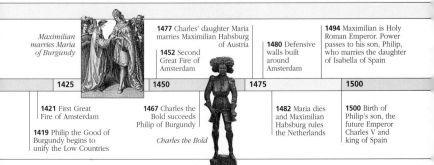

Maximilian marries Maria of Burgundy

1477 Charles' daughter Maria marries Maximilian Habsburg of Austria

1452 Second Great Fire of Amsterdam

1480 Defensive walls built around Amsterdam

1494 Maximilian is Holy Roman Emperor. Power passes to his son, Philip, who marries the daughter of Isabella of Spain

1425	1450	1475	1500

1421 First Great Fire of Amsterdam

1419 Philip the Good of Burgundy begins to unify the Low Countries

1467 Charles the Bold succeeds Philip of Burgundy

Charles the Bold

1482 Maria dies and Maximilian Habsburg rules the Netherlands

1500 Birth of Philip's son, the future Emperor Charles V and king of Spain

The Age of Intolerance

By 1500, Amsterdam had outpaced rivals to become the main power in the province of Holland. Trade in the Baltic provided wealth and the city grew rapidly. Spain's Habsburg rulers tried to halt the Protestant Reformation sweeping northern Europe. Dutch resistance to Philip II of Spain resulted in 80 years of civil war and religious strife. Amsterdam sided with Spain but switched loyalties in 1578 – an event known as the Alteration – to become the fiercely Protestant capital of an infant Dutch Republic.

EXTENT OF THE CITY

	1500		Today

Anabaptists' Uprising *(1535)*
An extremist Protestant cult of Anabaptists seized the Stadhuis. Many were executed after eviction.

Nieuwe Kerk **(1395)**

Rokin

Dam square

Oudezijds Voorburgwal

Oude Kerk **(1306)**

PERSPECTIVE OF AMSTERDAM

This painted woodcut is a bird's-eye view of Amsterdam by Cornelis Anthonisz (1538). It is a critically important, detailed and precise map, heralding a centuries-long tradition of world-class map making in the city *(see p146)*.

Schreiers-toren

William of Orange
William, portrayed in 1555 by Anthonius Mor, led the Dutch against the Spanish until his assassination in Delft (see p195).

Much of the farmland in the Netherlands is below sea level.

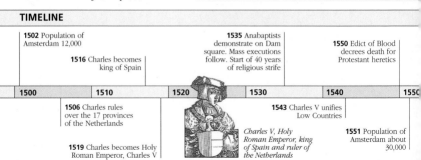

TIMELINE

1502 Population of Amsterdam 12,000		**1535** Anabaptists demonstrate on Dam square. Mass executions follow. Start of 40 years of religious strife	**1550** Edict of Blood decrees death for Protestant heretics
	1516 Charles becomes king of Spain		

| **1500** | **1510** | **1520** | **1530** | **1540** | **1550** |

1506 Charles rules over the 17 provinces of the Netherlands		**1543** Charles V unifies Low Countries	
		Charles V, Holy Roman Emperor, king of Spain and ruler of the Netherlands	**1551** Population of Amsterdam about 30,000
1519 Charles becomes Holy Roman Emperor, Charles V			

The Guild of St George *(1533)*
Guilds set up to keep order in the growing city later formed the Civic Guard (see pp82–3). Map-maker Cornelis Anthonisz painted this guild at supper.

Nieuwezijds Voorburgwal

Singel

Damrak

Wind-powered pump

Sea

WHERE TO SEE 16TH-CENTURY AMSTERDAM

Few buildings of early 16th-century provenance remain, but No. 1 Zeedijk *(see p67)* was built mid-century as a hostel for sailors. The Civic Guards' Gallery at the Amsterdams Historisch Museum *(pp80–83)* contains a series of splendid group portraits of 16th-century militia companies and guilds.

Montelbaanstoren
The lower section of the tower was built in 1512 (see p66), forming part of the city defences.

The Third Expedition
Gerrit de Veer's copper engraving (1597) shows Willem Barentsz on his search for a passage to the Arctic Sea.

Silver Drinking Horn
As the guilds grew richer, ceremony played a larger part in their lives. This ornate drinking horn shows St George defending the hapless maiden against the dragon.

Draining the Polders
"Gangs" of windmills were built to drain the low-lying land. Each mill scooped water up, stage by stage, until it drained away into the sea (see p173).

Duke of Alva

1555 Charles V abdicates. Philip II of Spain succeeds

1567 Duke of Alva introduces heavy taxation in Amsterdam

1578 Calvinists take civil power and expel Catholics from Amsterdam in the Alteration

1581 Philip II becomes king of Portugal

1596–7 Explorer Willem Barents finds route to Arctic Sea

1598 Philip II dies, unable to subdue Dutch Protestants

1560	1570	1580	1590	1600

1566 Calvinist iconosts demolish religious art in *Beeldenstorm*

1568 Beginning of Dutch Revolt under Protestant William of Orange

1579 Northern provinces sign Union of Utrecht

1584 William of Orange assassinated in Delft

1580 Spain absorbs Portugal, and Dutch establish new trade routes to the east

William was shot on the staircase of his headquarters in Delft in 1584 (see p195).

The Golden Age of Amsterdam

The 17th century was truly a Golden Age for Amsterdam. The population soared; three great canals, bordered by splendid houses, were built in a triple ring round the city; and scores of painters and architects were at work. Fortunes were made and lost, and this early capitalism produced paupers who were cared for by charitable institutions – a radical idea for the time. In 1648, an uneasy peace was formalized with Catholic Spain, causing tension between Amsterdam's Calvinist burgomasters and the less religious House of Orange, dominant elsewhere in the country.

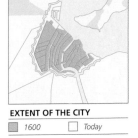

EXTENT OF THE CITY

▩ 1600   ☐ Today

Livestock and grain trading

Self-Portrait as the Apostle Paul *(1661) Rembrandt (see p62) was one of many artists working in Amsterdam in the mid-17th century.*

Nieuwe Kerk (1395)

The new Stadhuis (now the Koninklijk Paleis) was being constructed behind wooden scaffolding.

The Love Letter *(1666) Genre painting (see p194), such as this calm domestic interior by Jan Vermeer, became popular as society grew more sophisticated.*

DAM SQUARE IN 1656
Money poured into Amsterdam at this time of civic expansion. Jan Lingelbach (c. 1624–74) painted Dam square as a busy, thriving and cosmopolitan market, full of traders and wealthy merchants.

Delft Tiles
Delicate flower paintings were popular themes on 17th-century Delft tiles (see p195), used as decoration in wealthy households.

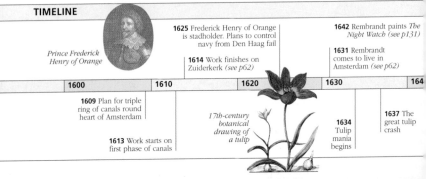

TIMELINE

Prince Frederick Henry of Orange

1625 Frederick Henry of Orange is stadholder. Plans to control navy from Den Haag fail

1642 Rembrandt paints *The Night Watch (see p131)*

1614 Work finishes on Zuiderkerk *(see p62)*

1631 Rembrandt comes to live in Amsterdam *(see p62)*

1600	1610	1620	1630	164

1609 Plan for triple ring of canals round heart of Amsterdam

17th-century botanical drawing of a tulip

1634 Tulip mania begins

1637 The great tulip crash

1613 Work starts on first phase of canals

Flora's Bandwagon *(1636)*
Many allegories were painted during "tulip mania". This satirical oil by HG Pot symbolizes the idiocy of investors who paid for rare bulbs with their weight in gold, forcing prices up until the market collapsed.

Commodities weighed at the Waag (see p60)

Ships sailing up the Damrak

Cargo unloaded by cranes **Turkish traders**

Giving the Bread
The painting by Willem van Valckert shows the needy receiving alms. A rudimentary welfare system was introduced in the 1640s.

WHERE TO SEE 17TH-CENTURY AMSTERDAM

Many public buildings sprang up as Amsterdam grew more wealthy. The Westerkerk *(see p90)* was designed by Hendrick de Keyser in 1620, the Luthers Kerk *(p78)* by Adriaan Dortsman in 1671. Elias Bouman built the Portugese Synagoge *(p66)* in 1675 for members of the immigrant Sephardic Jewish community *(p64)*.

Apollo *(c. 1648)*
Artus Quellien's statue is in the South Gallery of the Koninklijk Paleis (see p74).

Rembrandthuis *(1606)*
Jacob van Campen added the pediment in 1633 (see p66).

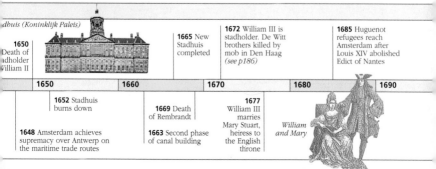

dhuis (Koninklijk Paleis)

1650 Death of stadholder William II

1652 Stadhuis burns down

1648 Amsterdam achieves supremacy over Antwerp on the maritime trade routes

1665 New Stadhuis completed

1669 Death of Rembrandt

1663 Second phase of canal building

1672 William III is stadholder. De Witt brothers killed by mob in Den Haag *(see p186)*

1677 William III marries Mary Stuart, heiress to the English throne

William and Mary

1685 Huguenot refugees reach Amsterdam after Louis XIV abolished Edict of Nantes

1650	1660	1670	1680	1690

The Golden Age Overseas

Coat of arms of the VOC

Supremacy in the Netherlands led to success overseas for Amsterdam. The Dutch colonized the Indonesian Archipelago, establishing a profitable empire based on spice trading in the East. The Dutch East India Company (VOC) thrived, using vast wooden ships called East Indiamen. In the New World, the Dutch ruled large parts of Brazil and bought Manhattan from its native owners, naming it New Amsterdam. However, war with England radically trimmed Dutch sea-power by the end of the 17th century.

Purchase of Manhattan
In 1626, explorer Pieter Minuit bought the island of Manhattan from the Native Americans for $24.

Salvaged Silverware
The Batavia *sank off the coast of western Australia in 1629. This bedknob, ewer and plate were salvaged in 1972.*

World Map *(1676)*
Joan Blaeu's map charted the known world, with parts of Asia and Australia missing.

Main mast — Steering stand

Officers' cabin

Mizzen mast

Poop deck

THE BATAVIA
Owned by the VOC, the *Batavia* was an East Indiaman, with three main masts. She was 45 m (148 ft) in length and carried a complement of about 350, including crew, soldiers and families.

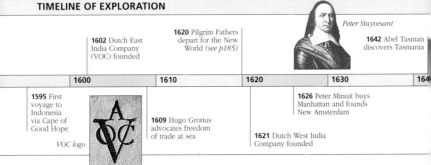

TIMELINE OF EXPLORATION

Peter Stuyvesant

1600	1610	1620	1630	164
1602 Dutch East India Company (VOC) founded	**1620** Pilgrim Fathers depart for the New World *(see p185)*			**1642** Abel Tasman discovers Tasmania
1595 First voyage to Indonesia via Cape of Good Hope	**1609** Hugo Grotius advocates freedom of trade at sea	**1621** Dutch West India Company founded	**1626** Peter Minuit buys Manhattan and founds New Amsterdam	

VOC logo

Dutch Battle Ships *(1683)*
Ludolf Backhuysen (1631–1708) painted the Dutch battle fleet routing the rival Portuguese navy off the coast of northern Spain.

THE DUTCH EAST INDIA COMPANY

Founded in 1602, the VOC had a monopoly on all profits from trade east of the Cape of Good Hope. It became a public company and many a Dutch merchant's fortune was made. By 1611, it was the leading importer of spices into Europe, with ships ranging as far as China, Japan and Indonesia. For nearly 200 years the VOC ran a commercial empire more powerful than some countries.

The Nederlands Scheepvaart Museum (see pp146–7) *has a hall devoted to the VOC. A replica of the East Indiaman, the* Amsterdam, *is moored outside.*

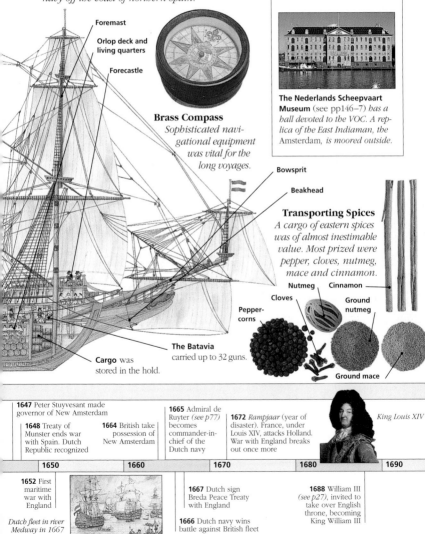

Foremast

Orlop deck and living quarters

Forecastle

Brass Compass
Sophisticated navigational equipment was vital for the long voyages.

Bowsprit

Beakhead

Transporting Spices
A cargo of eastern spices was of almost inestimable value. Most prized were pepper, cloves, nutmeg, mace and cinnamon.

Nutmeg   Cinnamon

Cloves

Peppercorns

Ground nutmeg

The Batavia
carried up to 32 guns.

Cargo was stored in the hold.

Ground mace

1647 Peter Stuyvesant made governor of New Amsterdam

1648 Treaty of Munster ends war with Spain. Dutch Republic recognized

1664 British take possession of New Amsterdam

1665 Admiral de Ruyter *(see p77)* becomes commander-in-chief of the Dutch navy

1672 *Rampjaar* (year of disaster). France, under Louis XIV, attacks Holland. War with England breaks out once more

King Louis XIV

| 1650 | 1660 | 1670 | 1680 | 1690 |

1652 First maritime war with England

Dutch fleet in river Medway in 1667

1667 Dutch sign Breda Peace Treaty with England

1666 Dutch navy wins battle against British fleet

1688 William III *(see p27)*, invited to take over English throne, becoming King William III

The Age of Consolidation

Though the Dutch Empire declined, the Netherlands remained wealthy. Amsterdam's ships became commercial cargo carriers and by the mid-18th century, the city was the world's financial capital. Tolerance prevailed and the city was flooded with immigrants, including Jews from all across Europe. Dissatisfaction with the ruling House of Orange intensified; although Prussian troops crushed a Patriot uprising in 1787, the Patriots established a short-lived republic, with French backing, only to see Napoleon take over, making his brother Louis king of the Netherlands.

Silver Torah finials *(see p64)*

EXTENT OF THE CITY

▨ 1700   ☐ Today

Drying room with Japanese screen

Bathroom

Receiving Visitors *(c. 1713)*
Amsterdam was cosmopolitan and decadent; in Cornelis Troost's satire, the ladies of a brothel parade before Prince Eugène of Savoy.

Drawing room

DOLLS' HOUSE

Costly dolls' houses were designed for show rather than play, and are a fitting symbol of the extravagance of the age. This example is a miniature replica of the house of an Amsterdam merchant. Now in the Frans Hals Museum in Haarlem *(see pp178–9)*, it was made around 1750 for Sara Rothé.

Wintertime in Amsterdam *(c. 1763)*
Petrus Schenk's print shows people skating on the frozen canals. The ice-breaking barges in the background are bringing fresh water to the city.

TIMELINE

1702 Death of William III. Second stadholderless period begins in the Netherlands

1713 Treaty of Utrecht signed. Dutch Republic becomes isolated

French musketeer

1748 Tax collector riots

1744 France invades Southern Provinces

| 1700 | 1710 | 1720 | 1730 | 1740 | 17 |

1697 Tsar Peter the Great of Russia visits Amsterdam to study shipbuilding

Portrait of Tsar Peter the Great (1727) on gold snuff box

1716 Second meeting of the Grand Assembly meets in Den Haag *(see p186)*. Radical government reforms imposed

1747 Stadholdership becomes hereditary under William IV

1751 Death of William IV. Start of 40 years of political strife

Prussian Troops Enter Amsterdam *(1787)*
A lithograph by an unknown artist shows Prussian troops entering the city on 10 October 1787, coming to the aid of the House of Orange after pro-French Patriot upheavals.

Pavilioned bed with green canopy

Lying-in room

Library

Florin *(1781)*
By 1750, Amsterdam possessed the most sophisticated and successful banking and broking system in the world.

WHERE TO SEE 18TH-CENTURY AMSTERDAM

De Gooyer windmill *(see p144)* produced corn for the growing city from 1725. A clandestine church was opened in 1735 in today's Museum Amstelkring *(pp84–5)*, in response to the Alteration *(pp24–5)*. Fine canal houses include No. 465 Herengracht *(p112)* and the Felix Meritis Building *(p113)*, designed by Jacob Otten Husly in 1787. Museum van Loon was renovated in 1752 *(p122)*.

Museum Willet-Holthuysen
The elaborate, gilded staircase *(see p121)* was built in 1740.

Tax Collector Riots *(1748)*
This print by Simonsz Fokke shows an angry mob raiding the house of a tax collector in June 1748.

Ceramic Plate *(c. 1780)*
The wealthy lived in great style, sparing no expense. This hand-painted plate is decorated with mythological figures and ornate gold leaf.

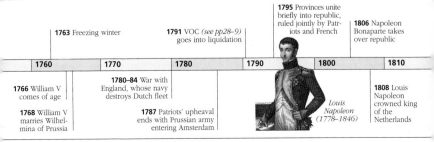

1763 Freezing winter

1791 VOC *(see pp28–9)* goes into liquidation

1795 Provinces unite briefly into republic, ruled jointly by Patriots and French

1806 Napoleon Bonaparte takes over republic

| 1760 | 1770 | 1780 | 1790 | 1800 | 1810 |

1766 William V comes of age

1780–84 War with England, whose navy destroys Dutch fleet

1768 William V marries Wilhelmina of Prussia

1787 Patriots' upheaval ends with Prussian army entering Amsterdam

Louis Napoleon (1778–1846)

1808 Louis Napoleon crowned king of the Netherlands

The Age of Industrialization

By the end of Louis Napoleon's rule, Amsterdam had stagnated. The decline continued, with little sign of enterprise and scant investment. Industrialization came late and attempts to revive the city's fortunes by digging a canal to the North Sea were less than effective. Politically, the country regrouped round the House of Orange, bringing the family back from exile and declaring a monarchy in 1813. The mid-century saw growth of the liberal constitution; by 1900 the Socialist tradition was well established.

EXTENT OF THE CITY

| 1800 | Today |

CENTRAAL STATION

The station *(see p79)* was completed in 1889. It became a symbol of the emergent industrial age – a sign that Amsterdam was finally moving towards the future rather than looking back to the Golden Age.

Van Houten

Cocoa Trading
Cocoa was one of Amsterdam's main exports in the 1890s.

Dutch Renaissance-style façade

The gilded "clock" shows the wind direction, acknowledging Amsterdam's earlier reliance on the wind to power her sailing ships.

Main concourse

Diamond Cutting
The diamond trade thrived in the late 19th century, when precious stones were imported from South Africa.

The Sweatshop by H Wolter
As industrialization increased, sweatshops, with their attendant poverty, became commonplace.

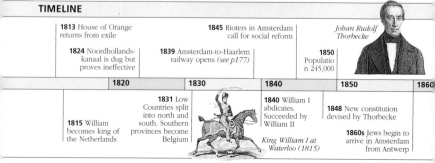

TIMELINE

1813 House of Orange returns from exile

1824 Noordhollands-kanaal is dug but proves ineffective

1845 Rioters in Amsterdam call for social reform

1839 Amsterdam-to-Haarlem railway opens *(see p177)*

Johan Rudolf Thorbecke

1850 Populatio n 245,000

| 1820 | 1830 | 1840 | 1850 | 1860 |

1831 Low Countries split into north and south. Southern provinces become Belgium

1815 William becomes king of the Netherlands

1840 William I abdicates. Succeeded by William II

King William I at Waterloo (1815)

1848 New constitution devised by Thorbecke

1860s Jews begin to arrive in Amsterdam from Antwerp

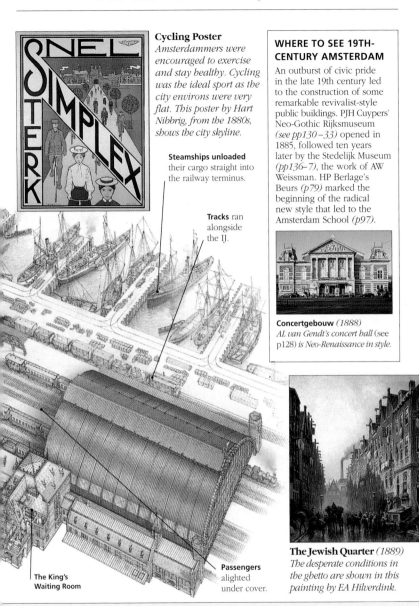

Cycling Poster
Amsterdammers were encouraged to exercise and stay healthy. Cycling was the ideal sport as the city environs were very flat. This poster by Hart Nibbrig, from the 1880s, shows the city skyline.

Steamships unloaded their cargo straight into the railway terminus.

Tracks ran alongside the IJ.

The King's Waiting Room

Passengers alighted under cover.

WHERE TO SEE 19TH-CENTURY AMSTERDAM

An outburst of civic pride in the late 19th century led to the construction of some remarkable revivalist-style public buildings. PJH Cuypers' Neo-Gothic Rijksmuseum *(see pp130–33)* opened in 1885, followed ten years later by the Stedelijk Museum *(pp136–7)*, the work of AW Weissman. HP Berlage's Beurs *(p79)* marked the beginning of the radical new style that led to the Amsterdam School *(p97)*.

Concertgebouw *(1888)*
AL van Gendt's concert hall (see p128) is Neo-Renaissance in style.

The Jewish Quarter *(1889)*
The desperate conditions in the ghetto are shown in this painting by EA Hilverdink.

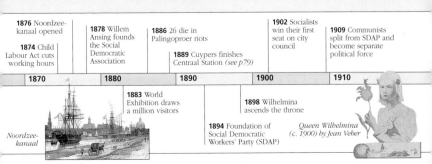

1876 Noordzee-kanaal opened

1874 Child Labour Act cuts working hours

1878 Willem Ansing founds the Social Democratic Association

1886 26 die in Palingoproer riots

1889 Cuypers finishes Centraal Station *(see p79)*

1902 Socialists win their first seat on city council

1909 Communists split from SDAP and become separate political force

| 1870 | 1880 | 1890 | 1900 | 1910 |

1883 World Exhibition draws a million visitors

Noordzee-kanaal

1894 Foundation of Social Democratic Workers' Party (SDAP)

1898 Wilhelmina ascends the throne

Queen Wilhelmina (c. 1900) by Jean Veber

Amsterdam at War

The Netherlands remained neutral in World War I. After the war, political unrest was rife and the city council embarked on a programme of new housing projects and, in the 1930s, the Amsterdamse Bos was created to counter unemployment. When World War II broke out, the Netherlands again opted for neutrality – only to be invaded by Germany. The early 1940s were bitter years, and many died of starvation in the winter of '44–5. During this time, most of the Jewish population was deported; many, like Anne Frank, tried to avoid detection by going into hiding.

EXTENT OF THE CITY

▢ 1945 ▢ Today

"Vote Red" Poster (1918)
The Social Democrats (Labour Party) were responsible for the introduction of a welfare state after World War II.

Attic

The van Pels' room

Anne's bedroom

The Franks' bedroom

Bathroom

Revolving bookcase (entrance to hideout)

ANNE FRANK'S HOUSE

In July 1942, 13-year-old Anne Frank, her family and the van Pels (renamed van Daans in Anne's diary) went into hiding at the rear of this house (*see p90*). Anne had already begun her diary. She made her last entry in August 1944, three days before being arrested. She died in Bergen-Belsen concentration camp in March 1945.

Potato Riots (1917)
Daan Bout's drawing shows desperate women fighting for vegetables during World War I. Rioting followed and the army was brought in to quell the uprising.

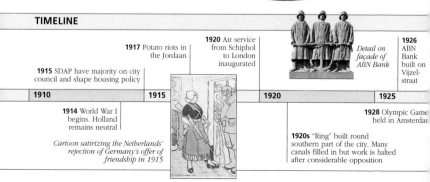

TIMELINE

1915 SDAP have majority on city council and shape housing policy

1917 Potato riots in the Jordaan

1920 Air service from Schiphol to London inaugurated

Detail on façade of ABN Bank

1926 ABN Bank built on Vijzelstraat

1910	1915	1920	1925

1914 World War I begins. Holland remains neutral

Cartoon satirizing the Netherlands' rejection of Germany's offer of friendship in 1915

1920s "Ring" built round southern part of the city. Many canals filled in but work is halted after considerable opposition

1928 Olympic Games held in Amsterdam

Het Schip by Michel de Klerk
*At the end of World War I, Amsterdam School architects
(see p97) designed new housing projects such as "the
ship", to replace the slums in the west of the city.*

Amsterdamse Bos
*In 1930, as part of a
job-creation scheme,
5,000 unemployed
Dutch citizens were
drafted in to help
develop a woodland
and leisure area to
the southwest of
the city.*

Offices at the front
of the building

Façade of No. 263
Prinsengracht

**Dockworker
Statue**
*The statue (see
p53) by Mari
Andriessen commem-
orates the February
1941 protest by dockers
and transport workers
against the Nazis'
treatment of Jews.*

The Deportation of Jews
*Pamphlets were distributed by the
Resistance vilifying those who stood by
and let the Nazis round up the Jews.*

WHERE TO SEE EARLY-20TH-CENTURY AMSTERDAM

Innovative Amsterdam School architecture is found to the south of the city. HP Berlage, PL Kramer and Michel de Klerk collaborated on De Dageraad *(see p151)* and were largely responsible for the Nieuw Zuid *(p154)*. Much of this was built in the run up to the 1928 Olympics; it boasts spectacular housing develop-ments and civic buildings.

Tuschinski Theater *(1921)*
*The interior of this exotic
complex is awash with colour.*

1930 Population 750,000. Unemployment worsens. Work on public project of Amsterdamse Bos begins

1939 Outbreak of World War II. The Netherlands chooses neutrality

1935 Work parties sent to Germany

1942 Deportation of Jews begins

1944 D-Day Landings. "Hunger Winter"

1945 Germany surrenders and western part of the Netherlands finally liberated

1930	1935	1940	1945

1934 Riots in Jordaan over reduction in social security. Seven die

1940 Germany bombs Rotterdam. The Dutch surrender

1932–7 Rise of Dutch Nazi Party under Anton Mussert

1941 450 Jews arrested. Dockworkers strike

Yellow Star of David, which Jews had to wear during Nazi Occupation

Amsterdam Today

Amsterdam tram

After World War II, Amsterdam suffered a series of social problems: its tolerance made it a haven for the 1960s hippy culture, it became a centre of drug use and trafficking, and the left-wing Provos challenged social order. In the 1970s, riots over squatting and urban redevelopment led to measures that alleviated the social issues. Now Amsterdam is again a tranquil city for all to visit. Programmes of urban expansion and sympathetic architectural developments have made the city an exciting hub of modernity.

EXTENT OF THE CITY

▨ *1950*	☐ *Today*

Football
The fans were ecstatic when the Dutch national team beat England 3:1 in 1988 in the European Championships.

Het Lieverdje
The statue of the Little Urchin by Carel Kneulman is in Spui. It became a symbol for the Provos in the 1960s.

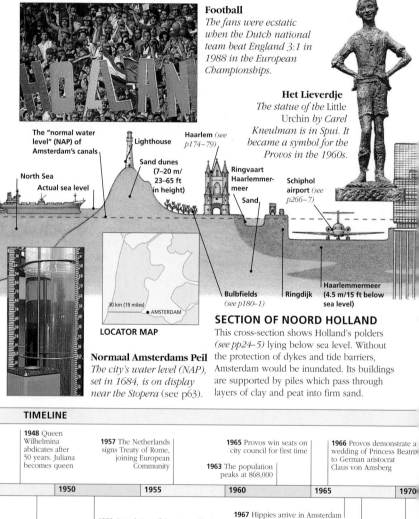

The "normal water level" (NAP) of Amsterdam's canals

Lighthouse

Haarlem *(see p174–79)*

Sand dunes (7–20 m/ 23–65 ft in height)

North Sea

Actual sea level

Ringvaart Haarlemmer- meer

Sand

Schiphol airport *(see p266–7)*

Bulbfields *(see p180–1)*

Ringdijk

Haarlemmermeer (4.5 m/15 ft below sea level)

LOCATOR MAP

30 km (19 miles)
● AMSTERDAM

Normaal Amsterdams Peil
The city's water level (NAP), set in 1684, is on display near the Stopera (see p63).

SECTION OF NOORD HOLLAND
This cross-section shows Holland's polders *(see pp24–5)* lying below sea level. Without the protection of dykes and tide barriers, Amsterdam would be inundated. Its buildings are supported by piles which pass through layers of clay and peat into firm sand.

TIMELINE

1948 Queen Wilhelmina abdicates after 50 years. Juliana becomes queen	**1957** The Netherlands signs Treaty of Rome, joining European Community	**1965** Provos win seats on city council for first time **1963** The population peaks at 868,000	**1966** Provos demonstrate at wedding of Princess Beatrix to German aristocrat Claus von Amsberg	
1950	**1955**	**1960**	**1965**	**1970**
1949 Indonesia officially independent from the Netherlands	**1952** Completion of the Amsterdam-Rhine Canal allows increased trade	**1967** Hippies arrive in Amsterdam **1968** First residents move to the vast Bijlmermeer housing estate	**1971** Ajax wins European Cup	

Queen Beatrix
*Born in 1938, Beatrix
was crowned in the
Nieuwe Kerk (see
pp76–7) in 1980
following the abdication
of her mother Juliana.*

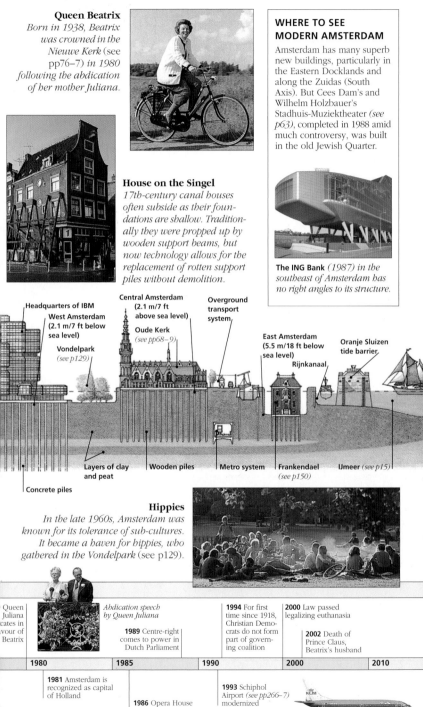

**WHERE TO SEE
MODERN AMSTERDAM**

Amsterdam has many superb
new buildings, particularly in
the Eastern Docklands and
along the Zuidas (South
Axis). But Cees Dam's and
Wilhelm Holzbauer's
Stadhuis-Muziektheater *(see
p63)*, completed in 1988 amid
much controversy, was built
in the old Jewish Quarter.

The ING Bank *(1987) in the
southeast of Amsterdam has
no right angles to its structure.*

House on the Singel
*17th-century canal houses
often subside as their foundations are shallow. Traditionally they were propped up by
wooden support beams, but
now technology allows for the
replacement of rotten support
piles without demolition.*

Headquarters of IBM

West Amsterdam
(2.1 m/7 ft below
sea level)

Vondelpark
(see p129)

Central Amsterdam
(2.1 m/7 ft
above sea level)

Oude Kerk
(see pp68–9)

Overground
transport
system

East Amsterdam
(5.5 m/18 ft below
sea level)

Rijnkanaal

Oranje Sluizen
tide barrier

Layers of clay
and peat

Wooden piles

Metro system

Frankendael
(see p150)

IJmeer *(see p15)*

Concrete piles

Hippies
*In the late 1960s, Amsterdam was
known for its tolerance of sub-cultures.
It became a haven for hippies, who
gathered in the Vondelpark (see p129).*

Queen
Juliana
cates in
vour of
Beatrix

*Abdication speech
by Queen Juliana*

1989 Centre-right
comes to power in
Dutch Parliament

1994 For first
time since 1918,
Christian Demo-
crats do not form
part of govern-
ing coalition

2000 Law passed
legalizing euthanasia

2002 Death of
Prince Claus,
Beatrix's husband

1980	1985	1990	2000	2010

1981 Amsterdam is
recognized as capital
of Holland

1986 Opera House
(see p63) opens in
Stopera

1993 Schiphol
Airport *(see pp266–7)*
modernized

975 Nieuwmarkt riots
ıpt against destruction
Jewish Quarter

KLM – the Dutch national airline

NO... KERT... ...LAN... | DIRCK DE VLA MINGH... | IACOB BACKER | PIETER HASSE LAUR 1635 | GERRIT SCHAP SYMON... | GER... CLAE...

CORNELIS DE GRAEF | DWOVTER VALCKENIER | CORNELIS BICKER VANSWIE | DALBERT BAS | NICOLAES CORVER | FRAN... ANNO...

RAN... ANDER MEER | IAN BICKER | D CORNELIS WITSEN | IAN VAN DER POLA | D NICOLAES TVLP... | ALB... DIRCKS...

NELIS DE VI NCH VAN NOUDIS | ANDRIES DE GRAEF Anno 1657 | SYMON V... HO... | HENDRICK HOFT Anno 1662 | IAN HALLAO... | GILLIS VE...

...rabus... | Pieter Reael 1699 | Jan van Waveren | Jan Munter 1676 | Johannis Hudd... 1672 | Corn... Gee...

IAN CORVER | Nicolaes Opmeer | Nicolaes ...SCH | Gerard Bors v Waveren | Joan de Vries 1686 | Willem

Iacob Borel 1691 | Jacob ...tloopen | Jeronimo de Haze george | Cornelis Valckenier | Dirck Bas | Fru... De

...RANT... | JAN GRAAF | Cornelio van Bam... | Cornelis... | Alexander... | Jan...

AMSTERDAM AT A GLANCE

There are more than 100 places of interest described in the *Area by Area* section of this book. The broad spectrum of entries covers recreational as well as cultural sights and ranges from sublime buildings, such as the Oude Kerk, to oddities like the Hash Marihuana Museum *(see p61)*. The Golden Bend *(see p112)* and other impressive canalscapes also feature,

along with suggested walks past some of Amsterdam's finest architecture and notable sights, such as Anne Frankhuis. To help you make the most of your stay, the following 12 pages are a time-saving guide to the best Amsterdam has to offer. Museums, canals and bridges, and cafés and bars all have their own sections. Below is a selection of attractions that no visitor should miss.

AMSTERDAM'S TOP TEN ATTRACTIONS

Nederlands Scheepvaartmuseum
See pp146–7

Van Gogh Museum
See pp134–5

Oude Kerk
See pp68–9

Begijnhof
See p75

Rijksmuseum
See pp130–33

Koninklijk Paleis
See p74

Stedelijk Museum
See pp136–7

Museum Amstelkring
See pp84–5

Magere Brug
See p119

Anne Frank Huis
See pp34–5 & 90–91

◁ Stained-glass coats of arms in the Lady Chapel of the Oude Kerk

Amsterdam's Best: Museums

For a fairly small city, Amsterdam has a surprisingly large number of museums and galleries. The quality and variety of the collections are impressive and many are housed in buildings of historical or architectural interest. The Rijksmuseum, with its Gothic façade, is a city landmark, and Rembrandt's work is exhibited in his original home. For more information on museums see pages 42–3.

Anne Frank Huis
Anne Frank's photo is exhibited in the house where she hid during World War II.

Amsterdams Historisch Museum
A wealth of historical information is on display here. Once an orphanage, it is depicted in Governesses at the Burgher Orphanage *(1683) by Adriaen Backer.*

Western Canal Ring

Rijksmuseum
An extensive collection of paintings by Dutch masters, including Jan van Huysum's Still Life with Flowers and Fruit *(c.1730), is held at the Rijksmuseum. The main building is closed for renovation until 2008* (see p130).

Central Canal Ring

Museum Quarter

Stedelijk Museum
Gerrit Rietveld's simple Steltman chair (1963) is one of many exhibits at this ever-changing contemporary art museum.

Van Gogh Museum
Van Gogh's Self-portrait with Straw Hat (1870) hangs in this large, stark museum, built in 1973 to house the bulk of his work.

Museum Amstelkring

Three 17th-century merchant's houses conceal in their attics Amsterdam's only remaining clandestine church. The buildings have been restored as the Museum Amstelkring.

Nederlands Scheepvaartmuseum

This national maritime museum is decorated with reliefs relating to the city's maritime history. Moored alongside is a replica of the East Indiaman, Amsterdam.

Nieuwe Zijde

Oude Zijde

Tropenmuseum

On display here are exhibits from former Dutch colonies in the tropics, including this wooden Nigerian fertility mask portraying a mother and twins.

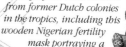

Eastern Canal Ring

Plantage

| 0 metres | | 500 |
| 0 yards | | 500 |

Museum Willet-Holthuysen

An impressive collection of furniture, silverware and paintings is housed in this beautifully preserved 17th-century canalside mansion.

Joods Historisch Museum

Four adjoining synagogues are linked to form this museum. The Holy Ark in the Grote Synagoge is the centrepiece of an exhibition on Judaism in the Netherlands.

Exploring Amsterdam's Museums

Wall plaque in St Luciensteeg

The richness of Amsterdam's history and culture is reflected by its wide range of museums, which cover everything from bibles, beer and African masks to ship-building and space travel. Its national art galleries house some of the world's most famous paintings, including Rembrandt's *The Night Watch*. The Nederlands Scheep-vaart Museum has the largest collection of model ships in the world, while the Anne Frank Huis is a stark reminder of the horrors of World War II.

View of a French-style garden from the Museum van Loon

PAINTING AND DECORATIVE ARTS

The world's most important collection of Dutch art is on display at the **Rijksmuseum**. This vast museum contains approximately 5,000 paintings, including works by Rembrandt, Vermeer, Frans Hals and Albert Cuyp as well as a significant collection of sculptures, prints, artifacts and Asiatic art. The main building is undergoing renovation until 2008.

A short stroll across Museumplein will bring you to the **Van Gogh Museum**. Besides a large collection of Van Gogh's paintings and drawings, which traces his entire career, you can see hundreds of his original letters to his brother Theo and the artist's private collection of Japanese prints. Works by other 19th-century Dutch painters are also displayed here.

Modern art is the focus of the **Stedelijk Museum**. While the collection features works by artists such as and Henri Matisse and Vassily

Kandinsky, the emphasis is on paintings, sculptures, drawings, graphics and photographs completed after 1945. Andy Warhol, Edward Kienholz and the Dutch Cobra artist Karel Appel are all represented.

The house where Rembrandt lived for 20 years opened as the **Museum Het Rembrandt-huis** in 1911. As well as providing an insight into the artist's life, it contains an important collection of his work, including a series of self-portraits.

The **Museum van Loon**, housed in a beautiful 17th-century mansion, is based on the outstanding private collections of the wealthy van Loon family.

Other wonderful collections of art can also be enjoyed by travelling from Amsterdam to the **Frans Hals Museum** in Haarlem, the **Mauritshuis** in Den Haag and the **Museum Boijmans Van Beuningen Rotterdam.**

Rembrandt's *The Jewish Bride* (1663) in the Rijksmuseum

Indonesian mask at the Tropenmuseum

HISTORY

Various aspects of Amsterdam's absorbing history is documented in several of the city's museums. The **Amsterdams Historisch Museum** covers the growth of Amsterdam from its origins as a fishing village in the 13th century, by means of maps, paintings and archaeological objects. The city's glorious maritime history is recalled at the **Nederlands Scheepvaartmuseum**. Its vast collection of model ships includes a life-size replica of an 18th-century sailing ship. The mechanics of more modern boats is the focus of the **Museum 't Kromhout**, which is housed in one of the few working shipyards left in the city. In the **Museum Willet-Holthuysen**, the richly decorated rooms and collection of Dutch paintings, Venetian glass, silverware and furniture reflects the wealth of Amsterdam in the Golden Age. Catholic ingenuity is revealed at the **Museum Amstelkring**, where a secret church is preserved in the attic of a 17th-century merchant's home. The history of the Dutch trade unions is documented at the **De Burcht (Vakbondsmuseum)**.

Jewish life in the city is remembered in the fascinating **Joods Historisch Museum**. The famous **Anne Frankhuis** provides a poignant reminder that Amsterdam's Jewish community was almost wiped out in World War II, and its secret annexe shows what life was like for those living in hiding. Displays on the activities of the Dutch Resistance at the **Verzetsmuseum Amsterdam** provide more fascinating insights on life in the Netherlands during the Nazi occupation.

Outside the city, the **Zuiderzeemuseum** recreates the life and traditions of the people who once fished these waters.

SPECIALIST MUSEUMS

Mummies, sarcophagi and effigies of ancient Egyptian gods are just a few of the displays at the **Allard Pierson Museum**. The **Bijbels Museum**, in adjoining canal houses, also focuses on the archaeology of Egypt and the Middle East, and contains the oldest Bible ever printed in the Netherlands.

The **Theatermuseum** traces the history of Dutch theatre through costumes, posters and props, while the **Nederlands Filmmuseum** screens more than 1,000 films a year. **Foam** is a lively and welcoming photography museum.

The **Heineken Experience** offers a history of beer-making as part of a tour of this former brewery and free samples at the end. More facts can be absorbed at the **Hash Marijuana Hemp Museum**, which shows the many uses this product has had through the ages.

The sounds and sights of anything from a North African village to an Indonesian rainforest are recreated at the **KIT Tropenmuseum**, devoted to cultures from around the world.

The open-air reconstruction village at the Zuiderzeemuseum

TECHNOLOGY AND NATURAL HISTORY

A hands-on approach is encouraged by **Nemo**, Holland's national science centre, to explain, for instance, how photography works or how computers process information. The centre is housed in a striking modern building.

Along with hundreds of live animals, the **Artis** complex (the oldest zoo in the Netherlands, founded in 1838) contains a variety of museums. Rock collectors will be tempted by a huge range of minerals, rocks, fossils and helpful models in the Geologisch Museum. There is also a collection of skulls, skeletons and stuffed animals in the Zoölogisch Museum, which is housed in the zoo's Aquarium, and a Planetarium. The Hortus Botanicus is a tranquil botanical garden with a three-climate greenhouse and a stunning collection of trees.

Model showing the process of precipitation in the Geologisch Museum at Artis

Amsterdam's Best: Canals and Waterways

From the grace and elegance of the waterside mansions along the *Grachtengordel* (Canal Ring) to the rows of converted warehouses on Brouwersgracht and the charming houses on Reguliersgracht, the city's canals and waterways embody the very spirit of Amsterdam. They are spanned by many beautiful bridges, including the famous Magere Brug *(see p119)*, a traditionally styled lift bridge. You can also relax at one of the many canalside cafés or bars and watch an array of boats float by.

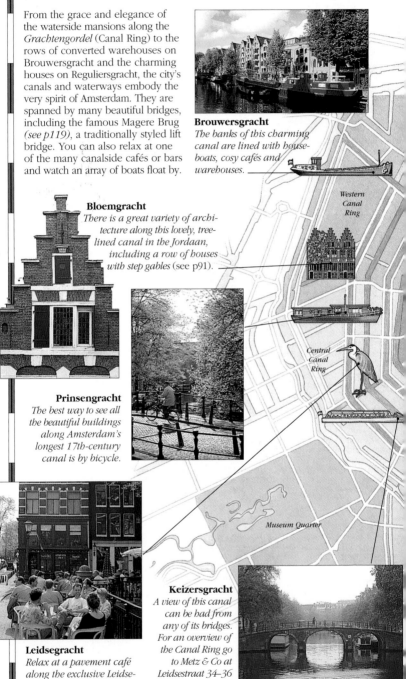

Brouwersgracht
The banks of this charming canal are lined with houseboats, cosy cafés and warehouses.

Bloemgracht
There is a great variety of architecture along this lovely, tree-lined canal in the Jordaan, including a row of houses with step gables (see p91).

Prinsengracht
The best way to see all the beautiful buildings along Amsterdam's longest 17th-century canal is by bicycle.

Western Canal Ring

Central Canal Ring

Museum Quarter

Leidsegracht
Relax at a pavement café along the exclusive Leidsegracht (see p111).

Keizersgracht
A view of this canal can be had from any of its bridges. For an overview of the Canal Ring go to Metz & Co at Leidsestraat 34–36 (see p112).

Singel

The Poezenboot, *a boat for stray cats, is just one of the many sights to be found along the Singel, whose distinctive, curved shape established the horseshoe contours of the Canal Ring.*

Entrepotdok

The warehouses on the Entrepotdok (see p144) were redeveloped in the 1980s. The quayside is now lined in summer with lively café terraces that overlook an array of houseboats and pleasure craft.

Nieuwe Zijde

Oude Zijde

0 metres	500
0 yards	500

Plantage

Eastern Canal Ring

Herengracht

Known as "the twin brothers", these matching neck-gabled houses at Nos. 409–411 are two of the prettiest houses on the city's grandest canal.

Reguliersgracht

Many crooked, brick buildings line this pretty canal, which was cut in 1664. The statue of a stork, located at No. 92, is symbolic of parental responsibility and commemorates a 1571 by-law protecting this bird.

Amstel

This river is still a busy commercial thoroughfare, with barges carrying grain and coal to the city's port.

Amsterdam's Best: Cafés and Bars

Amsterdam is a city of cafés and bars, about 1,500 in all. Each area has something to offer, from friendly and relaxed brown cafés to lively and crowded designer bars. The cafés and bars vary and each has some special attraction: a large range of beers, live music, canalside terraces, art exhibitions, board games and pool tables or simply a brand of *gezelligheid*, the unique Dutch concept of "cosiness". Further details of Amsterdam's cafés and bars are given on pages 48–9. Addresses are given in the directory on page 237.

De Tuin
This large brown café in the Jordaan is always crowded with regular customers, often local artists.

Western Canal Ring

Central Canal Ring

Van Puffelen
A smart and fashionable clientele is attracted to this intimate canalside café, with its impressive 19th-century interior, reading room and restaurant.

Vertigo
The café terrace of the Nederlands Filmmuseum has a splendid view across Vondelpark.

Museum Quarter

Café Americain
The American Hotel's grand café has a beautiful Art Deco interior, and is the place to go to be seen.

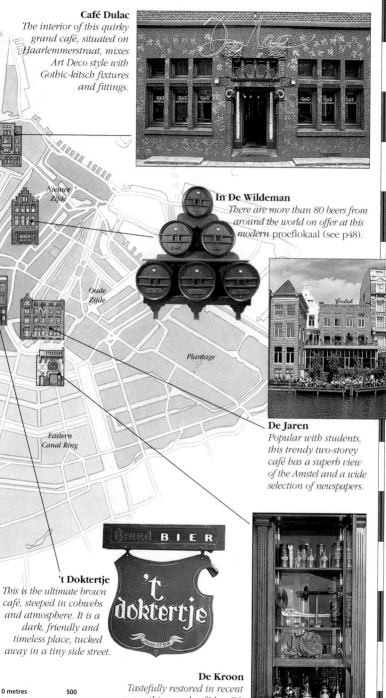

Café Dulac
The interior of this quirky grand café, situated on Haarlemmerstraat, mixes Art Deco style with Gothic-kitsch fixtures and fittings.

Nieuwe Zijde

In De Wildeman
There are more than 80 beers from around the world on offer at this modern proeflokaal (see p48).

Oude Zijde

Plantage

De Jaren
Popular with students, this trendy two-storey café has a superb view of the Amstel and a wide selection of newspapers.

Eastern Canal Ring

't Doktertje
This is the ultimate brown café, steeped in cobwebs and atmosphere. It is a dark, friendly and timeless place, tucked away in a tiny side street.

De Kroon
Tastefully restored in recent years, this grand café has DJs Thursday to Sunday.

| 0 metres | 500 |
| 0 yards | 500 |

Exploring Amsterdam's Cafés and Bars

Wherever you go in this vibrant city, you are never far from a café or bar. Amsterdammers are at their most friendly over a beer or a Dutch gin, so exploring the city's drinking establishments is an easy way to meet the locals. Table service is standard in most cafés and bars, though not universal. Instead of paying for each drink, bars keep a running total which you settle as you leave. The exception is outdoor terraces, where you pay as you order. Most places are open from about 11am until 1am, but some around the Leidseplein and Rembrandtplein stay open until 4 or 5am at the weekends.

Sportcafé Ajax-Arena, decorated with football memorabilia

BROWN CAFÉS

The traditional Dutch "local pub", the brown café, is characterized by dark wooden panelling and furniture, low ceilings, dim lighting and a fog of tobacco smoke. It is a warm and friendly place and often a social focus for the neighbourhood. Some of the best brown cafés are found in old 17th-century canal houses or tucked away on side streets. The tiny and characterful **'t Doktertje**, just off the Kalverstraat shopping street, is worth a visit, as is the cheap and cheerful **Pieper**, close to Leidseplein. **De Tuin,** in the heart of the Jordaan, is popular with the local artistic community. Most brown cafés are more than just places to drink at and many serve good, reasonably priced food (see pp236–7).

PROEFLOKALEN AND MODERN TASTING BARS

Literally meaning "tasting houses", *proeflokalen* go back to the Dutch Golden Age of the 17th century. In order to increase sales, wine and spirit importers would invite merchants to taste their wares. Today, *proeflokalen* denote bars specializing in either wine, spirits or beer. One of the oldest tasting bars, **De Drie Fleschjes**, dates from 1650, and *jenever* (Dutch gin) is its speciality. **Mulliner's** offers a superb range of vintage wines and ports, while **In De Wildeman** serves beers from around the world, many of them on draught. See the directory on page 237 for other good *proeflokalen*.

Sampling the wide range of beers in the popular modern tasting bar, Gollem

WHAT TO DRINK

The Dutch national drink is beer. A standard *pils* (a lager-like beer) is served in bars and cafés – the main brands are Heineken and Grolsch. Darker beers like De Koninck have a stronger flavour, and the wheat-brewed *witbiers* like Hoegaarden are white and cloudy. Beers from Amsterdam's 't IJ brewery, such as Columbus, are widely available. The most popular spirit, *jenever*, is the slightly oily Dutch gin. There is either the sharp tasting *jonge* (young), or the smoother *oude* (old) variety. For the complete Dutch experience, drink *jenever* in a single gulp or order a refreshing *pils* with a *jenever* chaser.

Bottle of *jonge* jenever

Traditional *oude jenever*

Hoegaarden, brewed in Belgium

Tarwebok, a strong type of Heineken

GRAND CAFÉS AND DESIGNER BARS

Grand cafés first emerged in the 19th century. Today, these large and opulent venues are the haunts of the upwardly mobile and fashion-conscious. **Café Luxembourg** has a street terrace for people-watching, while **Café Schiller** is more intimate and has a beautiful Art Deco interior. Designer bars cater for a similar clientele, but they are modern, stark and bright in style. Some of the best are the chic **Het Land Van Walem**, **De Balie**, **Vert-igo** and the trendy **De Jaren**.

The beautifully restored De Jaren

Café Schiller, one of Amsterdam's Art Deco grand cafés

SMOKING COFFEESHOPS

Smoking coffeeshops are ones where cannabis is openly sold and smoked. Although technically illegal, the sale of soft drugs is tolerated by the Dutch authorities if it remains discreet *(see p259)*. Many of these cafés are recognizable by their loud music and often psychedelic decor. Smoking coffeeshops appeal to a surprising range of people – old and young alike (under 16s are not permitted) from every social and professional background. **Rusland** and **Siberië** are two of the smaller, more relaxed places, while **The Bulldog Palace** is commercial and tourist-filled. As well as coffee, soft drinks and snacks are generally available. **Chocolata** even specializes in hash confectionery, such as hash cakes. If tempted to smoke, ask for the menu listing what is on sale. The cannabis is strong, especially the local "skunk". Be wary of hash cakes and cookies as there is no way to gauge their strength. See the directory on page 237 for other good smoking coffeeshops.

COFFEESHOPS AND SALONS DE THÉ

The more conventional type of coffeeshop is where well-to-do ladies go for a chat over coffee and cake. A number of these places use the Dutch spelling, *koffieshop*, or the French *salons de thé* to distinguish themselves from the many smoking coffeeshops, although the differences are obvious. Many, such as **Arnold Cornelis** and **Pompadour**, are attached to confectioners, patisseries or delicatessens, and have a tempting range of cakes and sweets on offer. Several of the city's larger stores and hotels also have tearooms, ideal places to sit down in comfort and relax after a busy day sightseeing or shopping. **Metz & Co** has a comfortable sixth-floor café that offers one of the most impressive canal views in Amsterdam *(see p112)*. Another canalside experience not to be missed is **Flores**, which has delicious German specialities. For something slightly different, try **Back Stage**, a wonderfully offbeat café run by an eccentric former cabaret artist called Mr. Christmas.

WHERE TO FIND THE BEST CAFÉS

All the cafés and bars described on these pages are listed in the directory on page 237. The best, as shown on pages 46–7, are also listed below.

Café Americain
American Hotel, Leidsekade 97.
Map 4 E2.
Tel 556 3000.

Café Dulac
Haarlemmerstraat 118.
Map 1 C3. *Tel* 624 4265.

't Doktertje
Rozenboomsteeg 4. **Map** 7 B4.
Tel 626 4427.

In de Wildeman
Kolksteeg 3. **Map** 7 C1.
Tel 638 2348.

De Jaren
Nieuwe Doelenstraat 20.
Map 7 C4.
Tel 625 5771.

De Kroon
Rembrandtplein 17. **Map** 7 C5.
Tel 625 2011.

De Tuin
2e Tuindwarsstraat 13 (near Anjeliersstraat). **Map** 1 B3.
Tel 624 4559.

Van Puffelen
Prinsengracht 377. **Map** 1 B5.
Tel 624 6270.

Vertigo
Nederlands Filmmuseum, Vondelpark 3. **Map** 4 D2.
Tel 612 3021.

De Koninck, a dark Belgian beer

Amstel Bockbier, a dark winter beer

Columbus, brewed in Amsterdam

AMSTERDAM THROUGH THE YEAR

Although there is no guarantee of good weather in Amsterdam, the cosmopolitan ambience of this 700-year-old city and the congeniality of the Dutch make it an appealing place to visit whatever time of year you go. Most tourists flock into the city from April to September, when temperatures are mild. Amsterdammers, however, are undaunted by the weather and maintain

Herons nest on the canals

an active programme of festivals and outdoor pursuits throughout the year. Crisp autumn days invite long walks along the city's stately canals, followed by a cosy chat in one of Amsterdam's brown cafés. About twice a decade, the winter temperatures drop so low that the canals freeze over. When this occurs a skating race is held between 11 Dutch cities.

SPRING

Spring begins in late March when daffodils and crocuses blossom overnight all over the city. Flower lovers descend on Amsterdam, using it as a base for day trips to Keukenhof, the Netherlands' 28-hectare (69-acre) showcase for Dutch bulb growers (see pp180–81).

MARCH

Stille Omgang (second or third Sat), Rokin. Silent night-time procession celebrating the Miracle of Amsterdam (see p22).

Opening of Keukenhof (21 Mar). One of the world's largest flower gardens (see p181).

APRIL

National Museum Weekend (second weekend of Apr). Cut-price or free admission to many state-run museums.
Koninginnedag (30 Apr). Amsterdam becomes the world's biggest flea market-cum-street party as the Dutch celebrate Queen Beatrix's official birth-day. Transport grinds to a halt as more than 2 million people throng the streets during the day and dance the night away.

Revellers celebrating in the streets to commemorate Koninginnedag

World Press Photo (end Apr– early Jun), Oude Kerk. Exhibition of the very best press photographs from around the world.

MAY

Herdenkingsdag (4 May). Commemorations throughout the city for the victims of World War II. Largest in Dam square.
Bevrijdingsdag (5 May). Con-certs and speeches around the city celebrate the end of the German occupation.
Kunst RAI (see p151) (second week). A massive exhibition of contemporary art held in Amsterdam RAI.
Nationale Molendag (second Sat). Windmills all over the Netherlands are opened to the public and their sails unfurled.
Boeken op de Dam (third or fourth Sun of May until September). Dam square fills with book stalls, and sometimes along the Amstel at Muziektheater (see p63) – Boeken aan de Amstel.

Tulip fields in bloom near Alkmaar

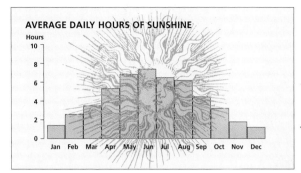

AVERAGE DAILY HOURS OF SUNSHINE

Hours

Sunshine Chart
The summer months are the sunniest, but this is no guarantee of good weather. Amsterdammers will often carry an umbrella even on the hottest of July days as summer rain in the morning often precedes the arrival of bright sunshine later.

SUMMER

Summer, which starts with the three week-long Holland Festival, is a hectic cultural roller-coaster ride. As well as the events listed below, classic European drama is staged in the Amsterdamse Bos (p155), and open-air concerts are held in the Vondelpark (pp128–9). This is the best time for people-watching in one of Amsterdam's street-side cafés and bars.

A rower training on the Bosbaan in the Amsterdamse Bos

JUNE

Open Garden Days *(mid-June)*. For one weekend in June, some of Amsterdam's most elegant private gardens open their gates to the public. Visit www.grachtenmusea.nl for more information.
Open Air Theatre in Vondel-park *(early Jun–end Aug)*. Theatre, music and children's shows *(see p128)*.
Holland Festival *(3 weeks of June)*. In venues throughout Amsterdam and in other major cities in the Netherlands, a varied programme of concerts, plays, operas and ballets.
Amsterdam Roots Festival *(late June)*, De Melkweg *(pp110–11)*, Tropenmuseum *(pp152–3)*, Oosterpark, and Concertgebouw *(p128)*. An ethnic programme of music, dance, film and theatre from Africa and other non-Western countries.

JULY

North Sea Jazz Festival *(mid-Jul)*, the Ahoy Exhibition Centre. Weekend of jazz ranging from Dixieland to jazz rock a short train ride away in Rotterdam.
Summer Concerts *(Jul–Aug)*, Concertgebouw *(see p128)*. Annual showcase of classical music.

Orchestral performance at the Prinsengracht Concert

AUGUST

Uitmarkt *(mid-Aug)*. A weekend of music and theatre performances at Leidseplein and Museumplein launches the start of the cultural season.
Grachtenfestival *(Wed–Sun, around third Sat)*. Classical concerts on Herengracht, Keizersgracht and Prinsengracht. The main concert is on Saturday on a barge in front of the Pulitzer Hotel *(see p220)*.

Café-goers relaxing and soaking up the sun at de Jaren Terrace

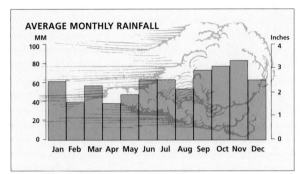

AVERAGE MONTHLY RAINFALL

Rainfall Chart
Expect rain all year round in Amsterdam. The pattern, however, is broadly seasonal. Visit the city in spring to enjoy the driest weather of the year. The heaviest rainfall occurs in autumn, reaching a peak in the windy and wet month of November.

AUTUMN

Temperatures drop quickly at the end of August, but the cultural heat is maintained with the diary of music, dance, opera and drama promoted in the Uitmarkt *(see p51)*. The Autumn is also a busy time for more sporting types. There is a range of spectator sports to watch, and it is a good time of year to enjoy brisk walks in one of the city's many parks or along the Amstel. By November, many Amsterdammers retreat indoors on rainy evenings to cafés like Schaakcafé Het Hok in the Lange Leidsedwarsstraat.

SEPTEMBER

Bloemen Corso *(first Sat)*. Crowds gather to watch a parade of flower-laden floats around Amsterdam. In the evening, there is an illuminated floral procession through the southern suburb of Aalsmeer.
Open Monumentendagen *(first or second weekend)*. A chance to see inside some historic, listed buildings which are normally closed to the public.
Car-Free Sunday *(second Sun)*. No cars are allowed in the historic centre, so hire a bike or walk around soaking up the beauty of traffic-free Amsterdam.
Jordaan Festival *(third weekend, including Fri)*. Festivals are held around Westerkerk and elsewhere in this picturesque district, with fairs, street parties, talent contests and music.

Barges moored along an Amsterdam waterfront in autumn

OCTOBER

Roeisloepengrachtentocht *(second Sat)*, Oosterdok. One of many rowing competitions.
ING Amsterdam Marathon *(third Sun)*. Some 1,500 runners circle the city before converging on the Olympic stadium in this 42-km (26-mile) run. A further 10,000 people join in for a 10-km (6-mile) stretch of the race.
Camping and Caravan RAI *(end Oct)*, Amsterdam RAI *(p151)*. Annual fair for open-air holiday enthusiasts.

NOVEMBER

PAN *(Nov–Dec)*. Art and antiques fair in RAI *(see p151)*.
Museumnacht *(first Sat)*. Many museums stay open during the night. There are often theatrical and musical events, too, as well as a special guided tour.
Sinterklaas' Parade *(second or third Sat)*. The Dutch equivalent of Santa Claus arrives by boat near St Nicholaaskerk *(see p79)* accompanied by *Zwarte Piet* (Black Peter) and distributes sweets to Amsterdam's waiting children.

Sinterklaas parading through Amsterdam

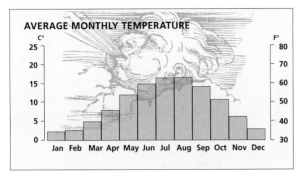

AVERAGE MONTHLY TEMPERATURE

Temperature Chart
The chart shows the average temperature for each month in Amsterdam. Summer is often cooled by the North Sea wind, both spring and autumn can be chilly, and temperatures in winter are frequently freezing.

WINTER

Christmas is a busy tourist season, with visitors and residents thronging to watch Christmas trees being hawked from barges on the main canals. Barrows appear throughout the city, tantalizing passers-by with the smell of freshly fried *oliebollen* and *appelflappen*, two sugary treats not to be missed. After Christmas, the talk of the town is whether or not it will be cold enough for the city authorities to permit skating on the city's canals. If the green light is given – which is rare – whole neighbourhoods turn out to skate under the stars.

DECEMBER

Sinterklaasavond *(5 Dec).* The traditional Dutch gift-giving day when Sinterklaas and his Moorish helpers visit Dutch children to leave a sack of presents. Friends give poems caricaturing each other.

Amsterdammers ice skating on the Keizersgracht

Christmas Day *(25 Dec).* Increasingly accepted as the main gift-giving day.
New Year's Eve *(31 Dec).* Firework celebrations throughout the city with an organized display over the Amstel.

JANUARY

Jumping Amsterdam *(Jan–Feb),* Amsterdam RAI *(p151).* International indoor showjumping competitions.
Chinese New Year *(Jan or Feb),* Nieuwmarkt. Traditional lion dance, fireworks, Chinese exhibitions and stage art.

FEBRUARY

Februaristaking *(25 Feb),* JD

The Dokwerker Monument in JD Meijerplein

Meijerplein. Commemoration of dockworkers' action against the deportation of Jewish residents during World War II.

PUBLIC HOLIDAYS

New Year's Day (1 Jan)
Tweede Paasdag (Easter Monday) *
Koninginnedag (30 April)
Bevrijdingsdag (5 May)
Hemelvaartsdag (Ascension Day) *
Pinksteren (Whitsun) *
Eerste Kerstdag (Christmas Day) (25 Dec)
Tweede Kerstdag (26 Dec)
* Dates change in accordance with church calendar.

AMSTERDAM AREA BY AREA

OUDE ZIJDE

The eastern half of Amsterdam became known as the Oude Zijde (Old Side). Originally it occupied a narrow strip on the east bank of the Amstel river, running between Damrak and the Oudezijds Voorburgwal *(see pp44–5)*. At its heart was built the Oude Kerk, the oldest church in the city. In the early 1400s the Oude Zijde began an eastward expansion which continued into the 17th century. This growth was

Aäron from Mozes en Aäronkerk

fuelled by an influx of Jewish refugees from Portugal. The oldest of the four synagogues, now containing the Joods Historisch Museum, dates from this period. These were central to Jewish life in the city for centuries. During the Golden Age *(see pp26–9)*, the Oude Zijde was an important commercial centre. Boats could sail up the Geldersekade to Nieuwmarkt, where goods were weighed at the Waag before being sold at the market.

SIGHTS AT A GLANCE

Historic Buildings and Monuments
Agnietenkapel ❺
Oostindisch Huis ❼
Oudemanhuispoort ❻
Pintohuis ⓰
Montelbaanstoren ⓱
Scheepvaarthuis ⓲
Schreierstoren ⓳
Trippenhuis ❽
Waag ❷

Opera Houses
Stadhuis-Muziektheater ⓫

Museums
Hash Marijuana Hemp Museum ❹
Joods Historisch Museum pp64–5 ⓮
Museum Het Rembrandthuis ❿

Churches and Synagogues
Mozes en Aäronkerk ⓭
Portugees-Israëlitische Synagoge ⓯
Oude Kerk pp68–9 ㉑
Zuiderkerk ❾

Streets and Markets
Nieuwmarkt ❸
Red Light District ❶
Waterlooplein ⓬
Zeedijk ⓴

GETTING THERE
The best way to reach the Oude Zijde is to get a tram to the Dam (trams 4, 9, 14, 16, 24 and 25) and then walk along Damstraat. Alternatively, take tram 9 or 14 directly to Waterlooplein, or the metro to Nieuwmarkt.

KEY

	Street-by-Street map *See p58–9*
🚊	Tram stop
Ⓜ	Metro station
⛴	Museum boat boarding point

0 metres   250
0 yards   250

◁ Some of the many exotic items to be found at the Waterlooplein flea market

Street-by-Street: University District

The University of Amsterdam, founded in 1877, is predominantly located in the peaceful, southwestern part of the Oude Zijde. The university's roots lie in the former Atheneum Illustre, which was founded in 1632 in the Agnieten-kapel. Beyond Damstraat, the bustling Red Light District meets the Nieuw-markt, where the 15th-century Waag evokes a medieval air. South of the Nieuwmarkt, Museum Het Rembrandt-huis gives a fascinating insight into the life of the city's most famous artist.

★ Red Light District
The sex industry brings billions of euros to Amsterdam every year ❶

Hash Marijuana Hemp Museum
Marijuana through the ages
❹

Agnietenkapel
Like many buildings in this area, the cloisters, which house a museum, belong to the University of Amsterdam ❺

House (1610), unusually, facing three canals

Oudemanhuispoort
Spectacles on the gateway into this 18th-century alms-house for elderly men symbolize old age ❻

STAR SIGHTS

★ Red Light District

★ Museum Het Rembrandthuis

Lift bridge over Groenburgwal

Nieuwmarkt

Despite redevelopment southeast of this once-important market square, the Nieuwmarkt itself is still bordered by many fine 17th- and 18th-century gabled houses ③

Trippenhuis

Although it appears to be a single 17th-century mansion, this building is in fact two houses, the middle windows being false to preserve the symmetry ⑧

LOCATOR MAP
See Street Finder maps 7 and 8

Waag

Amsterdam's only remaining medieval gatehouse now houses a restaurant ②

Oostindisch Huis

Now part of the University of Amsterdam, this former Dutch East India Company (VOC) building has a fine example of an early 17th-century façade ⑦

Zuiderkerk

This prominent city landmark now houses the city's planning information centre ⑨

| 0 metres | 50 |
| 0 yards | 50 |

KEY

– – – Suggested route

★ Museum Het Rembrandthuis

Hundreds of Rembrandt's etchings, including many self-portraits, are on display in the artist's former home ⑩

Red Light District ❶

Map 8 D2. 🚊 4, 9, 14, 16, 24, 25.

Barely clad prostitutes bathed in a red neon glow and touting for business at their windows is one of the defining images of modern Amsterdam. The city's Red Light District, referred to locally as de Walletjes (the little walls), is concentrated on the Oude Kerk (see pp68–9), although it extends as far as Warmoesstraat to the west, the Zeedijk to the north, the Kloveniersburgwal to the east and then along the line of Damstraat to the south.

Prostitution in Amsterdam dates back to the city's emergence as a port in the 13th century. By 1478, prostitution had become so widespread, with increasing numbers of sea-weary sailors flooding into the city, that attempts were made to contain it. Prostitutes straying outside their designated area were marched back to the sound of pipe and drum.

A century later, following the Alteration (see pp24–5), the Calvinists tried to outlaw prostitution altogether. Their attempts were half-hearted, and by the mid-17th century prostitution was openly tolerated. In 1850, Amsterdam had a

Entrance to one of the clubs in the Red Light District

population of 200,000, and more than 200 brothels. The most famous of these, like the luxurious Madame Traese's, catered for rich clients.

Today, the whole area is criss-crossed by a network of narrow lanes, dominated by garish sex shops and seedy clubs, and peppered with junkies, dealers and pickpockets. At night, the little alleys assume a somewhat sinister aspect, and it is not wise to wander away from the main streets. But by day, hordes of visitors crowding in generate a festive buzz, and among the sleaze there are interesting cafés, bars, restaurants and beautiful canal-side houses to be discovered.

Waag ❷

Nieuwmarkt 4. **Map** 8 D3. **Tel** 422 7772. 🚊 9, 14. Ⓜ Nieuwmarkt. 🔘 upper rooms closed to the public.

The multi-turreted Waag is Amsterdam's oldest surviving gatehouse. Built in 1488, it was then, and often still is, called St Antoniespoort. Public executions were held here, and prisoners awaited their fate in the "little gallows room". In 1617, the building became the public weigh house (waaggebouw). Peasants had their produce weighed here and paid tax accordingly. Various guilds moved into the upper rooms of each tower. From 1619 the Guild of Surgeons had their meeting room and anatomy theatre here. They added the central octagonal tower in 1691. Rembrandt's Anatomy Lesson of Dr Tulp, now in the Mauritshuis (see pp188–9), and The Anatomy Lesson of Dr Jan Deijman, in the Amsterdams Historisch Museum (see pp80–1), were commissioned by the guild and hung here.

After the weigh house closed in the early 1800s, the Waag served as a fire station and two city museums. It is now home to the café-restaurant In de Waag (see p228).

The 15th-century Waag dominating the Nieuwmarkt, with an antique market on the left

Part of the commemorative photo display in Nieuwmarkt metro

Nieuwmarkt ❸

Map 8 D3. 🚋 *9, 14.*
Ⓜ *Nieuwmarkt.* **Antiques market**
○ *May–Sep: 9am–5pm Sun.*
Organic market ○ *9am–4pm Sat.*

An open, paved square, the Nieuwmarkt is flanked to the west by the Red Light District. With the top end of the Geldersekade, it forms Amsterdam's Chinatown. The Waag dominates the square, and construction of this gateway led to the site's development in the 15th century as a marketplace. When the city expanded in the 17th century *(see pp26–7)*, the square took on its present dimensions and was called the Nieuwmarkt. It retains an array of 17th- and 18th-century gabled houses. True to tradition, an antiques market is held on Sundays during the summer.

The old Jewish Quarter leads off the square down St Antoniesbreestraat. In the 1970s, many houses were demolished to make way for the metro, sparking off clashes between protesters and police. The action of conservationists persuaded the city council to renovate rather than redevelop old buildings. In tribute to them, photographs of their protests decorate the metro.

Hash Marijuana Hemp Museum ❹

Oudezijds Achterburgwal 148.
Map 7 C3. *Tel* 623 5961. 🚋 *4, 9, 14, 16, 24, 25.* Ⓜ *Nieuwmarkt.*
○ *11am–10pm daily.* 🎦 ⊙ ♿
📷 www.hashmuseum.com

This museum is the only one in Europe to chart the history of hemp (marijuana). Exhibits refer back 8,000 years to early

Asiatic civilizations, which used the plant for medicines and clothing. It was first used in the Netherlands, according to a herbal manual of 1554, as a cure for earache.

Until the late 19th century, however, hemp was the main source of fibre for rope, and was therefore important in the Dutch shipping industry. Other exhibits relate to the psychoactive properties of this plant. They include an intriguing array of pipes and bongs (smoking devices), along with displays that explain smuggling methods. The museum also has a small cultivation area where plants are grown under artificial light. Police sometimes raid and take away exhibits, so there may be occasional gaps in displays.

Agnietenkapel ❺

Oudezijds Voorburgwal 231.
Map 7 C4. *Tel* 525 3339.
🚋 *4, 9, 14, 16, 24, 25.* ● *closed for renovations until 2007.*

Now home to the University Museum, the Agnieten-kapel was part of the convent of St Agnes until 1578 when it was closed after the Alteration *(see pp24–5)*. In 1632, the Athenaeum Illustre, the precursor of the University of Amsterdam, took it over and by the mid-17th century it was a centre of scientific learning. It also housed the municipal library until the 1830s. While the museum focuses on the history of the University of Amsterdam, the main attraction is the Agnietenkapel itself, dating from 1470. It is one of the few Gothic chapels to have survived the Alteration. During restoration from 1919 to 1921, elements of Amsterdam School architecture were introduced *(see p97)*. Despite these changes and long periods of secular use, the building still has the feel of a Franciscan chapel. The large auditorium on the first

floor is the city's oldest, and is used for university lectures. It has a lovely ceiling, painted with Renaissance motifs and a portrait of Minerva, the Roman goddess of wisdom and the arts.

The chapel will eventually become a conference centre which will not be open to the public.

Entrance to Agnietenkapel, home to the University Museum

Oudemanhuispoort ❻

Between Oudezijds Achterburgwal and Kloveniersburgwal. **Map** 7 C4.
🚋 *4, 9, 14, 16, 24, 25.* **Book market** ○ *10am–6pm Mon–Sat.*

The Oudemanhuispoort was once the entrance to old men's almshouses (Oudemannenhuis), built in 1754. Today the building is part of the University of Amsterdam. The pediment over the gateway in the Oudezijds Achterburgwal features a pair of spectacles, a symbol of old age. Trading inside this covered walkway dates from 1757 and today there is a market for second-hand books. Although the building is closed to the public, visitors may enter the 18th-century courtyard via the arcade.

Crest of Amsterdam, Oudemanhuispoort

The spire of the Zuiderkerk, a prominent city landmark

Oostindisch Huis ❼

Oude Hoogstraat 24 (entrance on Kloveniersburgwal 48). **Map** 7 C3. 🚊 4, 9, 14, 16, 24, 25. Ⓜ Nieuwmarkt. ◯ noon–5pm Tue, 9am–5pm Wed, unless there is a graduation ceremony.

The Oostindisch Huis, former headquarters of the Dutch East India Company or VOC *(see pp28–9)*, is now part of the University of Amsterdam. Built in 1605, it is attributed to Hendrick de Keyser *(see p90)*. The premises have been expanded several times, in 1606, 1634 and 1661, to house spices, pepper, porcelain and silk from the East Indies.

The VOC was dissolved in 1800 *(see p31)*, and for a while the Oostindisch Huis was taken over by the customs authorities. Later, the state tax offices also moved in, and the VOC medallion carved in the stone gate was replaced with a lion, the traditional heraldic symbol of the Netherlands.

Major restyling in the 1890s destroyed much of the interior decoration, but the façade has remained

largely intact, and the former meeting room of the VOC lords has been restored to its 17th-century state.

Trippenhuis ❽

Kloveniersburgwal 29. **Map** 8 D3. 🚊 4, 9, 14, 16, 24, 25. Ⓜ Nieuwmarkt. ◯ to the public.

Justus Vingboons designed this ornate Classical mansion, completed in 1662. It appears to be one house: it is in fact two. The façade, outlined by eight Corinthian columns, features false middle windows. The house was designed for the wealthy arms merchants Lodewijk and Hendrick Trip, and hence the chimneys look like cannons. The city's art collection was housed here

from 1817 to 1885, when it moved to the Rijksmuseum *(see pp130–33)*. The Trippenhuis now houses the Dutch Academy. Opposite at No. 26 is the Kleine Trippenhuis, built in 1698. It is only 2.5 m (7 ft) wide and has very detailed cornicing, which includes two carved sphinxes.

Zuiderkerk ❾

Zuiderkerkhof 72. **Map** 8 D4. **Tel** 680 6806. 🚊 9, 14. Ⓜ Nieuwmarkt. ◯ 9am–4pm Mon–Fri, noon–4pm Sat. 📷 ♿ **Tower** 🎫 📷 hours vary; phone 689 2565 for up-to-date information.

Designed by Hendrick de Keyser in 1603, the Renaissance-style Zuiderkerk was the first Calvinist church to open in Amsterdam after the Alteration *(see pp24–5)*. The spire, with its columns, decorative clocks and onion dome, is a prominent city landmark.

The Zuiderkerk ceased to function as a church in 1929. Restored in 1988, it is now a public housing exhibition centre. The surrounding community housing includes Theo Bosch's modern apartment building, the "Pentagon", completed in the mid-1980s.

Museum Het Rembrandthuis ❿

Jodenbreestraat 4. **Map** 8 D4. **Tel** 520 0400. 🚊 9, 14. Ⓜ Nieuwmarkt. ◯ 10am–5pm Mon–Sat, 11–5pm Sun and public hols. ◯ 1 Jan. 🎫 📷 📷 www.rembrandthuis.nl

Rembrandt worked and taught in this house from 1639 until 1656. He lived in the ground-floor rooms with his wife, Saskia, who died here in 1642, leaving the artist with a baby son, Titus *(see p200)*.

Many of Rembrandt's most famous paintings were created in the first-floor studio.

A fine collection of Rembrandt's drawings includes various self-portraits in different moods and guises. The interior has been restored to its former

Ornate balustrade of the Oostindisch Huis

Façade of Museum Het Rembrandthuis

glory, and furnished with objects and art works using the original inventory drawn up when Rembrandt sold the house in 1656. A new wing was added recently, with a shop and two floors used for temporary exhibitions.

Stadhuis-Muziektheater ⓫

Waterlooplein 22. **Map** 8 D4.
🚋 9, 14. Ⓜ *Waterlooplein.*
Stadhuis Tel 552 9111.
◯ **offices** 8:30am–5pm Mon–Fri
*(free concerts Sep–May: 12:30pm
Tue).* **Muziektheater Tel** 625 5455.
See *Entertainment pp246–51.*
♿ 🎫 www.hetmuziektheater.nl

Few buildings in Amsterdam caused as much controversy as the new Stadhuis (city hall) and Muziektheater (opera house). Nicknamed the "Stopera" by protesters, the scheme required the destruction of dozens of medieval houses, which were virtually all that remained of the original Jewish quarter. This led to running battles between squatters and police *(see pp36–7)*.

The building was completed in 1988, a massive confection of red brick, marble and glass. A mural illustrating the Normaal Amsterdams Peil *(see pp36–7)* is shown on the arcade linking the two parts of the complex. The Stopera has the largest auditorium in the country, with a seating capacity for 1,689

people, and it is now home to the Netherlands' national opera and ballet companies. There are guided backstage tours.

Waterlooplein ⓬

Map 8 D5. 🚋 9, 14. Ⓜ *Waterlooplein.* **Market** ◯ 9am–5pm Mon–Fri, 8:30am–5pm Sat.
Holland Experience 3D Movie Theatre Tel 422 2233. ◯ 10am–5:30pm daily (a show every hour). 🖥 www.holland-experience.nl

The Waterlooplein dates from 1882, when two canals were filled in to create a large market square in the heart of the Jewish quarter. The site was originally known as Vlooyenburg, an artificial island built in the 17th century to house the Jewish settlers *(see p64).*

It is now the setting for the new Holland Experience, a spectacular multi-media show taking visitors on a 30-minute tour of the country.

Despite encroachment by the Stadhuis-Muziektheater,

the northern end of the Waterlooplein still operates a lively market, selling anything from bric-a-brac and army-surplus clothing to Balinese carvings.

Mozes en Aäronkerk ⓭

Waterlooplein 205. **Map** 8 E4.
Tel 622 1305. 🚋 9, 14.
Ⓜ *Waterlooplein.* ◉ to the public except for exhibitions.

Designed by the Flemish architect T. Suys the Elder in 1841, Mozes en Aäronkerk was built on the site of a clandestine Catholic church. The later church took its name from the Old Testament figures of Moses and Aaron depicted on the gable stones found on the original building. These are now set into the rear wall.

The church was restored in 1990, when its twin wooden towers were painted to look like sandstone. It is now used for exhibitions, public meetings, concerts and celebrations.

Clothes on offer at the Waterlooplein market

Joods Historisch Museum ⑭

This complex of four synagogues was built by Ashkenazi Jews in the 17th and 18th centuries and opened as a museum in 1987. The synagogues were central to Jewish life in Amsterdam, until the devastation of World War II left them empty. They were restored in the 1980s and connected by internal walkways. Displays of art and religious artifacts depict Jewish culture and the history of Judaism in the Netherlands.

The Star of David, worn by all Jews in the Nazi occupation

The Nieuwe Synagoge was built in 1752.

Charlotte Salomon, Self-Portrait *(1940)*
In 2006, a climate-controlled print room was added under the Nieuwe Synagoge. The remarkable gouaches by Charlotte Salomon are regularly exhibited here.

JEWS IN AMSTERDAM

The first Jew to gain Dutch citizenship was a member of the Portuguese Sephardic community in 1597. The Ashkenazi Jews from eastern Europe came to Amsterdam later, in the 1630s. They were restricted to working in certain trades, but were granted full civil equality in 1796. With the rise of Zionism in the 19th century, Jewish identity re-emerged, but the Nazi occupation decimated the community *(see pp34–5)*.

18th-century Torah scroll finial in shape of the Westerkerk tower

★ Festival Prayer Book
Presented to Amsterdam's Jewish community by printer Uri Phoebus ha-Levi in 1669, this Festival Prayer Book was one of the few to survive the late Middle Ages.

MUSEUM GUIDE

Temporary exhibitions are shown in the Nieuwe Synagoge. The Grote Synagoge has a permanent collection illustrating the religion, culture and history of the Jews in the Netherlands. The museum's focus on children is illustrated by the Children's Museum and events.

Hanukah Lamp
Nine-branched candelabra are placed in synagogues during Hanukah – the Festival of Lights. Similar lamps are lit to mark the beginning of the Jewish Sabbath on Friday evenings.

VISITORS' CHECKLIST

Nieuwe Amstelstraat 1. **Map** 8 E5.
Tel *531 0310.* 9, 14.
Muziektheater. Waterlooplein. 11am–5pm daily.
Yom Kippur.
on request, incl. for the visually
disabled. www.jhm.nl

Obbene Shul (1685)

Café

Dritt Shul (1778)

Torah Mantle
This beautiful 18th-century cover for the Torah is heavily woven with gold and silver thread. It was used by Amsterdam's community of Portuguese Sephardic Jews.

Main entrance

STAR FEATURES

★ Grote Synagoge

★ Festival Prayer Book

The *mikveh*, or bath for ritual purification

★ Grote Synagoge
Designed by Elias Bouman (see p66). The Ark was given to the synagogue by Rabbi Abraham Auerbach when it opened in 1671. The neoclassical entrance was added during the 1822–1823 renovations.

Portugees-Israëlitische Synagoge ⑮

Mr Visserplein 3. **Map** 8 E5. **Tel** 624 5351. 🚊 9, 14. Ⓜ Waterlooplein. ◯ Apr–Oct: 10am–4pm Sun–Fri; Nov–Mar: 10am–4pm Sun–Thu, 10am–3pm Fri. ● Jewish hols. 📷 🚻 🛍 🖼 by arrangement at the Joods Historische Museum (see pp64–5).

Elias Bouman's design for this synagogue was inspired by the architecture of the Temple of Solomon in Jerusalem. Built for the Portuguese Sephardic community of Amsterdam (see p64) and inaugurated in 1675, the huge building has a rectangular ground plan with the Holy Ark in the southeast corner facing Jerusalem, and the *tebah* (the podium from which the service is led) at the opposite end.

The wooden, barrel-vaulted ceiling is supported by four Ionic columns. The interior of the synagogue is illuminated by more than 1,000 candles and 72 windows.

Italianate façade of the 17th-century Pintohuis

Pintohuis ⑯

Sint Antoniesbreestraat 69. **Map** 8 D4. **Tel** 624 3184. 🚊 9, 14. Ⓜ Nieuwmarkt. ◯ Call for up-to-date information. ● public hols.

Isaac de Pinto, a wealthy Portuguese merchant, bought the Pintohuis in 1651 for the then enormous sum of 30,000 guilders. He had it

remodelled over the next decades to a design by Elias Bouman, and it is one of the few private residences in Amsterdam to follow an Italianate style. The exterior design was reworked from 1675 to 1680. Six imposing pilasters break up the severe, cream façade into five recessed sections, and the cornice is topped by a blind balustrade concealing the roof.

In the 1970s, the house was scheduled for demolition because it stood in the way of a newly planned main road. However, concerted protest saved the building. Visitors can still admire the painted ceiling, which is decorated with birds and cherubs.

Montelbaanstoren ⑰

Oude Waal /Oudeschans 2. **Map** 8 E3. 🚊 9, 14. Ⓜ Nieuwmarkt. ● to the public.

The lower portion of the Montelbaanstoren was built in 1512 and formed part of Amsterdam's medieval fortifications. It lay just beyond the city wall, protecting the city's wharves on the newly built St Antoniesdijk (now the Oudeschans) from the neighbouring Gelderlanders.

The octagonal structure and open-work timber steeple were both added by Hendrick de Keyser (see p90) in 1606. His decorative addition bears a close resemblance to the spire of the Oude Kerk, designed by Joost Bilhamer, which was built 40 years earlier (see pp68–9). In 1611, the tower began to list, prompting Amsterdammers to attach ropes to the top and pull it right again.

Sailors from the VOC (see pp28–9) would gather at the Montelbaanstoren before being ferried in small boats down the IJ to the massive East Indies-bound sailing ships, anchored further out in deep water to the north.

The building appears in a number of etchings by Rembrandt, and is still a popular subject for artists. It now houses the offices of the Amsterdam water authority.

One of many stone carvings on the Scheepvaarthuis façade

Scheepvaarthuis ⑱

Prins Hendrikkade 108. **Map** 8 E2. 🚊 1, 2, 4, 5, 9, 13, 16, 17, 24, 25. 🚌 22, 59. Ⓜ Centraal Station. ● to the public.

Built as an office complex in 1916, the Scheepvaarthuis (Shipping House) is regarded as the first true example of Amsterdam School architecture (see p97). It was designed by Piet Kramer (1881–1961), Johan van der May (1878–1949) and Michel de Klerk (1884–1923) for a group of shipping companies which no longer wanted to conduct business on the quay.

The imposing triangular building has a prow-like front and is crowned by a statue of Neptune, his wife and four female figures representing

The medieval Montelbaanstoren, with its decorative timber steeple

the four points of the compass. No expense was spared on the construction and internal decoration of the building, and local dock workers came to regard the building as a symbol of capitalism. The doors, stairs, window frames and interior walls are festooned with nautical images, such as dolphins and anchors. Beautiful stained-glass skylights are also decorated with images of sailing ships and compasses.

The Scheepvaarthuis is now home to the municipal transport department. Although closed to the public, Archivisie *(see p270)* will arrange architectural tours of the building.

Schreierstoren ⑲

Prins Hendrikkade 94–95. **Map** 8 E1. 🚋 *1, 2, 4, 5, 9, 13, 16, 17, 24, 25.* Ⓜ *Centraal Station.* 🌐 *to the public.* **VOC Café *Tel*** *428 8291.* ⭕ *10am–11pm.*

The Schreierstoren (Weepers' Tower) was a defensive structure forming part of the medieval city walls, and dates from 1480. It was one of the few fortifications not to be demolished as the city expanded beyond its medieval boundaries in the 17th century. The building now houses a nautical equipment shop.

Popular legend states that the tower derived its name from the weeping (*schreien* in the original Dutch) of women who came here to wave their men off to sea. It is more likely, however, that the title has a less romantic origin and comes from the tower's position on a sharp (*screye* or *scherpe*), 90-degree bend in the old town walls. The earliest of four wall plaques, dated 1569, adds considerably to the confusion by depicting a weeping woman alongside the inscription *scrayer hovck*, which means sharp corner.

In 1609, Henry Hudson set sail from here in an attempt to discover a new and faster trading route to the East Indies. Instead, he unintentionally "discovered" the river in North America which still bears his name. A bronze plaque, laid in 1927, commemorates his voyage.

The Schreierstoren, part of the original city fortifications

Zeedijk ⑳

Map 8 D2. 🚋 *1, 2, 4, 5, 9, 13, 16, 17, 24, 25.* Ⓜ *Centraal Station.*

Along with the Nieuwendijk and the Haarlemmerdijk, the Zeedijk (sea dyke) formed part of Amsterdam's original fortifications. Built in the early 1300s, some 30 years after Amsterdam had been granted its city charter, these defences took the form of a canal moat with piled-earth ramparts reinforced by wooden palisades. As the city grew and the boundaries expanded, the canals were filled in and the dykes became obsolete. The paths that ran alongside them became the streets and alleys which bear their names today.

One of the two remaining wooden-fronted houses in Amsterdam can be found at No. 1. It was built in the mid-16th century as a hostel for sailors and now houses Café In 't Aepjen (Tel 626 8401). Opposite is St Olofskapel, built in 1445 and named after the first Christian king of Norway and Denmark.

By the 1600s, the Zeedijk had become a slum. The area is on the edge of the city's Red Light District, and in the 1960s and 1970s it became notorious as a centre for drug-dealing and street crime. Following a clean-up campaign in the 1980s, the Zeedijk is now much improved.

Plaques on the gables of some of the street's cafés reveal their former use – the red boot at No. 17 indicates that it was once a cobbler's.

Plaque on the Café 't Mandje (Little Basket), a gay bar at No. 63 Zeedijk

Oude Kerk ㉑

The origins of the Oude Kerk date from the early 13th century, when a wooden church was built in a burial ground on a sand bank *(see pp20–21)*. The present Gothic structure is 14th-century and it has grown from a single-aisled church into a basilica. As it expanded, the building became a gathering place for traders and a refuge for the poor. Its paintings and statuary were destroyed after the Alteration *(see pp24–5)* in 1578, but the gilded ceiling and stained-glass windows were undamaged. The Great Organ was added in 1724, and the stark interior has changed little since.

Carving on 15th-century choir misericord

The spire of the bell tower was built by Joost Bilhamer in 1565. François Hemony added the 47-bell carillon in 1658.

Tomb of Saskia, first wife of Rembrandt *(see pp62–3)*

The Oude Kerk Today
The old church, surrounded by shops, cafés and houses, remains a calm and peaceful haven at the heart of the frenetic Red Light District.

Christening Chapel

Tomb of Admiral Abraham van der Hulst (1619–66)

★ **Great Organ** *(1724)*
Christian Vater's oak-encased organ has eight bellows and 54 gilded pipes. Marbled-wood statues of biblical figures surround it.

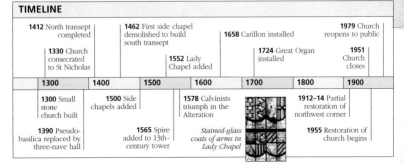

TIMELINE

1412 North transept completed	**1462** First side chapel demolished to build south transept	**1658** Carillon installed	**1979** Church reopens to public
1330 Church consecrated to St Nicholas	**1552** Lady Chapel added	**1724** Great Organ installed	**1951** Church closes

1300	1400	1500	1600	1700	1800	1900

1300 Small stone church built	**1500** Side chapels added	**1578** Calvinists triumph in the Alteration	**1912–14** Partial restoration of northwest corner
1390 Pseudo-basilica replaced by three-nave hall	**1565** Spire added to 13th-century tower	*Stained-glass coats of arms in Lady Chapel*	**1955** Restoration of church begins

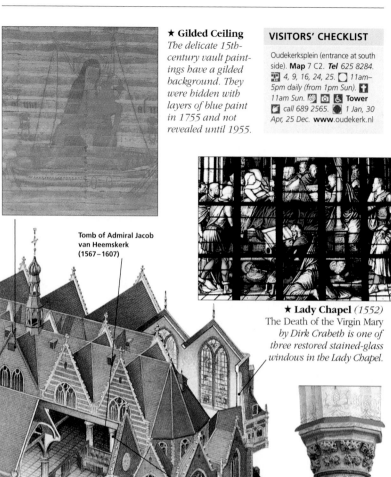

★ **Gilded Ceiling**
The delicate 15th-century vault paintings have a gilded background. They were hidden with layers of blue paint in 1755 and not revealed until 1955.

VISITORS' CHECKLIST

Oudekerksplein (entrance at south side). **Map** 7 C2. **Tel** 625 8284. 4, 9, 16, 24, 25. 11am–5pm daily (from 1pm Sun). 11am Sun. **Tower** call 689 2565. 1 Jan, 30 Apr, 25 Dec. www.oudekerk.nl

Tomb of Admiral Jacob van Heemskerk
(1567–1607)

★ **Lady Chapel** *(1552)*
The Death of the Virgin Mary by Dirk Crabeth is one of three restored stained-glass windows in the Lady Chapel.

Brocaded Pillars
Decorative pillars originally formed niches holding a series of statues of the Apostles, all destroyed by the iconoclasts in 1578.

17th- and 18th-century houses

Former sacristy

The Red Door
The inscription on the lintel above the door into the former sacristy warns those about to enter: "Marry in haste, repent at leisure."

STAR FEATURES

★ Great Organ
★ Gilded Ceiling
★ Lady Chapel

NIEUWE ZIJDE

The western side of medieval Amsterdam was known as the Nieuwe Zijde (New Side). Together with the Oude Zijde it formed the heart of the early maritime settlement. Nieuwendijk, now a busy shopping street, was originally one of the earliest sea defences. As Amsterdam grew, it expanded eastwards, leaving large sections of the Nieuwe Zijde, to the west, neglected and in decline. With its many wooden houses, the city was prone to fires and in 1452 much of the area was burnt down. During rebuilding, a broad moat, the Singel, was cut, along which warehouses, rich merchants' homes

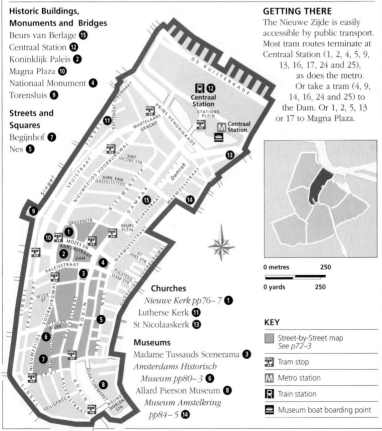

"The calf" emblem on a house in the Begijnhof

and fine quays sprang up. The Amsterdams Historisch Museum, which is now housed in a splendid, converted orphanage, has scores of maps and paintings charting the growth of the city from these times to the present day. One room is devoted to the Miracle of Amsterdam *(see p22),* which made the city a place of pilgrimage, and brought commerce to the Nieuwe Zijde. Nearby lies Kalverstraat, Amsterdam's main shopping street, and also the secluded Begijnhof. This pretty courtyard is mostly fringed by narrow 17th-century houses, but it also contains the city's oldest surviving wooden house.

SIGHTS AT A GLANCE

Historic Buildings, Monuments and Bridges
Beurs van Berlage ⑮
Centraal Station ⑫
Koninklijk Paleis ②
Magna Plaza ⑩
Nationaal Monument ④
Torensluis ⑨

Streets and Squares
Begijnhof ⑦
Nes ⑤

Churches
Nieuwe Kerk pp76–7 ①
Lutherse Kerk ⑪
St Nicolaaskerk ⑬

Museums
Madame Tussauds Scenerama ③
Amsterdams Historisch Museum pp80–3 ⑥
Allard Pierson Museum ⑧
Museum Amstelkring pp84–5 ⑭

GETTING THERE

The Nieuwe Zijde is easily accessible by public transport. Most tram routes terminate at Centraal Station (1, 2, 4, 5, 9, 13, 16, 17, 24 and 25), as does the metro. Or take a tram (4, 9, 14, 16, 24 and 25) to the Dam. Or 1, 2, 5, 13 or 17 to Magna Plaza.

| 0 metres | 250 |
| 0 yards | 250 |

KEY

⬚ Street-by-Street map See p72–3

🚊 Tram stop

Ⓜ Metro station

🚉 Train station

🚢 Museum boat boarding point

◁ *The Fatal Fall of Icarus,* one of the many Classical sculptures in the Koninklijk Paleis

Street-by-Street: Nieuwe Zijde

Although much of the medieval Nieuwe Zijde has disappeared, the area is still rich in buildings that relate to the city's past. The Dam, dominated by the Koninklijk Paleis and Nieuwe Kerk, provides examples of architecture from the 15th to the 20th century. Around Kalverstraat, the narrow streets and alleys follow the course of some of the earliest dykes and footpaths. Here, most of the traditional gabled houses have been turned into bustling shops and cafés. Streets such as Rokin and Nes are now home to financial institutions, attracted by the nearby stock and options exchanges. Nes is also known for its venues which feature alternative theatre.

Kalverstraat, now a busy tourist shopping area, took its name from the livestock market which was regularly held here during the 15th century.

★ **Amsterdams Historisch Museum**
Wall plaques and maps showing the walled medieval city are on display in this converted orphanage that dates from the 16th century ❻

★ **Begijnhof**
Two churches and one of the few remaining wooden houses in the city nestle in this secluded, tree-filled courtyard ❼

| 0 metres | 50 |
| 0 yards | 50 |

KEY

– – – Suggested route

Caffè Esprit
(see p237)

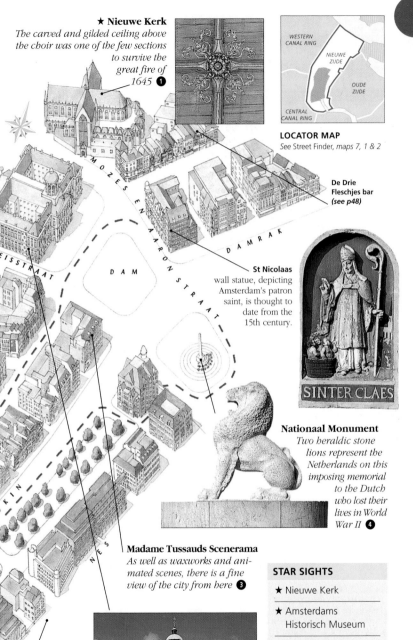

★ **Nieuwe Kerk**
The carved and gilded ceiling above the choir was one of the few sections to survive the great fire of 1645 ❶

LOCATOR MAP
See Street Finder, maps 7, 1 & 2

De Drie Fleschjes bar *(see p48)*

St Nicolaas wall statue, depicting Amsterdam's patron saint, is thought to date from the 15th century.

SINTER CLAES

Nationaal Monument
Two heraldic stone lions represent the Netherlands on this imposing memorial to the Dutch who lost their lives in World War II ❹

Madame Tussauds Scenerama
As well as waxworks and animated scenes, there is a fine view of the city from here ❸

STAR SIGHTS

★ Nieuwe Kerk

★ Amsterdams Historisch Museum

★ Begijnhof

Nes
This street is one of Amsterdam's oldest and has been a centre for theatre for 150 years ❺

Koninklijk Paleis
Built as the town hall, the building's Classical façade and fine sculptures were intended to glorify the city and its government ❷

The vast marble-floored Burgerzaal in the Koninklijk Paleis

Nieuwe Kerk ❶

See pp76–7.

Koninklijk Paleis ❷

Dam. **Map** 7 B2. **Tel** 624 8698.
🚊 1, 2, 4, 5, 9, 13, 14, 16, 17, 24, 25. ⬤ *for restoration until 2008. Phone 620 4060 or visit the website for up-to-date information.* 📷 ⬤ ♿ 🚻 🎫 *2pm Wed & Sun* (**Tel** *624 8698 to reserve a private group tour).* **www**.koninklijkhuis.nl

The Koninklijk Paleis, still used occasionally by the Dutch royal family for official functions, was built as the Stadhuis (town hall). Work began in 1648, after the end of the 80 Years War with Spain (*see pp28–9*). It dominated its surroundings and more than 13,600 piles were driven into the ground for the foundations. The Classically inspired design by Jacob van Campen (1595–1657) reflects Amsterdam's mood of confidence after the Dutch victory. Civic pride is also shown in the allegorical sculptures by Artus Quellien (1609–68), which decorate the pediments, and in François Hemony's statues and carillon.

The full magnificence of the architecture is best seen in the vast Burgerzaal (citizen's hall). Based on the assembly halls of ancient Rome, this 30-m (95-ft) high room runs the length of the building. It boasts a marble floor inlaid with maps of the eastern and western hemispheres, as well as epic sculptures by Quellien.

Most of the furniture on display, including the chandeliers, dates from 1808, when Louis Napoleon declared the building his royal palace (*see pp30–31*).

Madame Tussauds Scenerama ❸

Peek & Cloppenburg Building, Dam 20. **Map** 7 B3. **Tel** 522 1010.
🚊 4, 9, 14, 16, 24, 25. ⬤ *10am–5:30pm daily.* ⬤ *30 Apr.* 📷 ⬤ ♿ 🚻
www.madametussauds.nl

Located above the Peek & Cloppenburg department store, Madame Tussauds offers an audiovisual tour of Amsterdam's history, plus projected future developments. Some of the displays, such as the animated 5-m (16-ft)

figure of "Amsterdam Man", are bizarre, but the wax models of 17th-century people give an insight into life in the Golden Age (*see pp26–7*).

Nationaal Monument ❹

Dam. **Map** 7 B3.
🚊 4, 9, 14, 16, 24, 25.

Sculpted by John Raedecker and designed by architect JJP Oud, the 22-m (70-ft) obelisk in the Dam commemorates Dutch World War II casualties. It was unveiled in 1956, and is fronted by two lions, heraldic symbols of the Netherlands. Embedded in the wall behind are urns containing earth from all the Dutch provinces and the former colonies of Indonesia, the Antilles and Surinam.

Nes ❺

Map 7 B3. 🚊 4, 9, 14, 16, 24, 25.

This quiet, narrow street is home to several theatres. In 1614, Amsterdam's first bank was opened in a pawnshop at No. 57. A wall plaque marks the site, and pawned goods still clutter the shop window. At night, Nes can be dangerous for the unguarded visitor.

De Engelenbak, one of several theatres located along Nes

Amsterdams Historisch Museum ❻

See pp80–83.

Begijnhof 7

Spui (entrance at Gedempte Begijnensloot). **Map** 7 B4. ⚇ 1, 2, 5, 9, 14, 16, 24, 25. **Tel** 623 3565. **Gates** ◯ 9am–5pm daily.

The Begijnhof was originally built in 1346 as a sanctuary for the Begijntjes, a lay Catholic sisterhood who lived like nuns, although they took no monastic vows. In return for lodgings within the complex, these worthy women undertook to educate the poor and look after the sick. Nothing survives of the earliest dwellings, but the Begijnhof still retains a sanctified atmosphere. The rows of beautiful houses that overlook its well-kept green include Amsterdam's oldest surviving house at No. 34. On the adjoining wall, there is a fascinating collection of wall plaques with a biblical theme taken from the houses.

The southern fringe of the square is dominated by the Engelse Kerk (English Church), which dates from the 15th century. Directly west stands the Begijnhof Chapel, a clandestine church in which the Begijntjes and other Catholics worshipped in secret until religious tolerance was restored in 1795. It once housed relics of the Miracle of Amsterdam (see pp22–3). Four splendid stained-glass windows and paintings depict scenes of the Miracle. The occupants request that noise be kept to a minimum and no tour groups are allowed.

Plaque on the Engelse Kerk

The Begijnhof Chapel, a clandestine church (Nos. 29–30), was completed in 1680. It contains many reminders of Amsterdam's Catholic past.

No. 19 has a plaque depicting the exodus of the Jews from Egypt.

Houses in the Begijnhof are still occupied by single women.

Biblical plaques cover the wall behind No. 34.

Spui entrance

Main entrance from Gedempte Begijnensloot

Het Houten Huis at No. 34 is Amsterdam's oldest house, dating from around 1420. It is one of only two wooden-fronted houses in the city, as timber houses were banned in 1521 after a series of catastrophic fires. Most of the houses in the Begijnhof were not built until after the 16th century.

Engelse Kerk was built around 1419 for the Begijntjes. The church was confiscated after the Alteration (see pp24–5) and rented to a group of English and Scottish Presbyterians in 1607. The Pilgrim Fathers (see p185) may have worshipped here.

Nieuwe Kerk ❶

Dating from the 14th century, Amsterdam's second parish church was built as the population outgrew the Oude Kerk *(see pp68–9)*. During its turbulent history, the church has been destroyed several times by fire, rebuilt and then stripped of its finery after the Alteration *(see pp24–5)*. It reached its present size in the 1650s. Since 1814 all the Dutch monarchs have been crowned here. Nowadays, it is also a cultural centre.

Gilded Cherubs
Grimacing gilded cherubs struggle to support the corners of the wooden barrel vault above the transept crossing.

Baptistry

Box pews around the carved pulpit

The New Stadhuis, Dam Square
The Nieuwe Kerk is in the background, at the corner of Dam square, in this painting by Jan van de Heyden (1637–1712). It shows the newly completed Stadhuis, which is now the Koninklijk Paleis (see p74).

Ornate blind windows

★ Great Organ *(1645)*
Marbled-wood cherubs and angels adorn the elaborate gilded casing of the Great Organ, which was designed by Jacob van Campen.

★ Carved Pulpit *(1664)*
It took Albert Vinckenbrinck 15 years to carve the pulpit, which is unusually flamboyant for a Dutch Protestant church.

STAR FEATURES

★ Great Organ

★ Tomb of De Ruyter

★ Carved Pulpit

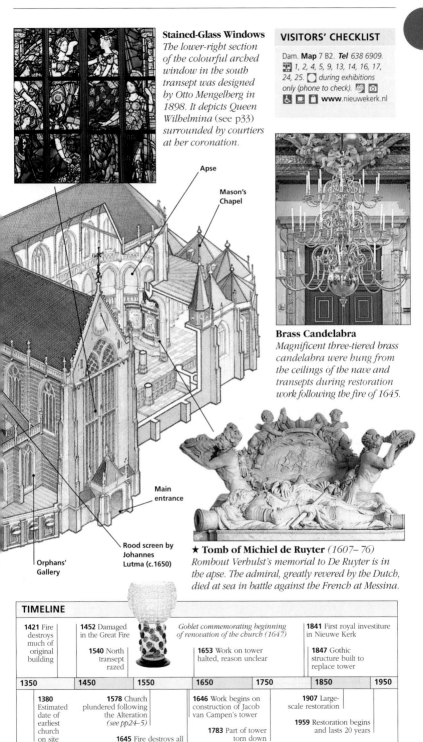

Stained-Glass Windows
The lower-right section of the colourful arched window in the south transept was designed by Otto Mengelberg in 1898. It depicts Queen Wilhelmina (see p33) surrounded by courtiers at her coronation.

VISITORS' CHECKLIST

Dam. **Map** 7 B2. **Tel** 638 6909.
1, 2, 4, 5, 9, 13, 14, 16, 17, 24, 25. during exhibitions only (phone to check).
www.nieuwekerk.nl

Apse

Mason's Chapel

Brass Candelabra
Magnificent three-tiered brass candelabra were hung from the ceilings of the nave and transepts during restoration work following the fire of 1645.

Main entrance

Rood screen by Johannes Lutma (c.1650)

Orphans' Gallery

★ **Tomb of Michiel de Ruyter** (1607–76)
Rombout Verhulst's memorial to De Ruyter is in the apse. The admiral, greatly revered by the Dutch, died at sea in battle against the French at Messina.

TIMELINE

1350	1450	1550	1650	1750	1850	1950

1421 Fire destroys much of original building

1452 Damaged in the Great Fire

1540 North transept razed

Goblet commemorating beginning of renovation of the church (1647)

1653 Work on tower halted, reason unclear

1841 First royal investiture in Nieuwe Kerk

1847 Gothic structure built to replace tower

1380 Estimated date of earliest church on site

1578 Church plundered following the Alteration (*see pp24–5*)

1645 Fire destroys all but façade and walls

1646 Work begins on construction of Jacob van Campen's tower

1783 Part of tower torn down

1907 Large-scale restoration

1959 Restoration begins and lasts 20 years

Allard Pierson Museum ❽

Oude Turfmarkt 127. **Map** 7 B4.
Tel 525 2556. 🚃 4, 9, 14, 16,
24, 25. ⭕ 10am–5pm Tue–Fri,
1–5pm Sat, Sun & pub hols. ⭘ 1
Jan, Easter Sun & Mon, Ascension
Day, 30 Apr, Whitsun, 25 Dec. 🅿
📷 ♿ 🖥 www.uba.uva.nl/apm

**Allard Pierson Museum's Neo-Classical façade
made of Bremer and Bentheimer stone**

Amsterdam's only specialist
archaeological collection
is named after Allard Pierson
(1831–96), a humanist and
scholar. The collection was
moved into this handsome
Neo-Classical building in 1976.

The museum contains Cyp-
riot, Greek, Egyptian, Roman,
Etruscan and Coptic artifacts.
Look out for a case of rather
gruesome Egyptian mummy
remains, a computer that en-
ables you to write your name
in hieroglyphics, a jointed
Greek doll from 300 BC and
some fine Roman jewellery.

Torensluis ❾

Singel between Torensteeg and Oude
Leliestraat. **Map** 7 B2. 🚃 1, 2, 5,
13, 14, 17.

The Torensluis is one of the
widest bridges in Amsterdam.
It was built on the site of a
17th-century sluice gate and

took its name from a tower
that stood on the bridge until
demolished in 1829 (its outline
is marked in the pavement). A
jail was built in its foundations.

In summer, visitors can sit
out at café tables on the bridge
and enjoy pleasant views down
the Singel. The statue dominating the bridge is of Multa-
tuli, the 19th-century Dutch
writer who wrote the well-
known book *Max Havelaar*.

Magna Plaza ❿

Nieuwezijds Voorburgwal 182.
Map 7 B2. **Tel** 626 9199.
🚃 1, 2, 5, 13, 14, 17.
⭕ 11am–7pm Mon, 10am–7pm
Tue–Sat, noon–7pm Sun. ⭘ public
hols. 📷 ♿ www.magnaplaza.nl

A post office building has
been sited here since 1748.
A wall panel on the current
building's façade depicts the
original office, which was taken
out of service in 1854. The

present building was com-
pleted in 1899. CH Peters,
the architect, was ridiculed
for the extravagance of its
Neo-Gothic design. Critics
dubbed the Postkantoor's
elaborately decorated style
and spindly towers "post-
office Gothic". It has been
redeveloped, and in 1990
opened as the city's first shopping mall, the Magna Plaza.
The grand dimensions and
arched galleries of Peters' design have been well preserved.

Ronde Lutherse Kerk ⓫

Kattengat 2. **Map** 7 C1.
Tel 621 2223. 🚃 1, 2, 5, 13, 17.
⭕ for concerts only.

Designed by Adriaan Dortsman (1625–82) and opened
in 1671, this is the first Dutch
Reformed church to feature
a circular ground plan and
two upper galleries, giving
the whole congregation a
clear view of the pulpit.

In 1882 a fire destroyed
everything except the
exterior walls. When the
interior and entrance were
rebuilt in 1883, they were
made squarer and more
ornate, in keeping with the

An outdoor café on the Torensluis bridge overlooking the Singel canal

church architectural style of that time. The church suffered another fire in 1993 and reopened the following year with a new copper dome.

Closed since 1935 due to falling attendances, the church is now used by the Amsterdam Renaissance Hotel *(see p217)* as a conference centre and banqueting chamber. It is occasionally open to the public in winter for concerts on Sunday afternoons.

Centraal Station ⑫

Stationsplein. **Map** 8 D1.
Tel *0900 9292.* 🚊 *1, 2, 4, 5, 9, 11, 13, 16, 17, 24, 25.*
Ⓜ *Centraal Station.* **Information**
◯ *6:30am–9pm daily.* 📷 ♿

Weather vane on Centraal Station

When the Centraal Station opened in 1889, it re-placed the old harbour as the symbolic focal point of the city *(see pp32–3)* and effectively curtained Amsterdam off from the sea. The Neo-Renaissance red-brick railway terminus was designed by PJH Cuypers, who was also responsible for the Rijksmuseum *(see pp130–31)* and AL van Gendt, who designed the Concertgebouw *(see p128)*.

Three artificial islands were created, using 8,600 wooden piles to support the structure. In the design of the station's twin towers and imposing central section there are architectural echoes of a triumphal arch. The imposing façade is adorned with elaborate gold and coloured decoration showing allegories of

Decorative brickwork on the façade of the Beurs van Berlage

maritime trade – a tribute to the city's past. Today it is a major meeting point as well as the transport hub of the capital, with 1,400 trains operating daily *(see p268)*, and buses and trams terminating here. The station is currently undergoing major renovation.

Sint Nicolaaskerk ⑬

Prins Hendrikkade 73. **Map** 8 D1. ***Tel*** *624 8749.* 🚊 *1, 2, 4, 5, 9,13, 16, 17, 24, 25.* Ⓜ *Centraal Station.* ◯ *noon–3pm Mon & Sat, 11am–4pm Tue–Fri.* ✝ *12:30pm Mon–Sat (also 10:30am Fri in Spanish); 10:30am, 1pm (in Spanish), 5pm Sun.* 📷
www.nicolaas-parochie.nl

Sint Nicolaas, the patron saint of seafarers, is an important icon in Holland. Many churches are named after him, and the Netherlands' principal day for the giving of presents, 5 December, is known as Sinterklaasavond *(see p53)*.

The Sint Nicolaaskerk was designed by AC Bleys (1842–1912), and completed in 1887. It replaced some clandestine Catholic churches set up in the city when Amsterdam was officially Protestant *(see p84)*.

The exterior is forbidding, its twin towers dominating the skyline. The monumental interior was recently enlivened by the replacement of stained-glass windows in the dome.

Museum Amstelkring ⑭

See pp84–5.

Beurs van Berlage ⑮

Damrak 2. **Map** 7 C2. ***Tel*** *530 4141.* 🚊 *4, 9, 16, 24, 25.* ◯ *only during exhibitions.* ● *1 Jan.* 📷 🚫 ♿
🏠 **www**.beursvanberlage.nl

Hendrik Berlage's stock exchange was completed in 1903. Its clean, functional appearance marked a departure from late 19th-century revivalist architecture. Many of its design features were adopted by the Amsterdam School *(see p97)*. It has an impressive frieze showing the evolution of man from Adam to stockbroker. Now used for concerts and shows, it is home to the Nederlands Philharmonic Orchestra. The Beurs houses a variety of changing exhibitions.

Neo-Renaissance façade of the Sint Nicolaaskerk

Amsterdams Historisch Museum ⑥

The Convent of St Lucien was turned into a civic orphanage two years after the Alteration of 1578 *(see pp24–5)*. The original red brick convent has been enlarged over the years, with new wings added in the 17th century by Hendrick de Keyser *(see p90)* and Jacob van Campen *(see p76)*. The present building is largely as it was in the 18th century. Since 1975 the complex has housed the city's historical museum.

Lecture Room

Museum Attic

★ **The Anatomy Lesson of Dr Jan Deijman** *(1656)*
In this painting, Rembrandt depicts the dissection of Black Jack, an executed criminal.

Second floor

Orphans' Relief *(1581)*
The relief above the gateway to Kalverstraat is a copy of Joost Bilhamer's original, kept in the main entrance hall. Its inscription asks people to contribute to the upkeep of the orphans.

Library

Kalverstraat main entrance

MUSEUM GUIDE

The permanent exhibitions are housed around the complex's inner courtyards. Clear signposting allows the visitor to either concentrate on a specific period – The Young City, The Mighty City or The Modern City – or to take a Grand Tour through Amsterdam's entire history. A new multimedia map offers a concise overview. There are also temporary exhibitions.

Goliath *(c.1650)*
This massive statue is one of a trio of biblical figures dominating the museum's café.

STAR FEATURES

★ The Flower Market and the Town Hall by Gerrit Berckheijde

★ Civic Guards' Gallery

★ The Anatomy Lesson of Dr Jan Deijman

KEY TO FLOORPLAN

- ☐ Civic Guards' Gallery
- ☐ Regents' Room
- ☐ Introduction & The First Amsterdammers
- ☐ The Young City: 1350-1550
- ☐ The Mighty City: 1550-1815
- ☐ The Modern City: 1815-Today
- ☐ Temporary exhibition space
- ☐ Non-exhibition space

★ **The Flower Market and the Town Hall** *(1673)*
This scene by Gerrit Berckheijde (1638–98) shows the city's original flower market on the Nieuwezijds Voorburgwal, which was filled in in the late 1800s. In the background is the Koninklijk Paleis (see p74).

VISITORS' CHECKLIST

Kalverstraat 92, Nieuwezijds Voorburgwal 357, St Luciensteeg 27. **Map** 1 C5. *Tel* 523 1822. 🚊 1, 2, 4, 5, 9, 13, 14, 16, 17, 24, 25. ◯ 10am–5pm Mon–Fri, 11am–5pm Sat & Sun. ● 1 Jan, 30 Apr, 25 Dec. 🎫 📷 ♿ ✉ 🖥 🍴 🏪 **www**.ahm.nl

Gilded Silver City Keys *(1810)*
These two silver keys were presented to Napoleon upon his entry into Amsterdam on 9 October 1811 (see p31).

First floor

★ **The Governesses (seated) and two Wardresses of the Spinhuis**
This was painted in 1638 by D.D. Santvoort.

Ground floor

17th-century red brick façade

Entrance in girls' courtyard

Entrance on Nieuwezijds Voorburgwal

St Luciensteeg entrance

Hunting Day *(1926)*
Johan Braakensiek's illustration shows the lively carnival atmosphere in Zeedijk during the celebrations for this day, which took place on the third Monday of August.

Exploring the Amsterdams Historisch Museum

The museum charts the development of Amsterdam from its humble origins as a small fishing village at the mouth of the Amstel in the Middle Ages to today's cosmopolitan city. The main focus of the museum is on trade, commerce and culture in Amsterdam's Golden Age during the 17th century, when the city's population and prosperity exploded *(see pp26–7)*. Three main exhibitions cover the various stages of the city's growth, from 1350 through to the present day. A series of Civic Guard group portraits are a highlight of the collection.

CIVIC GUARDS' GALLERY

This covered walkway is accessible to all during museum hours. Queen Juliana opened the gallery in 1975 to house the group portraits which were popular during the 16th century. The Civic Guard comprised three guilds of marksmen, which merged in 1580. This is a rare collection as few portraits were commissioned after 1650. Best-known are Rembrandt's works; highlights are by Dirck Barendsz *(see p81)* and Cornelis Anthonisz, such as *The Meal of the 17 Guardsmen of Company H* (1533).

REGENTS' CHAMBER

Built in 1634, this room was the meeting place of the orphanage's directors (regents). Its fine ceiling, added in 1656, shows the orphans receiving charity. Portraits of the regents hang on

17th-century coats of arms on wooden panel

the walls alongside Abraham de Verwer's two paintings of *The Battle of Slaak* (1633). The long table and cabinets are 17th-century.

THE FIRST AMSTERDAMMERS

The first rooms of the museum contain a series of displays explaining the growth of early Amsterdam around the Amstel river. A map of the city illuminates each area in turn to show when it was developed and how the buildings, roads, water and green spaces have combined to form the city as it is today. Visitors can choose to explore a specific period, or can take the 'Grand Tour' of the entire history of Amsterdam.

THE YOUNG CITY: 1350–1550

Amsterdam's rise to prominence in trade and commerce began at this time *(see pp22–3)*. Scale models and archeological finds such as a cauldron used to soften tar for shipbuilding, and many household items such as shoes and tools, help to explain what the city was like. In addition, there is a huge map on the ground showing where the important areas in the city were. A fervent religious

Bronze dagger (c. 1500)

revival took place during this period, spurred on by the Miracle of Amsterdam in 1345. A dying man was given the Sacrament, which he regurgitated, but when thrown on the fire the Host would not burn. Many churches were built and thousands of pilgrims flocked to the city.

THE MIGHTY CITY: 1550–1815

Between 1500 and 1560 the city's population tripled (in 1502 it had been just 12,000). The Civic Guard became defenders of law and order in the overcrowded city and there is a display of its armour and weaponry shown here. Cornelis Anthonisz's bird's-eye *View of Amsterdam (see pp24–5)* is the oldest city plan to survive, dated 1538. A number of churches and convents are clearly marked. It is during this time that the inner horseshoe of canals was constructed and the Town Hall on the Dam was built. Hendrick Cornelisz Vroom's oil painting (1615) of the fortified Haarlemmerpoort shows how the city defended itself against any outside attack from its political rivals.

The Golden Age *(see pp26–9)* and the importance of overseas trade and colonial expansion forms a large part of this exhibition and includes the globe of the famous cartographer Willem Blaeu *(see p146)*. A late 18th-century model of an East Indiaman is shown resting on a primitive floating dock known as a "camel". This ingenious piece of marine engineering enabled heavily laden ships to travel through the very shallow waters of the Zuiderzee.

Portraits and busts of a variety of dignitaries abound, as well as a collection of official silverware and a 1648 model of the town hall, designed by Jacob van Campen (1595–1657), now the Koninklijk Paleis *(see p74)*.

The great discrepancy between the rich and poorer

The First Steamship on the IJ (1816) by Nicolaas Baur

inhabitants of the city is shown in a room with walls hung with huge and rather gloomy canvases depicting the wealthy governors of Amsterdam's poor houses.

The patronage of art flourished in the city's Golden Age and artists flooded into the city. Contemporary paintings, often allegorical in nature, portray rich families and their lives such as Jacob de Wit's *Maid of Amsterdam* (1741). This and other paintings by great masters such as Pieter de Hooch and Rembrandt, as well as magnificent sculpture are just a few of the exhibits bringing the rich and varied history of Amsterdam to life.

THE OLD ORPHANAGE

Orphan Girls Going to Church (c. 1880) by Nicolaas van der Waaij

The orphanage moved to St Lucien's convent in 1580. It was open only to the children of burghers, excluding the poorest children. As the city grew, so did the number of orphans. In the 17th century, two wings were built to accommodate more children, and a separate entrance for girls was added on St Luciensteeg. The building was used as an orphanage until 1960, but the formal uniform was abandoned in 1919.

THE MODERN CITY: 1815–TODAY

Decline in trade resulted in poverty in the 19th century and charitable institutions grew up to deal with the problem. Art began to reflect the social problems such as the squalour and slum conditions in the city. Melancholic late Hague School works by George Breitner *(see p133)* and sombre black-and-white photographs reflect the city's demise. A series of unrealized plans for the expansion of Amsterdam highlight this stagnation.

A spectacular presentation, including interactive multimedia exhibits, documents more recent history. The museum shows a series of evocative photographs taken during the Depression of the early 1930s and the war years *(see pp34–5)*, when the city was under Nazi occupation.

Photographs, videos and computers allow modern city life to be explored in detail. One of the main themes is the 'Young in Amsterdam'. Temporary exhibitions cover aspects of 20th-century and contemporary Amsterdam and the Amsterdammers.

Museum Amstelkring ⑭

Tucked away on the edge of the Red Light District is a restored 17th-century canal house, with two smaller houses to the rear. The combined upper storeys conceal a secret Catholic church known as Our Lord in the Attic which was originally built in 1663. After the Alteration *(see pp24–5)*, when Amsterdam officially became Protestant, many such hidden churches were built throughout the city. The whole building became a museum in 1888, and today contain elegantly refurbished and decorated rooms, as well as a fine collection of church silver, religious artifacts and paintings.

Christ and the Dove of Peace in silver

Wooden viewing gallery of church

A chaplain's tiny box bedroom is hidden off a bend in the stairs. There was a resident chaplain in the church from 1663.

Amstelkring Façade
The house on the canal has a simple spout gable and includes the two smaller houses behind. It was built by bourgeois merchant Jan Hartman in 1661.

Main entrance

House on the canal

Antechamber in late 18th-century style

★ The Parlour
Restored to its former opulence, the Parlour is an unusually fine example of a living room decorated and furnished in the Dutch Classical style of the 17th century.

STAR FEATURES

★ Our Lord in the Attic

★ Altar Painting by Jacob de Wit

★ The Parlour

Sacristy

VISITORS' CHECKLIST

Oudezijds Voorburgwal 40. **Map**
8 D2. **Tel** 624 6604. 🚊 4, 9, 16,
24, 25. ◯ 10am–5pm Mon–
Sat, 1–5pm Sun and public hols.
⬤ 1 Jan, 30 Apr. 📷 🔲 🛡 ⬛

Confessional
*The landing where the tiny
wooden confessional stands
was formerly the living room
of the rear house.*

★ Altar Painting
The Baptism of Christ *(1716) hanging above
the mock marble altar is by Jacob de Wit (1695–
1754). It is one of three altar paintings that
were designed to be interchangeable.*

Rear
house

17th-Century Kitchen
*The kitchen was originally part of
the sacristan's secret living quarters.
The Delft tiles, fireplace and black-
and-white floor are all original.*

Middle
house

★ Our Lord in the Attic
*The original hidden church was
extended in c. 1735 to create more
seating space. It served the Catholic
community until St Nicolaaskerk
(see p79) was finished in 1887.*

WESTERN CANAL RING

At the start of the 17th century, construction of the *Grachtengordel* began here, just west of the Singel. At the same time, city planner Hendrick Staets laid out the marshy area beyond these fashionable canals as an area for workers whose industries were banned from the town centre. Its network of narrow streets and oblique canals followed the course of old paths and drainage ditches. Immigrants fleeing

"Writing hand" emblem on Claes Claeszhofje

religious persecution also settled here. It is thought that Huguenot refugees called the district *jardin* (garden), later corrupted to "Jordaan". Historically a poor area, it is famous for its almshouses *(hofjes)*, and the Claes Claeszhofje is a fine early example. Recently, the Jordaan has taken on a more bohemian air. Further north are the characterful Western Islands, created in the mid-17th century to meet the demand for warehouses.

SIGHTS AT A GLANCE

Historic Buildings and Monuments
Haarlemmerpoort ⑬
Huis met de Hoofden ④

Museums
Anne Frank Huis ③
Pianola en Piano Museum ⑪
Theatermuseum ①

Canals and Islands
Bloemgracht ⑥
Brouwersgracht ⑫
Egelantiersgracht ⑤
Western Islands ⑭

Churches
Noorder-
  kerk ⑨
Westerkerk ②

Markets
Noordermarkt ⑩

Hofjes
Claes Claeszhofje ⑦
De Star and Zon's Hofje ⑧

GETTING THERE
It is a 10–15-minute walk from the Dam and Centraal Station to the Jordaan. Trams 13, 14 and 17 go to Rozengracht; 3 follows Marnixstraat to Haarlemmerpoort and 10 goes halfway.

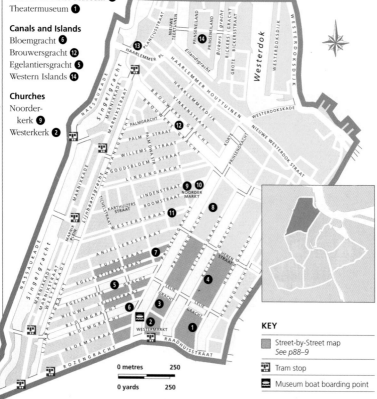

KEY

▨	Street-by-Street map See p88–9
🚊	Tram stop
⛴	Museum boat boarding point

◁ **View of Prinsengracht with its densely packed houseboats and the Westerkerk in the distance**

Street-by-Street: Around the Jordaan

West of the *Grachtengordel*, the Jordaan still retains a network of narrow, characterful streets and delightful canals. Among the 17th-century workers' houses are dozens of quirky shops, which are well worth a browse, selling anything from designer clothes to old sinks, and lively brown cafés and bars, which spill on to the pavements in summer. A stroll along the *Grachtengordel* provides a glimpse into some of the city's grandest canal houses, including the Bartolotti House.

★ Anne Frank Huis
For two years, the Frank family and four others lived in a small upstairs apartment that was hidden behind a revolving bookcase ❸

Bloemgracht
This quiet, pretty canal was once a centre for makers of paint and dye ❻

★ Westerkerk
Hendrick de Keyser's church is the site of Rembrandt's unmarked grave, and was the setting for the wedding of Queen Beatrix and Prince Claus in 1966 ❷

Egelantiersgracht
This charming tree-lined Jordaan canal is overlooked by an interesting mixture of old and new architecture. Pretty views are provided from its numerous bridges

Huis met de Hoofden

The name "House with the Heads" refers to the six Classical busts at the entrance, depicting Apollo, Ceres, Mars, Minerva, Bacchus and Diana ❹

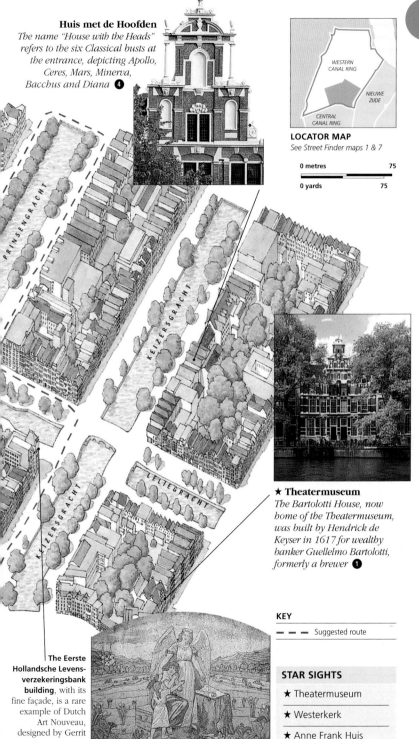

LOCATOR MAP
See Street Finder maps 1 & 7

| 0 metres | 75 |
| 0 yards | 75 |

★ **Theatermuseum**
The Bartolotti House, now home of the Theatermuseum, was built by Hendrick de Keyser in 1617 for wealthy banker Guellelmo Bartolotti, formerly a brewer ❶

KEY

– – – Suggested route

The Eerste Hollandsche Levensverzekeringsbank building, with its fine façade, is a rare example of Dutch Art Nouveau, designed by Gerrit van Arkel in 1905.

STAR SIGHTS

★ Theatermuseum

★ Westerkerk

★ Anne Frank Huis

Theatermuseum interior, with 18th-century staircase and stuccowork

Theatermuseum ❶

Herengracht 168. **Map** 7 A2.
Tel 551 3300. 🚋 13, 14, 17. 🚌
Prinsengracht. ⬜ 11am–5pm Mon–Fri,
1–5pm Sat & Sun. ⬤ 1 Jan, 30 Apr, 25
Dec. 🎫 ∅ 🖥 ♿ 🎧 www.tin.nl

Two fine buildings house
the theatre museum, which
contains costumes, sets and
memorabilia. You can even
play with antique sound effects
and create your own storm.
The museum entrance is in
the White House, No. 168, a
Neo-Classical house designed
by Philips Vingboons (see p99)
in 1638. The interior was re-
styled in about 1730, and has

a magnificent spiral staircase,
stuccowork by Van Logteren
and rich ceiling paintings by
Jacob de Wit (see p122).
The museum extends into
Bartolotti House (Nos. 170–
172). Built by Hendrick de
Keyser (1565– 1621) in 1617,
its elaborate Renaissance
façade contrasts sharply with
the austerity of the White
House. Its interior decoration
was carried out by Jacob de
Wit and Isaac de Moucheron.

Westerkerk ❷

Prinsengracht 281. **Map** 1 B4.
Tel 624 7766. 🚋 13, 14, 17.
⬜ Easter–Sep: 11am–3pm Mon–Fri
& Sat (Aug–Sep only, except during
services). 🎫 629 7766. 📷 **Tower**
⬤ for restoration. Phone 689 2565 for
up-to-date information and to arrange
guided tours. 🎫 www.westerkerk.nl

Built as part of the development of the Canal Ring (see
pp44–5), this church has the
tallest tower in the city at 85 m
(272 ft), and the largest nave of
any Dutch Protestant church.
It was designed by Hendrick
de Keyser, who died in 1621,
a year after work began.
Rembrandt was buried here
but his grave has never been
found. The organ shutters
(1686) were painted, by Gérard

de Lairesse, with lively scenes
showing King David, the
Queen of Sheba and the Evan-
gelists. The spire is topped by
the Imperial Crown of Maximilian (see pp22–3). The stunning views justify the climb.

Anne Frank Huis ❸

Prinsengracht 267. **Map** 1 B4.
Tel 556 7105. 🚋 13, 14, 17.
🚌 Prinsengracht. ⬜ 9am–9pm
daily (Oct–Feb: to 7pm); 1 Jan &
25 Dec: noon–5pm; 21 & 31 Dec:
9am–5pm; 4 May: 9am–7pm.
⬤ Yom Kippur. 🎫 ∅ 🖥 🎧
www.annefrank.org

**Anne's picture display in her
room in the Anne Frank Huis**

For two years during World
War II, the Frank and van
Pel families, both Jewish,
hid here until their betrayal
to the Nazis. In 1957, the
Anne Frank Stichting (foundation) took over the house,
to carry out "the ideals set

The Westerkerk in the 18th century, a view by Jan Ekels

down in the *Diary of Anne Frank*. The 13-year-old Anne began her now-famous diary in July 1942. It gives a unique account of growing up under persecution, and of life in confinement (*see pp34–5*). It was first published in 1947 as *Het Achterhuis (The Annexe)*.

Visitors to the Anne Frank Huis climb to the second floor and enter the annexe via the revolving bookcase that hid its entrance. Its rooms are now empty, except for the film-star pin-ups in Anne's room, and Otto Frank's model of the annexe as it was during the occupation. At the front of the house, Otto Frank's office has been re-created using period furniture. Original documents concerning the Frank family are on display. Get here early or late in the day – with more than 900,000 visitors a year, the museum gets very crowded. Last admittance is half an hour before closing time.

Huis met de Hoofden ❹

Keizersgracht 123. **Map** 7 A1.
Tel 552 4888. 🚊 *13, 14, 17.*
🌐 *to the public.*

Built in 1622, the Huis met de Hoofden (house with the heads) is one of the largest double houses of the period. It has a fine step gable and takes its name from the six heads placed on pilasters along the façade. Legend has it that they commemorate a housemaid who, when left alone in the house, surprised six burglars and cut off their heads. The sculptures are in fact portrayals of six Classical deities (from left to right): Apollo, Ceres, Mars, Minerva, Bacchus and Diana.

The design of the building is sometimes attributed to Pieter de Keyser (1595–1676), the son of Hendrick de Keyser.

Bikes and boats along the tranquil Bloemgracht

Egelantiersgracht ❺

Map 1 B4. 🚊 *13, 14, 17.*

Many canals in the Jordaan were named after trees or flowers, and this includes the Egelantiersgracht (sweetbrier or eglantine). The canal was cut in the 17th century along a drainage ditch. The houses in this area, built for artisans, are on a more intimate scale than the grand mansions along Herengracht, Keizersgracht and Prinsengracht. As a result, demand for canalside residences in the Jordaan has boomed. Despite some development, the Egelantiersgracht retains much of its original character and one of the most charming spots along the canal is the St Andrieshofje at Nos. 107–114. This

Head of Apollo on the Huis met de Hoofden

hofje was built in 1617, and the passage through to its courtyard is decorated with splendid blue-and-white tiles.

Bloemgracht ❻

Map 1 B4. 🚊 *13, 14, 17.*

The Bloemgracht (flower canal) was a centre for dye and paint manufacture in the 17th century. Today, only one paint maker remains, and this quiet canal is called the Herengracht (gentlemen's canal) of the Jordaan, because of the fine gable houses along its banks.

The most beautiful are the three houses at Nos. 87 to 91. Built in 1642 in the traditional "burgher" style of the period, they feature stepped gables and a strong use of glass. Their gable stones, which served as house names until numbering was introduced in the 19th century, depict a farmer, a townsman and a seaman.

Stone plaque on the *hofje* founded in 1616 by the merchant Anslo

Claes Claeszhofje **⑦**

1e Egelantiersdwarsstraat. **Map** 1 B3. 🚊 *3, 10, 13, 14, 17.* ⬜ *on & off.*

This is a group of *hofjes*, the earliest of which was founded in 1616 by a textile merchant, Claes Claesz Anslo. They were renovated by the Stichting Diogenes, a foundation which now rents out the houses to art students.

One of the oldest and most distinctive is the "Huis met de Schrijvende Hand" (house with the writing hand), Egelantiersstraat 52. Once the home of a teacher, it dates from the 1630s.

De Star Hofje and Zon's Hofje **⑧**

De Star Hofje: Prinsengracht 89–133; Zon's Hofje: Prinsengracht 159–171. **Map** 1 C3. 🚊 *3, 10, 13, 14, 17.* **Star** ⬜ *6am–6pm Mon–Fri, 6am–2pm Sat.* **Zon** ⬜ *10am–5pm Mon–Fri.*

These two charming *hofjes* are within a short walk of each other. De Star was built on the site of the Star Brewery in 1804 and is officially known as Van Brienen *hofje*. Legend has it that a merchant, Jan van Brienen, founded this almshouse in gratitude for his release from a vault in which he had been accidentally imprisoned. The peaceful courtyard has a lovely flower garden.

Zon's *hofje* was built on the site of a clandestine church, known as Noah's Ark, now indicated by a plaque in the courtyard. The church's original name of Kleine Zon (Little Sun) gave the *hofje* its name.

Noorderkerk **⑨**

Noordermarkt 44–48. **Map** 1 C3. **Tel** *626 6436.* 🚊 *3, 10, 13, 14, 17.* ⬜ *10:30am–3pm Mon & Wed, 11am–1pm Sat.* ✝ *10am & 7pm Sun.*

Built for poor settlers in the Jordaan, the recently renovated North Church was the first in Amsterdam to be constructed in the shape of a Greek cross. Its layout around a central pulpit allowed everyone in the encircling pews to see and hear well.

The church was designed by Hendrick de Keyser *(see p90)*, who died in 1621, a year after building began. It was completed in 1623. The church is still well attended by a Calvinist congregation, and bears many reminders of the working-class origins of the Jordaan. By the entrance is a sculpture of three bound figures, inscribed: "Unity is Strength". It commemorates the Jordaanoproer (Jordaan Riot) of 1934 *(see pp34–5)*. On the south façade is a plaque recalling the strike of February 1941, a protest at the Nazis' deportation of Jews.

There are regular concerts on Saturday afternoons.

Noordermarkt **⑩**

Map 1 C3. 🚊 *3, 10, 13, 14, 17.* **General Market** ⬜ *9am–1pm Mon;* **Boerenmarkt** (organic fruit and vegetables) ⬜ *9am–5pm Sat.*

Visitors to the Saturday morning fair in Noordermarkt

Since 1627, the square that surrounds the Noorderkerk has been a market site. At that time, it sold pots and pans and *vodden* (old clothes), a tradition that continues today with a flea market. Since the 18th century, the area has been a centre for bed shops, and bedding, curtains and fabrics are still sold on Monday morning along the Westerstraat. On Saturday mornings, the *vogel-tjes* (small birds) market sells various birds and rabbits. Around 10am, the *boerenmarkt* takes over, selling health foods, ethnic crafts and candles.

Pianola en Piano Museum **⑪**

Westerstraat 106. **Map** 1 B3. **Tel** *627 9624.* 🚊 *3, 10, 13, 14, 17.* ⬜ *2–5pm Sun (Mon–Sat by appt only).* 📷 📷 **www**.pianola.nl

Fifteen instruments and some 15,000 piano rolls are on show here, celebrating the automatic pianos that were introduced in 1900. There are regular performances often with live pianists.

The lush garden in the courtyard of De Star *hofje*

A flower-filled houseboat on Brouwersgracht

Brouwersgracht ⑫

Map 1 B2. 🖪 *3*.

Brouwersgracht (brewers' canal) was named after the breweries established here in the 17th and 18th centuries. Leather, spices, coffee and sugar were also processed and stored here. Today, most of the warehouses are smart residences that look out on an array of houseboats moored between the canal's picturesque hump-backed bridges.

Prime examples of these functional buildings, with their spout gables *(see pp96–7)* and shutters, can be seen at Nos. 188 to 194. The last distillery in the area, the Ooievaar, is just off Brouwersgracht on Driehoekstraat (Triangle street). The Dutch gin, *jenever*, has been made here since 1782. Visit one of the many *proeflokalen* or tasting houses *(see p48)* around the city to sample it.

Haarlemmerpoort ⑬

Haarlemmerplein 50. **Map** 1 B1. 🖪 *3*. 🚫 *to the public.*

Originally a defended gateway into Amsterdam, the Haarlemmerpoort marked the beginning of the busy route to Haarlem. The present gateway, dating from 1840, was built for King William II's triumphal entry into the city *(see pp32–3)* and officially named Willemspoort. However, as the third gateway to be built on or close to this site, it is still referred to as the Haarlemmerpoort by Amsterdammers.

Designed by Cornelis Alewijn (1788–1839), the Neo-Classical gatehouse was used as tax offices in the 19th century and was made into flats in 1986. Traffic no longer goes through the gate, since a bridge has been built over the adjoining Westerkanaal. Beyond the Haarlemmerpoort is the peaceful Westerpark *(see p151)*, a pleasant retreat.

Western Islands ⑭

Map 1 C1. 🖪 *3*.

Plaque with shipping motif on a house in Zandhoek, Realeneiland

This district comprises three islands built on the IJ in the early 17th century to provide space for warehouses and shipyards. Some of these are still in use and many of the period houses have survived.

Bickerseiland was bought in 1631 by the merchant Jan Bicker, who then developed it. Today, the island is residential with a mix of colourful apartment blocks on one side of its walkway and a jumble of tugs and houseboats on the other.

Photogenic Realeneiland has one of the city's prettiest spots, the waterside street of Zandhoek. Here, a row of 17th-century houses built by the island's founder, Jacobsz Reaal, overlook the sailboats moored along Westerdok.

Prinseneiland, the smallest island, is dominated by characterful warehouses, many of which are now apartments. The walk on pages 158–9 explores the area in more detail.

DUTCH HOFJES

Before the Alteration *(see pp24–5)*, the Catholic Church usually provided subsidized housing for the poor and elderly, particularly women. During the 17th and 18th centuries, rich merchants and Protestant organizations took on this charitable role and built hundreds of almshouse complexes, which were planned around courtyards and known as *hofjes*. Behind their street façades lie pretty houses and serene gardens. Visitors are admitted to some but are asked to respect the residents' privacy. Many *hofjes* are found in the Jordaan and some still serve their original purpose *(see p75)*.

The "house with the writing hand" (c. 1630) in Claes Claeszhofje

A CANAL WALK AND GUIDE TO ARCHITECTURE

With the increase in wealth and civic pride in Amsterdam during the 17th century, an ambitious plan was formed to build a splendid ring of canals round the city *(see pp26–7)*. Conceived in 1609, and added to in 1664 by Daniel Stalpaert, the scheme grew

Wall plaque, No. 1133 Prinsengracht

to encompass wide canals lined with opulent town houses in a variety of architectural styles *(see pp96–7)*. The houses on the canals of Singel, Keizersgracht, Herengracht, Reguliersgracht and Prinsengracht, illustrated on pp98–105, form a fascinating walk through Golden Age Amsterdam.

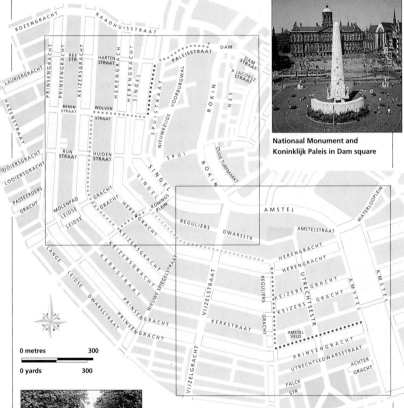

Nationaal Monument and Koninklijk Paleis in Dam square

0 metres   300
0 yards   300

A picturesque stone hump-back bridge on the Reguliersgracht

FOLLOWING THE ROUTE

The walk begins at Dam square and should be followed from left to right across the next two pages, always walking on the left-hand side of the canal. The coloured dots correspond to the stretch of canal illustrated, the grey dots trace interconnecting roads forming part of the route, but are not illustrated.

KEY TO WALK ROUTE

• • • Singel
• • • Keizersgracht
• • • Herengracht
• • • Reguliersgracht
• • • Prinsengracht
• • • Connecting streets

◁ *Keizersgracht (c. 1750) by Hendrick Keun* – a scene of beauty and tranquillity

A Guide to Canal House Architecture

Amsterdam has been called a city of "well-mannered" architecture because its charms lie in intimate details rather than in grand effects. From the 15th century on, planning laws, plot sizes and the instability of the topsoil dictated that façades were largely uniform in size and built of lightweight brick or sandstone, with large windows to reduce the weight. Canal house owners stamped their own individuality on the buildings, mainly through the use of decorative gables and cornices, ornate doorcases and varying window shapes.

Broken pediment and vase, **"Broken handle" window surrounds**

Bartolotti House *(1617)*
The contrasting brick and stone, flamboyant step gable, with its marble obelisk and scrolls, is typical of the Dutch Renaissance style of Hendrick de Keyser (see p90).

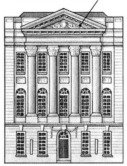

Pediment carvings symbolize the arts and sciences.

Felix Meritis Building *(1778)*
The Corinthian columns and triangular pediment are influenced by Classical architecture. This marks the building (see p113) by Jacob Otten Husly as Dutch Classical in style.

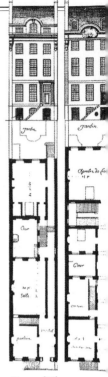

Ground Plans
Taxes were levied according to width of façade, so canal houses were often long and narrow, with an achterhuis (back annexe) used for offices and stora...

CORNICES

Decorative top mouldings, called cornices, became popular from 1690 onwards when the fashion for gables declined. By the 19th century, they had become unadorned.

Louis XV-style with rococo balustrade (1739)

19th-century cornice with mansard roof

19th-century dentil (tooth-shaped) cornice

GABLES

The term gable refers to the front apex of a roof. It disguised the steepness of the roof under which goods were stored *(see pp22–3)*. In time, gables became decorated with scrolls, crests, and even coats of arms.

Simple triangular gable

No. 34 Begijnhof *(c. 1420)* is one of few remaining timber houses *(see pp22–3)*.

Warehouse-style spout gable

Dutch Renaissance style

The style of gable on No. 213 Leliegracht *(c. 1620)* was used for warehouses.

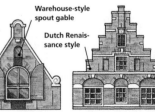

Step gables like the one on No. 2 Brouwersgracht were in vogue between 1600–65.

eaning Façades
*anal houses were often built
ith a deliberate tilt, allowing
oods to be winched up to the
ttic without crashing against
e windows. A law dating from
565 restricted this lean to 1:25,
limit the risk of buildings
ollapsing into the streets.*

AMSTERDAM SCHOOL ARCHITECTURE

Members of the Amsterdam School, a loose grouping of like-minded and idealistic architects, built many distinctive housing estates between 1911 and 1923 *(see p151).* They believed in the ability of unusual architecture to enhance residents' lives, many of whom were rehoused from appalling slums. Michel de Klerk's development, Het Schip (1921), is on the corner of Zaanstraat Spaarndammerplantsoen in northwest Amsterdam (www.hetschip.nl). It is typical of the lively style of the Amsterdam School.

**Michel de Klerk
(1884–1923)**

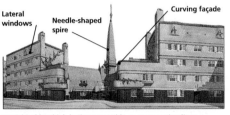

Lateral windows — Needle-shaped spire — Curving façade

Het Schip (the ship), built to resemble an ocean-going liner

utch Hofjes
*lmshouses (hofjes) were built
roughout the Netherlands by
ich benefactors in the 17th and
8th centuries. By providing
ccommodation for the elderly
nd infirm (see p93), the hofjes
arked the beginning of the
utch welfare system.*

Sign of a sailor's hostel

Symbol of a dairyman

Noah's Ark – a refuge for the poor

WALL PLAQUES

Carved and painted stones were used to identify houses before street numbering was introduced in the 19th century. Many reflect the owner's occupation.

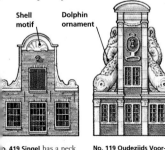

Shell motif — Dolphin ornament

Unadorned bell gable

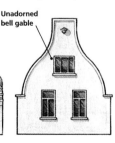

Stonework with cornucopia decoration

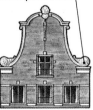

. 419 Singel has a neck
ble, a common feature
om 1640 to around 1840.

**No. 119 Oudezijds Voor-
burgwal** has an ornate
17th-century neck gable.

No. 57 Leliegracht has a plain
bell gable, popular from the
late 17th century.

**No. 298 Oudezijds Voorburg-
wal** has a bell gable dating
from the 18th century.

Dam Square to Herengracht 487

The walk along Amsterdam's finest canals begins in Dam square *(see pp74)*. Following the grey dots on the map, leave the square past the Koninklijk Paleis *(see p74)*, cross Nieuwezijds Voorburgwal and Spuistraat down Paleisstraat, and turn left along the left bank of Singel, marked by purple dots. Further directions are incorporated into the route below.

LOCATOR MAP

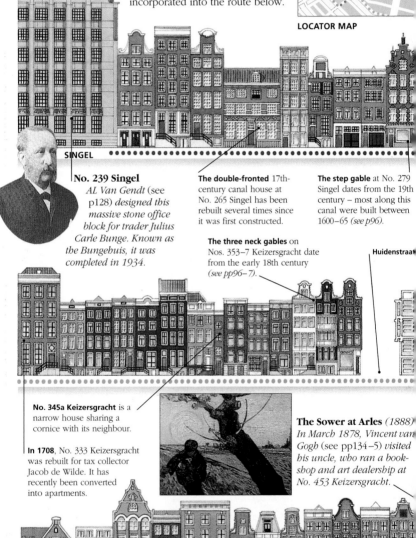

SINGEL

No. 239 Singel
AL Van Gendt (see p128) designed this massive stone office block for trader Julius Carle Bunge. Known as the Bungehuis, it was completed in 1934.

The double-fronted 17th-century canal house at No. 265 Singel has been rebuilt several times since it was first constructed.

The step gable at No. 279 Singel dates from the 19th century – most along this canal were built between 1600–65 *(see p96)*.

The three neck gables on Nos. 353–7 Keizersgracht date from the early 18th century *(see pp96–7)*.

Huidenstraat

No. 345a Keizersgracht is a narrow house sharing a cornice with its neighbour.

In 1708, No. 333 Keizersgracht was rebuilt for tax collector Jacob de Wilde. It has recently been converted into apartments.

The Sower at Arles *(1888)*
In March 1878, Vincent van Gogh (see pp134–5) visited his uncle, who ran a book-shop and art dealership at No. 453 Keizersgracht.

Tsar Peter (see p101) stayed at No. 527 Herengracht, home of the Russian ambassador, after a night of drunken revelry at No. 317 Keizersgracht in 1716.

Herengracht (1790)
A delicate watercolour by J Prins shows the "gentlemen's canal" from Koningsplein.

The asymmetrical building at Nos. 533–7 Herengracht was built in 1910 on the site of four former houses. From 1968–88 it was the Registry of Births, Marriages and Deaths.

The façades of Nos. 37 and 39 Reguliersgracht lean towards the water, showing the danger caused by subsidence when building on marshland.

Reguliersgracht Bridges
Seven arched stone bridges cross the can which was originally designed to be a stre

Keizersgracht

Nos. 1059 and 1061 Prinsengracht have tiny basement entrances, rare amid the splendour of the *Grachtengordel*, where the height of the steps was considered an indication of wealth.

The sober spout-gabled building at No. 1075 Prinsengracht was built as a warehouse in 1690.

My Domestic Companions
Society portraitist Thérèse van Duyl Schwartze painted this picture in 1916. She owned Nos. 1087, 1089 and 1091 Prinsengracht, a handsome row of houses where she lived with her extended family.

Nos. 289–293 Singel
These houses stand on an alley once called Schoorsteenvegersteeg (chimney sweeps' lane), home to immigrant chimney sweeps.

Yab Yum Brothel
The huge lantern is the only sign that this famous brothel operates at No. 295 Singel.

The doorway of No. 365 Keizersgracht was taken from an almshouse on Oudezijds Voorburgwal in the 19th century.

Jacob de Wit
The artist (see p122) bought Nos. 383 and 385 Keizersgracht, living in No. 385 until his death in 1754.

: & Co is an elegant ...rtment store at No. 34–36 ...estraat on the corner Keizersgracht *(see p112).*

Gerrit Rietveld
Rietveld (see p136) designed the cupola on Metz & Co, and a line of plain, inexpensive furniture for the store.

De Vergulde Ster (gilded star), at No. 387 Keizersgracht, was built in 1668 by the municipal stone-masons' yard. It has an elongated neck gable *(see p96–7)* and narrow windows.

DIRECTIONS TO HERENGRACHT
Turn left on to Leidsestraat, and walk to Koningsplein, then take the left bank of the Herengracht eastwards towards Thorbeckeplein.

HERENGRACHT

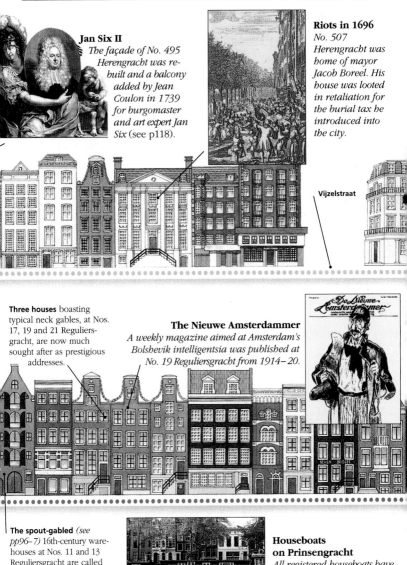

Jan Six II
The façade of No. 495 Herengracht was rebuilt and a balcony added by Jean Coulon in 1739 for burgomaster and art expert Jan Six (see p118).

Riots in 1696
No. 507 Herengracht was home of mayor Jacob Boreel. His house was looted in retaliation for the burial tax he introduced into the city.

Vijzelstraat

Three houses boasting typical neck gables, at Nos. 17, 19 and 21 Reguliersgracht, are now much sought after as prestigious addresses.

The Nieuwe Amsterdammer
A weekly magazine aimed at Amsterdam's Bolshevik intelligentsia was published at No. 19 Reguliersgracht from 1914–20.

The spout-gabled *(see pp96–7)* 16th-century warehouses at Nos. 11 and 13 Reguliersgracht are called the Sun and the Moon.

Café Marcella, at No. 1047a Prinsengracht, is a typical local bar which has seating outside in summer.

Houseboats on Prinsengracht
All registered houseboats have postal addresses and are connected to the electricity mains.

Utrechtsestraat

Keizersgracht
This photograph of the "emperor's canal" is taken at dusk, from the corner of Leidsegracht. The Wester-kerk (see p90) is in the distance.

Behind the contrasting 18th-century façades at Nos. 317 and 319 Singel are two second-hand bookshops, which are well worth browsing through.

DIRECTIONS TO KEIZERSGRACHT
At Raamsteeg, cross the bridge, take the Oude Spiegelstraat, cross Herengracht and walk along Wolven-straat to the left bank of Keizersgracht.

KEIZERSGRACHT

No. 399 Keizersgracht dates from 1665, but the façade was rebuilt in the 18th century. Its *achter-huis (see p96)* has been perfectly preserved.

No. 409 Keizersgracht
Built in 1671 on a triangular piece of land, this house contains a newly discovered, highly decorated wooden ceiling.

No. 401 Kaizersgracht houses a museum of photography known as Huis Marseille.

The plain, spout-gabled building *(see pp96–7)* at No. 403 Keizersgracht was originally a warehouse – a rarity in this predominantly residential area.

No. 469 Herengracht
The modern office block by KL Sijmons replaced the original 18th-century houses in 1971.

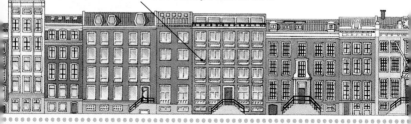

The unusual office block at No. 313 Keizersgracht was built in 1914 by CN van Goor.

No. 319 Keizersgracht was built by the architect Philips Vingboons (1608–78) in 1639. It has a rare, highly decorated façade covered with scrolls, vases and garlands.

Peter the Great *(1716)*
The Russian tsar sailed up Keizersgracht to No. 317, the home of his friend Christoffel Brants. Legend says the tsar got drunk and kept the mayor waiting while at a civic reception.

Leidsegracht
This canal marked the end of Daniel Stalpaert's city expansion plan of 1664 (see p26). It has a mixture of fine 17th- and 18th-century canal houses.

The Louis XIV-style house at No. 323 Keizersgracht was built in 1728. It has a raised cornice embellished with two hoisting beams, one functional and the other to provide symmetry.

Art patron Jan Gildemester bought No. 475 Herengracht in 1792. Attributed to Jacob Otten Husly *(see p113)*, it has a stuccoed entrance hall.

Jan Corver
Burgomaster of Amsterdam 19 times, Corver built No. 479 Herengracht in 1665.

Turn over to continue walk at top of page 102

Herengracht 489 to the Amstel

The second half of the walk takes you along Herengracht, winding past grand, wide-fronted mansions. It then follows Reguliersgracht and Prinsengracht down to the Amstel. Many of the fine houses have recently been converted into banks, offices and exclusive apartment blocks.

LOCATOR MAP

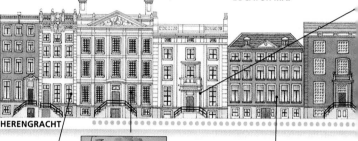

HERENGRACHT

The house at No. 491 Herengracht was built in 1671. The façade, rebuilt in the 18th century, is decorated with scrolls, vases and coats of arms.

No. 493 Herengracht *This 17th-century house was given a Louis XV-style façade in 1767 by Anthony van Hemert.*

The Kattenkabinet at No. 497 Herengracht was created by financier B Meijer in 1984. It is devoted to exhibits featuring the cat in art.

DIRECTIONS TO REGULIERSGRACHT

At Thorbeckeplein, take the bridge to the right, which marks the beginning of Reguliersgracht. Follow the left bank.

REGULIERSGRACHT

Amstelveld in the 17th Century *This etching shows the construction of a wooden church at Amstelveld, with sheep grazing in front of it.*

Restaurant Janvier *The Amstelkerk (see p119) now contains a restaurant and offices, while the square itself is a popular play area for local children.*

DIRECTIONS TO PRINSENGRACHT

Turn left by the church, take the left bank of Prinsengracht and walk to the Amstel river.

PRINSENGRACHT

Herengracht *(c. 1670)*
A Berckheijde's etching shows one side of the canal bare of trees. Elms were later planted, binding the topsoil, to strengthen the buildings' foundations.

No. 543 Herengracht was built in 1743 under the supervision of owner Sibout Bollard. It has a double-fronted façade with an ornate balustrade and decorated balcony.

The small houses at the corner of Herengracht and Thorbeckeplein contrast with the grand neighbouring buildings.

Isaac Gosschalk
The architect designed Nos. 57, 59 and 63 Reguliersgracht in 1879. They have ornate stone, brick and wood-work façades.

Reguliers Monastery
This engraving by J Wagenaar (1760) shows the monastery that once stood on the canal.

The Amstel
Turn left and follow the broad sweep of the Amstel river, up past the Magere Brug (see p119) on up in and back to the Dam, where the walk began.

CENTRAL CANAL RING

The extension of Amsterdam's three major canals continued from the early 17th century *(see pp26–7)*, as the merchant classes sought to escape the overcrowding and industrial squalor in the old city, around the Amstel. They bought plots of land along the new extensions to the Herengracht, Keizersgracht and Prinsengracht, and in the 1660s the wealthiest built opulent houses on a stretch of Herengracht known as the

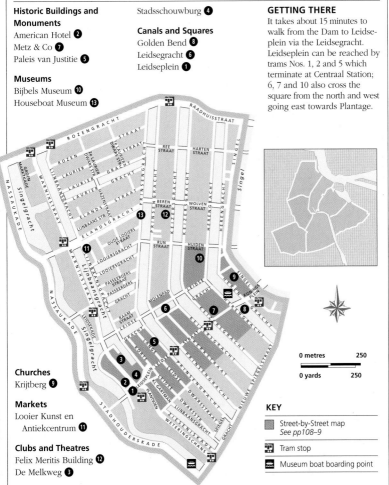

Pillar decoration on the Felix Meritis Building

Golden Bend. Designed and decorated by the best architects of the day, such as Philips Vingboons *(see p101)*, the mansions built here were often twice the width of standard canal houses *(see p96)*. Today, many of these grand buildings are owned by institutions. Other architectural landmarks include the Neo-Gothic Krijtberg, with its soaring steeples, the imposing Paleis van Justitie and the Art Nouveau American Hotel overlooking the busy Leidseplein.

SIGHTS AT A GLANCE

GETTING THERE
It takes about 15 minutes to walk from the Dam to Leidseplein via the Leidsegracht. Leidseplein can be reached by trams Nos. 1, 2 and 5 which terminate at Centraal Station; 6, 7 and 10 also cross the square from the north and west going east towards Plantage.

KEY

	Street-by-Street map See pp108–9
🚏	Tram stop
🚢	Museum boat boarding point

0 metres 250
0 yards 250

◁ **Cyclist crossing one of the many bridges on Leidsegracht**

Street-by-Street: Leidsebuurt

The area around Leidseplein is one of Amsterdam's busiest nightspots. There are various films to be seen at the many cinemas, plays at the Stadsschouwburg and lively programmes of music at De Melkweg. In contrast, there is fine architecture to admire around **Leidseplein street-performer** the Canal Ring, such as the imposing Paleis van Justitie on Prinsengracht, the lavish De Krijtberg on the Singel and scores of grand houses on the Golden Bend.

Bijbels Museum
In addition to bibles, there are several archaeological finds from Egypt and the Middle East on display here ❿

Leidsegracht
Cut in 1664, this canal was the main waterway for barges heading for Leiden ❻

Paleis van Justitie
This vast Empire-style building contains Amsterdam's Court of Appeal ❺

Stadsschouwburg
The city's football team, Ajax, uses the theatre's balcony to greet supporters after winning important games ❹

★ American Hotel
The hotel's Café Americain has a fine Art Deco interior and is a popular place to while away an afternoon (see p110) ❷

De Melkweg
This converted milk-processing factory and former hippie hang-out survives as one of Amsterdam's key venues for alternative entertainment ❸

Leidseplein
Young people flock to this square to watch street performances and enjoy the vibrant nightlife ❶

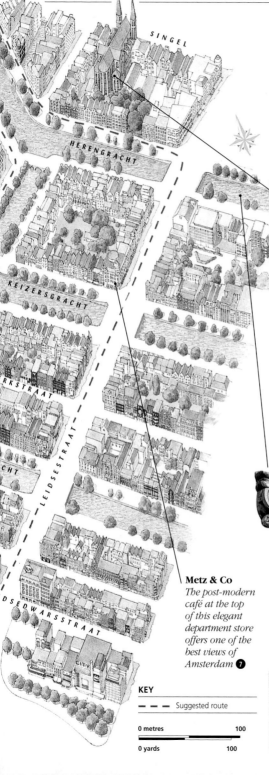

LOCATOR MAP
See Street Finder, maps 4 & 7

★ **De Krijtberg**
This Neo-Gothic church houses an ornate wooden carving of the Immaculate Conception **9**

★ **Golden Bend**
Classical columns and façades on this part of the Herengracht powerfully recall the city's wealth **8**

Metz & Co
The post-modern café at the top of this elegant department store offers one of the best views of Amsterdam **7**

KEY

- - - Suggested route

| 0 metres | 100 |
| 0 yards | 100 |

STAR SIGHTS

★ American Hotel

★ Golden Bend

★ De Krijtberg

Leidseplein ❶

Map 4 E2. 🚋 *1, 2, 5, 6, 7, 10.*

Amsterdam's liveliest square, Leidseplein is also a busy tram intersection and centre of night-time transport.

The square developed in the 17th century as a wagon park on the outskirts of the city – farmers and peasants would leave their carts here before entering the centre. It takes its name from the Leidsepoort, the massive city gate demolished in 1862, which marked the beginning of the route out to Leiden.

During the day, the square is buzzing with fire-eaters, buskers and other street performers playing to café audiences. It is also popular with pickpockets. At night, it is the focal point for the city's youth, who hang out in the many bars, cafés, restaurants, nightclubs and cinemas in and around the square.

Street performer in Leidseplein

American Hotel ❷

Leidsekade 97. **Map** 4 E2. *Tel 556 3000.* 🚋 *1, 2, 5, 6, 7, 10.* 🖵 🍴

Leidseplein was fast becoming a fashionable entertainment area when the American Hotel was built overlooking it in 1882. The hotel got its name because its architect, W Steinigeweg, studied hotel design in the United States, and adorned his Neo-Gothic creation with a bronze eagle, wooden figures of native Indians and murals of American landscapes. Within 20 years it was deemed *passé* and the hotel was demolished. The present building is by Willem Kromhout (1864–1940) and was completed in 1902. His design marked a radical departure, interpreting the Art Nouveau style in an angular Dutch fashion. The building's turreted exterior and elaborate brickwork anticipated the progressive Amsterdam School (*see p97*). A carved stone plaque on the Leidseplein side of the hotel shows the original building.

The Café Americain (*see p46*), decorated in Art Deco style, remains one of the most elegant in Amsterdam. It retains its period furnishings and stained-glass windows. The rest of the hotel was redecorated in the 1980s. Samples of the original furnishings are in the Rijksmuseum (*see pp130–33*).

De Melkweg ❸

Lijnbaansgracht 234a. **Map** 4 E2. *Tel 531 8181.* 🚋 *1, 2, 5, 6, 7, 10.* **Box office** ⭘ *1–5pm Mon–Fri, 4–6pm Sat & Sun; also open evenings for performances.* **Performances**: *8:30pm approx.* 🈂 🎦 *See* **Entertainment** *p249.* **www**.melkweg.nl

De Melkweg (Milky Way) is a multimedia centre situated in a former dairy behind the Stadsschouwburg. It opened in 1970 and soon gained a dazzling reputation as an alternative cultural meeting place. Nowadays, it offers a wide range of entertainment,

The American Hotel seen from Singelgracht

including live music, film, video, theatre, dance and a photographic gallery. The theatre has a stage for new international acts, and De Melkweg's annual Amsterdam Roots Festival *(see p51)* promotes the latest in world music.

De Melkweg's star-lit façade

Stadsschouw- burg ❹

Leidseplein 26. **Map** 4 E2. *Tel 624 2311.* 🚊 *1, 2, 5, 6, 7, 10.* **Box office** ⬜ *10am–6pm Mon–Sat; two hours before performance Sun. See* **Entertainment** *p246.* 🚹 ⏁ ♿ **www.**stadsschouwburgamsterdam.nl

This Neo-Renaissance building is the most recent of three successive municipal theatres in the city, its predecessors having burned down. The theatre was designed by Jan Springer and AL van Gendt, who was also responsible for the Concertgebouw *(see p128)*. The planned exterior ornamentation was never carried out because of budget cuts. This, combined with a hostile public reaction to his theatre, forced Springer into virtual retirement. Public disgust was due, however, to the theatre management's policy of restricting use of the front door to patrons who had

bought expensive tickets. The whole building is currently undergoing a face-lift.

Until the Muziektheater was completed in 1986 *(see p63)*, the Stadsschouwburg was home to the Dutch national ballet and opera companies. Today, the theatre stages plays by local groups such as the resident Toneelgroep Amsterdam, and international companies, including some English-language productions. The theatre has now become a favourite venue for Amsterdam's premier football club Ajax. Whenever this team wins an important competition, the players gather on the theatre's balcony to greet their fans.

A new auditorium is due to open between the Melkweg and the Stadsschouwburg in autumn 2007. It will be used by both centres.

Paleis van Justitie ❺

Prinsengracht 434–436. **Map** 4 E1. *Tel 541 2111.* 🚊 *1, 2, 5, 6, 7, 10.* ⬜ *with restrictions.*

Conversion of the former city orphanage into the Empire-style Palace of Justice, designed by the city architect Jan de Greef, was completed in 1829. Balustrades run along the roofline and the monotony of the imposing Neo-Classical façade is broken up by Corinthian pilasters. The building houses Amsterdam's Court of Appeal, and the courtrooms inside are set around two open yards.

The orphanage opened in 1666 with space for 800 chil-

dren. By 1811, the building housed more than 2,000, over half of the city's orphans. To control their rising numbers, a royal decree was passed permitting the relocation of orphans to other towns. When this act was implemented in 1822, there was widespread protest from local people and accusations that the authorities had stolen children. Once all the children were relocated, the orphanage was closed.

Leidsegracht ❻

Map 4 E1. 🚊 *1, 2, 5, 6, 7, 10.*

No. 39 Leidsegracht, on the right

The Leidsegracht was for a few years the main route for barges from Amsterdam to Leiden. It was cut in 1664 to a plan by city architect Daniel Stalpaert, and is now one of the city's smartest addresses.

Cornelis Lely, who drew up the original plans for draining the Zuiderzee *(see p165)*, was born at No. 39 in 1854. A wall plaque shows Lely poised between the Zuiderzee and the newly created IJsselmeer.

The elongated Neo-Classical façade of the Paleis van Justitie, converted from the city orphanage

Metz & Co ●

Leidsestraat 34–36. **Map** 7 A5.
Tel 520 7020. 🚊 1, 2, 5. ☐ 11am–
6pm Mon, 9:30am–6pm Tue–Sat,
noon–5pm Sun. ⬤ public hols.
🖥 See **Cafés** p49.

On its completion
in 1891, Metz & Co was
the tallest commercial
building in Amsterdam,
measuring 26 m (85 ft)
in height. It was
designed by J van
Looy and was built
for the New York
Life Insurance
Company. Since 1908,
it has housed the
luxury store Metz
& Co. In 1933, a
splendid glass cupola
by Gerrit Rietveld
(see p136) was
added. Liberty of

**The 1891 turret
of Metz & Co**

London, which bought Metz
& Co in 1973, renovated the
building and commissioned
Cees Dam to design a café
on the sixth floor. The views
from the café across the city
are superb.

Golden Bend ●

Map 7 A5. 🚊 1, 2, 4, 5, 9, 14, 16,
24, 25. Kattenkabinet Herengracht
497. **Tel** 626 5378. ☐ 11am–5pm
Tue–Sun. ⬤ public hols.

The stretch of the Heren-
gracht between Leidsestraat
and Vijzelstraat was first
called the Golden Bend in
the 17th century, because of
the great wealth of the ship-
builders,
merchants
and poli-
ticians who
originally
lived along
here. Most
of the man-
sions have
been
converted
into offices
or banks, but
their former
elegance
remains. The
majority of the
buildings are

**Window decor-
ation on No. 475
Herengracht**

faced with
sandstone,
which was

more expensive than brick
and had to be imported.
The earliest mansions date
from the 1660s. One very
fine and largely untouched
example, designed by
Philips Vingboons in 1664
(see p99), stands at No.
412. Building continued
into the 18th century,
with the Louis XIV style
predominating. No.
475 is typical of this
trend. Built in 1730,
it is often called
the jewel of canal
houses. Two
sculpted female
figures over the
front door adorn its
monumental sand-
stone façade. The
ornate mansion at
No. 452 is a good
example of a 19th-
century conversion.
The Kattenkabinet (cat
museum) at No. 497 Heren-
gracht is one of the few
houses on the Golden Bend
which is accessible to the
public. The museum is
well worth visiting for its
interesting collection of
feline artifacts.

De Krijtberg ●

Singel 448. **Map** 7 A4. **Tel** 623
1923. 🚊 1, 2, 5. ☐ half an hour
before the services; 1:30–5pm
Tue–Thu & Sun. ✝ 12:30pm, 5:45pm
Mon–Fri; 12:30 pm, 5:15pm, Sat;
9.30am, 11am, 12:30pm, 5:15pm
Sun. ♿ www.krijtberg.nl

An impressive Neo-Gothic
church, the Krijtberg (or
chalk hill) replaced a clandestine Jesuit chapel (see p84) in
1884. It is officially known as
Franciscus Xaveriuskerk, after
St Francis Xavier, one of the
founding Jesuit priests.
Designed by Alfred Tepe,
the church was constructed
on the site of three houses;
the presbytery beside the
church is on the site of two
other houses, one of which
had belonged to a chalk
merchant – hence the
church's nickname. The back
of the church is wider than
the front, extending into
the space once occupied by
the original gardens. The

narrowness of the façade is
redeemed by its two magnificent, soaring, steepled towers.
The ornate interior of the
building contains some good
examples of Neo-Gothic
design. The stained-glass
win-dows, walls painted
in bright colours and liberal
use of gold are in striking
contrast to the city's austere
Protestant churches. A statue
of St Francis Xavier stands
in front and to the left of
the high altar; one of St
Ignatius, founder of the
Jesuits, stands to the right.
Near the pulpit is an 18th-
century wooden statue of
the Immaculate Conception,
showing Mary trampling the
serpent. It used to be housed
in the original hidden chapel.

**The twin-steepled façade of the
Neo-Gothic Krijtberg**

Bijbels Museum ●

Herengracht 366–368. **Map** 7 A4.
Tel 624 2436. 🚊 1, 2, 5.
🚊 Herengracht/Leidsegracht. ☐
10am–5pm Mon–Sat, 11am–5pm
Sun & public hols. ⬤ 1 Jan, 30 Apr.
📷 ♿ 🖥 www.bijbelsmuseum.nl

Reverend Leendert Schouten
founded the Bijbels Museum
in 1860, when he first put his
private collection of biblical
artifacts on public display. In

1975, the museum moved to its present site, two 17th-century houses in a group of four designed by Philips Vingboons.

The Bible Museum is packed with artifacts that aim to give historical weight to Bible stories. Displays feature models of historical sites, and there are archaeological finds from Egypt and the Middle East. Highlights include a copy of the Book of Isaiah from the Dead Sea Scrolls, and the Delft Bible, dating from 1477. The museum also has a beautiful garden, two ceiling paintings by Jacob de Wit and two well-preserved 17th-century kitchens.

Looier Kunst en Antiekcentrum ⓫

Elandsgracht 109. **Map** 4 D1.
Tel 624 9038. 🚋 *7, 10, 13, 14, 17.*
⏹ *11am–5pm Sat–Thu.* ⬤ *public hols.* ⓧ ♿ www.looier.nl

A vast network of ground-floor rooms in a block of houses has been turned into the Looier Antiques Centre. The market, named after its location near the Looiersgracht (tanners' canal), boasts the largest collection of art and antiques in the Netherlands.

It has around 100 stalls selling everything from glassware to dolls. On Saturdays, anyone can rent a stall here and once a month the facility is rent-free. Lively bridge sessions, open to all, are always on the go.

The Palladian façade of the 18th-century Felix Meritis Building

Felix Meritis Building ⓬

Keizersgracht 324. **Map** 1 B5. *Tel* 623 1311. 🚋 *1, 2, 5, 10, 13, 14, 17.* Box office & enquiries ⏹ *9am–7pm Mon–Fri, if there is an event, 9am–start of event; Sat–Sun 90 mins before start. See **Entertainment** p246.* 📷 ⓧ ♿ www.felix.meritis.nl

This Neo-Classical building is best viewed from the opposite side of the canal (*see p96*). Designed by Jacob Otten Husly, it opened in 1787 as a science and arts centre set up by the Felix Meritis society. The name means "happiness through merit". An association of wealthy citizens, the society was founded by watchmaker Willem Writs in 1777, at the time of the Dutch Enlightenment (*see pp30–31*).

Five reliefs on the façade proclaim the society's interest in natural science and art. The building was fitted out with an observatory, library,

laboratories and a small concert hall. Mozart, Edvard Grieg and Johannes Brahms are among the distinguished musicians who have given performances here.

In the 19th century, it became Amsterdam's main cultural centre, and its concert hall inspired the design of the Concertgebouw (*see p128*).

The Dutch Communist Party (CPN) occupied the premises from 1946, but cultural prominence was restored in the 1970s when the Shaffy Theatre Company used the building as a theatre and won acclaim for its avant-garde productions.

The building is now used as a European Centre for Arts and Sciences, a place where politics and culture meet.

Houseboat Museum ⓭

Prinsengracht, opposite no. 296. **Map** 1 B5. *Tel* 427 0750. 🚋 *1, 2, 5, 7, 10, 13, 14, 17.* ⏹ *Mar–Oct: 11am–5pm Tue–Sun, Nov–Feb: 11am–5pm Fri–Sun.* ⬤ *Jan, 30 Apr, 25, 26 & 31 Dec.* 📷 📷 www.houseboatmuseum.nl

Moored on the Prinsengracht canal on the edge of the Jordaan, the *Hendrika Maria* is a showcase of life aboard an Amsterdam houseboat. Built in 1914, it served as a barge and transported coal, sand and gravel until the 1960s when it was converted into a houseboat. Coffee is served in the spacious living room.

Vintage robots on sale at the Looier Kunst en Antiekcentrum

EASTERN CANAL RING

Sun motif on a café in Reguliersdwarsstraat

Stretching south from Munttoren, part of a former city gate, this area lies wholly beyond the line of the medieval city wall. From the 1660s, the *Grachtengordel* was extended further east towards the Amstel. One of Amsterdam's prettiest canals, Reguliersgracht with its seven bridges, was cut at this time. Today, houses on the major Canal Ring, such as the Van Loon, with its grand façade and fine interior, convey a sense of life in the Golden Age *(see pp26–9)*. Beyond is the 19th-century De Pijp, a working-class district built to relieve the overcrowded Jordaan. De Pijp is now a lively multicultural area, and home to the Albert Cuypmarkt, the city's biggest street market.

SIGHTS AT A GLANCE

Historic Buildings and Bridges
Blauwbrug ③
Gemeentearchief Amsterdam ⑤
Magere Brug ⑥
Amstelkerk ⑦
Munttoren ⑫

Squares and Markets
Rembrandtplein ①
Albert Cuypmarkt ⑧
Bloemenmarkt ⑬

Cinemas
Tuschinski Theater ⑪

Museums
Museum Willet-Holthuysen pp120–21 ②
Foam Museum ④
Heineken Experience ⑨
Museum van Loon ⑩

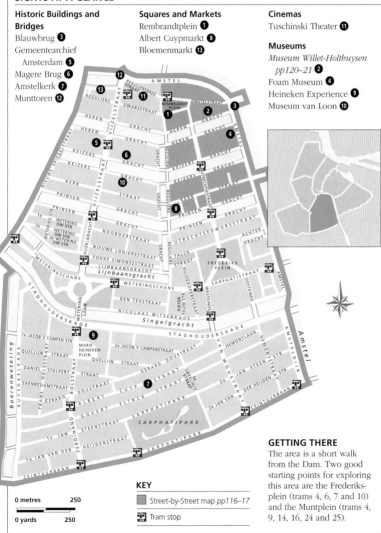

GETTING THERE
The area is a short walk from the Dam. Two good starting points for exploring this area are the Frederiksplein (trams 4, 6, 7 and 10) and the Muntplein (trams 4, 9, 14, 16, 24 and 25).

KEY

Street-by-Street map *pp116–17*

Tram stop

| 0 metres | 250 |
| 0 yards | 250 |

◁ Colourful display of flowers at the Albert Cuypmarkt, including roses, lilies and sunflowers

Street-by-Street: Amstelveld

The eastern end of the *Grachtengordel* is quiet and
largely residential, especially around the Amstelveld,
with its pretty wooden church and houseboats.
A short walk will take you past shops
and numerous cafés, particularly
on the bustling
Rembrandtplein. As
you wander down
the broad sweep of the
Amstel river, Amster-
dam suddenly loses its
village atmosphere and
begins to feel like a city.

★ Rembrandtplein
*Looking on to the former Botermarkt
(butter market) and the cast-iron statue
of Rembrandt, there are dozens of cafés
dating from the 19th century, including
the De Kroon at No. 17 (see p47)* ❶

Café Schiller
(see p49)

**★ Museum Willet-
Holthuysen**
*This double canal house
contains a number of
period rooms, including
the fine 19th-century-style
garden room which looks
out on to the restored 18th-
century formal garden* ❷

Amstelkerk
*This wooden church was
meant to be a temporary
structure while money was
raised to build a big new
church on Rembrandtplein,
but the grand scheme fell
through. Today, the church
houses offices and a
restaurant (see p119)* ❼

Blauwbrug
*This cast-iron and stone bridge,
inspired by the Alexander III bridge
in Paris, is adorned with
sculptures on nautical
and marine themes* ❸

LOCATOR MAP
See Street Finder maps 5 & 8

At Amstel 216, the walls of
the building still show
the mysterious scribbles
left by former resident
Coenraad van Beuningen, city
mayor in the mid-1600s.

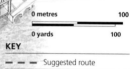

| 0 metres | 100 |
| 0 yards | 100 |

KEY

– – – Suggested route

STAR SIGHTS

★ Rembrandtplein

★ Museum Willet-
Holthuysen

★ Magere Brug

The Market Crier statue
commemorates Professor
Kokadorus (1867–1934),
one of Amsterdam's most
famous street traders.

★ Magere Brug
*The current wooden bridge is a 20th-century
replica of the 17th-century original, but its
mechanical drive was only installed in 1994* ❻

Rembrandtplein ❶

Map 7 C5. 🚊 *4, 9, 14.*

Formerly called the Botermarkt, after the butter
market held here until the
mid-19th century, this square
acquired its present name
when the statue of Rembrandt
was erected in 1876.

Soon afterwards,
Rembrandtplein developed
into a centre for nightlife
with the opening of various
hotels and cafés. The Mast
(renamed the Mille Colonnes
Hotel) dates from 1889, and
the Schiller Karena hotel *(see
p220)* and the Café Schiller
(see p49) both opened in
1892. De Kroon *(see p47)*,
which epitomizes a typical
grand café, dates from 1898.
The popularity of Rembrandtplein has persevered, and the
café terraces are packed
during summer with people
enjoying a pleasant drink and
watching the world go by.

Museum Willet-Holthuysen ❷

See pp120–21.

Blauwbrug ❸

Amstel. **Map** 8 D5. 🚊 *9, 14.*
Ⓜ *Waterlooplein.*

The Blauwbrug (Blue Bridge)
is thought to have taken its
name from the colour of
the wooden bridge that
originally crossed this
particular stretch of the
Amstel in the 17th

Outdoor café on Rembrandtplein

century. The present bridge
is made of stone. It was built
in preparation for the World
Exhibition, which attracted
thousands of visitors to
Amsterdam in 1883.

The Blauwbrug is decorated
with sculptures of medieval
boats, fish and the imperial
crown of Amsterdam and is
surmounted by ornate lamps.
The design was inspired by
the plans for the elaborate
Alexander III bridge in Paris.

Foam Museum ❹

Kaizersgracht 609. **Map** 5 A3.
Tel 551 6500. 🚊 *16, 24, 25.*
⭘ *10am–5pm Sat–Wed,
10am–9pm Thu & Fri.*
⭘ *1 Jan, 30 Apr.* 🖼 📷
☐ ▯ *www.*foam.nl

Three elegant canal houses
have been joined together
and renovated to create a
labyrinth of rooms filled
with photographs. Foam
(Fotografiemuseum
Amsterdam) is dedicated
to exhibiting every form
of photography, from

**Detail of the ornate stone carving
on the Blauwbrug**

historical to journalistic, to
cutting-edge and artistic.

The museum holds four
major exhibitions a year and
15 smaller ones, showcasing
both established figures of
the art form and emerging
local talent. Some of the
most recent exhibitions
have included Annie
Leibovitz's "American Music",
a retrospective on Henri
Cartier-Bresson and "50
Years of World Press Photo".

More than just a museum,
though, Foam prides itself
for being an interactive
centre for photography, a
place where amateurs can
learn more about the art
by meeting professionals,
attending lectures and taking
part in discussion evenings,
or just stop for a coffee
and a browse of the well-
stocked bookshop.

Gemeentearchief Amsterdam ❺

Vijzelstraat 32. **Map** 4 F2. **Tel** 572
0202. 🚊 *16, 24, 25.* ⭘ *10am–5pm
Mon–Sat.* ⬤ *public holidays.* ♿
📷 *(with permission).* **www**.
gemeentearchief.amsterdam.nl

The Gemeentearchief, which
houses the city's municipal
archives, has moved from its
former location in Amsteldijk
to this monumental building.
Designed by KPC de Bazel,
one of the principal
representatives of the
Amsterdam school of
architecture, the edifice
was completed in 1926 for
the Netherlands Trading
Company. In spite of much
renovation work at the end
of World War II and in the
1970s, the building retains
many attractive original
features, such as the
colourful floor mosaics
(designed by de Bazel
himself) and the wooden
panelling in the boardrooms
on the second floor. There
are also some interesting
paintings of the Amsterdam
and Rotterdam harbours in
the third-floor meeting room.

In 1991 the building,
affectionately known as
"The Bazel", was declared
a national monument.

Magere Brug 6

Amstel. **Map** 5 B3. ⬛ 4.

Of Amsterdam's 1,400 or so bridges, the Magere Brug (Skinny Bridge) is undoubtedly the city's best-known, instantly associated with Amsterdam. The original drawbridge was constructed in about 1670. The traditional story has it that it was named after two sisters called Mager, who lived on either side of the Amstel. However, it appears more likely that the bridge acquired the name from its narrow *(mager)* design.

The present drawbridge was in fact put up in 1969 and, though wider than the original, it still conforms to the traditional double-leaf style. It is constructed from African azobe wood (an extremely dense wood), and was intended to last for at least 50 years. About every 20 minutes, the bridge master has to let boats through the bridge. He then jumps on his bicycle and opens up the Amstelsluizen *(see p145)* and Hoge Sluis.

Magere Brug, a traditional double-leaf Dutch drawbridge

The Amstelkerk, built as a temporary church in the 17th century

Amstelkerk 7

Amstelveld 10. **Map** 5 A3.
Tel 520 0060. ⬛ 4. ☐ 9am–5pm Mon–Fri. ● public hols.

Designed by Daniel Stalpaert in 1668, the wooden Amstelkerk was originally intended to be only a temporary structure, while in the meantime money was going to be raised for a large new church on the Botermarkt (now Rembrandtplein). Unfortunately, the necessary funds for the grand scheme were never forthcoming, and so the temporary Amstelkerk had to be kept and maintained. In 1825, the Protestant church authorities attempted to raise money to renovate the Amstelkerk's plain interior in a Neo-Gothic style. It was not until 1840, however, when Frederica Elisabeth Cramer donated 25,000 guilders to the project, that work could begin. The interior walls, pulpit, pews, and organ, which cost some made by Jonathan Batz, all date from this period. The windows, however, are older and date from 1821.

In the late 1980s, the Amstelkerk underwent a substantial and radical conversion, which cost some 4 million guilders. Glass-walled offices were installed inside the building. However, services and concerts are still held in the Amstelkerk, and the nave, which was preserved in all its Neo-Gothic magnificence, now houses the excellent modern Janvier restaurant *(see p233)*.

HOW THE MAGERE BRUG WORKS

Steel cables

The balance is made up of two counterweighted beams.

The arched wooden portal provides a pivot for the balance.

Mechanical chain-drive

Each deck has a span of about 5 m (16 ft).

Museum Willet-Holthuysen ❷

Named after its last residents, the museum allows the visitor a glimpse into the lives of the merchant class who lived in luxury along the *Grachtengordel* (Canal Ring). The house was built in 1685 and became the property of coal magnate Pieter Holthuysen (1788–1858) in 1855. It passed to his daughter Louisa (1824–95) and her husband, Abraham Willet (1825–88), both fervent collectors of paintings, glass, silver and ceramics. When Louisa died childless and a widow in 1895, the house and its many treasures were left to the city. Some of the rooms remain unchanged, while others, such as the kitchen and Garden Room, have been restored in the style of the 18th century.

Statue of Paris on stairway

Portrait of Abraham Willet
Painted in 1877 by André Mniszech, this full-length portrait shows the master of the house dressed in a 17th-century costume.

Temporary exhibitions are on display in the second-floor rooms. The bedroom has the only permanent exhibition.

Ballroom

Front room

Entrance

Ticket office

STAR FEATURES

★ Blue Room

★ Dining Room

★ Blue Room
Hung with heavy blue damask, the room boasts a chimney piece by Jacob de Wit (see p122), and was the exclusive preserve of the men of the house.

Garden Room
Now repainted in its original green, the Garden Room offers views over the intricate knot garden, laid out in 18th-century French style. It was used by the family to entertain guests to tea.

VISITORS' CHECKLIST

Herengracht 605. **Map** 8 D5.
Tel 523 1822. 4, 9, 14.
 10am–5pm Mon–Fri, 11am–
5pm Sat & Sun. 1 Jan,
30 Apr, 25 Dec.
www.willetholthuysen.nl

Bedroom

Staircase
The staircase was built in 1740 and has an elaborate gilded balustrade. The lower walls are painted to look like marble.

Hall

★ Dining Room
The wallpaper is a careful copy of the 18th-century silk original. The elaborate 275-piece Meissen dinner service provided up to 24 places.

The Blue Room porcelain collection includes Chinese vases made during the Kangxi dynasty (1662–1722).

Kitchen
The 18th-century kitchen has been restored using items salvaged from similar houses, including the sink and pump.

Albert Cuypmarkt **8**

Albert Cuypstraat. **Map** 5 A5.
🚊 4, 16, 24, 25. 🕐 9:30am–5pm Mon–Sat.

The market running along Albert Cuypstraat began trading in 1904, shortly after the expansion of the city was completed. The wide street, once a canal, is named after the Dutch landscape painter Albert Cuyp (1620–91). It is located in the Pijp district, originally built for workers.

Described by the stallholders as "the best-known market in Europe", it attracts some 20,000 visitors on weekdays and often twice as many on Saturdays. The goods on sale at the 325 stalls range from fish, poultry, cheese, fruit and vegetables to clothes, and prices are among the cheapest in Amsterdam.

Smoked fish in Albert Cuypmarkt

Heineken Experience **9**

Stadhouderskade 78. **Map** 4 F3. **Tel** 523 9666. 🚊 6, 7, 10, 16, 24, 25. 🕐 10am–6pm Tue–Sun. **Box office** 10am–5pm. 🕐 25 Dec, 1 Jan 📷 www.heinekenexperience.com

Gerard Adriaan Heineken founded the Heineken company in 1864 when he bought the 16th-century Hooiberg (haystack) brewery on the Nieuwezijds Voorburgwal. The original Stadhouderskade

Formal rose garden at Museum van Loon

building was erected in 1867. His readiness to adapt to new methods and bring in foreign brewers established him as a major force in Amsterdam's profitable beer industry.

In 1988, the company finally stopped producing beer in its massive brick brewery on Stadhouderskade, as it was unable to keep up with the demand. Production is now concentrated in two breweries, one in Zoeterwoude, near Den Haag, another in Den Bosch. Today, Heineken produces around half of the beer sold in Amsterdam, has production facilities in dozens of countries and exports all over the world.

The Stadhouderskade building now houses the Heineken Reception Centre, launched in 1991. Visitors can walk through the tiled brewhouse, with its enormous brewing coppers, and on through the renovated stables where the splendid dray horses are once more on show. Visitors to the museum can learn about the history of the company and of beer-making in general. The offer of free beer makes a popular end to the tour, which is open to anyone over 18 years old.

Museum van Loon **10**

Keizersgracht 672. **Map** 5 A3. **Tel** 624 5255. 🚊 16, 24, 25. 🕐 11am–5pm Wed–Mon. 🔴 public hols. 📷 📷 📷 **www**.museumvanloon.nl

Van Loon was the name of one of Amsterdam's foremost families in the 17th century. They did not move into this house on the Keizersgracht, however, until 1884. Designed by Adriaan Dortsman, No. 672 is one of a pair of symmetrical houses built in 1672 for the Flemish merchant Jeremias van Raey. It was redecorated in 1752 when Dr Abraham van Hagen and his wife Catharina Elisabeth Trip moved in. Their surnames are incorporated in the copper staircase railing.

The house was opened as a museum in 1973, after many years of restoration. It is now a delightful canalside museum, retaining the original charming character of the house. It contains a collection of Van Loon family portraits, stretching back to the early 1600s. The period rooms are adorned with fine pieces of furniture, porcelain and sculpture. Some of the upstairs rooms contain sumptuous illusionistic wall paintings, which were popular in the 17th and 18th centuries. Four were painted by the classicist artist Gérard de Lairesse (1641–1711). Outside, in the formal rose garden, is a beautiful 18th-century coach house, now a private residence.

Dray horse and beer wagon at the Heineken Brouwerij

Tuschinski Theater ⓫

Reguliersbreestraat 26–28.
Map 7 C5. **Tel** 0900 1458. 🚋 4,
9, 14. **Box office** ⏰ 12:15–10pm.
🎫 📷 ♿

Abraham Tuschinski's cinema
and variety theatre caused
a sensation when it opened in
1921. Until then, Amsterdam's
cinemas had been sombre
places, but this was an exotic
blend of Art Deco and Amsterdam School architecture *(see
pp96–7)*. Its twin towers are
26 m (85 ft) in height. Built
in a slum area known as the
Duivelshoek (Devil's Corner),
it was designed by Heyman
Louis de Jong and decorated
by Chris Bartels, Jaap Gidding
and Pieter de Besten. In its
heyday, Marlene Dietrich and
Judy Garland performed here.

Now converted into a six-
screen cinema, the building
has been meticulously
restored, both inside and out.
The carpet in
the entrance
hall, replaced
in 1984, is an
exact copy of
the original.
Visitors may
take a guided
tour, but the
best way to
appreciate
the opulence
of the
Tuschinski
Theater is to
go and see a film. For just a
few extra euros, you can take
a seat in one of the exotic
boxes that make up the back
row of the huge semi-
circular, 1,472-seater main
auditorium.

View of the Munttoren at the base of Muntplein

**Detail of Tuschinski
Theater façade**

Munttoren ⓬

Muntplein. **Map** 7 B5. 🚋 4, 9, 14,
16, 24, 25. **Tower** 🚫 to the public.
Shop ⏰ 10am–6pm Mon–Sat.

The polygonal base of the
Munttoren (mint tower)
formed part of the Reguliers-
poort, a gate in Amsterdam's
medieval city wall. The gate
was destroyed by fire in 1618,
but the base survived. In the
following year, Hendrick de
Keyser *(see p90)* added the
clock tower, capped with a
steeple and openwork orb.
The carillon was designed by
François Hemony *(see p68)*
in 1699, and rings every 15
minutes. The tower acquired
its name in 1673, during the
French occupation of Amsterdam, when the city mint was
temporarily housed here. Up-
market gift shops are now
found in the base of the tower.

Bloemenmarkt ⓭

Singel. **Map** 7 B5.
🚋 1, 2, 4, 5, 9, 14, 16, 24, 25.
⏰ 9:30am–5pm daily.

On the Singel, west of Muntplein, is the last of the city's
floating markets. In the past,
nurserymen sailed up the
Amstel from their smallholdings
and moored here to sell cut
flowers and plants directly
from their boats. Today, the
stalls are still floating but are
permanent. Despite the sellers'
tendency to cater purely for
tourists, the displays of fragrant seasonal flowers and
bright spring bedding-plants
are always beautiful to look at.

Florist arranging his display at the Bloemenmarkt

MUSEUM QUARTER

Until the late 1800s, the Museum Quarter was little more than an area of farms and small-holdings. At this time, the city council designated it an area of art and culture and plans were conceived for constructing Amsterdam's great cultural monuments: the Rijksmuseum, the Stedelijk Museum and the Concertgebouw. The Van Gogh Museum followed in 1973, its striking extension

"Russia" gablestone in Roemer Visscherstraat

being added in 1999. The Museumplein has two memorials to the victims of World War II. The *plein* is still used as a site for political demonstrations. To the north and south are turn-of-the-century houses, where the streets are named after artists and intellectuals, such as the 17th-century poet Roemer Visscher. To the west, the Vondelpark offers a pleasant, fresh-air break from all the museums.

SIGHTS AT A GLANCE

Museums and Workshops
Coster Diamonds ❷
Nederlands Filmmuseum ❾
Rijksmuseum pp130–33 ❶
Stedelijk Museum
  pp136–7 ❹
Van Gogh Museum
  pp134–5 ❸

Concert Halls
Concertgebouw ❺

Historic Buildings
Hollandsche Manege ❼
Vondelkerk ❽

Parks
Vondelpark ❻

GETTING THERE
Trams 2 and 5 are all convenient for the Rijksmuseum and other museums, while trams 3 and 12 stop outside the Concertgebouw. The area has a mixture of parking areas and meters. The museum boat stops near the Rijksmuseum, on the Singelgracht.

| 0 metres | 250 |
| 0 yards | 250 |

KEY

	Street-by-Street map *See pp126–7*
	Tram stop
	Museum boat boarding point

◁ Statue of the painter Pieter Aertsen (1509–75) on the façade of the Stedelijk Museum

Street-by-Street: Museum Quarter

Statue on façade of Stedelijk

The green expanse of Museumplein was once bisected by a busy main road known locally as the "shortest motorway in Europe". But dramatic renovation between 1996 and 1999 has transformed it into a stately park, fringed by Amsterdam's major cultural centres. The district is one of the wealthiest in the city, with wide streets lined with grand houses.

After the heady delights of the museums, it is possible to window-shop at the up-market boutiques along the exclusive PC Hooftstraat and Van Baerlestraat, or watch the diamond polishers at work in Coster Diamonds.

★ Van Gogh Museum
The new wing of the museum, an elegant oval shape, was designed by Kisho Kurokawa and opened in 1999. It is dedicated to temporary exhibitions of 19th-century art ❸

Van Baerlestraat contains exclusive clothing shops *(see p238).*

★ Stedelijk Museum
Housing the civic collection of modern art, this museum also stages controversial contemporary art exhibitions. Temporarily relocated (see p136) ❹

Concertgebouw
Designed by AL van Gendt, the building has a Classical façade and a concert hall with near-perfect acoustics ❺

VAN DER VELDESTR

PAULUS POTTERSTRAAT

VAN BAERLESTRAAT

Coster Diamonds
Diamonds have been cut, polished and sold at Coster since 1840. The firm now occupies three splendid adjoining villas, built on Museumplein in 1896 ❷

LOCATOR MAP
See Street Finder, map 4

Light lines

HOBBEMASTRAAT

Pond/ice rink

★ Rijksmuseum
The heavily ornamented Neo-Gothic Rijksmuseum holds the magnificent Dutch national art collection of some 5,000 paintings, 30,000 pieces of applied art and 17,000 historical artifacts ❶

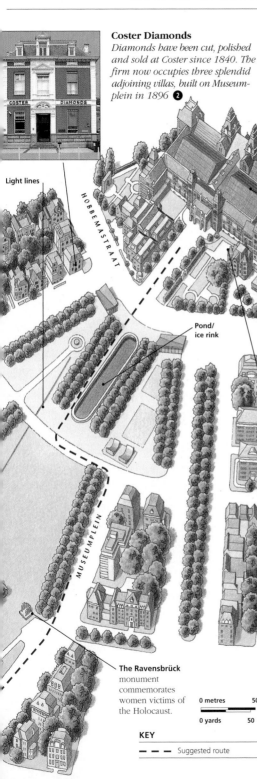

The Rijksmuseum
is surrounded by gardens which contain statuary. This weathered bronze of Mercury, designed by Ferdinand Leenhoff (1841–1914), is found in the southeast garden.

MUSEUMPLEIN

The Ravensbrück
monument commemorates women victims of the Holocaust.

0 metres	50
0 yards	50

KEY

--- Suggested route

STAR SIGHTS

★ Rijksmuseum

★ Van Gogh Museum

★ Stedelijk Museum

Rijksmuseum ❶

See pp130–33.

Coster Diamonds ❷

Paulus Potterstraat 2–8.
Map 4 E3. **Tel** 305 5555. 🚊 *2, 5.*
🕐 *9am–5pm daily.* 📷 📵 ♿
www.costerdiamonds.com

One of Amsterdam's oldest diamond factories, Coster was founded in 1840. Twelve years later, Queen Victoria's consort, Prince Albert, honoured the company by giving them the task of repolishing the enormous *Koh-i-Noor* (mountain of light) diamond. This blue-white stone is one of the treasures of the British crown jewels and weighs in at 108.8 carats. A replica of the coronation crown, which incorporates a copy of the fabulous stone, is found in Coster's spacious entrance hall.

More than 2,000 people visit the factory each day to witness the processes of grading, cutting and polishing the stones. The goldsmiths and diamond-cutters work together to produce customized items of jewellery, in a range of styles, which are available over the counter. For serious diamond-buyers, such as the jewellers who come to Amsterdam from all over the world, there is a series of private sales rooms where discretion is assured.

A potential sale under discussion at Coster Diamonds

Van Gogh Museum ❸

See pp134–5.

Stedelijk Museum ❹

See pp136–7.

Façade of the award-winning Concertgebouw (1881) by AL van Gendt

Concertgebouw ❺

Concertgebouwplein 2–6. **Map**
4 D4. **Tel** 671 8345. 🚊 *2, 3, 5, 12, 16.* Box office 🕐 *10am–7pm daily.* 📷 📵 ♿ *by arrangement.*
www.concertgebouw.nl

Following an open architectural competition held in 1881, AL van Gendt (1835–1901) was chosen to design a vast new concert hall for Amsterdam. The resulting Neo-Renaissance building boasts an elaborate pediment and colonnaded façade, and houses two concert halls. Despite Van Gendt's lack of musical knowledge, he managed to produce near-perfect acoustics in the Grote Zaal (main concert hall), which is renowned the world over.

The inaugural concert at the Concertgebouw was held on 11 April 1888, complete with an orchestra of 120 musicians and a choir of 600. A resident orchestra was established at the hall seven months later.

The building has been renovated several times over the years, most recently in 1983, when some serious subsidence threatened the building's entire foundation. To remedy this, the whole superstructure had to be lifted up off the ground while the original supporting piles, which rested on sand 13 m (43 ft) underground, were removed and replaced by concrete piles sunk into the ground to a depth of 18 m (59 ft). A glass extension and new entrance were added by Pi de Bruijn in 1988. The original entrance was relocated round to the side of the building. Though primarily designed to hold concerts, the Concertgebouw has become a multi-functional building. It has played host to business meetings, exhibitions, conferences, political meetings and occasional boxing matches.

Bandstand in Vondelpark

Vondelpark ❻

Stadhouderskade. **Map** 4 E2.
🚊 *1, 2, 3, 5, 6, 12.* Park
🕐 *24hrs daily.* Open-air theatre
🕐 *Jun–last week Aug: Wed–Sun.*

In 1864, a group consisting of prominent Amsterdammers formed a committee with the aim of founding a public park, and they raised enough money to buy 8 hectares (20 acres) of land. JD and LP Zocher, a father-and-son team of landscape architects, were then commissioned to design the park in typical English landscape style. They used vistas, pathways and ponds to create the illusion of a large natural area, which was opened to the public on 15 June 1865, as the Nieuwe Park. The park's present name was adopted in 1867, when a statue of Dutch poet Joost van den Vondel

(1586–1679) was erected in the grounds. The committee soon began to raise money to enlarge the park, and by June 1877 it had reached its current dimensions of 45 hectares (110 acres). The park now supports around 100 plant species and 127 types of tree. Squirrels, hedgehogs, ducks and garden birds mix with a huge colony of greedy, bright green parakeets, which gather in front of the pavilion every morning to be fed. Herds of cows, sheep, goats and even a lone llama graze in the pastures.

Vondelpark welcomes about 8 million visitors a year, and is popular with the locals for dog-walking, jogging, or just for the view. Free concerts are given at the *openluchttheater* (open-air theatre) or at the bandstand in the summer.

Hollandsche Manege ❼

Vondelstraat 140. **Map** 3 C2.
Tel 618 0942. 🚊 *1, 6.*
🕐 *9am–midnight Mon–Fri,
9am–6pm Sat & Sun.* 📷 💻

The Dutch Riding School was originally situated on the Leidsegracht *(see p111)*, but in 1882 a new building was opened, designed by AL van Gendt and based on the Spanish Riding School in Vienna. The riding school was threatened with demolition in the 1980s, but was saved after a public outcry. Reopened in 1986 by Prince Bernhard, it has been restored to its former

Façade of the Hollandse Manege

glory. The Neo-Classical indoor arena boasts gilded mirrors and moulded horses' heads on its elaborate plasterwork walls. Some of the wrought-iron stalls remain and sound is muffled by sawdust. At the top of the staircase, one door leads to a balcony overlooking the arena, another to the café.

Vondelkerk ❽

Vondelstraat 120. Map 3 C2.
🚊 *1, 3, 6, 12.* 🚫 *to the public.*

The Vondelkerk was the largest church designed by PJH Cuypers, architect of the Centraal Station *(see pp32–3)*. Work began on the building in 1872, but funds ran out by the following year. Money gathered from public donations and lotteries allowed the building to be completed by 1880.

When fire broke out in November 1904, firefighters saved the nave of the church by forcing the burning tower to fall away into Vondelpark. A new tower was added later by the architect's son, JT Cuypers. The church was deconsecrated in 1979 and converted into offices in 1985.

Nederlands Filmmuseum ❾

Vondelpark 3. **Map** 4 D2. **Tel** 589
1400. 🚊 *1, 3, 6, 12.* Library
🕐 *1–5pm Mon–Fri.* ● *public hols.*
Box Office 🕐 *9am–10:15pm
Mon–Fri, 1 hour before first screening
Sat–Sun. Screenings: from 7:30pm
daily, and 1:45pm Wed & Sun
(for children).* 💳 *for cinema.*
🚫 💻 🍴 www.filmmuseum.nl

Vondelpark's pavilion was designed by the architects PJ Hamer (1812–87), and his son, W Hamer (1843–1913), and opened on 4 May 1881 as a café and restaurant. After World War II, it was restored and then reopened in 1947 as an international cultural centre. In 1991, the pavilion was renovated once more. The complete Art Deco interior of the Cinema Parisien, Amsterdam's first cinema, built in 1910, was moved into one of the rooms. It is now an important national film museum, showing more than 1,000 films a year. The museum owns a film poster collection, runs a public film library at Nos. 69–71 Vondelstraat and holds free outdoor screenings during summer.

The terrace of Café Vertigo at the Filmmuseum

Rijksmuseum ❶

The Rijksmuseum, an Amsterdam landmark, possesses an unrivalled collection of Dutch art, begun in the early 19th century. The huge museum opened in 1885 to bitter criticism from Amsterdam's Protestant community for its Neo-Gothic style. The main building is undergoing extensive renovation between 2003 and 2008. However, the highlights from the Golden Age are on show in the Philips Wing during this period.

Second floor

Winter Landscape with Skaters *(1618)*
Dumb painter Hendrick Avercamp specialized in intricate icy winter scenes.

The Gothic façade
of Cuypers' building is red brick with elaborate decoration, including coloured tiles.

★ The Kitchen Maid *(1658)*
The light falling through the window and the stillness of this scene are typical of Johannes Vermeer (see p194).

Stair

Entrance

KEY TO FLOORPLAN

- ☐ Dutch history
- ☐ Dutch painting
- ☐ European painting
- ☐ Sculpture and decorative art
- ☐ Prints and drawings
- ☐ Asiatic art
- ☐ Temporary exhibitions
- ☐ Non-exhibition space

STAR PAINTINGS

- ★ The Night Watch by Rembrandt
- ★ St Elizabeth's Day Flood
- ★ The Kitchen Maid by Vermeer

★ St Elizabeth's Day Flood *(1500)*
An unknown artist painted this altarpiece, showing a disastrous flood in 1421. The dykes protecting Dordrecht were breached, and 22 villages were swept away by the flood water.

Entrance

Study collections

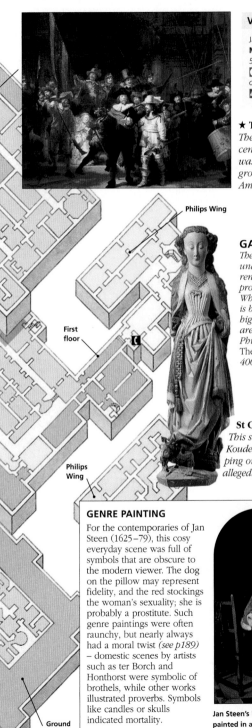

VISITORS' CHECKLIST

Jan Luykenstraat 1 (Philips Wing).
Map 4 E3. **Tel** 674 7047. 🚊 2,
5, 6, 7, 10. 🚋 Stadhouderskade.
⬜ 9am–6pm daily (Philips Wing
only). 🌑 1 Jan. 📷 🚫 👪 📹
🔒 🅿 📷 **www**.rijksmuseum.nl

★ **The Night Watch** *(1642)*
*The showpiece of Dutch 17th-
century art, this vast canvas
was commissioned as a
group portrait of an
Amsterdam militia company.*

Philips Wing

First
floor

GALLERY GUIDE

*The museum is currently
undergoing the biggest
renovation and rebuilding
programme in its history.
Whilst the main building
is being renovated, all the
highlights of the Golden Age
are on show throughout the
Philips Wing, under the title of
The Masterpieces. More than
400 pieces are on display.*

St Catherine *(c.1465)*
*This sculpture by the Master of
Koudewater shows the saint stamping on Emperor Maxentius, who
allegedly killed her with his sword.*

Philips
Wing

GENRE PAINTING

For the contemporaries of Jan
Steen (1625–79), this cosy
everyday scene was full of
symbols that are obscure to
the modern viewer. The dog
on the pillow may represent
fidelity, and the red stockings
the woman's sexuality; she is
probably a prostitute. Such
genre paintings were often
raunchy, but nearly always
had a moral twist *(see p189)*
– domestic scenes by artists
such as ter Borch and
Honthorst were symbolic of
brothels, while other works
illustrated proverbs. Symbols
like candles or skulls
indicated mortality.

Jan Steen's *Woman at her Toilet* **was
painted in about 1660**

Ground
floor

Exploring the Rijksmuseum

The Rijksmuseum is almost too vast to be seen in a single visit, though the key pieces can be found in the Philips Wing. It is famous for owning probably the best collection of Dutch art in the world, from early religious works to the masterpieces of the Golden Age. However, the applied art and sculpture sections, and the Asiatic artifacts, are equally wonderful, and the Dutch history section only slightly less rewarding. If time is short, start with the incomparable 17th-century paintings, taking in Frans Hals, Vermeer and scores of other Old Masters, to arrive finally at Rembrandt's *The Night Watch*.

Feeding the Hungry **from a series of seven panels by the Master of Alkmaar**

DUTCH HISTORY

The turbulent history of the Netherlands is encapsulated in this section. In the opening room is the medieval altar painting of *St Elizabeth's Day Flood (see p130)*. The central room has 17th-century models of ships, artifacts salvaged from shipwrecks and paintings of factories and townscapes from the days of the Dutch Empire. Later displays recall battles in naval history; exhibits from the 18th century deal with the impact of revolutionary France on Amsterdam, ending in 1815 after the Napoleonic Wars.

EARLY PAINTING AND FOREIGN SCHOOLS

Alongside a small collection of Flemish and Italian art, including portraits by Piero di Cosimo (1462–1521), are the first specifically "Dutch" paintings. These works are mostly religious, such as *The Seven Works of Charity* (1504) by the Master of Alkmaar, Jan van Scorel's quasi-Mannerist *Mary Magdalene* (1528) and Lucas van Leyden's triptych, *Adoration of the Golden Calf* (1530). As the 16th century progressed, religious themes were superseded by pastoral subjects; by 1552, paintings like Pieter Aertsen's *The Egg Dance* were full of realism, by then the keystone of much Dutch art.

17TH-CENTURY PAINTING

By the Alteration in 1578 *(see pp24–5)*, Dutch art had moved away completely from religious to secular themes. Artists turned to realistic portraiture, landscapes, still lifes, seascapes, domestic interiors, including genre work *(see p131)*, and animal portraits.

Rembrandt *(see p62)* is the most famous of many artists who lived and worked around Amsterdam at this time. Examples of his work hanging in the Rijksmuseum include *Portrait of Titus in a Monk's Habit* (1660), *Self Portrait as the Apostle Paul* (1661), *The Jewish Bride (see p42)* and the incredible *Night Watch (see p131)*. Look out too for the work of his many pupils, who included Nicolaes Maes and Ferdinand Bol.

Don't miss Jan Vermeer's (1632–75) serenely light-filled interiors including *The Kitchen Maid, (see p130)*, and *The Woman Reading a Letter* (1662). Of several portraits by Frans Hals *(see pp178–9)* the best known are *The Wedding Portrait* and *The Merry Drinker* (1630). *The Windmill at Wijk* by Jacob van Ruisdael (1628–82) is a great landscape by an artist at the very height of his power. Other artists whose works contribute to this unforgettable collection include Pieter Saenredam, Jan van de Capelle, Jan Steen *(see p131)* and Gerard ter Borch.

18TH- AND 19TH-CENTURY PAINTING

In many ways, 18th-century Dutch painting merely continued the themes and quality of 17th-century work.

The Wedding Portrait **(c. 1622) by Frans Hals**

This is particularly true of portraiture and still lifes, with the evocative *Still Life with Flowers and Fruit* by Jan van Huysum (1682–1749) standing out. A trend developed later for elegant "conversation pieces" by artists such as Adriaan van der Werff (1659–1722) and Cornelis Troost (1696–1750). Most had satirical undertones, like *The Art Gallery of Jan Gildemeester Jansz* (1794) by Adriaan de Lelie (1755–1820), showing an 18th-century salon whose walls are crowded with 17th-century masterpieces.

HAGUE SCHOOL AND THE IMPRESSIONISTS

The so-called Hague School was made up of a group of Dutch artists who came together around 1870 in Den Haag. Their landscape work, which earned them the alternative title the "Grey" School for their overcast skies, captures the atmospheric quality of subdued Dutch sunlight. One of the prizes of the Rijksmuseum's 19th-century collection is *Morning Ride on the Beach* (1876) by Anton Mauve (1838–88), painted in soft pearly colours. Alongside hangs the beautiful polder landscape, *View near the Geesthbrug* by Hendrik Weissenbruch (1824–1903). In contrast, the Dutch Impressionists, closely linked to the French Impressionists, preferred active subjects such as *The Bridge over the Singel at Paleisstraat, Amsterdam* (1890) by George Hendrik Breitner (1857–1923).

SCULPTURE AND APPLIED ARTS

Beginning with religious medieval sculpture, this section moves on to the splendour of Renaissance furniture and decoration. Highlights that capture the wealth of the Golden Age include an exquisite collection of glassware, Delftware *(see p195)* and diamond-encrusted jewellery. A late 17th-century 12-leaf Chinese screen incorporates European figures on one side, a phoenix on the other; and two dolls'

Still Life with Flowers and Fruit (c. 1730) by artist Jan van Huysum (1682–1740), one of many still lifes exhibited in the Rijksmuseum

houses are modelled on contemporary town houses. Some outstanding 18th-century Meissen porcelain and Art Nouveau glass complete the collection.

PRINTS AND DRAWINGS

The Rijksmuseum owns about a million prints and drawings. Although the emphasis is on Dutch works (most of Rembrandt's etchings as well as rare works by Hercules Seghers (c. 1589–1637) are here), there are prints by major European artists, including Dürer, Tiepolo, Goya, Watteau and Toulouse-Lautrec as well as a set of coloured Japanese woodcuts. Small exhibitions are held on the ground floor of the museum, but particular prints can be viewed with special permission from the Study Collection in the basement.

ASIATIC ART

Rewards of the Dutch imperial trading past are on show in this department, which has a separate entrance at the rear of the museum. Some of the earliest artifacts are the most unusual: tiny bronze Tang dynasty figurines from 7th-century China and gritty, granite rock carvings from Java (c. 8th century). Later exhibits include a lovely – and extremely explicit – Hindu statue entitled *Heavenly Beauty*, luscious Chinese parchment paintings of tigers, inlaid Korean boxes and Vietnamese dishes painted with curly-tailed fish. This is a veritable hoard of delights and, above all, a monument to the sophistication and skill of craftsmen and artists in early Eastern cultures.

Late 7th-century Cambodian *Head of Buddha*

Van Gogh Museum ❸

The Van Gogh Museum is based on a design by De Stijl architect Gerrit Rietveld (*see p136*) and opened in 1973. A new, freestanding wing, designed by Kisho Kurokawa, was added in 1999. When Van Gogh died in 1890, he was on the verge of being acclaimed. His younger brother Theo, an art dealer, amassed a collection of 200 of his paintings and 500 drawings. These, combined with around 850 letters by Van Gogh to Theo, and selected works by his friends and contemporaries, form the core of the museum's outstanding collection.

KEY TO FLOORPLAN

☐ Works by Van Gogh
☐ Study collection & Print room
☐ Other 19th-century paintings
☐ Temporary exhibitions

★ Vincent's Bedroom in Arles (*1888*)
One of Van Gogh's best-known works, this was painted to celebrate his achievement of domestic stability at the Yellow House in Arles. He was so delighted with the colourful painting that he did it twice.

★ Sunflowers
(*1888*)
The vivid yellows and greens in this version of Van Gogh's Sunflowers have been enriched by broad streaks of bright mauve and red.

Third floor

Stairwell

Second floor (study collection)

First floor

19th-century art

Entrance

Ground floor

Shop

STAR PAINTINGS

★ Sunflowers

★ Vincent's Bedroom in Arles

★ Wheatfield and Crows

MUSEUM GUIDE

Paintings from Van Gogh's Dutch period and from his time in Paris and Provence are on the first floor. The study collection, occasional exhibits of Van Gogh's drawings and other temporary exhibitions are on the second floor. Works by other 19th-century artists are on the ground floor and third floor, along with the bookshop and café. The new wing houses temporary exhibitions.

AN ARTIST'S LIFE

Vincent Van Gogh (1853–90), born in Zundert, began painting in 1880. He worked in the Netherlands for five years before moving to Paris, later settling at Arles in the south of France. After a fierce argument with Gauguin, he cut off part of his own ear and his mental instability forced him into an asylum in Saint-Rémy. He sought help in Auvers, where he shot himself, dying two days later.

Van Gogh in 1871

VISITORS' CHECKLIST

Paulus Potterstraat 7. **Map** 4 E3.
Tel 570 5200. 🚊 2, 3, 5, 12
🕐 10am–6pm Mon–Thu, Sat & Sun; 10–10pm Fri. 🚫 1 Jan.
📷 🚫 🎧 🚻 📖 🍽 🎁
www.vangoghmuseum.nl

Pietà (after Delacroix) (1889)
Van Gogh painted this work while in the asylum at Saint-Rémy. The figure of Christ is thought to be a self-portrait.

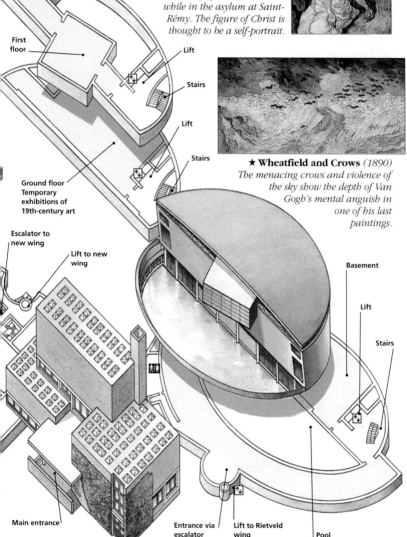

First floor

Lift

Stairs

Lift

Stairs

★ Wheatfield and Crows (1890)
The menacing crows and violence of the sky show the depth of Van Gogh's mental anguish in one of his last paintings.

Ground floor
Temporary exhibitions of 19th-century art

Escalator to new wing

Lift to new wing

Basement

Lift

Stairs

Main entrance

Entrance via escalator

Lift to Rietveld wing

Pool

Stedelijk Museum ❹

Built to house a collection left to the city by Sophia de
Bruyn in 1890, the Stedelijk Museum on Museumplein
became the national museum of modern art in 1938. The
building is currently closed for renovation, meaning that
classics by the likes of Picasso, Chagall and Cézanne are
out of bounds. A temporary venue, the Stedelijk Museum
CS, has been set up near Centraal Station to display
works of art and design created after 1968. The museum's
website gives details of the changing exhibitions.

**Portrait of the Artist with
Seven Fingers** *(1912)*
*Marc Chagall's self-portrait
is heavily autobiographical;
the seven fingers of the title
allude to the seven days of
Creation and the artist's
Jewish origins. Paris and
Rome, the cities Chagall
lived in, are inscribed in
Hebrew above his head.*

**Solidaridad con
America Latina** *(1970)*
*The Stedelijk's collection of
rare posters comprises some
17,000 works, including
this graphic image by the
Cuban human rights
campaigner Asela Perez.*

THE MUSEUM BUILDING

The Neo-Renaissance building
was designed by AW Weissman
(1858–1923) in 1895. The façade is
adorned with turrets and gables and
with niches containing statues of
artists and architects. Inside, it is
ultra-modern. The museum will
be undergoing major renovation
between 2004 and 2008.

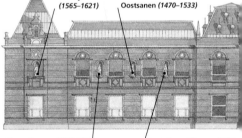

Hendrick
de Keyser
(1565–1621)

Jacob Cornelisz van
Oostsanen (1470–1533)

Pieter Aertsen (1509–75)

Joost Jansz Bilhamer (1541–

Gerrit Rietveld's *Red Blue Chair* (1918)

DE STIJL MOVEMENT

The Dutch artistic movement known as De Stijl (The
Style) produced startlingly simple designs which have
become icons of 20th-century abstract art. These include
Gerrit Rietveld's famous *Red Blue Chair* and Pieter
Mondriaan's *Composition in Red, Black, Blue, Yellow
and Grey* (1920). The movement was formed in 1917 by
a group of artists who
espoused clarity in their
work, which embraced
the mediums of painting,
architecture, sculpture,
poetry and furniture des-
ign. Many De Stijl artists,
like Theo van Doesburg,
split from the founding
group in the 1920s, and
their legacy can be seen
in the work of the Bau-
haus and Modernist
schools which followed.

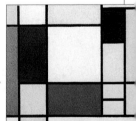

*Composition in Red, Black, Blue,
Yellow and Grey by Mondriaan*

Dancing Woman (1911)
Ernst Ludwig Kirchner (1880–1938) was inspired by the primitive art of African and Asian cultures, and by the natural qualities of the materials he worked with.

Elaborate bell tower

Man and Animals (1949)
Karel Appel (born 1921) was a member of the short-lived, experimental Cobra movement. The human figure, dog fish and mythical creature are painted in the naive style of a child.

Thomas de Keyser
(1596–1667)

Jan van der Heyden
(1637–1712)

Jacob van Campen
(1595–1657)

STAR COLLECTIONS

★ Works by Mondriaan

★ Cobra Collection

★ Works by Malevich

Untitled (1965)
Jasper Johns (born 1930) believed viewers should draw their own conclusions from his work. This huge canvas, with its bold rainbow (red, blue and yellow streaks and slabs), invites the viewer to think about the symbolism of colour.

PERMANENT ARTISTS

Works by inventive photographer Man Ray, Russian artist Kazimir Malevich and sculptor Jean Tinguely are usually on show in the museum.

Man Ray (1890–1977) *elevated photography to an art form, and was a major influence on the Surrealists.*

Kazimir Malevich (1878–1935) *founded Suprematism, an abstract movement which experimented with colour.*

Jean Tinguely (1925–1991) *created humorous, moving sculptures, welded together from junk and recycled metal.*

PLANTAGE

Pillar decoration on Theater Carré

Known as the "plantation", this area was once green parkland beyond the city wall, where 17th-century Amsterdammers spent their leisure time. From about 1848, it became one of Amsterdam's first suburbs. The tree-lined streets around Artis and Hortus Botanicus are still popular places to live. In the 19th century, many middle-class Jews prospered in the area, mainly in the diamond-cutting industry. They formed a large part of the Diamond Workers' Union, whose history is recorded at the Nationaal Vakbondsmuseum. From the Werf 't Kromhout, once a thriving shipyard, there is a fine view of De Gooyer Windmill, one of the few in Amsterdam to survive. The national maritime collection is kept at the Scheepvaart Museum, a former naval storehouse.

SIGHTS AT A GLANCE

Museums
De Burcht
  (Vakbondsmuseum) **2**
Geologisch Museum **5**
Hermitage Amsterdam **16**
Hollandsche Schouwburg **3**
Museum 't Kromhout **11**
Nederlands Scheepvaart-
  museum pp146–7 **12**
Verzetsmuseum **15**

**Historic Buildings
and Structures**
Amstelsluizen **14**
Entrepotdok **8**
De Gooyer Windmill **10**
Muiderpoort **9**

Sights of Scientific Interest
Aquarium **7**
Artis **4**
Planetarium **6**

Botanical Gardens
Hortus Botanicus Amsterdam **1**

Theatres
Koninklijk Theater Carré **13**

GETTING THERE
Trams 6, 9 and 14 pass Artis and Hortus Botanicus; buses 22 and 32 stop at the Scheepvaartmuseum. Weesperplein metro station is located in the southwest of Plantage. It can be intimidating at night, so use the nearby Waterlooplein station.

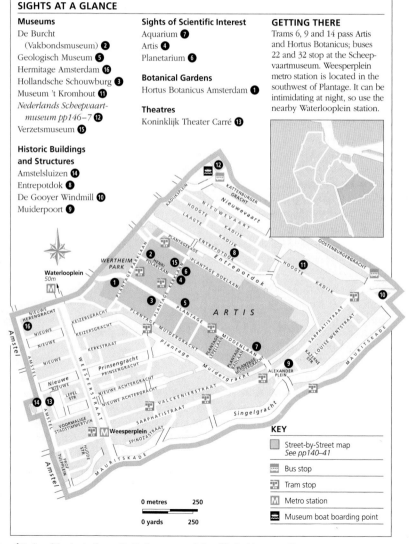

KEY

	Street-by-Street map *See pp140–41*
	Bus stop
	Tram stop
M	Metro station
	Museum boat boarding point

0 metres 250
0 yards 250

◁ Replica of the *Amsterdam*, an East Indiaman, moored alongside the Scheepvaart Museum

Street-by-Street: Plantage

Elephant from Artis zoo

With its wide, tree-lined streets and painted, sandstone buildings, the Plantage is a graceful and often over-looked part of the city. Though it seems like a quiet part of town, there is a lot to see and do. The area is dominated by the Artis complex. It has a diverse range of popular attractions which can get very busy on sunny days. The area has a strong Jewish tradition, and several monuments commemorate Jewish history in Amsterdam, including a basalt memorial in the Hollandsche Schouwburg. The cafés of the Entrepotdok offer a pleasant setting for a relaxing coffee, within earshot of the zoo.

De Burcht (Vakbondsmuseum)
Inspired by an Italian palazzo, its museum displays trade-union memorabilia ➋

PLANTAGE PARKLAAN

PLANTAGE KIRKLAAN

Planetarium
Part of the Artis complex, the domed Planetarium explores man's relationship with the stars. Interactive displays show the positions of the planets ➏

Moederhuis, Aldo van Eyck's refuge for pregnant women, has a colourful, modern façade intended to draw people inside.

★ Hortus Botanicus Amsterdam
The old glasshouses have been restored, and this new one put up to hold tropical and desert plants ➊

STAR SIGHTS

★ Artis

★ Hollandsche Schouwburg

★ Hortus Botanicus Amsterdam

★ Hollandsche Schouwburg
Little remains of this former theatre, now a sombre monument to the deported Jews of World War II ➌

Entrepotdok
This was the largest warehouse development in Europe during the 19th century. It has recently been redeveloped and transformed into an attractive quayside housing, office and leisure complex **8**

LOCATOR MAP
See Street Finder maps 5 & 6

★ Artis
More than 5,000 species, including a variety of reptiles, live in the zoo complex, which occupies a beautifully laid out garden site **4**

Geologisch Museum
This updated exhibition covers planet earth, dinosaurs and fossils **5**

Artis restaurant

E MIDDENLAAN

St Jacob's incorporates the stone portal from an old peoples' home formerly on this site.

Aquarium
The fine Neo-Classical building is home to thousands of aquatic species, ranging from tiny, fluorescent tropical fish to gigantic, European moray eels **7**

| 0 metres | | 100 |
| 0 yards | | 100 |

Tropical plants in the Hortus Botanicus

Hortus Botanicus Amsterdam ❶

Plantage Middenlaan 2. **Map** 6 D2.
Tel 625 8411. �· 6, 9, 14.
Ⓜ *Waterlooplein.* ◯ 9am–5pm
Mon–Fri; 10am–5pm Sat, Sun &
public hols (to 9pm Jul–Aug, to 4pm
Dec–Jan). ● 1 Jan, 25 Dec. 🖾 ⬛
🔕 📷 *in English by arrangement.*
🖥 📖 **www**.dehortus.nl

This botanical garden began as
a small apothecaries' herb garden in 1682, and now boasts
one of the world's largest botanical collections. Its range
of flora expanded when
tropical plants were brought
back by the Dutch East India
Company *(see pp28–9)*. In
1706, it became the first place
outside Arabia to succeed in
cultivating the coffee plant.

The glass-domed Palm
House, built in 1912, contains
a 400-year-old cycad (palm
fern). Art shows with a botanical theme are held here. The
restored Orangery has a museum, café and terrace and is
open for dinner July to August.

A modern glass and alu-
minium construction, designed
by Moshé Zwarts and Rein
Jansma, was opened in 1993
to make room for the tropical,
sub-tropical and desert plants.
There is also a butterfly house.

De Burcht (Vakbondsmuseum) ❷

Henri Polaklaan 9. **Map** 5 C2.
Tel 624 1166. �· 6, 9, 14.
◯ 11am–5pm Tue–Fri, 1–5pm Sun.
● public hols. 🖾 📷 🔕 🖥 📖
www.deburcht-vakbondsmuseum.nl

This small museum, housed
in the headquarters of the
General Dutch Diamond
Workers' Union (ANDB), outlines the history of the Dutch

trade union movement.
Founded in 1894, the
ANDB was the first,
largest and wealthiest
union in the Netherlands.

The red-brick crenel-
lated building, known
locally as "the castle",
was designed by HP
Berlage *(see p79)* in
1900. It has a beautiful
interior, with murals by
the socialist artist Richard
Ronald Holst of the Amsterdam
School *(see p97)*, and a spectacular arched foyer. But the
material on show will be best
enjoyed by Dutch speakers.

Hollandsche Schouwburg ❸

Plantage Middenlaan 24. **Map** 5 C2.
Tel 531 0340. �· 6, 9, 14. ◯
11am–4pm daily. ● Rosh Hashanah
(Jewish New Year), Yom Kippur. 📷
🔕 **www**.hollandscheschouwburg.nl

Formerly a theatre, this is now
a memorial to the 104,000
Dutch Jewish victims of World
War II. Thousands of them

were detained here before
being deported to concentration camps. After the war, the
building was abandoned until
1962, when a garden was laid
out in the former auditorium.
A basalt column with a base
in the shape of the Star of
David was erected on the site
of the stage and behind it is
written: "To the memory of
those taken from here".

The façade and foyer were
restored in 1993, and became
an education centre. On the
ground floor, a candle illuminates the names of the war
victims. Upstairs, exhibits explain the theatre's dark role.

Artis ❹

Plantage Kerklaan 38–40. **Map** 6 D2.
Tel 523 3400. �· 6, 9, 14. ◯
9am–5pm daily (Apr–Sep: to 6pm,
Jul–Aug: till sunset). 🖾 📷 🔕 🍴
🖥 📖 11am Sun. **www**.artis.nl

Artis is the oldest surviving
zoological complex in the
Netherlands. It was founded
in 1838 by Dr GF Westerman,

Decorative tiles on the staircase of the Vakbondsmuseum

Seals basking in their pool in Artis zoo complex

president of the Natura Artis Magistra (Nature the Teacher of Art) association. Since its inception biologists have worked here and later the general public were allowed in to admire the collection of plants, trees and animals.

The complex has more than 5,000 animal species, as well as three greenhouses, the Planetarium, Geologisch Museum, Aquarium, Amfibarium, Insectarium and Zoölogisch Museum.

The zoo's attractions include big cats, giraffes, polar bears, penguins, hippos and seals. It also contains a steamy reptile house, nocturnal house, aviary, ape house, butterfly house and flamingo lake. Also, the African savannah and South American pampas habitats have been re-created. Children can clamber on model animals in the playground or pat the sheep and goats in the farmyard.

Geologisch Museum ❺

Plantage Kerklaan 40. **Map** 6 D2. *Tel 523 3400.* 🚊 *6, 9, 14.* ⬜ *9am–5pm daily (Apr–Sep: until 6pm).* 📷 ♿ 📹

Located at the southwest corner of the Artis complex, the Geologisch Museum offers an entertaining introduction to planet earth. The admission charge is automatically covered by the entry ticket to Artis.

The first gallery on the ground floor is devoted to the evolution of life on earth. Displays trace the gigantic leap from single-cell life forms, via dinosaurs, to mammals. The

second gallery on the ground floor deals imaginatively with the interacting elements of the earth and the forces which control it. The gallery's central attraction is the Earth Machine, which features rotating components to represent the biosphere (the area inhabited by living things), hydrosphere (water), atmosphere (air) and geosphere (the earth's solid crust). Upstairs, there is an extensive display of fossils, minerals and stones.

Ammonite fossil at the Geologisch Museum

Planetarium ❻

Plantage Kerklaan 40. **Map** 6 D2. *Tel 523 3452.* 🚊 *6, 9, 14.* ⬜ *9am–5pm daily (Apr–Sep: until 6pm) (shows every hour).* 📷 ♿ 📹

Budding astronomers should not miss the show at the Planetarium, which takes place on the hour every hour. In this large, domed building a powerful projector reproduces the night sky and shows how the planets constantly change positions in relation to the constellations. Adult and children's programmes are shown alternately and, although the commentary is in Dutch, there are summaries in English, French and German.

Around the edge of the Planetarium, stellar and planetary systems are mapped out using models, photographs,

videos and push-button exhibits. There are also educational computer games and displays on exploration and astronomy.

Aquarium ❼

Plantage Kerklaan 40. **Map** 6 D3. *Tel 523 3400.* 🚊 *6, 9, 14.* **Aquarium** ⬜ *9am–5pm daily (Apr–Sep: until 6pm).* **Zoölogisch Museum** ⬜ *9am–5pm daily.* 📷 ♿ 📹

Perhaps the best feature of the Artis complex is its Aquarium, which opened in 1882 in a grand Neo-Classical building. Mainly housed on the first floor, there are now four separate aquatic systems: one freshwater and three saltwater. Together they hold almost a million litres (220,000 gallons) of water. These tanks, each kept at a different temperature, contain almost 500 species of fish and marine animals that can be viewed at close quarters. They range from simple invertebrates to piranhas, sharks and massive marine turtles. Look out for the vivid coral fish and charming sea horses housed at the far end of the gallery.

The Amfibarium is housed in the basement of the Aquarium building. This hall contains a substantial collection of frogs, toads and salamanders in all shapes, sizes and colours.

The building also houses the small Zoölogisch Museum, which is as old as the park itself. The museum has a more academic flavour, and its exhibition halls hold temporary shows on such themes as the history of the dodo or aspects of animal behaviour.

Tropical fish at the Aquarium, home to almost 500 marine species

Spout-gable façades of former warehouses along Entrepotdok

Entrepotdok ❽

Map 6 D2. 🚊 *6, 9, 14, 22, 32.*

The redevelopment of the old VOC *(see pp28–9)* warehouses at Entrepotdok has revitalized this dockland area. It was once the greatest warehouse area in Europe during the mid-19th century, being a customs-free zone for goods in transit. The quayside buildings of Entrepotdok are now a lively complex of offices, homes and eating places. Some of the original façades of the warehouses have been preserved, unlike the interiors, which have been opened up to provide an attractive inner courtyard. Café tables are often set out alongside the canal. On the other side, brightly coloured houseboats are moored side by side, and herons doze at the water's edge.

Muiderpoort ❾

Alexanderplein. **Map** 6 E3. 🚊 *7, 9, 10, 14.* 🚫 *to the public.*

Formerly a city gate, the Muiderpoort was designed by Cornelis Rauws in about 1770. The central archway of this Classical structure is topped with a dome and clock tower. Napoleon entered the city through this gate in 1811 and, according to legend forced the citizens to feed and house his ragged troops.

De Gooyer Windmill ❿

Funenkade 5. **Map** 6 F2. 🚊 *7, 10.* 🚫 *to the public.*

Of the six remaining windmills within the city's boundaries, De Gooyer, also known as the Funenmolen, is the most central. Dominating the view down the Nieuwevaart, the mill was built around 1725, and was the first corn mill in the Netherlands to use streamlined sails.

It first stood to the west of its present site, but the Oranje Nassau barracks, built in 1814, acted as a windbreak, and the

The grand dome and clock tower of the Muiderpoort

mill was then moved piece by piece to the Funenkade. The octagonal wooden structure was rebuilt on the stone foot of an earlier water-pumping mill, demolished in 1812.

By 1925, De Gooyer was in a very poor state of repair and was bought by the city council, which fully restored it. Since then, the lower part of the mill, with its neat thatched roof and tiny windows, has been a private home, though its massive sails still creak into action sometimes. Next to the mill is the IJ brewery *(see p48)*, one of two independent breweries in the city.

Museum 't Kromhout ⓫

Hoogte Kadijk 147. **Map** 6 D1. **Tel** 627 6777. 🚊 *6, 9, 10, 14.* 🚌 *22, 32.* 🚢 *Oosterdok or Kattenburgergracht.* 🕐 *10am–3pm Tue.* **www**.machinekamer.nl

The Museum 't Kromhout is one of the oldest working shipyards in Amsterdam, and is also a museum. Ships were built here as early as 1757. In the second half of the 19th century, production changed from sailing ships to steamships. As ocean-going ships got bigger, the yard, due to its small size, turned to building lighter craft for inland waterways. It is now used only for restoration and repair work. The museum is largely dedicated to the history of marine engineering, concentrating on work carried out at the shipyard, with engines, maritime photographs and ephemera, and a well-equipped forge.

Werf't Kromhout Museum and working shipyard

Nederlands Scheepvaartmuseum ⑫

See pp146–7.

Koninklijk Theater Carré ⑬

Amstel 115–125. **Map** 5 B3. *Tel 0900 252 5255.* 4, 6, 7, 9, 10, 14. Weesperplein. **Box office** 4–9pm daily. *See Entertainment p246.* 11am Sat (phone in advance). www.theatercarre.nl

During the 19th century, the annual visit of the Carré Circus was a popular event. In 1868, Oscar Carré built wooden premises for the circus on the banks of the Amstel river. The city council considered the structure a fire hazard, so Carré persuaded them to accept a permanent building modelled on his other circus in Cologne. Built in 1887, the new structure included both a circus ring and a stage. The Classical façade is richly decorated with sculpted heads of dancers, jesters and clowns.

The Christmas circus is still one of the annual highlights at the theatre, but for much of the year the recently enlarged stage is taken over by concerts and big-show musicals.

Amstelsluizen ⑭

Map 5 B3. 4, 6, 7, 9, 10, 14. Weesperplein.

The Amstelsluizen, a row of sturdy wooden sluice gates spanning the Amstel river, form part of a complex system of sluices and pumping stations that ensure Amsterdam's canals do not stagnate. Four times a week in summer and twice a week in winter, the sluices are closed while fresh water from large lakes north of the city, is allowed to flow into Amsterdam's canals. Sluices to the west of the city are left open, allowing the old water to flow, or be pumped, into the sea.

The Amstelsluizen date from the 18th century, and were operated manually until 1994, when they were mechanized.

Verzetsmuseum ⑮

Plantage Kerklaan 61. *Tel 620 2535.* 6, 9, 14. 10am-5pm Tue–Fri, noon–5pm Sat–Mon & public hols. 1 Jan, 30 Apr, 25 Dec. www.verzetsmuseum.org

Carving on façade of Koninklijk Theater Carré

Previously based in a former synagogue in Nieuw Zuid (New South), now moved to this site in the Plantage, the Resistance Museum holds a fascinating collection of memorabilia recording the activities of Dutch Resistance workers in World War II. It focuses on the courage of the 25,000 people actively involved in the movement. On display are false documents, film clips, slide shows, photographs, weaponry and equipment.

By 1945 there were 300,000 people in hiding in the Netherlands, including Jews and anti-Nazi Dutch. Subsequent events organized by the Resistance, like the February Strike against deportation of the Jews *(see p35)*, are brought to life by exhibits showing where the refugees hid and how food was smuggled in. Voted the best historic museum in 2002 and 2003, it complements the Anne Frank Huis *(see p90)* perfectly.

Hermitage Amsterdam ⑯

Nieuwe Herengracht 14. **Map** 8 E5. *Tel 530 8751.* 4, 9, 14. Waterlooplein. Muziektheater. 10am–5pm daily (during exhibitions only). free for under 16s. 1 Jan, 30 Apr, 25 Dec. www.hermitage.nl

In the early 1990s the State Hermitage Museum in St Petersburg decided upon Amsterdam as the ideal city to open a branch of the Russian museum. This satellite museum would display rotating temporary exhibitions drawn from the Hermitage's rich collection.

The Hermitage Amsterdam opened in early 2004 with a spectacular exhibition of fine Greek gold jewellery from the 6th to the 2nd century BC. Other exhibitions have included the collection of the last Tsars Nicholas and Alexandra.

Currently, the Hermitage Amsterdam consists of six galleries over two floors and is housed in the Neerlandia building, part of Amsterdam's Amstelhof complex. The whole complex will be in use by the museum by late 2008.

De Neerlandia building, home of the Hermitage Amsterdam, overlooking De Nieuwe Herengracht canal

Nederlands Scheepvaartmuseum 🄬

Once the arsenal of the Dutch Navy, this vast Classical sandstone building was built by Daniel Stalpaert in 1656 round a massive courtyard. It was supported by 18,000 piles driven into the bed of the Oosterdok. The Navy stayed in residence until 1973, when the building was converted into the Netherlands Maritime Museum. The museum is under renovation until 2009, but the VOC ship *Amsterdam*, moored nearby, remains open and part of the collection is on show at other locations.

Ornate 17th-century brass sextant

Ajax
This figurehead is from a ship built in 1832. It portrays Ajax, a hero of the Trojan War, who killed himself in despair when Achilles' armour was given to Odysseus.

First floor

★ The Orrery of Jan van den Dam *(1750)*
With a copper ball at its centre to represent the Sun, this is the oldest working orrery in the Netherlands.

MUSEUM GUIDE
The museum is arranged chronologically. The first floor covers the early maritime history of the Netherlands. The second floor spans merchant shipping from the 19th century to date, including technical developments. A cinema is on the first floor, and a full-size model of the East India-man, Amsterdam, is docked at the quayside.

STAR EXHIBITS

★ Royal Barge

★ The Amsterdam

★ The Orrery of Jan van den Dam

Classical sandstone façade

Map of the World
This map of Asia forms part of a series of five published in the Netherlands in 1780. Too inaccurate for navigation, they were used as wall decorations.

Main entrance

VISITORS' CHECKLIST

Kattenburgerplein 1. **Map** 6 D1.
Tel 523 2222. 22, 32.
Oosterdok, Kattenburgergracht.
10am–5pm Tue–Sun & pub
hols; mid-Jun–mid-Sep also
10am–5pm Mon. 1 Jan, 30
Apr, 25 Dec.
www.scheepvaartmuseum.nl

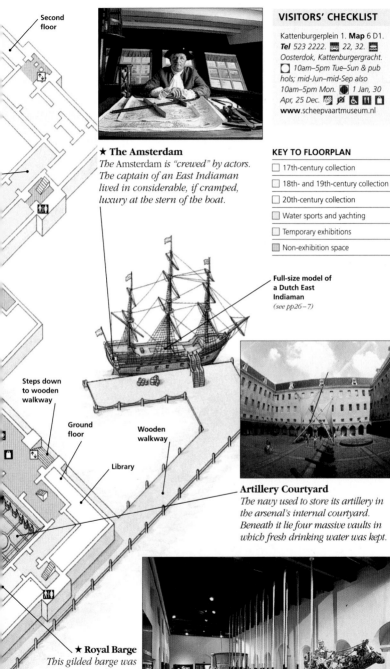

★ The Amsterdam
*The Amsterdam is "crewed" by actors.
The captain of an East Indiaman
lived in considerable, if cramped,
luxury at the stern of the boat.*

KEY TO FLOORPLAN

- 17th-century collection
- 18th- and 19th-century collection
- 20th-century collection
- Water sports and yachting
- Temporary exhibitions
- Non-exhibition space

**Full-size model of
a Dutch East
Indiaman**
(see pp26–7)

Second floor

**Steps down
to wooden
walkway**

**Ground
floor**

**Wooden
walkway**

Library

Artillery Courtyard
*The navy used to store its artillery in
the arsenal's internal courtyard.
Beneath it lie four massive vaults in
which fresh drinking water was kept.*

★ Royal Barge
*This gilded barge was
made in 1818 for King
William I. It is 17 m (54 ft) long
and was propelled by 20 oars-
men. It was last used in 1962,
during Queen Juliana's 25th wedding anniversary celebrations.*

FURTHER AFIELD

Sculpture on the fountain at Frankendael

Great architecture and good town planning are not confined to central Amsterdam. Parts of the Nieuw Zuid (New South) bear testament to the imagination of the innovative Amsterdam School architects *(see p97)* under the auspices of the Municipal Councils. Many fine buildings can be found in De Dageraad Housing complex and the streets around the Olympic Quarter. If you are seeking old-world charm, the historic small town of Ouderkerk aan de Amstel, nestling on the southern fringes of the city, prides itself on being older than Amsterdam. There are also fine parks just a short tram ride from the city centre, which offer a whole host of leisure activities. Visitors can view the lakes, woods and parkland of the Amsterdamse Bos *(see pp34–5)* from the deck of an antique tram which tours the park from the Electrische Museumtramlijn. The more formal horticulture of the Amstelpark can be viewed aboard a miniature train. There is also a clutch of instructive museums to be found in the suburbs of Amsterdam.

SIGHTS AT A GLANCE

Historic Monuments, Buildings and Districts
De Dageraad Housing ❺
Frankendael ❶
Olympic Quarter ❾
Ouderkerk aan de Amstel ❽

Museums and Exhibition Halls
Amsterdam RAI ❻

Electrische Museumtramlijn ❿
Nemo ❸
Schiphol Airport ⓬
Tropenmuseum see pp152–3 ❷

Parks and Gardens
Amstelpark ❼
Amsterdamse Bos ⓫
Westerpark ❹

KEY

	Central Amsterdam
	Greater Amsterdam
✈	Airport
═	Major road
═	Minor road

0 kilometres   2
0 miles   2

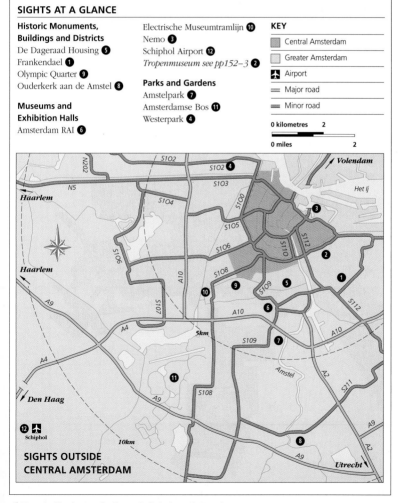

SIGHTS OUTSIDE CENTRAL AMSTERDAM

◁ **Moored sailing boat on the river at Ouderkerk aan de Amstel**

Frankendael ❶

Middenweg 72. **Map** 6 F5. 📷 9.
🚊 59, 120, 126, 136. **Gardens**
Tel 774 4480. ☐ dawn–dusk.

During the early part of the 18th century, many of Amsterdam's wealthier citizens built country retreats south of Plantage Middenlaan on reclaimed land called the Watergraafsmeer. The elegant Louis XIV-style Frankendael is the last survivor. The house is closed to the public and the best views of the ornamented façade are from Middenweg. This is also the best place to view the fountain made by Ignatius van Logteren in 1714, complete with reclining river gods, in the front garden.

The formal gardens at the back of the Frankendael are open to the public. They have been painstakingly reconstructed over the past few years and offer a peaceful refuge of shrubs and ancient trees.

The back of the Frankendael, with its well-tended formal gardens

Ignatius van Logteren's fountain in the grounds of the Frankendael

Tropenmuseum ❷

See pp152–3.

Nemo Science Center Amsterdam ❸

Oosterdok 2. **Map** 2 F4. **Tel** 0900 919 1100. 🚊 22, 32. ☐ 10am–5pm Tue–Sun (daily during public hols). ● 1 Jan, 30 Apr, 25 Dec. 📷 🎦 📷 ♿ 🍴 📷 www.e-nemo.nl

In June 1997 Holland's national science centre moved to this dazzling curved building which protrudes 30 m (99 ft) over water. Nemo presents technological innovations in a manner which allows visitors' creativity full expression. You can interact with virtual reality, operate the latest industrial equipment under expert supervision and harness science to produce your own art. The Centre is divided into five themed zones (Interactivity, Technology, Energy, Science and Humanity), each of which is revamped every three years to keep pace with scientific evolution. Visitors – who in this setting might equally be

Striking architecture of Nemo Science and Technology Centre

termed explorers – can participate in games, experiments, demonstrations and workshops or take in lectures, films and even educational stage shows.

In July and August the roof is turned into a beach and visitors are welcome to bring picnics and enjoy the views.

Westerpark ❶

Haarlemmerweg 8–10. **Map** 1 A1. 3, 10. 18, 22, 46. **Wester-gasfabriek** *Tel* 586 0710. **Museum Het Schip** Spaarndammerplantsoen 140. **Map** 1 B1. *Tel* 475 0924 or 418 2885. 1–5pm Wed–Sun (also by appt). hourly. **www**.wester park.amsterdam.nl; **www**.westergas fabriek.com; **www**.hetschip.nl

The wasteland around Amsterdam's former gas-works (Westergasfabriek) was transformed into a 14-hectare park in the early 2000s. Facilities in this green area include playgrounds, bars and restaurants, and several performance spaces.

The gasworks itself has been redeveloped and is being rented out to various associations that organize festivals, performances and exhibitions. The Westergasfabriek is now the city's foremost cultural destination.

Nearby is Het Schip (The Ship), one of the most iconic buildings by the Amsterdam architectural school. Designed by Michel de Klerk, this apartment block plays host to the documentation centre for public housing.

Het Schip, a standard of the Amsterdam architectural school

De Dageraad Housing ❺

Pieter Lodewijk Takstraat. 4, 12, 25. to the public.

One of the best examples of Amsterdam School architecture *(see p97)*, De Dageraad housing project was developed for poorer families following the revolutionary Housing Act of 1901 by which the city council was forced to condemn slums and rethink housing policy.

Socialist architect HP Berlage *(see p79)* drew up ingenious plans for the suburbs, aiming to integrate rich and poor by juxtaposing their housing. After Berlage's death, Piet Kramer and Michel de Klerk of the Amsterdam School adopted his ideas. Between 1918 and 1923, they designed this complex for a housing association known as De Dageraad (the Dawn).

Imposing corner block of De Dageraad public housing

They used a technique called "apron architecture" in which an underlayer of concrete allows for tucks, folds and rolls in the brick exterior, which was then subtly coloured and interspersed with decorative doors and windows. Each house mirrors the one opposite and there is a corner tower at the end of every block. The façades of the buildings were designed to give the impression of horizontal movement, an effect which is produced by the streamlined windows and the undulating roofs.

Amsterdam RAI ❻

Europaplein. *Tel* 0900 267 8373. 4. **M** RAI. 15, 66, 199. depending on exhibition. with assistance. **www**.rai.nl

Amsterdam RAI is one of the largest exhibition and conference centres in the country. It hosts more than a thousand events annually, from cabaret to horse shows and trade fairs.

The first Amsterdam trade fair was a bicycle exhibition held in 1893. Subsequent shows included cars and became an annual event known as the "RAI" (Rijwiel Automobiel Industrie). The present complex on Europaplein opened in 1961. It has undergone several extensions since then and now boasts a total of 11 exhibition halls, 22 congress halls and seven restaurants.

KIT Tropenmuseum ❷

Built to house the Dutch Colonial Institute, this vast complex was finished in 1926 by architects MA and JJ Nieukerken. The exterior is decorated with symbols of imperialism, such as stone friezes of peasants planting rice. When the building's renovation was completed in 1978, the Royal Tropical Institute opened a museum, with a huge central hall and three levels of galleries. The institute's aims are to study and to help improve the lives of the indigenous populations of the tropics. The displays reflect this, focusing on development issues regarding daily life, education and colonization.

Moroccan Bride
The gold embroidery is one of the most remarkable aspects of this Moroccan wedding dress.

★ Pustaha – Book of Divinations
Made of wood and tree bark, this volume contains prescriptions applied by the village healer-priest.

Great hall

★ Bisj Poles
The roots of massive mangrove trees were used to make these exotic, painted ritual totem poles from New Guinea.

GALLERY GUIDE
Temporary exhibitions are held in the Great hall on the ground floor. On the upper floors, the permanent exhibitions combine static and interactive displays covering diverse topics. The shop on the ground floor has a wide range of gifts and in the basement are a restaurant, café and theatre.

Main entrance

Basement

STAR EXHIBITS

★ Bisj Poles

★ Diorama

★ Pustaha – Book of Divinations

Second floor

Park Hall

★ **Diorama** *(1819)*
Gerrit Schouten used papier-mâché and painted wood to create this colourful scene of life in Surinam.

First floor

VISITORS' CHECKLIST

Linnaeusstraat 2. **Map** 6 E3.
KIT Tropenmuseum *Tel* 568 8215. 🚊 7, 9, 10, 14. ⬜ 10am–5pm daily, 10am–3pm 5 Dec, 24 Dec, 31 Dec. ⬤ 1 Jan, 30 Apr, 5 May, 25 Dec.
Tropenmuseum Junior
Tel 568 8233. ⬜ for Junior, Family & Workshop programmes, Wed, Sat, school hols and most public hols, in Dutch language only (phone for further information or see website). ⬤ As Tropenmuseum.
🅿 📷 ♿ 🚻 🍴 🛒 🎁
www.tropenmuseum.nl;
www.tropenmuseumjunior.nl

Javanese Stone Friezes
The stone friezes decorating the main stairs are copies from a Javanese monument from about AD 800. This section shows two Buddhas praying under ornate temple awnings.

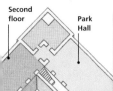

Wooden Hook
This wooden hook is carved in the shape of a naked male figure wearing a tribal mask. The item comes from New Guinea, in the South Pacific.

KEY TO FLOORPLAN

- ⬜ SE Asia & Textiles in Indonesia
- ⬛ W Asia & N Africa
- ⬜ Latin America & the Carribean
- ⬜ Man & the Environment
- ⬜ Music, Dance & Theatre
- ⬜ Africa
- ⬜ Dutch Colonialism
- ⬜ Dutch New Guinea
- ⬜ Tropenmuseum Junior
- ⬜ Temporary exhibition space
- ⬜ Non-exhibition space

Jeepney
Old army trucks left behind by the Americans after World War II are used as taxibuses, or jeepneys, in Manila, in the Philippines. The one housed here is a typically colourful example.

Amstelpark's Rieker windmill

Amstelpark ❼

Europaboulevard. 🚊 4. Ⓜ 🚉 RAI.
🚌 66, 199. ◯ dawn–dusk.

Situated in the suburb of Buitenveldert, southwest of Amsterdam, this large park was created in 1972. Among its attractions are a rose garden, rhododendron walk and model garden with nursery.

The park offers good facilities for children, including a playground, pony rides, mini-golf and mini-football. The well-preserved Rieker windmill (1636) stands at the southern tip of the park, and art exhibitions are held in the Glazen Huis (Glass House) and the Papillon Gallery. From Easter to October, you can tour the park in a miniature train.

Ouderkerk aan de Amstel ❽

Ⓜ 🚉 Bijlmer. 🚌 175 from Bijlmer station. **Wester Amstel Garden** ◯ mid-Apr–mid-Oct: 10am–8pm daily; mid-Oct–mid-Apr: 10am–4pm daily.

This pretty village at the junction of the Amstel and the Bullewijk rivers has been a favourite with Amsterdammers since the Middle Ages. They had no church of their own until 1330 (see pp66–7), and worshippers had to travel to the 11th-century Ouderkerk that gave the village its name. The Old Church was destroyed in a tremendous storm in 1674, and a fine 18th-century church now stands on its site. Opposite is the Beth Haim Jewish cemetery, where more than 27,000 Jews from Amsterdam have been buried since 1615. The elders of the Jewish community bought this land to use as a burial ground because Jews were forbidden to bury their dead inside the city.

Today Ouderkerk aan de Amstel is popular with cyclists who come to enjoy the ambience of its waterfront cafés and restaurants. The skyline is dominated by the 50-m (160-ft) spire of the Urbanuskerk, a Catholic church designed by PJH Cuypers (see pp32–3) and consecrated in 1867.

A short walk upriver along Amsteldijk, there are two 18th-century country houses. While there is no access to the first, the restful wooded garden of the second house, Wester Amstel (built in 1720), is open to the public.

Olympic Quarter ❾

🚊 6, 16, 24. 🚌 15, 23, 65, 142, 165, 170, 172.

Development of the western side of the Nieuw Zuid (New South) began during the run up to the Olympic Games, held here in 1928. Many of the streets and squares were given Grecian names, like Olympiaplein and Herculesstraat.

The Stadium was designed by J Wils and C van Eesteren. Its stark vertical lines and soaring torch tower recall the work of the American architect Frank Lloyd Wright. Once threatened with demolition, it has recently been renovated.

The sturdy bridge across the Noorder Amstel Kanaal at Olympiaplein is typical Amsterdam School design. It is the work of PL Kramer and the sculptor H Krop. Beyond the bridge, the Amsterdams Lyceum (a secondary school) shows the style at its best.

The peaceful waterfront at Oudekerk aan de Amstel, south of Amsterdam

Pedalos on a lake in the Amsterdamse Bos

Electrische Museumtramlijn ❿

Amstelveenseweg 264. **Tel** 673 7538. 🚋 6, 16, 24. 🚌 15, 23, 170, 172. ⏰ Easter–Oct: 11am–5pm Sun (Jul–Aug: also 1–3pm Wed). ♿ 📷 **www**.museumtram.nl

Not a museum, as the name suggests, but a tram ride that operates from Haarlemmer-meerstation and the southern tip of the Amsteldamse Bos. The

Classic tram from the Museumtramlijn

tramcars, which date from 1910 to 1950, come from all over the Netherlands, Vienna, Prague and Berlin. The fleet is run by a group of enthusiasts along traditional lines and cars depart regularly from either terminus. A one-way journey takes about 20 minutes and provides a good view of the Olympic Stadium.

Amsterdamse Bos ⓫

Amstelveenseweg. 🚋 Electrische Museumtramlijn (see entry 10). 🚌 170, 172. **Theatre Tel** 643 3286 (after 6pm Jul & Aug). **www**.bostheater.nl

This woodland park is the largest recreational area in Amsterdam. It was laid out in the 1930s in a bid to reduce unemployment in the city (see p35). Extensive wooded areas, interspersed with grassy meadows, lakes, waterways and even a hill, were created on reclaimed land that lies 3 m (13 ft) below sea level. The park was enlarged periodically until 1967, when it reached its present size of more than 800 ha (2,000 acres).

Today, the marshy areas around Nieuwe Meer and the lakes at Amstelveense Poel and Kleine Poel are nature reserves. Other highlights include an animal enclosure, a goat farm, the Vogeleiland botanical gardens and the Bos-museum, with its exhibits on the natural and social history of the park.

Among the facilities are an extensive network of planned walks, cycle paths and bridle ways, as well as water sports and an open-air theatre (see p245) during the summer.

Schiphol Airport ⓬

Evert van Beekstraat 202. **Tel** 0900 7244 7465. 🚉 Schiphol Airport. **www**.schiphol.nl

Attracting over 110,000 people each day, this modern, forward-thinking airport (official name: Amsterdam Airport Schiphol) is one of the world's most efficient and user-friendly, with different colour-coded signs to help visitors navigate around this huge area (see pp266–7).

The airport has a wide variety of exciting extras to help pass the time while waiting for a flight. In 2002, an annex of the Rijksmuseum was opened on Holland Boulevard at Schiphol airport, where a small selection of classic works of art are on show. The museum is situated beyond passport control, and entrance is free to everyone with a boarding pass.

The airport also boasts a small casino between gates E and F (open 6am–8pm) to help pass the time, as well as a haven for the sore and weary traveller in the form of a chair massage.

The "Silence Centre", is open between 9am and 5pm. This is a place of worship for all religions, or simply a place for quiet contemplation.

In addition to the vast number of shops, bars and restaurants there is also a Panorama Terrace offering great views of the aircraft.

The entrance to Amsterdam's modern Schiphol Airport

TWO GUIDED WALKS

Many of Amsterdam's most important historical landmarks, and several fine examples of 16th- and 17th-century architecture, can be enjoyed on both of these walks. The first takes the visitor through the streets of the Jordaan, a peaceful quarter known for its narrow, pretty canals, houseboats and traditional architecture. The route winds through to the man-made Western Islands of Bickerseiland, Realeneiland and Prinseneiland, built in the 17th century to accommodate the expansion in Amsterdam's overseas trade. The area, with its rows of warehouses and

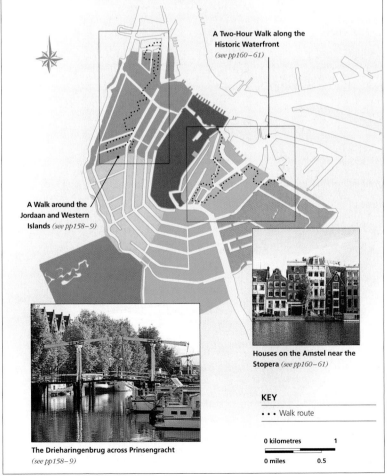

Wall plaque at No. 6 Zandhoek

wharves, is a reminder of the city's erstwhile supremacy at sea. The city's maritime heritage is also evident on the second walk, which starts off from the Schreierstoren, where women waved their husbands off to sea in the 17th century, and finishes at the Nederlands Scheepvaart Museum. On the way, the walk passes the original city boundaries, countless converted warehouses and along streets named after the spices brought in by the East India Company (VOC). On any weekday, there is also the opportunity to spend a few pleasurable hours browsing round the Waterlooplein flea market.

A Two-Hour Walk along the Historic Waterfront *(see pp160–61)*

A Walk around the Jordaan and Western Islands *(see pp158–9)*

Houses on the Amstel near the Stopera *(see pp160–61)*

The Drieharingenbrug across Prinsengracht *(see pp158–9)*

KEY

• • • Walk route

0 kilometres 1

0 miles 0.5

◁ View from the tower of the Westerkerk across the Jordaan, with Prinsengracht in the foreground

A Walk around the Jordaan and Western Islands

The Jordaan is a tranquil part of the city, crammed with canal houses, old and new galleries, restaurants, craft shops and pavement cafés. The walk route meanders through narrow streets and along enchanting canals. It starts from the Westerkerk and continues past Brouwersgracht, up to the IJ river and on to the Western Islands. These islands have now been adopted by the bohemian artistic community as a fashionable area to live and work.

Plaque on No. 8 Zandhoek, a former sailors' hostel

Prinsengracht to Westerstraat

Outside Hendrick de Keyser's Westerkerk ① *(see p90)* turn left up Prinsengracht, past the Anne Frankhuis ② *(see p90)*, and cross over the canal. Turn left down the opposite side of Prinsengracht and walk along Bloemgracht – the prettiest canal in the Jordaan. Before crossing the second bridge, look out for the three identical canal houses called the Drie Hendricken (the three Henrys) ③ *(see p91)*. Continue up 3e Leliedwarsstraat, with its cafés and old shops in the first half of the street, turn right and walk past the St Andrieshofje ④, one of the numerous well-preserved almshouses in the city. It is worth pausing to take a look across Egelantiersgracht at No. 360, a rare example of an Art Nouveau canal house.

Follow the bank to the end, turn left on to Prinsengracht, passing the Café 't Smalle, and turn left into Egelantiersstraat. In 1e Egelantiersdwarsstraat can be found a group of 17th-century almshouses, known as the Claes Claeszhofje ⑤ *(see p92).* Follow this tiny street past several cafés as well as many unusual shops selling clothes, bric-a-brac, pottery and paintings, to Westerstraat.

Simple wooden gable with hoisting hook on Westerstraat

Westerstraat to Bickerseiland

Cross the street – Westerstraat originally bordered a canal, now filled in – and turn right. The gabled houses are typical of the late-17th-century style of the Jordaan. Walk along for one block and take the first left into 1e Boomdwarsstraat, then right to the Noorderkerk ⑥ *(see p92)*. Each Monday morning, a lively flea market takes place in the Noordermarkt *(see p92)*. Continue on to the south side of the Lindengracht. To the left, at Nos. 149–163, is the Suyckerhofje ⑦, a former refuge for abandoned women. Turn right and you will pass a wall plaque on No. 55 Lindengracht depicting fish swimming in trees and echoing an inverted view of houses reflected in the city's canals. The statue on Lindengracht is of the writer and educationalist, Theo Thijssen. Turn left down Brouwersgracht *(see p93)*, which is lined with colourful houseboats. Cross the first lift bridge and go into Binnen Oranjestraat, then under the railway bridge onto Bickerseiland, which is named after one of the city's most wealthy 17th-century families.

Ornate step gables (1642) at Nos. 89 and 91 Bloemgracht

KEY

• • • Walk route

0 metres   200

0 yards   200

A view of houseboats and gabled houses from Galgenstraat ⑨

The Western Islands

The Western Islands are made up of Bickers-, Prinsen- and Realeneiland (see p93). They were created in the early 17th century to cope with the city's need for warehouses as a result of Amsterdam's maritime trading success. Their quays were lined with ships, while sailors and dockworkers lived in nearby canal houses.

Cross the Hendrik Jonkerplein ⑧ and go on to Bickersgracht where the boatyards are still operational. The first bridge to the left leads on to Prinseneiland and then into Galgenstraat (gallows street) ⑨, so called because the view from here in the 17th century was of the gallows across the IJ.

Turning right, follow the bend and cross the wooden drawbridge on to Realeneiland. Turn right along Realengracht, take the first left, then right into Jan Mensplein and through to Taanstraat, first looking back along Vierwindenstraat where there stands a series of sombre old warehouses, once used for storing grain, hemp and flax. At the end, turn right down Zandhoek (sand corner) ⑩ (see p93), with its rows of charming 17th-century houses. The name originates from the sand market which once took place here.

Follow Zandhoek and cross the wooden bridge (a 1983 replica of the original). Stay on the canal and follow the footpath that runs along Bickersgracht. Keep your eyes on the water and you might see a blue-grey heron looking for fish. Walk along Grote Bickersstraat and you will find yourself back where you started, at the bridge leading on to Prinseneiland. To leave the islands and return to the city centre, retrace your steps to Haarlemerdijk and turn left.

TIPS FOR WALKERS

Starting point: Outside the Westerkerk on the Prinsengracht.
Length: 4.5 km (2.8 miles).
Duration: One and a half hours.
Getting there: Buses 21, 142, 170 and 172. Trams 13, 14 and 17 from Centraal Station.
Stopping-off points: The Jordaan is packed with cafés and bars. On the Egelantiersgracht, 't Smalle is particularly atmospheric and there are bars in Noordermarkt, Haarlemmerdijk and Hendrik Jonkerplein. De Gouden Reaal in Zandhoek is ideal to rest in before the trip home.

The tranquil, tree-lined Egelantiersgracht

A Two-Hour Walk along the Historic Waterfront

Begin the walk at the Schreierstoren *(see p67)*, once a
defence tower in the medieval town wall. The route
follows the development of Amsterdam as a great trading
city, as wharves, warehouses and houses were built to
accommodate the boom in overseas trade and in population. The city's expansion was carefully planned; as
existing waterfronts became overcrowded, more islands
were created to the east, slowly reclaiming the surrounding marshy countryside. The walk takes in a number of
reminders of the Dutch East India Company (VOC) *(see
pp28–9)*, such as the streets named after spices, and ends
up at the imposing Nederlands Scheepvaart Museum.

**16th-century stone tablet near the
main door, Schreierstoren** ①

**Gables and façades along the
right bank of Krommewaal**

Schreierstoren to
St Antoniesbreestraat

From the Schreierstoren ①,
walk along Prins Hendrikkade,
turning at Kromme Waal and
following the right bank, with
its series of rich façades and
gables, to Lastageweg ②.
Lastage is an area which was
developed for trade after the
fire of 1452 *(see p23)*. The expansion which followed in the
16th century *(see p25)* brought
Lastage within the city walls.
 Continue to Rechtbooms-
sloot and turn right and keep
going until you reach Geldersekade, one of the town
boundaries in the 15th century.
Follow along Recht Boomssloot,
then along the side of Krom
Boomssloot, until you see the
Schottenburch warehouses ③
at Nos. 18–20. Built in 1636,
these are among the oldest in
the city and are now converted
into apartments. Next door is
an Armenian church, converted
from a warehouse in the mid-
18th century. Then follow
Snoekjesgracht, turning left
into St Antoniesbreestraat ④.

St Antoniesbreestraat to
Uilenburg Island

On St Antoniesbreestraat,
cross the road at Elias
Bouwman's Pintohuis ⑤
(see p66), the only surviving
building from the original
street. Enter the Zuider-
kerk ⑥ yard opposite
through its skull-
adorned gateway.
The church was
built by Hendrick
de Keyser *(see p90)*
in 1603 and now
hosts a permanent
exhibition on vari-
ous aspects of
urban renewal.

Schreierstoren

Montelbaanstoren

**Lift bridge on Staalstraat,
crossing Groenburgwal**

KEY

• • •   Walk route

Ⓜ   Metro station

0 metres   200

0 yards   200

Cross the square and continue to Zandstraat. Continue on to Kloveniersburgwal and turn left along the canal on to Staalstraat, where another left turn takes you past the Saaihal ⑦ (the draper's hall), with its unusual trapezoid gable. The first bridge crosses the Groenburgwal, with splendid views of the Amstel to the right and Zuiderkerk to the left. The next bridge leads to the Stopera ⑧ (see p63), and Waterlooplein flea market ⑨ (see p63). Follow the market stalls and half way along turn left towards Jodenbreestraat,

The 16th-century Montelbaanstoren, part of the city defences ⑫

Wall plaque at Museum Het Rembrandthuis

transformed since it was the heart of Jewish Amsterdam. To the left on Jodenbreestraat is the Museum Het Rembrandthuis ⑩ (see p62). Cross the road and continue on to Nieuwe Uilenburgerstraat and on to the island of Uilenburg, built in the late 16th century to take housing for the poor. On the right can be seen the vast Gassan Diamonds factory ⑪, with two synagogues in the yard, a reminder of the time when diamond polishing was one of the few trades open to Jews (see p64).

Uilenburg to the Eastern Islands

Turn left into Nieuwe Batavierstraat and then right at Oude Schans, a broad canal with former warehouses and quays full of eccentric-looking houseboats. On the opposite bank of the canal is the Montelbaanstoren ⑫ (see p66), an old defence tower. At the bend, cross over the Rapenburgwal bridge until

you reach Peperstraat. Like other streets on these man-made islands, Peperstraat was named after a commodity imported by the VOC (see pp28–9) in the 17th century. From here, turn right on to the main road of Prins Hendrikkade and then into Nieuwe Foeliestraat. Turn left onto Rapenburg, then left again onto Rapenburger Plein. Take the bridge across Nieuwe Herengracht to the gateway of the Entrepotdok ⑬ (see p144). Turn left into Kadijksplein, continue along Prins-Hendrikkade and across the Nieuwevaart bridge from which you can see Daniel Stalpaert's Oosterkerk. Continue on to the Eastern Islands, built in 1658 to create more shipyards. The Nederlands Scheepvaart Museum ⑭ (see pp146–7) dominates the Oosterdok to the left. To return to the centre, follow Prins Hendrikkade westwards.

TIPS FOR WALKERS

Starting point: The Schreierstoren on Prins Hendrikkade.
Length: 6 km (4 miles).
Duration: Two hours.
Getting there: Some buses go along Prins Hendrikkade, but it is easier to take a tram to Centraal Station (see p79) and walk along the IJ. To pick up the walk halfway, trams 9 & 14 go to Waterlooplein.
Stopping-off points: There are cosy brown cafés (see pp 48 and 236) along the start of the walk and at the Stopera (see p63). There are also bars on Schippersgracht and within the Entrepotdok.

Oosterdok

Oosterdok

Scheepvaart Museum ⑭

⑬

Antiques and bric-a-brac at Waterlooplein flea market ⑨

Tulips in full bloom in the Bloembollenstreek, near Leiden ▷

BEYOND AMSTERDAM

BEYOND AMSTERDAM

A msterdam is at the heart of a region known as the Randstad, the economic powerhouse of the Netherlands. The city is a haven for tourists; within easy reach are the ancient towns of Leiden and Utrecht, as well as Den Haag and Haarlem with their exceptional galleries and museums. The Randstad extends south as far as Rotterdam, a thriving modern city full of avant-garde architecture.

Much of the land comprising the Randstad has been reclaimed from the sea during the last 300 years, and the fertile soil is farmed intensively. Production is centred around early season greenhouse crops, like tomatoes and cucumbers and the incomparable Dutch bulbs. Spreading to the southwest in spring, dazzling colours carpet the fields, and the exquisite gardens at Keukenhof *(see p181)* are the showcase of the bulb industry.

Reclamation continues apace, and Flevoland, the Netherlands' newest province, consists entirely of polder. This flat marshy land, interspersed with drainage channels, has been created since 1950 by draining 1,800 sq km (695 sq miles) of the IJsselmeer. The flat terrain provides shelter for wild birds such as herons, swans and grebes, which nest along the reed-fringed canals. The area beyond Utrecht, to the east of Amsterdam, is much less populated than the Randstad, with vast tracts of unspoilt forest, moorland and peat bog, home to red deer and wild boar.

North of Amsterdam, the traditional fishing communities that depended on the Zuiderzee before it was closed off from the sea in 1932 *(see p170–71)*, have now turned to tourism for their income.

The coast round Zandvoort, lying to the west of Amsterdam, takes the full brunt of vicious North Sea storms in winter, but maritime vegetation and wild birds find shelter among the sandbanks of the exposed coastline.

Lift bridge and canalside café at Enkhuizen – a popular haunt for visitors to the Zuiderzee Museum

◁ Traditional working smock mills *(see p173)* at Zaanse Schans

Exploring the Netherlands

Amsterdam is at the centre of a part of the Netherlands where there are many places of interest within easy reach. Haarlem is just 15 minutes away, and it takes less than half an hour to get to the cheese markets of Edam and Gouda. To the north, the Zuiderzee Museum recreates an old fishing community, and to the south lies historic Utrecht. The east offers the wilderness of the Nationaal Park de Hoge Veluwe, and the stately Paleis Het Loo, a hunting lodge and summer residence of the Dutch royal family since 1692.

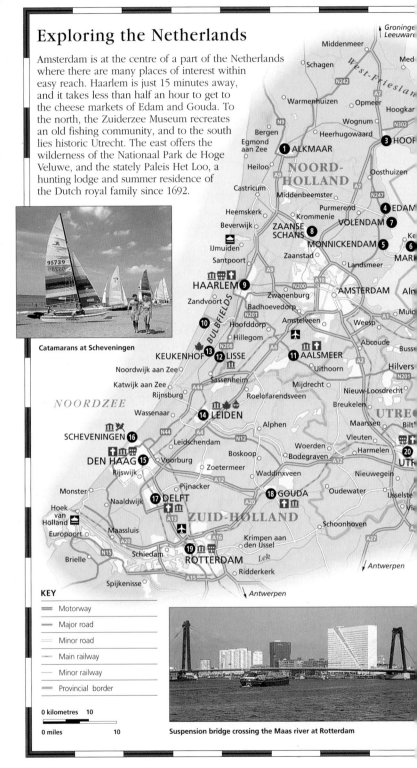

Catamarans at Scheveningen

Suspension bridge crossing the Maas river at Rotterdam

KEY

▬▬	Motorway
▬▬	Major road
▬▬	Minor road
▬▬	Main railway
—	Minor railway
▬▬	Provincial border

0 kilometres   10

0 miles   10

For additional map symbols *see back flap*

Traditional wooden fishing boats in the harbour at Hoorn

Enkhuizen
**ZUIDERZEE
MUSEUM**

N302

kermeer

Groningen,
Leeuwarden

Lelystad

A6

N302

FLEVOLAND

mere-Buiten

Trekkersveld

*Zuidelijk-
Flevoland*

Harderwijk

N305

en

N301 A28

hoten

Putten

Vaassen

A50

Zwolle

Nijkerk

Voorthuizen

N344

Apeldoorn

Enschede

Baarn

Hoevelaken

A1

A1

Soest

GELDERLAND

Beekbergen

sfoort

Barneveld

N312

N237 A28

Hoenderloo

A50

oesterberg

N30 Lunteren

Otterlo

Eerbeek

N226

Scherpenzeel

Ede

**NATIONALE PARK
DE HOGE VELUWE**

N224

Dieren

rn

Veenendaal

A12

Neder Rijn N225

Bennekom

Velp

*Vijk bij
urstede*

Wageningen

Oosterbeek

ARNHEM

Elden

Düsseldorf

Eindhoven

Duiven

A325

Nijmegen

**PALEIS
HET LOO**

GETTING AROUND

Amsterdam sits at the hub of the Dutch transport system, with fast road and rail links to towns and cities throughout the Netherlands. The A9 and A7 motorways connect the capital with Alkmaar and Hoorn in Noord Holland, and a network of motorways and first-class roads cuts across the provinces to the south and east. It is not vital to have a car, as regular buses run to all major towns from Amsterdam, and the rail service, using modern double-decker trains, is even better. Cycling is the ideal way to take in the beauty of the spring bulbfields.

**An elaborate
gabled façade in
Monnickendam**

SIGHTS AT A GLANCE

Children in national costume at the Zuiderzee Museum

Renaissance façade and bell tower of Alkmaar's Waaggebouw (1582)

Alkmaar ❶

40 km (25 miles) NW of Amsterdam.
🏠 94,000. 🚊 🛈 Waaggebouw,
Waagplein 2–3. (072) 511 4284.
🚩 🚢 cheese market: Apr–Sep:
10am–12:30pm Fri; main market:
Sat. www.vvvalkmaar.nl

Alkmaar is an attractive old town with tree-lined canals and an historic centre, scene of an unsuccessful siege by the Spanish in 1573. It is one of the few Dutch towns to maintain its traditional cheese market, held every Friday in summer. Local producers lay out Gouda cheeses and some rounds of Edam in the Waagplein, and from here porters take them off on sledges for weighing. The porters, who sport colourful straw hats, belong to an ancient guild and indulge in good-natured rivalry. The streets around the Waagplein are packed with stalls that sell everything from cheese to locally made pottery.

🏛 Waaggebouw
Waagplein 2. **Tel** (072) 511 4284.
Hollands Kaasmuseum 🚩 27
Mar–4 Nov: 10am–4pm Mon–Thu &
Sat, 9am–4pm Fri. 🖼 🛆
www.kaasmuseum.nl
The focal point of the cheese market is the imposing Waaggebouw (weigh house), which was altered in 1582 from a 14th-century chapel. It now contains the Hollandse Kaasmuseum, where local cheese-making techniques are revealed. Each day on the hour, mechanical knights, under the clock of the Waaggebouw, stage a jousting tournament while a clarion blower sounds his trumpet.

⛪ Grote Kerk
Kerkplein, Koorstraat. **Tel**
(072) 514 0707. 🚩 Jun–
Aug: 10am–5pm Tue–Sat,
1–5pm Sun (and during exhibitions).
This imposing Gothic church contains the tomb of Floris V (see p21), whose body was exhumed and brought here when the building was completed in 1520. The 17th-century organ, built by Jacob van Campen (see p74) and painted by Cesar van Everdingen, dominates the Grote Kerk's nave.

Zuiderzee-museum ❷

See pp170–71.

Hoorn ❸

40 km (25 miles) N of Amsterdam. 🏠
68,000. 🚊 🛈 Veemarkt 4. (072)
511 4284. 🚢 Sat; mid-Jun–Aug:
Wed (for tourists). www.vvvhoorn.nl

Hoorn was the capital of the ancient province of West Friesland and one of the great seafaring towns of the Golden Age (see pp26–9). The collection of ornate patrician houses around Rode Steen, Hoorn's main square, attests to the town's prosperous history. Several famous maritime heroes were born here, including Willem Schouten (1580–1625), who named the tip of South America Cape Horn after his birthplace, and Abel Tasman (see pp28–9). A statue in Rode Steen commemorates Jan Pietersz Coen (1587–1629), a famous explorer who went on to found Batavia, now known as Jakarta, the capital of Indonesia (see pp28–9).

Painted unicorn, Westfries Museum

🏛 Westfries Museum
Rode Steen 1. **Tel** (0229) 280 020.
🚩 11am–5pm Mon–Fri, 2–5pm Sat
& Sun. ⬤ 1 Jan, 30 Apr, 3rd Mon
in Aug, 25 Dec. 🖼 www.wfm.nl
The building that houses the Westfries Museum in Rode Steen was built in 1632 as a prison – the square takes its name, "red stone", from the blood spilt at executions there.
The three-tiered gable of the building is decorated with heraldic figures carrying the coats of arms of the towns that made up the province of West Friesland. Inside the museum, little has changed since 1925, when writer Aldous Huxley affectionately described it as "filled with mixed rubbish". There is much to enjoy here, from the archaeological displays in the basement to the 17th-century rooms filled with furniture and antique clocks.

Porters carrying cheese on sledges in Alkmaar's traditional market

Wooden clogs outside a restored fisherman's cottage in Monnickendam

Edam ❹

22 km (14 miles) N of Amsterdam.
🏘 7,200. 🚌 🛈 Damplein 1.
(0299) 315 125. 🧀 cheese market:
Jul & Aug: 10:30am–12:30pm Wed;
general market: every Wed.
www.vvv-edam.nl

The name of Edam is known
throughout the world for its
ball-shaped cheeses wrapped
in wax – red for export, and
yellow for local consumption.
In the summer, cheese lovers
should head for the *kaasmarkt*
(cheese market), held in the
main square, which is called
Jan van Nieuwenhuizenplein.
The *kaasmarkt's* single-gabled
weigh house dates from 1592
and has a gaudy painted
façade. Cheese-making is
now an automated process
and some factories around
the outskirts of the town
offer guided tours for visitors.

Edam itself is exceptionally
pretty, full of narrow canals
bordered by elegant, gabled
Golden Age canal houses and
crossed by wooden lift bridges.
The imposing Grote Kerk is
noted both for its 16th-century
carillon, and its outstandingly
beautiful stained-glass
windows (1606–24). The harbour to the east of the town
was built in the 17th century,
in the days when Edam was
a prominent whaling centre.

🏛 **Edams Museum**
Damplein 8. **Tel** (0299) 372 644.
◯ Apr–Oct: 10am–4.30pm
Tue–Sat, noon–4.30pm Sun. ◗ 30
Apr. 🖼 **www**.edamsmuseum.nl
This amazing Gothic building
(1530) is home to an eccentric
museum of local history. The

timbered interior and steep,
narrow stairs look like the
inside of a ship. The house is
said to have been built for a
retired sea captain who could
not bear sleeping on dry land.
The unusual floating cellar
has a floor that rises and falls
with fluctuations in the water
table. Just as strange are the
17th-century portraits of
odd-looking locals, such as
Trijntje Kever, who was said
to be almost 2.8 m (9 ft) tall.

Monnickendam ❺

16 km (10 miles) N of Amsterdam.
🏘 10,000. 🚌 🛈 Zeestraat 37,
Volendam. (0299) 363 747. 🧀 Sat.

Visitors flock to this beautifully
preserved port to admire the
gabled houses and the
renovated fishermen's cottages
in the narrow streets around
the harbour. Freshly smoked
local eel can be bought here,
and the fish restaurants are a
popular draw for tourists.

The **Museum de Speeltoren**
is dedicated to the history of
Monnickendam. It is housed in
the clock tower of the Stadhuis,
with its ornate 15th-century
carillon. When bells chime the
hour, the clockwork knights
in armour parade around the
exterior of the tower.

🏛 **Museum de Speeltoren**
Noordeinde 4. **Tel** (0299) 652 203.
◯ Apr & mid-Sep–Oct: 11am–
4:30pm Sat, 1–4:30pm Sun;
May–mid-Sep: 11am–4:30pm
Tue-Sat, 1–4:30pm Sun. ◗ public
hols. 🖼 **www**.despeeltoren.nl

Lift bridge on one of the canals at Edam

Zuiderzeemuseum ❷

Enkhuizen was one of several villages around the
edge of the Zuiderzee whose fishing-based economy
was devastated when access to the North Sea was
blocked by construction of the Afsluitdijk in 1932 *(see
p165)*. The village's fortunes were revived with the
opening of this museum complex. Seven centuries of
Zuiderzee history is depicted in the Binnenmuseum
(indoor museum). There is also a display of historic
boats. The Buitenmuseum (open air museum) consists
of rescued buildings, reconstructed to create a typical
Zuiderzee village, with demonstrations of local crafts.

★ Houses from Urk
*Buildings from the little island
of Urk have been rebuilt in the
open air museum. Daily life on
the island in 1905 is recreated
by actors in role play.*

Smoke-houses from
Monnickendam

Childrens's
Island

Reconstruction of
Marken harbour

★ Marine Hall
*Housed in an old ware-
house of the Dutch East
India Company (see
pp28–9), the indoor
museum's Marine Hall
contains sailing and
fishing boats. A small
pleasure boat is rigged
up for children to play in.*

The Church
*The builders of this
late 19th-century
church, from the
island of Wieringen,
disguised the organ
in a cupboard to
avoid the tax that
was then levied on
church organs.*

Main entrance

Barges carry
visitors to the
open air
museum.

Lime Kilns
*Bottle-shaped kilns were
used to burn shells dredged
from the sea bed. The
resulting quicklime was
used as an ingredient in
mortar for bricklaying.
These kilns are from
Akersloot in Noord Holland.*

★ **Apothecaries' Gapers**
The Apothecary has a wonderful Art Nouveau façade and, inside, a display of "gapers": brightly painted heads placed outside Dutch chemists' shops and used as advertising signs.

VISITORS' CHECKLIST

50 km (31 miles) NE of
Amsterdam. Wierdijk 12–22,
Enkhuizen. **Tel** *(0228) 351 111.*
Indoor ⬜ *10am–5pm Tue–Sun.*
⬤ *1 Jan, 25 Dec.* Open Air ⬜
Apr–Oct: 10am–5pm Tue–Sun.
⬤ *Nov–Mar.* 🚉 *Enkhuizen.*
🚌 *leaves from behind train
station.* 🖼️ 📷 ♿ 🍴 🛍️
www.zuiderzeemuseum.nl

Shed for refitting barges

Fish Smoking
Herrings, the main catch of the former Zuiderzee, are preserved by smoking them over smouldering woodchips. They are then ready for visitors to eat.

Houses brought from the nearby island of Urk

Houses in this area are from Zoutkamp, a fishing village once on the Zuiderzee.

A working windmill shows how excess water was cleared from the dykes to create polders *(see pp24–5).*

0 metres	50
0 yards	50

Keeping House in 1930
This interactive exhibition allows you to experience Zuiderzee life in the 1930s. A "housewife" sits down with visitors and describes her daily life over a cup of tea.

STAR FEATURES

★ Houses from Urk

★ Marine Hall

★ Apothecaries' Gapers

Marken ❻

16 km (10 miles) NE of Amsterdam.
🚶 *2,000.* 🚌 ⛴

Until recently, Marken was an island fishing community that had changed very little over 200 years. However, the construction of a causeway link between the village and the mainland in 1957 brought an abrupt end to its isolation.

The village is popular with tourists, who are drawn here by its old-world character. The locals sometimes wear traditional dress, and the gabled timber houses are painted in the rather sombre shades of black and green.

Marken's transition from fishing community to tourist centre is neatly symbolized by the local heritage centre, the **Marker Museum**, which consists of six historical houses, one of which is furnished as a traditional fisherman's abode.

🏛 **Marker Museum**
Kerkbuurt 44. **Tel** *(0299) 601 904.*
⏲ *Apr–Sep: 10am–5pm daily (from noon Sun); Oct: 11am–4pm Mon–Sat, noon–5pm Sun.* 🎟

Yachts and pleasure boats in Volendam's marina

Volendam ❼

18 km (11.5 miles) NE of Amsterdam.
🚶 *18,000.* 🚌 🛈 *Zeestraat 37. (0299) 363747.* 🏪 *Sat.*
www.vvv-volendam.nl

The harbour in Volendam is now overrun with tourists, but the village is still worth exploring for the narrow canals and streets behind the main dykes, an area known as the Doolhof. The residents wear traditional costume: tight bodices, winged lace caps and striped aprons for the women; baggy trousers and jerseys for the men.

Artists flocked to Volendam in the late 19th century to paint views of this pretty town. Many stayed at the Spaander Hotel at No. 15 Haven, and the walls of the hotel's café are covered with paintings accepted by the owners in lieu of payment.

Zaanse Schans ❽

Schansend 1, Zaandam 13 km (8 miles) N of Amsterdam.
🚉 *Koog-Zaandijk* 🚶 *50.*
🚌 *Zaandam.* **Tel** *(075) 6168 218.*
⏲ *9am–5pm daily (some attractions closed during the week in winter).*
🎟 *for some buildings and parking.*
www.zaanseschans.nl

Part of the town of Zaandam, Zaanse Schans was created in 1960 as a monument to village life in the 17th century. Shops, cottages, windmills, houses and historic buildings from all over the Zaan region have been relocated here to create a museum village in which people can live and work.

The local community is dedicated to preserving the traditional Dutch way of life, and Zaanse Schans is run as a piece of living history. The inhabitants operate the carefully restored windmills themselves; these include a mustard mill, the last working oil mill still in existence, and mills that generate power. The energy they produce goes to sawing logs for building timber, and to grinding minerals to make pigments used in paint.

In summer, cruises can be taken in open-topped boats along the surrounding dykes.

A typical 17th-century gabled timber house in Marken

Windmill Technology

Windmills have been a familiar feature of the Dutch landscape since the 13th century. They had many uses, including grinding corn, crushing seed to make oil and driving sawmills. However, as much of the Netherlands lies below sea level, their most vital function was to drain the land of lakes and marshes, and extend the shoreline to create fertile farmland called *polder*. Subsequently, the windmills have had to cope with

Miller in cap and apron

the constant threat of flooding. To help prevent this, canals were dug to drain water from the soil; the mills then pumped excess water via a series of stepped canals until it drained into the main river system. Today, most land drainage is carried out by electric pumps driven by wind turbines. Of the thousands of windmills that once dotted the Dutch countryside, about 950 survive, many preserved in working order.

Modern aerogenerators, *or wind turbines, are widely used in the Netherlands. They harness strong gusts of wind to create electricity without the pollution caused by burning fossil fuels such as gas or coal.*

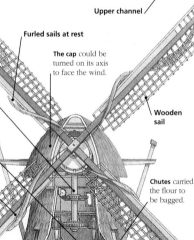

Trelliswork and canvas sail

Smock mills, *shaped like peasants' smocks, were drainage mills used, from the 17th century, in groups known as gangs. The Archimedes' screw rotated to force the water upwards.*

Drive shaft

Archimedes' screw

Upper channel

Furled sails at rest

The cap could be turned on its axis to face the wind.

Main axle

Wooden sail

Grain was ground by two vast millstones.

Chutes carried the flour to be bagged.

Canvas cloth was stretched over the blades.

The sails *of this traditional windmill transmit power via mechanical gears. A rotating cog operates an adjacent wheel to drive the water pump.*

Flour mills, *thatched with reeds and shaped like giant pepperpots, were vital to Dutch daily life. Sophisticated internal mechanisms were used to grind the wheat, barley and oats which formed the basis of the community's diet.*

Street-by-Street: Haarlem **⑨**

Misericord in the Grote Kerk

Haarlem is the commercial capital of Noord Holland province and the eighth largest city in the Netherlands. It is the centre of the Dutch printing, pharmaceutical and bulb-growing industries, but there is little sign of this in the delightful pedestrianized streets of the historic heart of the city. Most of the sites of interest are within easy walking distance of the Grote Markt, a lively square packed with ancient buildings, cafés and restaurants. Old bookshops, antique dealers and traditional food shops are all to be discovered in nearby streets.

Statue of Laurens Coster
According to local legend, Haarlem-born Laurens Jansz Coster (1370–1440) invented printing in 1423, 16 years before Gutenberg. The 19th-century statue in the Grote Markt celebrates the claim.

No. 31 Nieuwe Groenmarkt is a quaint restaurant called "Ma Brown".

The Hoofdwacht is a 17th-century, former guard house.

Stadhuis
Lieven de Key's allegorical figure of Justice (1622) stands above the main entrance. She carries a sword and the scales of justice.

Vleeshal *(1603)*
The old meat market is part of the Frans Hals Museum (see pp178–9).

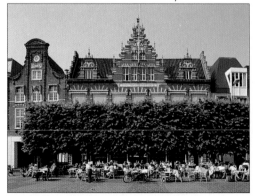

Grote Markt
The tree-lined market square is bordered with busy pavement restaurants and cafés. It has been the meeting point for the townspeople for centuries.

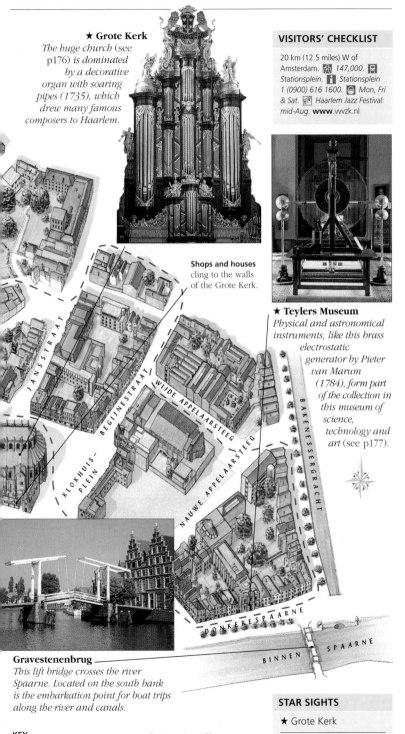

★ **Grote Kerk**
The huge church (see p176) is dominated by a decorative organ with soaring pipes (1735), which drew many famous composers to Haarlem.

VISITORS' CHECKLIST

20 km (12.5 miles) W of Amsterdam. 🚋 147,000. 🚆 *Stationsplein.* 🛈 *Stationsplein 1 (0900) 616 1600.* 🛒 *Mon, Fri & Sat.* 🎷 *Haarlem Jazz Festival: mid-Aug.* **www**.vvvzk.nl

Shops and houses cling to the walls of the Grote Kerk.

★ **Teylers Museum**
Physical and astronomical instruments, like this brass electrostatic generator by Pieter van Marum (1784), form part of the collection in this museum of science, technology and art (see p177).

JANSSTRAAT

BEGIJNESTRAAT

WIJDE APPELAARSTEEG

KLOKHUIS-PLEIN

NAUWE APPELAARSTEEG

BAKENESSERGRACHT

DONKERE SPAARNE

BINNEN SPAARNE

Gravestenenbrug
This lift bridge crosses the river Spaarne. Located on the south bank is the embarkation point for boat trips along the river and canals.

KEY

- - - Suggested route

0 metres   50
0 yards   50

STAR SIGHTS

★ Grote Kerk

★ Teylers Museum

Exploring Haarlem

Haarlem became a city in 1245, and had grown into a thriving clothmaking centre by the 15th century. But in the Spanish siege of 1572–3 the city was sacked, and a series of fires wreaked further destruction in 1576. The town's fortunes changed in the 17th century, when industrial expansion ushered in a period of prosperity lasting throughout the Golden Age *(see pp26–9)*. The centre was largely rebuilt by Lieven de Key (1560–1627) and still retains much of its character. The Grote Kerk continues to overlook the city's *hofjes* (almshouses), and the brick-paved lanes around the Grote Markt are little changed.

Grote Markt, Haarlem (c.1668) by Berckheyde, showing the Grote Kerk

🏛 Frans Hals Museum
See pp178–9.

⛪ Grote Kerk
Oude Groenmarkt 23. **Tel** *(023) 553 2040.* ⬜ *10am–4pm Mon–Sat.* 🖼 ♿ **www**.bavo.nl

The enormous Gothic edifice of Sint Bavo's great church, often referred to simply as the Grote Kerk, was a favourite subject of the 17th-century Haarlem School artists Pieter Saenredam (1597–1665) and Gerrit Berckheyde (1639–98). Built between 1400 and 1550, the church and its ornate bell tower dominate the market square. Clinging on to the exterior of the south wall is a jumble of 17th-century shops and houses. The rents raised from these ramshackle, untidy buildings contributed to the maintenance of the church.

Today, the entrance to the Grote Kerk is through one of the surviving shops, a tiny antechamber that leads straight into the enormous nave. The church has a high, delicately patterned, vaulted cedarwood ceiling, white upper walls, and 28 supporting columns painted

in greens, reds and golds. The intricate choir screen, like the magnificent brass lectern in the shape of a preening eagle, was made by master metal worker Jan Fyerens in about 1510. The choirstalls (1575) are painted with coats of arms, and the armrests and misericords are carved with caricatures of animals and human heads. Not far away is the simple stone slab covering the grave of Haarlem's most famous artist, Frans Hals.

The Grote Kerk boasts one of Europe's finest and most flamboyant organs, built in 1735 by Christiaan Müller. In 1738 Handel tried the organ and pronounced it excellent. It also found favour with the infant prodigy Mozart, who shouted for joy when he gave a recital on it in 1766. The organ is still often used for concerts, recordings and teaching.

🏛 Stadhuis
Grote Markt 2. **Tel** *(023) 511 3000.* ⬜ *by appt only.* ♿

Haarlem's Stadhuis (town hall) has grown rather haphazardly over the centuries and is an odd mixture of architectural styles dating from 1250. The oldest part of the building is the beamed medieval banqueting hall of the counts of Holland *(see p21)*, originally known as the Gravenzaal. Much of this was destroyed in two great fires in 1347 and 1351, but the 15th-century panel portraits of the counts of Holland can still be seen.

The wing of the town hall bordering the Grote Markt was designed by Lieven de Key in 1622. It is typical of Dutch Renaissance architecture, combining elaborate gables, ornate painted detail and Classical features, such as pediments over the windows.

In a niche above the main entrance is a plump allegorical figure of Justice, bearing a sword in one hand and scales in the other as she smiles benignly upon the pavement cafés in the market below. To the left, in Koningstraat, an archway leads to the university buildings behind the Stadhuis, where there is a 13th-century cloister and library.

🏛 De Hallen
(Vleeshal and Verweyhal)
Grote Markt 16. **Tel** *(023) 511 5775.* ⬜ *as Frans Hals Museum (p179).* 🖼 *1 Jan, 25 Dec.* 🖼 **www**.dehallen.com

De Hallen (the halls) is the collective name for two buildings in the Grote Markt which are part of the Frans Hals Museum *(see pp178–9)*. The more recent Verweyhal accommodates exhibitions of Dutch Expressionism, the Cobra School, Impressionism and contemporary works. It is named after the painter Kees Verwey, whose Impressionist still lifes are an important feature of the collection. The heavily ornamented Vleeshal (meat market) is situated just to the west of the church

Detail on Vleeshal façade by Lieven de Key

The west gate of the Amsterdamse Poort (1355)

and houses temporary exhibitions of modern art. It was built in 1602 by the city surveyor, Lieven de Key, and has a steep step gable which disguises the roof line. The extravagantly over-decorated miniature gables above each dormer window bristle with pinnacles. A giant painted ox's head on the building's façade signifies its original function.

🚪 Amsterdamse Poort
Nr Amsterdamsevaart. 🚫 to public.
The imposing medieval gateway that once helped protect Haarlem lies close to the west bank of the river Spaarne. The Amsterdamse Poort was one of a complex of 12 gates guarding strategic transport routes in and out of Haarlem. The gate was built in 1355,

though much of the elaborate brickwork and tiled gables date from the late 15th century.

The city defences were severely tested in 1573, when the Spanish, led by Frederick of Toledo, besieged Haarlem for seven months during the Dutch Revolt (see pp24–5). The city fathers agreed to surrender the town on terms that included a general amnesty for all its citizens. The Spanish appeared to accept, but once inside they slaughtered nearly 2,000 people – almost the entire population of the city.

🏛 Teylers Museum
Spaarne 16. **Tel** (023) 531 9010.
🕙 10am–5pm Tue–Sat, noon–5pm Sun & holidays. 🚫 1 Jan, 25 Dec. 🈳
♿ 📷 📱 **www**.teylersmuseum.nl
This was first major public museum to be founded in the Netherlands. It was established in 1778 by the silk merchant Pieter Teyler van der Hulst to encourage the study of science and art. The museum's eccentric collection of fossils, drawings and scientific paraphernalia is displayed in Neo-Classical splendour in a series of 18th-century rooms. The two-storey Oval Hall was added in 1779, and contains bizarre glass cabinets full of minerals and cases of intimidating medical instruments. A significant collection of sketches by Dutch and Italian masters are shown a few at a time. In 2002 a multimedia room was opened.

Tiles in Haarlem Station

🏛 Historisch Museum Haarlem
Groot Heiligland 47. **Tel** (023) 542 2427. 🕙 noon–5pm Tue–Sat, 1–5pm Sun. 🚫 1 Jan, 25 Dec.
www.historischmuseumhaarlem.nl
Haarlem is well known for its hofjes (almshouses) that were set up to minister to the poor and sick (see p93). Almshouses began to appear in the 16th century, and were run by rich guild members, who took over the role traditionally filled by the monasteries until the Alteration of 1578 (see pp24–5).

St Elisabeth's Gasthuis was built in 1610, around a pretty courtyard opposite what is now the Frans Hals Museum. A stone plaque carved above the main doorway in 1612 depicts an invalid being carried off to hospital. After extensive restoration this almshouse was opened in 1995 as Haarlem's principal historical museum.

🚉 Haarlem Station
Stationsplein. **Tel** 0900 92 92.
The first railway line in the Netherlands opened in 1839 and ran between Haarlem and Amsterdam (see pp32–3). The original station, built in 1842, was reworked in Art Nouveau style between 1905–8. It is a grandiose brick building with an arched façade and square towers. The green and beige interior is decorated with brightly coloured tiles depicting modes of transport. Other highlights include the timberwork of the offices.

17th- and 18th-century gabled houses along the river Spaarne in Haarlem

Frans Hals Museum

Hailed as the first "modern" artist, Frans Hals (c.1582–1666) introduced a new realism into painting. While contemporary painters aimed for an exact likeness, Hals captured the character of his sitters through a more impressionistic technique. In his eighties, he still painted passionate portraits, such as *The Governesses of the Old Men's Home* (1664). The Old Men's Home, one of many in Haarlem, became the Frans Hals Museum in 1913. Besides his work, there is a selection of Dutch painting and applied art from the 16th and 17th centuries.

Mother and Child
Following the Alteration (see pp24–5), artists like Pieter de Grebber (1600–53) often painted secular versions of religious themes. This painting (c.1630) of a woman suckling her baby recalls the Virgin Mary with Jesus.

STAR PAINTINGS

- ★ Banquet of the Officers by Frans Hals

- ★ Still Life by Floris van Dijck

- ★ Mercury by Hendrick Goltzius

KEY TO FLOORPLAN

- ☐ Works by Frans Hals
- ☐ Renaissance Gallery
- ☐ Old Masters
- ▨ History of 17th-century Haarlem
- ☐ Temporary exhibitions
- ▨ Non-exhibition space

Hals's Civic Guard portraits

18th-century doll's house

★ Banquet of the Officers of the Civic Guard of St George *(1616)*
The characteristics of each of the 12 Civic Guards and the opulence of their banqueting hall are superbly portrayed in this formal group portrait by Frans Hals.

Delft Dish *(1662)*
This blue-and-white earthenware dish by M Eems shows the Grote Kerk and Grote Markt in Haarlem (see p176).

Doll's House *(c. 1750)*
This 11 room house, which belonged to Sara Rothé, is made to a scale of 1:10. Its representation is so realistic that it offers a good view into what it was like inside an 18th-century canal-side mansion (see pp30–31).

★ **Mercury** *(1611)*
Hendrick Goltzius (1558–1617) painted a lot of biblical and mythological scenes. This canvas was commissioned by a wealthy Haarlem burgomaster as one of a series of three.

Small courtyard

Main entrance

MUSEUM GUIDE
The entrance leads into a modern wing with a museum shop. The best route is anti-clockwise; displays of Frans Hals' work, other portraits, still life and many other paintings are usually reordered each year. Exhibits of modern art are held in De Hallen (Vleeshal and Verweyhal) which are in the Grote Markt (see p176).

An Allegory on Tulip Mania *(c. 1640)*
Jan Breughel II's painting ridicules the obsession with tulips that was gripping Holland at the time.

★ **Still Life** *(1613)*
Precise attention to detail and texture was the hallmark of Floris van Dijck (1574–1651). The damask tablecloth shown in the painting was a product of Haarlem's thriving linen industry.

A Tour of the Bulbfields ⑩

Occupying a 30-km (19-mile) strip between Haarlem and Leiden, the Bloembollenstreek is the main bulb-growing area in the Netherlands. From late January, the polders bloom with a series of vividly coloured bulbs, beginning with early crocuses and building to a climax around mid-April when the tulips flower. These are followed by late-blooming flowers like lilies, which extend the season into late May. If you don't have a car, the VVV *(see p256)* has details on a variety of tours. Alternatively, hire a bicycle at Haarlem railway station, cycle to Leiden and take the bike back to Haarlem on the train.

TIPS FOR DRIVERS

Starting point: Haarlem.
Length: Approx 30 km (19 miles).
Stopping-off points: In addition to the places named below, all of which have a selection of restaurants, cafés and bars, it is worth diverting to Noordwijk aan Zee. This lively seaside town, with its lovely dune-backed beach, is a perfect picnic spot. Good viewpoints en route are marked on the map.

Sand dunes lining the coast

De Cruquius Museum ①
The museum contains exhibits that explain how polders and dams work and how they have kept sea and flood water at bay.

Linnaeushof ②
Named after an 18th-century botanist, this huge park contains one of Europe's largest adventure playgrounds.

Lisse ⑤
There is a small bulb-museum in Lisse and boat trips are available on Kager Plassen lake, nearby.

Vogelenzang ③
The first nurseries in Vogelenzang were established in 1789 – the Frans Bozen nurseries (sadly they recently went bankrupt).

Keukenhof ④
Visitors to this park are greeted by the heady scents and brilliant colours of millions of bulbs in bloom.

```
0 kilometres          5
0 miles          2.5
```

KEY

▰▰▰	Tour route
═ ═ ═	Roads
✹	Viewpoint

Katwijk ⑦
A rare, early-17th-century lighthouse is situated just to the north of this seaside town, which stands at the mouth of the Oude Rijn.

Sassenheim ⑥
West of the town lie the remains of Burcht Teylingen, an 11th-century castle where Jacoba of Bavaria, the deposed Countess of Holland, died in 1436.

Map labels: AMSTERDAM, A5, N208, HAARLEM, ZANDVOORT, N201, AALSMEER, Amsterdamse Waterleiding Duinen, N206, Hillegom, de Haarlemmermeerpolder, N208, Ringvaart van, AALSMEER, Noordwijk aan Zee, NOORDZEE, N206, A44, Kager Plassen, Rijnsburg, A44, LEIDEN DEN HAAG

A tulip field in the Bloembollenstreek

UTCH BULBS

he most cultivated bulbs in
e Netherlands include glad-
li, lilies, daffodils, hyacinths,
ses, crocuses and dahlias.
ulips, however, are still far
d away the country's most
ultivated flower. Originally
om Turkey, the tulip was
rst grown in Dutch soil by
arolus Clusius in 1593.

addin tulips

ina pink tulips

hiti daffodils

innow daffodils

ue jacket hyacinths

An array of bulbs in flower in the wooded Keukenhof park

Aalsmeer ⓫

10 km (6 miles) south of Amsterdam.
🏠 23,000. 🚇 ℹ️ *Driekolommen-
plein 1. (0297) 325 374.* 🔄 *Tue.*
www.hollandsmidden.nl

Aalsmeer is home to the largest
flower auction in the world,
the Bloemenveiling (see www.
vba.nl). Visitors can watch the
colourful proceedings from
a viewing gallery above the
trading floors. As the 3.5 billion
cut flowers and 400 million
pot plants sold here annually
all have a short shelf-life,
speed is of the essence. A
clock above the auctioneer's
head shows the prices falling
as the hand sweeps round,
from 100 to 1. When it reaches
the price that bidders are
willing to pay, the clock stops.

Lisse ⓬

35 km (22 miles) west of Amsterdam.
🏠 22,000. 🚇 ℹ️ *Grachtweg 53.
(0900) 222 2333.*

The best time to visit Lisse
is at the end of April, when
the town mounts a series of
colourful flower parades.
   The **Museum de Zwarte
Tulp** (the Black Tulip Museum) has displays on the
history and life cycle of bulbs.
Imported from Turkey in the

early 17th century, by the mid-
1630s "tulip mania" gripped the
nation *(see pp26–7)*. At the
height of the boom rare bulbs
were sold for their weight in
gold. By February 1637 however, the market had collapsed.

🏛 **Museum de Zwarte Tulp**
Grachtweg 2a. **Tel** *(0252) 417 900.*
🕐 *1pm–5pm Tue–Sun.* 🔴 *1 Jan,
last Thu in Sep, 25, 26 & 31 Dec.*
🖥 **www**.museumdezwartetulp.nl

Keukenhof ⓭

Stationsweg, Lisse. **Tel** *(0252) 465555.*
🚌 *54 (Leiden Centraal Station; ask for
the bus & entry deal)* 🕐 *late Mar–
mid-May: 8am–7:30pm daily (last
adm 6pm).* 🖥 **www**.keukenhof.nl

Set in a wooded park on the
outskirts of Lisse, Keukenhof
is one of the most spectacular
flower gardens in the world.
It was set up in 1949 as a showcase for Dutch bulb growers
and is now planted with some
7 million bulbs. It is at its most
spectacular from late March
to late May, when drifts of
daffodils, hyacinths or tulips
are in bloom. The flowers are
complemented by the snowy
blossom of Japanese cherry
trees early in the season, and
by splashes of azaleas and
rhododendrons later in the year.

Street-by-Street: Leiden ⑭

Leiden is a prosperous university town, with its origins in Roman times. It grew due to its position on a branch of the Rijn (Rhine) and is still an important commercial crossroads. During term-time, the streets are crowded with students cycling between lectures or packing the cafés and bookshops. A number of exceptional museums document Leiden's turbulent history, including the Golden Age, when the town was a centre for world-wide trade *(see pp26–7)*. The wall plaque on the façade of Rembrandt's house in Weddesteeg marks his birthplace in June 1606 *(see p62)*.

Statue of Justice on Stadhuis wall

★ **Rijksmuseum van Oudheden**
This squat statue of a kneeling treasury scribe is among the many Egyptian artifacts in the museum.

John Robinson *(see p185)* lived in the Jan Pesijnshofje.

★ **Hortus Botanicus**
The botanical gardens (see p184) are owned by Leiden University, and were laid out initially as a study aid for botany students in 1587.

Oude Rijn
Many of the gabled houses along Leiden's canals have shops and cafés on the ground floor.

Neo-Classical houses on Rapenburg

University library

Het Gravensteen
The university's law faculty lies behind the Classical façade of this complex of buildings, which grew up between the 13th and 17th centuries.

Hoogstraat

Crossing the meeting point of the Rijn (Rhine) canals, Hoogstraat is popular for its floating cafés and restaurants.

Pieterskerkhof is a cobbled lane with antiquarian bookshops.

VISITORS' CHECKLIST

35 km (22 miles) SW of Amsterdam. 👥 *119,000.* 🚉 *Stationsplein.* ℹ️ *Stationsweg 2D (0900 2222 333).* 🛒 *Wed, Sat.* 🎭 *Viering van Leidens Ontzet: 3 Oct.* **www**.vvleiden.nl

Korenbeursbrug

The stone bridge over the Nieuwe Rijn was roofed over in 1825 in Neo-Classical style to shelter corn merchants' stalls.

Stadhuis (1595) by Lieven de Key

★ Pieterskerk

This ethereal tombstone marks the oldest intact grave in the Netherlands – that of 15th-century merchant Floris van Boschuysen and his wife.

KEY

– – – Suggested route

0 metres	50
0 yards	50

STAR SIGHTS

★ Rijksmuseum van Oudheden

★ Pieterskerk

★ Hortus Botanicus

Exploring Leiden

Leiden is famous for its university, the oldest and most prestigious in the Netherlands. It was founded in 1575 by William of Orange, a year after he relieved the town from a year-long siege by the Spanish (*see pp24–5*). As a reward for their endurance, William offered the citizens of Leiden a choice of the building of a university or the abolition of tax. They chose wisely, and the city's reputation as a centre of intellectual and religious tolerance was firmly established. English Puritan dissidents, victims of persecution in their homeland, were able to settle here in the 17th century before undertaking their epic voyage to the New World.

Arched gazebo within a walled garden in the Hortus Botanicus

🏛 Stedelijk Museum De Lakenhal

Oude Singel 28–32. **Tel** (071) 516 5360. ☐ 10am–5pm Tue–Fri, noon–5pm Sat & Sun. ● 1 Jan, 25 Dec. 📷 ♿ ☐ ☐ 📷 www.lakenhal.nl

The Lakenhal (cloth hall) was the 17th-century headquarters of Leiden's cloth trade. Built in 1640 in Dutch Classical style by Arent van 's Gravesande, it houses the municipal museum, with temporary exhibitions of modern art and furniture from the 16th century onwards.

The pride of the collection is Lucas van Leyden's Renaissance triptych of *The Last Judgment* (1526–7), rescued from the Pieterskerk during the religious struggles of 1566 (*see pp24–5*).

A wing built in the 1920s offers a silver collection, furniture and exhibits covering the local weaving industry. Not to be missed is a big bronze *hutspot*, or

cauldron, allegedly left behind by the Spanish when William of Orange broke the siege in 1574. The cauldron contained a spicy stew which the starving people ate. This meal is now cooked every year on 3 October, to commemorate Dutch victory over the Spanish.

❀ Hortus Botanicus der Rijksuniversiteit Leiden

Rapenburg 73. **Tel** (071) 527 7249. ☐ Apr–Nov: 10am–6pm daily; Dec–Mar: 10–4pm Sun–Fri. ● 3 Oct, 25 Dec–1 Jan. 📷 ♿ partial. ☐ 📷 www.hortusleiden.nl

Leiden's botanical garden was founded in 1587 as part of the university. The varied trees and shrubs include a 350-year-old laburnum planted

shortly after the gardens were set up. Carolus Clusius, who was responsible for introducing the tulip to the Netherlands in 1593 (*see pp26–7*), became the first professor of botany at Leiden University. Today the Hortus Botanicus contains a modern reconstruction of his original walled garden, called the Clusiustuin. Other delights include hothouses full of exotic orchids, rose gardens and colourful beds of tulips planted around ponds.

🏛 Museum Boerhaave

Lange St Agnietenstraat 10. **Tel** (071) 521 4224. ☐ 10am–5pm Tue–Sat; noon–5pm Sun, pub hols. ● 1 Jan. 📷 ☐ www.museumboerhaave.nl

The Leiden physician Herman Boerhaave (1668–1738) wrote the definitive 18th-century medical textbook, called *Institutiones*

Lucas van Leyden's triptych of *The Last Judgment* in the Stedelijk Museum de Lakenhal

Medicae. The museum named after him is devoted to the development of science in the Netherlands and contains reconstructions of an anatomy theatre and hospital wards. The displays are arranged chronologically and include pendulum clocks made by Christiaan Huygens (1629–95), the discoverer of Saturn's rings, and thermometers by Gabriel Fahrenheit (1686–1736).

🏛 Rijksmuseum voor Volkenkunde

Steenstraat 1. **Tel** *(071) 516 8800.*
⏲ *10am–5pm Tue–Sun.*
● *1 Jan, 3 Oct, 25 Dec.*
🖼 ♿ 🖥 🎧 **www**.rmv.nl

This outstanding ethnological museum, founded in 1837, houses collections from non-western cultures. Individual displays are linked together to create a worldwide cultural journey that shows both the differences and connections between cultures. Temporary exhibitions feature living conditions across the world, from the Arctic wastes to the hills of China, adding to this eclectic museum's wide appeal to people of all age groups.

🏛 Stedelijk Molenmuseum de Valk

2e Binnenvestgracht 1. **Tel** *(071) 5165 353.* ⏲ *10am–5pm Tue–Sat, 1–5pm Sun.* ● *1 Jan, 3 Oct, 25 Dec.* 🖼 📷

This towering grain mill, built in 1743, is Leiden's last remaining mill. It is an imposing seven storeys high, and now restored to its original working state. A tour takes in the living quarters on the ground floor, the repair workshop and a retrospective exhibition on the history of Dutch windmills.

⛪ Pieterskerk

Pieterskerkhof 1a. **Tel** *(071) 512 4319.* ⏲ *opening times vary; phone in advance.* ● *3 Oct, 31 Dec.* ♿ **www**.pieterskerk.com

The magnificent Gothic church was built in the 15th century in rose-pink brick, and stands in a leafy square surrounded by elegant houses. Now a

community centre, the church is worth visiting for its austere interior and its organ, built by the Hagenbeer brothers in 1642 and enclosed in gilded woodwork. The floor of the nave is covered with worn slabs marking the burial places of 17th-century intellectuals like Puritan leader John Robinson and Golden Age artist Jan Steen *(see p133)*. Parts of the church may be screened off due to restoration.

♜ De Burcht

Nieuwe Rijn. **Battlements** ⏲ *daily.*

De Burcht is an odd 12th-century fortress with crenellated battlements. It sits between two channels of the Rijn (Rhine) atop a grassy, manmade mound, which is thought to be of Saxon origin. The top of the citadel offers superb views over Leiden.

Heraldic lion at De Burcht

🏛 Rijksmuseum van Oudheden

Rapenburg 28. **Tel** *(0900) 6600 600.* ⏲ *10am–5pm Tue–Fri, noon–5pm Sat & Sun.* ● *1 Jan, 30 Apr, 3 Oct, 25 Dec.* 🖼 ♿ 🖥 🎧 **www**.rmo.nl

The Dutch museum of antiquities, established in 1818, is Leiden's main attraction. The centrepiece of the collection is the Egyptian Temple of Taffeh, reassembled in the main exhibition hall in 1978. It dates from the 1st century AD, and was dedicated to Isis, Egyptian goddess of fertility, from the 4th century AD.

The museum's rich collection of Egyptian artifacts occupies the first two floors. There are also impressive displays of musical instruments, textiles and shoes, expressive Etruscan bronzework and fragments of Roman mosaic and frescoes.

The presentation has been designed with children in mind with interactive media reconstructing daily life in ancient Egypt, Greece and Rome.

A lift bridge across the Oude Rijn in Leiden

Den Haag ⑮

Statue in Binnenhof courtyard

Den Haag ('s-Gravenhage or The Hague) is the political capital of the Netherlands, home to prestigious institutions such as the Dutch Parliament and International Court of Justice, located in the Vredespaleis *(see p190)*. When Den Haag became the seat of government in 1586, it was a small town built around the castle of the counts of Holland. That same castle, much rebuilt, now stands at the heart of a city which is home to half a million people. It is surrounded by public buildings, such as the Mauritshuis *(see pp188–9)*, and protected to the north by the remains of a moat which forms the Hofvijver (lake). To the west is the seaside town of Scheveningen *(see p191)*.

🏛 Mauritshuis

See pp188–9.

▦ Ridderzaal

Binnenhof 8a. **Tel** (070) 364 6144.
⬜ *Mon–Sat (phone in advance).*
🌐 *Sun & public hols.* 🈲 📷
www.binnenhofbezoek.nl

By the side of the Hofvijver is the Binnenhof courtyard. In the centre of this stands the fairy-tale, double-turreted Gothic Ridderzaal (Hall of the Knights). This was the 13th-century dining hall of Floris V, Count of Holland *(see p21)*. Since 1904, the hall's function has been mostly ceremonial; it is used for the opening of the Dutch Parliament by the monarch (Prinsjesdag, the third Tuesday in September), and for other state occasions. It is open to visitors when parliament is not in session. A tour takes in the two former debating chambers.

🏛 Museum Bredius

Lange Vijverberg 14. **Tel** (070) 362 0729. ⬜ *noon–5pm Tue–Sun.*
🈲 *1 Jan & 25 Dec.* 🈲 *(free on Sat).*
📷 www.museumbredius.nl

Dr Abraham Bredius was an art historian and collector as well as director of the Mauritshuis *(see pp188–9)* from 1895 to 1922. On his death in 1946, he bequeathed his vast collection of 17th-century art to the city of Den Haag. This bequest is displayed in a distinguished 18th-century merchant's house on the north side of the Hof-vijver, and features around 200 Golden Age paintings – famous works by Dutch Masters such as Rembrandt *(see p66)* and Jan Steen *(see p133)*, and others by lesser-known artists.

The building itself has undergone considerable renovation and boasts a fine collection of antique furniture, delicate porcelain and elaborate silverware.

🔒 Grote Kerk

Rond de Grote Kerk 10.
Tel (070) 302 8630. ⬜ *during exhibitions only (usually Jul–Aug).*
♿ www.grotekerkdenhaag.nl

In its present form, the Grote Kerk dates mainly from 1539, but has undergone major re-building between 1985 and 1987. Its most impressive feature is a stained-glass window which depicts Charles V, the Holy Roman Emperor *(see pp24–5)*, kneeling at the feet of the Virgin Mary. The church is at the centre of Den Haag's shopping area.

Coat of arms on façade of Rijksmuseum Gevangenpoort

🏛 Rijksmuseum Gevangenpoort

Buitenhof 33. **Tel** (070) 346 0861.
⬜ *10am–5pm Tue–Fri, noon–5pm Sat–Sun.* 🈲 *1 Jan, 25, 26 Dec.* 🈲
📷 *(every hour: obligatory. Last tour: 4pm)* 📱 www.gevangenpoort.nl

The Gevangenpoort (prison gate) was originally the main gateway to the 14th-century castle of the counts of Holland. Later, it was turned into a jail, becoming infamous during a period of violent social unrest in the late 17th century when burgomaster Cornelis de Witt *(see p27)* was confined and tortured here. Both he and his brother Jan were subsequently tried for heresy, and torn limb from limb outside the prison gate by a rioting mob.

Now a prison museum, on display is a unique collection of torture instruments, accompanied by a stereo soundtrack of blood-curdling screams.

The Hofvijver and parliament buildings in Den Haag

Paintings in Galerij Prins Willem V

🏛 Galerij Prins Willem V

Buitenhof 35. **Tel** (070) 302 3456.
🔵 closed for renovations until 2007.
📧 🖥 www.mauritshuis.nl

In his youth, Prince William V
(see p30) was a collector of
Golden Age paintings. His
collection was opened to the
public in 1774, inside this
former inn, which the prince
had converted for use as his
kabinet – the 18th-century
Dutch word for an art gallery.
The Galerij is the oldest art
gallery in the Netherlands.
The 18th-century fashion for

covering every available inch
of wall space with paintings
has been retained, and so
several pictures are hung too
high and too close together.
Many of Prince William's
original purchases are still to
be seen. Old Master paintings
by Rembrandt, Jan Steen and
Paulus Potter (1625–54) are
included in a collection that
consists principally of
typically Dutch Golden Age
landscapes, genre works,
"conversation pieces" and
recreations of historical
events (see p132).

🏛 Haags Historisch Museum

Korte Vijverberg 7. **Tel** (070) 364
6940. 🔵 10am–5pm Tue–Fri,
noon–5pm Sat–Sun. 🔵 1 Jan, 3rd
Tue in Sep, 25 Dec. 📧 ♿ 🖥 📷
🌐 www.haagshistorisch
museum.nl

Den Haag's history museum
is in the Sebastiaansdoelen,
a Dutch Classical mansion
built in 1636 and the former
headquarters of the Civic
Guard of St Sebastian.
Exhibitions tell the story
of Den Haag's growth
since the Middle Ages.

The displays are changed
periodically and are drawn
from the city's collection of
landscapes, portraits and
genre paintings (see pp132–3)
as well as 17th- and 18th-
century furnishings.

The 17th-century façade of the Haags Historisch Museum

DEN HAAG CITY CENTRE

Galerij Prins Willem V ③
Grote Kerk ①
Haags Historisch Museum ⑥
Mauritshuis ⑦
Museum Bredius ④
Ridderzaal ⑤
Rijksmuseum
   Gevangenpoort ②

0 metres   250
0 yards   250

Key to Symbols see back flap

The Mauritshuis

The Count of Nassau, Johann Maurits, commissioned this graceful house while he was the governor of Brazil. It was completed in 1644 by Pieter Post and Jacob van Campen in Dutch Classical style with influences from Italian Renaissance architecture, and enjoys wonderful views across the Hofvijver *(see p186)*. The mansion was bequeathed to the state after Maurits's death in 1679, and has been the home of the Royal Picture Gallery since 1821. The collection is small, but almost every painting is a superb work by one of the Old Masters. This, combined with the exquisite presentation in elegant period rooms, makes the Mauritshuis one of the finest galleries in the Netherlands.

★ **The Anatomy Lesson of Dr Nicolaes Tulp** *(1632)*
Rembrandt's painting of surgeons examining a corpse reflects the burgeoning contemporary interest in anatomy and science.

GALLERY GUIDE

The Mauritshuis, a small gallery set on three floors, is packed with artworks. The arrangement of the paintings changes frequently in order to cover all aspects of the collection, but you can check the current display on the museum's website. Information sheets and an audio tour are available in English. If in doubt, ask for help from one of the gallery attendants. The permanent collection is subject to changes.

Vase with Flowers in a Niche *(c.1618)* Ambrosius Bosschaert the Elder captured the beauty of early summer flowers, but the flies buzzing around remind us of mortality.

Ground floor

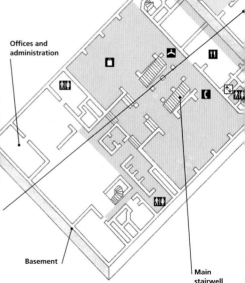

Offices and administration

Basement

Main stairwell

Portrait of a Man from the Lespinette Family *(c. 1485–90)*
Thought to be a work by Antonello da Messina until the 19th century, this tightly framed portrait has now been attributed to Hans Memling.

The Goldfinch *(1654)*
This tiny, delicate painting is by Carel Fabritius (1622–54), who was a pupil of Rembrandt.

Main stairs (first floor)

First floor

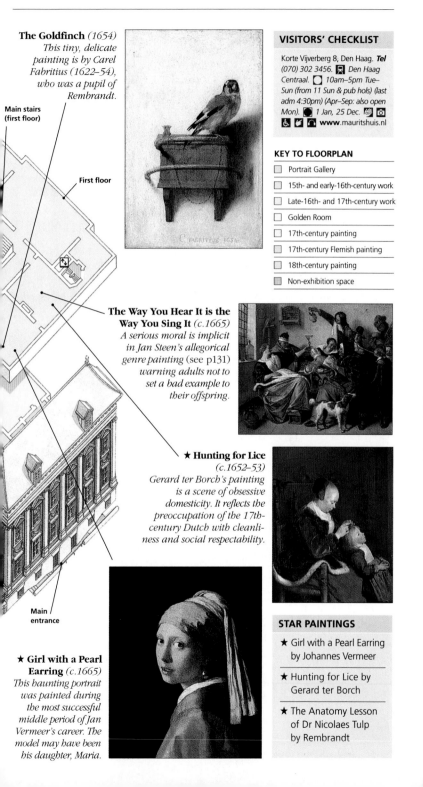

VISITORS' CHECKLIST

Korte Vijverberg 8, Den Haag. **Tel** (070) 302 3456. 🚉 Den Haag Centraal. ⏰ 10am–5pm Tue– Sun (from 11 Sun & pub hols) (last adm 4:30pm) (Apr–Sep: also open Mon). ⬤ 1 Jan, 25 Dec. 📷 📸 ♿ 📷 🎧 www.mauritshuis.nl

KEY TO FLOORPLAN

☐ Portrait Gallery

☐ 15th- and early-16th-century work

☐ Late-16th- and 17th-century work

☐ Golden Room

☐ 17th-century painting

☐ 17th-century Flemish painting

☐ 18th-century painting

☐ Non-exhibition space

The Way You Hear It is the Way You Sing It *(c.1665)*
A serious moral is implicit in Jan Steen's allegorical genre painting (see p131) warning adults not to set a bad example to their offspring.

★ Hunting for Lice *(c.1652–53)*
Gerard ter Borch's painting is a scene of obsessive domesticity. It reflects the preoccupation of the 17th-century Dutch with cleanliness and social respectability.

Main entrance

★ Girl with a Pearl Earring *(c.1665)*
This haunting portrait was painted during the most successful middle period of Jan Vermeer's career. The model may have been his daughter, Maria.

STAR PAINTINGS

★ Girl with a Pearl Earring by Johannes Vermeer

★ Hunting for Lice by Gerard ter Borch

★ The Anatomy Lesson of Dr Nicolaes Tulp by Rembrandt

Vredespaleis

Carnegieplein 2. **Tel** *(070) 302 4137.*
Mon–Fri. compulsory (phone
in advance). public hols and
when court is in session.
www.vredespaleis.nl

In 1899, Den Haag played host
to the first international peace
conference. This then led to
the formation of the Permanent
Court of Arbitration, which had
the aim of maintaining world
peace. To provide a suitably
august home for the court, the
Scottish-born philanthropist,
Andrew Carnegie (1835–1918)
donated £1 million towards the
building of the mock-Gothic
Vredespaleis (peace palace),
which was designed by French
architect Louis Cordonnier.

The enormous palace was
completed in 1913, and many
of the member nations of the
Court of Arbitration contributed
to the interior's rich decoration.
Today the Vredespaleis is the
seat of the United Nations'
International Court of Justice,
which was formed in 1946 as
successor to the Permanent
Court of Arbitration.

Vredespaleis, home to the International Court of Justice

Haags Gemeentemuseum

Stadhouderslaan 41. **Tel** *(070) 338
1111.* 11am–5pm Tue–Sun.
1 Jan, 25 Dec.
www.gemeentemuseum.nl

The Gemeentemuseum is one
of the town's finest museums.
The building was the last work
of HP Berlage, the father of the
architectural movement known
as the Amsterdam School *(see
p97)*. The museum was completed in 1935, a year after his
death, and is built in sandy-
coloured brick on two storeys
round a central courtyard.

The exhibits are displayed
in three sections. Highlights of
the superb applied arts section
include antique Delftware,

Islamic and Oriental porcelain
and the world's largest
collection of paintings by Piet
Mondriaan *(see p136)*. Musical
instruments and costumes worn
in the 18th century onwards,
including showcases on jewellery and fashion photography,
can be seen in the basement.

Probably the museum's main
attraction is the collection of
musical instruments which date
from the 15th to 19th centuries.
European instruments include
harpsichords and pocket-size
fiddles; more exotic is a Javanese *gamelan*, which consists
of gongs and drums.

Panorama Mesdag

Zeestraat 65. **Tel** *(070) 364 4544.*
10am–5pm Mon–Sat, noon–5pm
Sun. 1 Jan, 25 Dec.
www.panorama-mesdag.com

This painted cyclorama is
important both as a work of
Dutch Impressionism and as a
rare surviving example of 19th-
century entertainment. The
vast painting is 120 m (400 ft)
around, and lines the inside
wall of a circular, canopied pavilion. It shows the old fishing
village of Scheveningen, 4 km
(2.5 miles) north of Den Haag.

The astonishingly realistic
effect of the painting is
achieved through the brilliant
use of perspective, enhanced
by natural daylight from above.
Real sand and drift-wood
piled at the foot of the painting
add to the illusion. It was
painted in 1881 by members
of the Dutch Impressionist
School, led by HW Mesdag
(1831–1915) and his wife,
Sientje (1834–1909). George
Hendrik Breitner (1857–1923)
later added a group of cavalry
officers charging along the
beach on horseback.

Haags Gemeentemuseum (1935), designed by HP Berlage

🏛 Omniversum

President Kennedylaan 5.
Tel *(0900) 666 4837.* ⬜ *daily.*
🖼 ♿ 🚻 ⬛ www.omniversum.nl

The Omniversum is a cross between a planetarium and a space-age cinema, and is especially appealing to children. It has a high-tech sound system and a massive dome-shaped screen, on to which films and lasers are projected. These are combined to create stunning three-dimensional images of space exploration, volcanic eruptions and life beneath the ocean's surface.

🏛 Madurodam

George Maduroplein 1.
Tel *(070) 416 2400.* ⬜ *daily.* 🖼
♿ 🍴 🚻 www.madurodam.nl

Madurodam is a model of a composite Dutch city, built to a scale of 1:25. It incorporates replicas of the Vredespaleis and Binnenhof in Den Haag, the canal houses of Amsterdam, Rotterdam's Europoort *(see p199)* and Schiphol Airport *(pp266–7)*, along with windmills, polders, bulbfields and a nudist beach. At night the streets and buildings are illuminated by 50,000 tiny lights.

The model city was opened by Queen Juliana in 1952. It was conceived by JML Maduro as a memorial to his son George, who died at Dachau concentration camp in 1945.

Scale models in the miniature town of Madurodam

Scheveningen ⑯

45 km (28 miles) SW of Amsterdam.
🚶 *17,800.* 🚊 🏢 *Gevers Deijnoot-weg 1134 (0900 340 3505).* 🛍 *Thu.*

This resort is a 15-minute tram-ride from the centre of Den Haag. Like many Dutch seaside towns, it had its heyday in the 19th century, and is now a mixture of faded gentility and seediness. Even so, it has retained its popularity as a holiday destination, mainly due to stretches of clean, sandy beaches as well as a pier, built

earlier this century, which was recently renovated. There is no shortage of places to eat, including some good seafood restaurants. The imposing French Empire-style Kurhaus, now a luxury hotel with its own casino, was built in 1885 when Scheveningen was still an important spa town.

Modern amenities include the **Sea Life Centre**, nearby, where visitors can walk in see-through tunnels for under-water views of stingrays, sharks and other forms of sea life. It is also a sanctuary for all kinds of wounded marine creatures.

The town has swallowed up the original fishing village of Scheveningen Haven, which has still managed to maintain some of its traditional fishing industry. The south side of the harbour is the departure point for tourists' fishing trips.

Close by is the **MuZee Scheveningen**, which combines exhibits of marine life from around the world with displays on life in the village at the turn of the 20th century.

🏛 MuZee Scheveningen

Neptunusstraat 92. ***Tel*** *(070) 350 0830.* ⬜ *Tue–Fri & Sun.* ⬛ *1 Jan, 25 Dec.* www.museumscheveningen.nl

🍴 Sea Life Centre

Strandweg 13. ***Tel*** *(070) 354 2100.*
⬜ *daily.* ⬛ *25 Dec.* 🖼 ♿ 📷
🚻 www.sealife.nl

Holiday-makers on Scheveningen's popular sandy beach

Street-by-Street: Delft ⑰

19th-century Delft tile showing a church and barges

The origins of Delft date from 1075 and its prosperity was based on weaving and brewing. However, a massive explosion at the national arsenal destroyed much of the medieval town in October 1645. The centre was rebuilt in the late 17th century and the sleepy old town has changed little since then – gabled Gothic and Renaissance houses still line the tree-shaded canals. Activity centres on the market square, bordered by the landmarks of the Stadhuis and Nieuwe Kerk. Visitors can dip into the scores of shops selling antiques and expensive, hand-painted Delftware. Tours of local factories are available, and their shops are often reasonably priced.

★ Stedelijk Museum Het Prinsenhof
Here you can see bullet holes where William of Orange was murdered in 1584.

SCHOOLSTRAAT

ST AGATHA PLEIN

Volkenkundig Museum Nusantara

★ Oude Kerk
The 13th-century Oude Kerk contains tombs of eminent Delft citizens like Antonie van Leeuwenhoek, inventor of the microscope.

Oude Delft is lined with Renaissance canal houses.

HIPPOLYTUSBUURT

OUDE DELFT

NIEUWSTRAAT

BOTER BRUG

OUDE DELFT

Chapel of St Hippolytus
This simple, red-brick Gothic chapel (1396) was used as an ammunition store during the Alteration (see pp24–5).

PEPERSTR

0 metres	50
0 yards	50

STAR SIGHTS

★ Oude Kerk

★ Nieuwe Kerk

★ Stedelijk Museum Het Prinsenhof

KEY

- - - Suggested route

View of Delft (c.1660)
Jan Vermeer's painting captures the town of Delft on a gloomy summer afternoon. The original spire of the Nieuwe Kerk is clearly visible in the distance.

VISITORS' CHECKLIST

50 km (31 miles) SW of Amsterdam.
🏠 95,000. 🚉 Stationsplein. ℹ️
Hippolytusbuurt 4. (0900) 515 15
55. 🛒 Thu, Sat. 🎭 Chamber
Music Festival: 1st wk Aug; Jazz/
Blues Festival: mid-Aug; Delft
Dag: last Sat in Aug. **www**.delft.nl

The Waag
(1770) is now
a theatre.

Stadhuis (1618)
The Renaissance town hall was designed by Hendrick de Keyser and is adorned with stone lions' heads. It was built around a Gothic tower of the 13th-century.

★ **Nieuwe Kerk**
The church was built in erratic bursts over many years (see p194). Inside, this statue of Prince William of Orange reclines at the heart of his elaborate mausoleum.

Vleeshal (1650)
The façade of the old meat market is decorated with animal heads. After 1872 it was used as a corn exchange.

Exploring Delft

The charming town of Delft is known the world over for its blue-and-white pottery, but is equally famous as the resting place of William of Orange (1533–84), one of the most celebrated figures in Dutch history. He commanded the Dutch Revolt against Spanish rule from his headquarters in Delft, and his victory resulted in religious freedom and independence for the Dutch people *(see pp24–5)*. Delft was also the birthplace of artist Jan Vermeer (1632–75), whose talent was so underrated during his lifetime that he died in extreme poverty.

The imposing Renaissance pulpit (1548) of the Oude Kerk

🔒 Oude Kerk

Heilige Geestherkhof. *Tel (015) 212 3015.* ⬜ *9am–6pm Mon–Sat (Nov–Mar: 11am–4pm).* 🏷️ ♿
www.oudekerk-delft.nl

Although a church has existed on this site since the 13th century, the original building has been added to many times. The ornate, but leaning, clock tower was built in the 14th century, and the flamboyant Gothic north transept was added by Belgian architect Anthonis Keldermans in the early 16th century. The interior is dominated by the carved wooden pulpit with overhanging canopy. The floor is paved with 17th-century tomb slabs. The simple stone tablet at the east end of the north aisle marks the burial place of Jan Vermeer. In the north transept lies Admiral Maarten Tromp (1598–1653), who routed the English fleet in 1652. Admiral Piet Heyn (1577–1629), who captured the Spanish silver fleet in 1628, is in the chancel.

🔒 Nieuwe Kerk

Markt. *Tel (015) 212 3025.* ⬜ *9am–6pm Mon–Sat (Nov–Mar: 11am–4pm).* 🏷️ **www**.nieuwekerk-delft.nl

The Nieuwe Kerk was built between 1383 and 1510, but much of the original structure was restored following a fire in 1536 and an explosion at the national arsenal in 1645. Work on the church continued for many years, and it was not until 1872 that PJH Cuypers *(see pp32–3)* added the statuesque 100 m (320 ft) tower to the Gothic façade.

The burial vaults of the Dutch royal family are in the crypt of this empty, cavernous church, but the most prominent feature of the interior is the stately mausoleum of William of Orange. Set in the vast arched choir, the richly decorated tomb was designed by Hendrick de Keyser *(see p90)* in 1614 and is carved from black and white marble, with heavy gilded detailing. At its heart is a sculpture of William, resplendent in his battle dress, and at each corner stand bronze figures representing the Virtues. Close to William is the forlorn figure of his dog, who died days after him, and at the foot of the tomb is a trumpeting angel – symbol of Fame.

The Nieuwe Kerk in Delft's market square

DELFTWARE

The blue-and-white tin-glazed pottery, known as Delftware, was developed from majolica and introduced to the Netherlands by immigrant Italian potters in the 16th century. Settling around Delft and Haarlem, the potters made wall tiles, adopting Dutch motifs such as animals and flowers as decoration. Trade with the east brought samples of delicate Chinese porcelain to the Netherlands, and the market for coarser Dutch majolica crashed. By 1650, local potters had adopted the Chinese model and designed fine plates, vases and bowls decorated with Dutch landscapes, and biblical and genre scenes. In 1652, De Porceleyne Fles was one of 32 thriving potteries in Delft. Today, it is one of two Delftware factories still in production, and is open for guided tours (www.royaldelft.com).

Hand-painted 17th-century Delft tiles

🏛 Koninklijk Nederlands Legermuseum

Korte Geer 1. **Tel** (015) 215 0500. ☐ 10am–5pm Mon–Fri, noon–5pm Sat–Sun. ● 1 Jan, 25 Dec. ☐ ☐ www.legermuseum.nl

This army museum is housed in the Armamentarium, formerly the arsenal of the old provinces of West Friesland and Holland. Built in 1692, it is still full of weaponry, also military uniforms, battle models and armoured vehicles.

Coat of arms on façade of the Legermuseum

These exhibits trace developments in Dutch military history since the Middle Ages up to the present peace-keeping role of the Netherlands in the service of the United Nations.

🏛 Stedelijk Museum Het Prinsenhof

St Agathaplein 1. **Tel** (015) 260 2358. ☐ 10am–5pm Tue–Sat, 1–5pm Sun. ● 1 Jan, 25 Dec. 🎫 www.prinsenhof-delft.nl

This tranquil Gothic building, formerly a convent, now houses Delft's historical museum but is better known as the place where William of Orange was assassinated. He requisitioned the convent in 1572 for his headquarters during the Dutch Revolt. In 1584, by order of Philip II of Spain (see pp24–5), William was shot by Balthasar Geraerts. The bullet holes in the main staircase wall can still be seen.

The museum houses a rare collection of antique Delftware, displayed alongside tapestries, silverware, medieval sculpture and a series of portraits of the Dutch royal family.

🏛 Volkenkundig Museum Nusantara

St Agathaplein 4. **Tel** (015) 260 2358. ☐ 10am–5pm Tue–Sat, 1pm–5pm Sun. ● 1 Jan, 25 Dec. 🎫 ☐ www.nusantara-delft.nl

When William of Orange took over the Prinsenhof in 1572, the nuns moved into one of its wings across the square. This is now the home of the Nusantara ethnological museum. It is small, but has a wonderful collection of masks, carvings, textiles, jewellery and musical instruments brought back from Indonesia by traders working for the Dutch East India Company (see pp28–9). The shop sells unusual modern Indonesian crafts.

🏛 Museum Lambert van Meerten

Oude Delft 199. **Tel** (015) 260 2358. ☐ 10am–5pm Tue–Sat, 1pm–5pm Sun. ● 1 Jan, 25 Dec. 🎫 www.lambertvanmeerten-delft.nl

This small museum is located in an elegantly furnished 19th-century mansion, with paintings and architectural details recently salvaged from local 17th- and 18th-century buildings. Its main attraction is the antique hand-painted Delftware tiles and tile pictures.

Fine gabled façades along Binnenwaterslot in the centre of Delft

St Janskerk, Gouda

The original Catholic church of 1485 was rebuilt in Gothic style after it was razed by fire in 1552. Between 1555 and 1571, a series of remarkable stained-glass windows were donated to the church by wealthy Catholic benefactors such as Philip II of Spain. After the Alteration *(see pp24–5)* the church became Protestant, but even the iconoclasts could not bring themselves to destroy the windows – in fact Protestant patrons, such as the aldermen of Rotterdam, continued to donate windows until 1603. Depicting contemporary figures and events, the stained glass is rich in political symbolism, using biblical stories to make coded reference to the conflict between Catholic and Protestant, and Dutch and Spanish that led to the Dutch Revolt in 1572.

Donor's coat of arms (1601)

The Nave
At 123 m (403 ft), the nave is the longest in the Netherlands. Memorial slabs cover the floor.

The Adulterous Woman *(1601)*
Dressed as a Franciscan monk, Jesus begs the people in the temple to forgive the adulterous wife, who is heavily guarded by Spanish soldiers.

Baptism of Christ

North aisle

Visitors' entrance

Purification of the Temple

South aisle

Judith Slays Holofernes
This detail is taken from a window which portrays the biblical story of the slaying of Holofernes by Judith. The glazier, Dirck Crabeth, shows John the Baptist holding a lamb. Next to him is the kneeling figure of Jean de Ligne, Count of Aremberg, who commissioned the window.

The Relief of Leiden *(1603)*
William of Orange is pictured here directing Leiden's heroic resistance to the Spanish siege of 1574 (see p184).

VISITORS' CHECKLIST

Achter de Kerk 16. **Tel** (0182) 512
684. ☐ 9am–5pm Mon–Sat
(Nov–Feb: 10–4pm; pub hols
1–5pm). ● 1 Jan, 25 & 26 Dec.
🚹 🖼 ♿ **www**.sintjan.com

Purification of the Temple
*The window was donated by
William of Orange (see p24)
in 1567. The detail shows
dismayed traders watching
Jesus drive the moneylenders
from the temple. It represents
the Dutch desire to expel the
Spanish from their country.*

Baptism of Christ *(1555)
John the Baptist is shown
baptizing Christ in the river
Jordan. The window was donated by the Bishop of Utrecht.*

View over Gouda with St Janskerk in the background

Gouda ⑱

50 km (33 miles) S of Amsterdam.
🚶 72,000. 🚉 🚹 Markt 27. (0900)
468 3288. 🧀 cheese market: mid-
Jun–Aug: 10am–12.30pm Thu;
general market: Thu & Sat; antiques:
May–Sep, Wed. **www**.vvvgouda.nl

Gouda received its charter
from Count Floris V *(see p21)*
in 1272. Situated at the
confluence of two rivers, the
town became the centre of a
successful brewing industry in
the 15th century. The growth
of the cheese trade during the
17th century brought more
prosperity. Today, the name
of Gouda is synonymous with
its famous full-bodied cheese.
There is a cheese market in
summer, and the twice-weekly
general market offers local
cheeses and crafts. There is
also a Candle Festival the
second or third Tuesday in
December. All these markets
take place in the huge square
around the Stadhuis which,
dating from 1450, is one of the
oldest town halls in the Netherlands. The building bristles
with pinnacles and miniature
spires in Flemish Gothic style.
The elaborate façade includes
statues of Gouda's former
rulers. The principal attraction
of the town is the stained-
glass windows in St Janskerk.

🏛 Stedelijk Museum Het
Catharina Gasthuis
Oosthaven 9 (entrance Achter
de Kerk 14). **Tel** (0182) 331 000.
☐ 11am–5pm Tue–Sat. ● 1 Jan,
25 Dec. 🖼 **www**.museumgouda.nl
An arched gatehouse (1609)
leads into the leafy courtyard
of this delightful museum.
The Catharina Gasthuis was
built in the 14th century as
a hospice for travellers, later
becoming an almshouse for
the elderly. Converted into
a museum in 1910, it has a
series of Civic Guard portraits
and landscapes by Dutch
Impressionists.

🏛 Stedelijk Museum De
Moriaan/The Blackamoor
Westhaven 29. **Tel** (0182) 331 000.
☐ 11am–5pm Tue–Sat. ● 1 Jan,
25 Dec. 🖼 **www**.museumgouda.nl
This little tobacco museum
was once a sugar refinery
and later a coffee and tobacco
shop. Behind the 1617 façade
it is packed with tobacco jars
and traditional clay pipes with
long stems and tiny bowls.

**Gatehouse of the Stedelijk
Museum Het Catharina Gasthuis**

Rotterdam ⑲

Rotterdam occupies a strategic position where the Rijn (Rhine), Europe's most important river, meets the North Sea. Barges from Rotterdam transport goods deep into the continent, and ocean-going ships carry European exports around the world. This made Rotterdam a prime target for aerial bombardment during World War II, and the city's ancient heart was destroyed. Much of the city has been rebuilt in experimental styles, resulting in some of Europe's most original and innovative architecture. The Europoort is now the world's largest container port, stretching for 37 km (23 miles) along the river banks.

Cabin on the warship De Buffel

🏛 **Maritiem Museum Rotterdam**
Leuvehaven 1. *Tel* (010) 413 2680.
☐ 10am– 5pm Tue–Sat, 11–5pm Sun & public hols; Jul & Aug: also Mon.
🔲 1 Jan, 30 Apr, 25 Dec. 🔲 🔲 🔲
🔲 🔲 www.maritiemmuseum.nl
Prince Hendrik, brother of King William III *(see pp32–3)*, founded this museum in 1873. Its main highlight is an iron-clad warship called *De Buffel*, built in 1868. It boasts an opulent officers' quarters, which have the atmosphere of a gentleman's club. Other exhibits include a small fleet of barges and steamships.

🏛 **Historisch Museum Rotterdam**
Korte Hoogstraat 31. *Tel* (010) 217 6767. ☐ 10am–5pm Tue–Fri; 11am–5pm Sat, Sun & public hols.
🔲 1 Jan, 30 Apr, 25 Dec. 🔲 🔲 🔲
www.hmr.rotterdam.nl
Rotterdam's historical museum is in the Schielandshuis, a town house built in 1665 by Jacob Lois. The museum charts the development of the city, and the urbane lifestyles of its people, through displays of paintings, silverware and furniture in elegant rooms.

Oudehaven, with the futuristic Kubuswoningen houses in the background

Exploring Rotterdam

Much of Oudehaven, the old harbour area of Rotterdam, was destroyed in bombing raids during World War II. It has largely been rebuilt in daring and avant-garde styles. The pencil-shaped **Gemeente-bibliotheek** (public library) is similar to the Pompidou Centre in Paris: its yellow ventilation ducts and service piping are on the exterior of the building.

Piet Blom's **Kubuswoningen** (cube houses) of 1982 are extraordinary apartments, set on concrete stilts and tilted at a crazy angle. Residents have specially designed furniture to fit the sloping rooms. Pavement cafés have sprung up along the harbour quay-side, and apartment blocks

with undercover shopping arcades have now replaced the old wooden warehouses.

In the Golden Age, maritime trade brought wealth to Dutch towns with access to the sea. Delft *(see pp192–5)* lacked a harbour, so its citizens built a 12-km (7.5-mile) canal from the town to the Nieuwe Maas river, and constructed **Delfs-haven** – a purpose-built village complete with harbour. This has long been swallowed up by Rotterdam, but remains a pretty corner of the city, with 18th-century warehouses converted into apartments, galleries, restaurants and cafés.

🏛 **Museum Boijmans-van Beuningen**
See pp200–201.

Peaceful canal houses in a quiet corner of Delfshaven

🏛 Historisch Museum de Dubbelde Palmboom

Voorhaven 12. **Tel** *(010) 476 1533.*
⏱ *10am–5pm Tue–Fri; 11am–5pm Sat, Sun & public hols.* ⬤ *1 Jan, 30 Apr, 25 Dec.* 📷 ♿ 🍴 🛍
www.hmr.rotterdam.nl

The museum "of the double palm tree" is in a twin-gabled, wooden warehouse dating to 1825. Its five storeys are open-plan with vast, beamed rooms. These display arts and crafts, photographs and scale models depicting life at the mouth of the Nieuwe Maas river, from Iron Age fishing settlements to today's industrial port.

🏛 Wereldmuseum Rotterdam

Willemskade 25. **Tel** *(010) 270 7172.*
⏱ *10am–5pm Tue–Sun.* ⬤ *1 Jan, 30 Apr, 5 & 25 Dec.* 📷 ♿ 🍴 🛍
www.wereldmuseum.rotterdam.nl

During the 17th century, the city fathers amassed a superb ethnological collection. It is now in a museum, built in 1851, which uses audiovisual displays of theatre, film, dance and music. Permanent collections include Indonesian musical instruments, ancient folk art, masks and carvings.

Euromast against the skyline

📡 Euromast

Parkhaven 20. **Tel** *(010) 436 4811.*
⏱ *Apr–Sep: 9:30am–11pm daily; Oct–Mar: 10am–11pm daily.*
📷 ♿ 🍴 🛍 **www**.euromast.nl

Visitors ride a high-speed lift up the first 100 m (328 ft) of the Euromast to enjoy sweeping views of Rotterdam. This lower section, built in 1960, has a viewing platform with a restaurant and exhibition area.

VISITORS' CHECKLIST

65 km (40 miles) SW of Amsterdam. 🏠 600,000. 🚉 *Stationsplein.* ✈ *6 km (4 miles) NW.* 🛈 *Coolsingel 5. 0900 403 4065.* 🚢 *Tue, Fri, Sat.* 🎭 *Rotterdam Film Festival: end Jan–begin Feb; North Sea Jazz Festival: 2nd weekend of Jul.* **www**.rotterdam.info

In 1970 the Space Tower added another 85 m (272 ft) to make this the tallest construction in the Netherlands. A "space cabin" attached to the outside ascends 58 m (190 ft) up from the viewing platform.

Spido

Havenrondvaarten Willemsplein 85.
Tel *(010) 275 9988.* **Europoort** ⏱ *daily.* 🚢 *See Getting to Amsterdam By Ferry p268.* **Boat tours** ⏱ *Apr–Oct: daily.* 📷 **www**.spido.nl

The wharves and quays of the city's port service about 32,000 container ships a year. A boat tour is an ideal way of seeing the port, built between 1958 and 1975. Cyclists and motorists follow the 48-km (30-mile) Haven Route (harbour route) along the Nieuwe Maas.

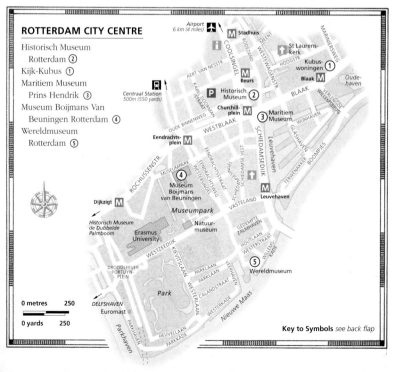

ROTTERDAM CITY CENTRE

Historisch Museum Rotterdam ②
Kijk-Kubus ①
Maritiem Museum Prins Hendrik ③
Museum Boijmans Van Beuningen Rotterdam ④
Wereldmuseum Rotterdam ⑤

0 metres 250
0 yards 250

Key to Symbols *see back flap*

Museum Boijmans Van Beuningen Rotterdam

The museum is named after two art connoisseurs, FJO Boijmans, who bequeathed his paintings to Rotterdam in 1847, and DG van Beuningen, who donated works between 1916 and 1954. The resulting collection is one of The Netherlands' finest. First displayed in the nearby Schielandshuis, the collection was moved to the present gallery in 1935. Known mainly for its supreme series of Old Master paintings, the collection also covers the whole spectrum of art, from the medieval works of Jan van Eyck to rare glassware and Surrealist paintings.

★ **The Pedlar** (c.1502)
Hieronymus Bosch's painting shows mankind travelling through life with sin trying to trap him at every turn.

Three Marys at the Open Sepulchre (1430)
Brothers Jan and Hubert van Eyck collaborated on this colourful work, which shows the three Marys at the tomb of the resurrected Christ.

Nautilus Cup (1590)
A beautiful example of Dutch Renaissance art, this cup contains ornamental motifs relating to the sea and is crowned with Neptune sitting on a dolphin.

First floor

STAR PAINTINGS

★ The Tower of Babel by Pieter Bruegel

★ The Pedlar by Hieronymus Bosch

★ Titus at his Desk by Rembrandt

La Méditerranée (1905)
Aristide Maillol's bronze was presented to the museum in 1961. He often used the female nude as a medium to express his philosophy of form.

MUSEUM GUIDE

The museum is vast and can be confusing, especially since the displays change regularly. Signposting to the museum's main sections is clear and attendants are adept at directing visitors. For Brueghel and Rembrandt follow signs to the Old Masters Collection, and for Dali and Magritte look for the Modern Art section.

★ **The Tower of Babel** *(c.1553)*
Pieter Bruegel took his theme from the Old Testament, and showed the elaborate ten-storey edifice teeming with frenetic activity.

VISITORS' CHECKLIST

Museumpark 18–20, Rotterdam.
Tel *(010) 441 9400.* 🚆 *Centraal Station.* 🕙 *11am–5pm Tue–Sun.* 🔴 *1 Jan, 30 Apr, 25 Dec.* 🅿 ⚬ ⚬ 🍴 ⚬
www.boijmans.rotterdam.nl

KEY TO FLOORPLAN

- ☐ Old Masters
- ☐ Art: 1750–1930
- ☐ Modern Art
- ☐ Print Gallery
- ☐ Surrealists
- ☐ Applied Art
- ☐ Temporary Exhibition space
- ☐ Non-exhibition space

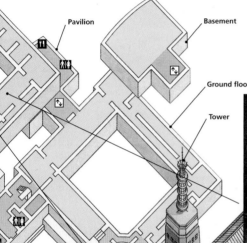

Pavilion

Basement

Ground floor

Tower

Courtyard

Main entrance

Entrances to courtyard

★ **Titus at his Desk** *(1655)*
Rembrandt portrayed his sickly son in introspective mood, bathed in a tender light which heightens the ghostly pallor of his brooding features.

Thetis Receives Achilles' Armour from Vulcanus
(1630–32)
This oil sketch by Peter Paul Rubens is one of a series inspired by Achilles' life.

Utrecht ⑳

Utrecht was founded by the Romans in AD 47 to protect an important river crossing on the Rijn (Rhine). The town was among the first in the Netherlands to embrace Christianity. In 700, St Willibrord (658–739), a missionary from northern England, established a bishopric here, known as Het Sticht. Utrecht grew in importance as a religious centre throughout the Middle Ages, extending its control over much of the Netherlands until 1527, when Bishop Hendrik of Bavaria was obliged to sell all his temporal powers to Charles V (see pp24–5). The city centre still retains many of its medieval churches and monasteries, but these now stand alongside modern blocks and a vast undercover shopping complex. The Oudegracht (old canal) threads its way through the city, flowing 5 m (16.5 ft) below ground level to prevent flooding. Today, it is lined with broad quays, cellar bars and cafés.

a superb railway museum. The Spoorwegmuseum is in the restored 19th-century Malie-baan station. Inside there are specialist technical displays, engines and modern rail accessories. Outside, children can explore steam engines, carriages, trams and signal boxes.

The newly renovated museum includes five new railway "worlds", each with its own theme.

Organ in the Speelklok museum

🎠 Domtoren

Via 'Rondom', Domplein 9. **Tel** (030) 233 3036. 🎫 every hour. Apr–Oct: 11am–5pm daily (from noon Mon,

The Gothic Domtoren

Sun; from 10am Sat); Nov–Mar: noon, 2pm & 4pm Mon–Fri; 10am–4pm Sat; noon–4pm Sun. 🚫 1 Jan, 25 Dec. 📷

The soaring Domtoren is a Gothic masterpiece and one of the tallest towers in the Netherlands at 112 m (367 ft) high. It was completed in 1382, on the site of the small, 8th-century church of St Willibrord. In 1674, the tower, which has always stood apart from the Domkerk, survived a massive hurricane that destroyed the nave of the cathedral. The Domtoren continues to dominate Utrecht's skyline.

⛪ Domkerk

Achter den Dom 1. **Tel** (030) 231 0403 🕐 daily; phone for times. ♿ 📷 🌐 www.domkerk.nl

Construction of the cathedral began in 1254. Today, only the north and south transepts, two chapels and the choir remain, along with the 15th-century cloisters and a chapter house (1495), now part of the university. It was here that the Union of Utrecht (see p25) was signed in 1579 by John, Count of Nassau, brother of William of Orange. Outside the church is a giant boulder, dated 980 and covered with runic symbols. It was presented to Utrecht by the Danish people in 1936, to commemorate Denmark's early conversion to Christianity by missionaries from Utrecht.

🏛 Nederlands Spoorwegmuseum

Maliebaanstation. **Tel** (030) 2306 206. 🕐 Tue–Sun. 🚫 pub hols. 📷 ♿ 🍴 🌐 www.spoorwegmuseum.nl

The headquarters of the Dutch railways are based in Utrecht, so it is fitting that the town has

🏛 Nationaal Museum van Speelklok tot Pierement

Buurkerk on Steenweg 6. **Tel** (030) 2312 789. 🕐 10am–5pm Tue–Sun. 🚫 1 Jan, 30 Apr, 25 Dec. 📷 📷 ♿ 📷 🌐 www.museumspeelklok.nl

This magical place – literally "from musical clock to street organ" – is located in the 13th-century Buurkerk, Utrecht's oldest church. It has a collection of mechanical musical instruments from the 18th century to the present day. Fairground organs compete with clocks, carillons, pianolas and automated birds. These instruments are demonstrated on guided tours, during which visitors are encouraged to sing and dance along.

🏛 Centraal Museum

Nicolaaskerkhof 10. **Tel** (030) 2362 362. 🕐 noon–5pm Tue–Sun (to 9pm Fri). 🚫 1 Jan, 30 Apr, 25 Dec. 📷 📷 📷 🌐 www.centraalmuseum.nl

Housed in an old convent, Centraal Museum is only a ten-minute walk from the city centre. At the heart of the collection is a series of portraits by artist

Steam engine and guard's box, Nederlands Spoorwegmuseum

Gerrit Rietveld's Schröderhuis (1924), part of the Centraal Museum

Jan van Scorel (1495–1562). On visiting Rome, van Scorel absorbed ideas from Italian Renaissance painting and he became the first Dutch artist to paint group portraits. These established the tradition leading to the superb 16th-century Civic Guard portraits *(see p81)*.

Another of the museum's highlights is Gerrit Rietveld's Schröderhuis, Prins Hendriklaan 50. Designed in 1924 and regarded as the apogee of De Stijl architecture *(see p136)* (tours by appointment).

There is also a display of Dutch interior design from the Middle Ages to the 18th century.

Pieterskerk

Pieterskerkhof. *Tel* (030) 2311 485. 11am–3pm 1st & 3rd Sat (Jul–mid-Sep: 11am–4:30pm Tue–Sat). Built of tufa (limestone) with red sandstone columns, the church was completed in 1048. A rare Dutch example of German Romanesque architecture.

Museum Catharijneconvent

Lange Nieuwstraat 38. *Tel* (030) 231 3835. 10am–5pm Tue–Sun (from 11am Sat, Sun & pub hols). www.catharijneconvent.nl The beautiful former convent of St Catherine (1562) is now home to this fascinating

museum. Recently revamped, it deals with the troubled history of religion in the Netherlands and owns an award-winning collection of medieval art. Sculptures, gold and silver work, manuscripts, paintings and jewel-encrusted miniatures are displayed in rooms round the cloister. On the upper floors is a series of model

Sculpture in Catharijneconvent

church interiors, highlighting the variety of Dutch religious philosophies through the ages. They range from the lavish statues, paintings and altar in a Catholic church to the plain interiors typical of Protestant churches.

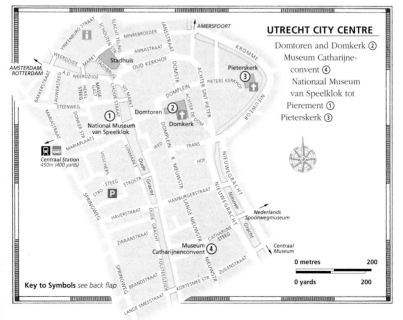

UTRECHT CITY CENTRE

Key to Symbols see back flap

Het Nationale Park De Hoge Veluwe ㉑

Made up of more than 5,500 ha (13,750 acres) of woodland, fen, heath and sand drifts, the Netherlands' largest nature reserve is home to thousands of rare plants, wild animals and birds. In order to preserve the natural habitat, cars are banned from large sections of the reserve. Also located in the park are the Museum Kröller-Müller, with 278 paintings by Van Gogh, and an outdoor sculpture garden, the Beeldentuin. Beneath the Visitors' Centre is the Museonder, with audiovisual displays about the earth's sub-surface, including an earthquake simulator.

Jachthuis St Hubertus
This hunting lodge was built in 1920 by HP Berlage (see p79) for the park's wealthy patrons, the Kröller-Müllers.

★ Museum Kröller-Müller
Besides Van Gogh's Café Terrace at Night *(1881), the museum has a collection of early Flemish masters and works by modern artists.*

★ Beeldentuin
Jean Dubuffet's Jardin d'Emaille, *shown here, is one of the striking modern sculpures on display in this 11-ha (27-acre) sculpture park. The Beeldentuin also provides an elemental setting for works by Auguste Rodin, Alberto Giacometti and Barbara Hepworth.*

OTTERLOSE ZAND

De Wetweg

Otterlo entrance

Houtkampweg

Moufflon

Kronkelweg

Visitors' Centre and Museonder

Nieuwe Plijmen game observation post

FRA... BE...

PLIJMEN

Roe Deer

OUD-REEMSTER ZAND

Wild Boar

Wildbaan...

Bosje van Staf game observation post

Reemsterweg

OUD-REEMST... VELD

Picnicking
Tables are provided near the Visitors' Centre. Picnicking is allowed everywhere except in areas set aside for the animals.

OUD-REEMST

Roe Deer

Free White Bicycles
At the Visitors' Centre bikes are available for exploring the park.

Camp site

Hoenderloo entrance

Roe Deer

Houtkampweg

De Klep game hide

Red Deer

DEELENSE WAS

LENSE ELD

Schaarsbergen entrance

RBERG

Game Hides and Observation Points
Special viewing areas (see map) allow the wildlife, like red deer, moufflon sheep and wild boar, to remain undisturbed.

VISITORS' CHECKLIST

80 km (50 miles) SE of Amsterdam. 108S from Apeldoorn, 108S or 110 from Ede-Wageningen. **Entrances** Otterlo, Schaarsbergen, Hoenderloo. **Nationale Park Visitors' Centre** Otterlo. **Tel** (0900) 464 3835. ☐ Apr: 8am–8pm; May, Aug: 8–9; Jun, Jul: 8–10; Sep: 9–8; Oct: 9–7; Nov–Mar: 9–6 (last adm: 1 hr before closing). **Regulations**: Do not camp, or disturb the animals. Vehicles must not leave the road. Do not light fires outside designated areas. Keep dogs on a leash. **Museum Kröller-Müller** Houtkampweg 6, Otterlo. **Tel** (0318) 591 241. ☐ 10am–5pm Tue–Sun & pub hols. ● 1 Jan. **www.** hogeveluwe.nl; **www**.kmm.nl

KEY

▬▬ Main road

●●● Walk route

┉ Cycle path

☐ Forest

☐ Heath

☐ Sand drifts

▨ No access

0 kilometres ▬▬▬▬ 2

0 miles ▬▬▬ 1

STAR SIGHTS

★ Museum Kröller-Müller

★ Beeldentuin

Arnhem ㉒

80 km (50 miles) SE of Amsterdam. 141,000. 🚊 🚌 ⓘ Velperbuiten-Singel 25. 0900 202 4075. ▦ 🍴 👪 🎪 🏠 Sat. **www**.vvvarnhem.nl

Capital of Gelderland province, Arnhem was all but destroyed between 17 and 27 September 1944, in one of the most famous battles of World War II. The city still retains a number of reminders of the conflict, such as the John Frost Bridge, scene of some of the heaviest fighting. The bridge is named after the commanding officer of the 2nd Parachute Battalion, which fought to hold the bridgehead for four days.

🏛 Airborne Museum

Utrechtseweg 232, Oosterbeek. **Tel** (026) 3337 710. ☐ 10am–5pm Mon–Sat, noon–5pm Sun (1 Nov–1 Apr: from 11am Mon–Sat). ● 1 Jan, 25 Dec. **www**.airbornemuseum.com
The museum traces the course of the struggle to take Arnhem, using models, slides, and taped commentaries. The collection is in a villa near Oosterbeek, used by the Commander of the 1st British Airborne Division, General Urquhart.

John Frost Bridge, Arnhem

🏛 Nederlands Openluchtmuseum

Schelmseweg 89. **Tel** (026) 357 6100. ☐ 10am–5pm daily (Dec–mid-Jan: noon–8pm; mid-Jan–Mar: 11am–4:30pm). ● 1 Jan, 24 Dec, Nov. 🚻 **www**.openluchtmuseum.nl
Situated in a wooded park, the Nederlands Openluchtmuseum recreates the traditional architecture and folklore of the Netherlands from 1800 to 1950. Founded in 1912, about 100 farmhouses, barns, windmills and workshops have since been erected here, many of them furnished in period style. The museum staff dress up in traditional costume.

Paleis Het Loo 🕗

Stadholder William III *(see p30)* built Het Loo in 1686 as a royal hunting lodge. Generations of the House of Orange used the lodge as a summer palace. Because of its magnificence, it was regarded as the "Versailles of the Netherlands". The main architect was Jacob Roman (1640–1716); the interior decoration and layout of the gardens were the responsibility of Daniel Marot (1661–1752). The building's Classical façade belies the opulence of its lavish interior; after extensive restoration work was completed on both in 1984, the palace was opened as a museum.

Coat of arms (1690) of William and Mary, future king and queen of England.

★ **Royal Bedroom of Stadholder William III** *(1713)*
Recently refurbished, the wall coverings and draperies in this luxurious bedroom are of rich orange damask and purple silk.

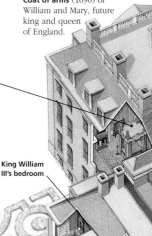

King William III's bedroom

King's Garden

Stadholder William III's Closet *(1690)*
The walls of William's private study are covered in embossed scarlet damask. His favourite paintings and Delftware pieces are exhibited here.

Classic Cars
This 1925 Bentley, nicknamed Minerva, was owned by Prince Hendrik, husband of Queen Wilhelmina. It is one of the royal family's many vintage cars, which are on display in the stable block (1910).

STAR FEATURES

★ Old Dining Room

★ Royal Bedroom

★ Formal Gardens

VISITORS' CHECKLIST

85 km (53 miles) SE of Amsterdam.
Koninklijk Park 1, Apeldoorn. **Tel**
(055) 577 2400. 🚉 *Apeldoorn,*
then bus 102, 104. **Palace & Gar-**
dens ⬭ *10am–5pm Tue–Sun.*
⬤ *1 Jan.* 📷 ⬤ *gardens only.*
♿ ⬭ 🍽 **www.paleishetloo.nl**

★ Old Dining Room *(1686)*
*In 1984, six layers of paint were
removed from the marbled walls,
now hung with tapestries depicting scenes from Ovid's poems.*

Queen's Garden

Picture gallery

Library

**The East
Wing** now
contains the
original plans
for the formal
gardens.

**Bedroom of
Queen Mary II**

Main entrance

★ Formal Gardens
*The gardens combine plants,
statuary and fountains in
Classical style. The Fountain
of the Celestial Sphere stands
in the Lower Garden.*

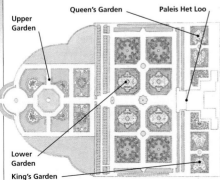

Upper
Garden

Queen's Garden   Paleis Het Loo

Lower
Garden

King's Garden

THE FORMAL GARDENS

Old prints, records and plans were
used as the guidelines for recreating Het
Loo's formal gardens, which lie in the
vast acres behind the palace. Grass was
planted over the original walled and knot
gardens in the 18th century, and this
was cleared in 1975. By 1983, the intricate
floral patterns had been re-established,
replanting had begun, the Classical
fountains were renovated and the water
supply fully restored. The garden reflects
the late 17th-century belief that art and
nature should operate in harmony.

Layout of the formal section of the gardens

TRAVELLERS' NEEDS

WHERE TO STAY

Amsterdam provides top-quality, city-centre accommodation to suit everyone's budget. It ranges from a clutch of luxurious five-star hotels that should impress the most hedonistic traveller to the many cheap hostels for those on a budget. In between there are scores of B&Bs, many occupying pretty gabled houses, often with a canal view. Accommodation can even be found on the water, in the form of canal-boat hotels. We have included dozens of hotels in all price ranges, selecting those which are particularly friendly, comfortable, interesting or good value. They are described in the listings on pages 216–23.

The Van Ostade Bicycle Hotel in southern Amsterdam *(see p223)*

CHOOSING A HOTEL

Most of Amsterdam's hotels are clustered in a few areas: the most popular place to stay, unsurprisingly, is along the scenic canals; the neighbourhood near the museums and Vondelpark is also popular. More suited to the budget traveller is the area around Centraal Station and the Red Light District, where you will find one or two gems studded amongst the general seediness.

Visitors often find accommodation in Amsterdam expensive, while at the same time rooms can be smaller than in other European cities. Hotels which are most beautiful and most typical of Amsterdam are found along the main canal belt, the *Grachtengordel*. Many of these buildings are listed monuments and thus cannot be altered, so you will often come across very steep stairs and no lifts.

Hotels in the Museum Quarter tend to be a little more spacious and are often in elegant villas. This sedate area is away from the bright lights, but near many of Amsterdam's cultural hotspots like the Rijksmuseum and the Concertgebouw.

Hotels which are aimed squarely at the business market are mostly clustered around the RAI exhibition centre in the south, and near the office blocks of Nieuw Zuid (New South).

Arena Hotel *(see p223)*

Wherever a hotel is situated in Amsterdam, however, seems to have little effect on price, so the cost of a hotel in a suburb will differ little from that of one in the same class in the very centre.

The **Amsterdam Tourist Board (VVV)** publishes a comprehensive list of accommodation in the city, available at Schiphol Airport and VVV offices, as well as

NBTC (Netherlands Board of Tourism and Conventions) offices around the world.

ROOM RATES

There are no hard and fast rules as to whether a hotel's advertised rates always include breakfast and the compulsory 5 per cent City Tax, though the price guide we include in the listings on pages 216–23 does factor all of this in. Generally, breakfast tends to be included, apart from at those hotels at the very top and bottom ends of the price scale.

If you are staying in *Grachtengordel*, be aware that rooms with canal views generally cost more, whatever class of hotel you are staying

Hotel de l'Europe, overlooking Muntplein *(see p216)*

◁ **People relaxing on the terrace of De Jaren café, in Nieuwe Zijde**

An airy breakfast room in an Amsterdam hotel

in, and hotels are increasingly starting to specify that weekend stays must be for a minimum of three nights.

There are a couple of tips that budget-conscious travellers should bear in mind. Firstly, if you are travelling in a group, many hotels have larger rooms for sharing, or will add beds for a fraction of the room price. Secondly, cheaper accommodation is available in budget hotels for those prepared to share sanitation. Lone travellers generally get a bad deal; the maximum reduction on single occupation of a double room is around 20 per cent – if there is any reduction at all, that is. The best option for visitors on their own is to make use of one of the many hostels. Some can be particularly quirky and charming – especially those located in canal boats along the picturesque waterways.

SPECIAL OFFERS

Many hotels – especially private ones – have lower rates between November and March, although they tend to peak again around Christmas and New Year. Some even throw in a complimentary boat trip and/or free museum admissions. When booking, it is always worthwhile making a point of asking about any special offers that might be available when you visit.

Chain hotels, of which there are many, almost always have promotions on, so if you shop around, it is unlikely that you will have to pay the standard rate. You will also find that many chains are aimed at businesses, so weekend rates are often substantially cheaper than weekday prices – **NH Hoteles** and **Best Western** are two of the best in Amsterdam. For good deals in all classes of hotels, whether chain or private, it is worth checking a reputable reservations website like www.hotels.nl or www.bookings.nl.

BOOKING AND PAYING

The busiest times of year for Amsterdam hotels are April to May (as it is tulip season), July and August and the Christmas and New Year period. If you want to visit during these times, it is worth bearing in mind, therefore, that it is often difficult to book a room last minute at any time of the year, and planning ahead – especially if you intend on staying in a *Grachtengordel* or canalside hotel – is recommended.

Booking a room via telephone, website or email is invariably straightforward, as hotel staff all speak excellent English. All the chains take credit card payments, as do an increasing number of privately-owned hotels. Many smaller establishments will ask for a deposit in the form of a cheque or postal order, usually for the full amount of the first night's stay, while some of these smaller and/or cheaper hotels are also able to secure room bookings on credit cards. There is, however, no guarantee that the final bill can be settled with a card – often, a cash payment will be necessary when checking out.

The **NRC (Netherlands Reservation Centre)** will book a room for you free of charge if you are already in the Netherlands, but it will charge a substantial fee should you reserve before you arrive in the country.

If you arrive in Amsterdam without a room already reserved, then the VVV (tourist board) at Schiphol Airport, Centraal Station (two branches) or Leidseplein will book one for you, but this service will incur a small fee.

HOTEL GRADINGS

The star system used by Benelux Hotel Classification ranges from one (may have shared sanitation facilities) to five stars (rooms must be of a minimum size and the hotel have plenty of amenities). These stars relate entirely to facilities and not to location or attractiveness, therefore you may find that a small, cheap hotel on a canal is more charming than a bland, corporate one in the suburbs, but that the more "appealing" of the two will have fewer stars.

The elegant foyer of the Inter-Continental Amstel *(see p223)*

Dining room of the Canal House in the Western Canal Ring *(see p218)*

WHAT TO EXPECT

The only hotels which have restaurants are the larger chains or very expensive hotels, the former are generally middle-of-the-road, the latter among the best in town. On the other hand, quite a few hotels – even the smallest – have bars. The rest provide just bed and breakfast, though bigger places may also have communal lounge areas.

Breakfast itself is a filling buffet which will always include rolls, jam, cheese and meats, a boiled egg and coffee. Only the most expensive hotels will provide hot dishes.

Make sure you get a description of the room when you book, or you may find you do not have that canal vista you had hoped for. Most rooms are on the small side and will come with a TV and telephone. Increasing numbers of hotels – even budget ones – now provide WiFi, though this is not always free of charge. Bathrooms can be tiny, and, as with Amsterdam apartments, bathtubs are a luxury rather than standard.

TRAVELLING WITH CHILDREN

Amsterdam is generally a child-friendly place, and although some of the most exclusive places positively discourage younger travellers, most places welcome them. Many of the chains and bigger hotels allow children (usually up to two) to stay free in parents' rooms and some offer free breakfasts. Other hotels may offer reduced rates or charge a small fee to rent out babies' cots. It is worth shopping around for the best deal. We have indicated which hotels cater for children in the listings on pages 216-23.

Wall plaque on the façade of the Radisson SAS *(see p216)*

GAY HOTELS

Amsterdam is a very gay-friendly city, so you may find you do not even want to stay in a specifically gay hotel. If you do, though, the most popular hotel among gay men is the **Golden Bear**, at the heart of the Kerkstraat gay scene. **ITC**, near Rembrandtplein, is also popular with both gay and lesbian travellers. The city lacks women-only accommodation, but many lesbians stay at the **Quentin**, near Leidesplein. *The Bent Guide to Amsterdam* gives a full overview of all things gay and lesbian in Amsterdam and is available at **Pink Point** and the **Vrolijk** bookshop.

DISABLED TRAVELLERS

Cobbled streets, tall, narrow houses and steep stairs are all things that make Amsterdam so charming for able-bodied visitors, but they can cause problems for disabled tourists. As so many hotels on the canal belt have a protected status and cannot be altered, there are few lifts, so wheelchair access is often only viable in chain hotels or top-price establishments. Our listings on pages 216-23 indicate which hotels have lifts and specially adapted rooms.

HOSTELS

There is a strong hostel scene in Amsterdam, catering to a young backpacking crowd, many of whom are attracted to Amsterdam's liberal attitude to marijuana smoking. Many hostels have cheap, cheerful bars, which are ideal for meeting like-minded people on the Interrail trail. Some good hostels are mentioned in our listings. Most hostels are privately owned (except **Stay-okay**) and have dorm accommodation, though some may have private rooms as well. There are often curfews and hostels near to Centraal Station are sometimes not as pleasant as elsewhere, so do exercise caution when booking.

CAMPING

Although Amsterdam is well served by campsites, none of them are in the city centre, though there are good public transport links. Open between March and November, **Gaasper Camping** is good for families and there are watersporting opportunities nearby. The **Amsterdamse Bos** site is set in acres of recreational woodland, perfect for children. To the north, **Vliegenbos** is great for exploring pretty Waterland villages, and **Zeeburg** is the nearest of all to the city centre. It has a tram-stop right outside, rental huts for the tentless and is open year-round.

SELF-CATERING

There are few self-catering options in Amsterdam since apartment space is at a premium. The VVV's hotel

brochure lists letting agents, who usually stipulate a minimum stay of a week. City Mundo's website (www. citymundo.nl) is also a good place to research possibilities. Of the hotels recommended in this guide, Best Western Eden (see p219), Hotel Acacia (see p218) and Houseboat Cecilia (see p220) offer the best self-catering options.

STAYING IN PRIVATE HOMES

Owing to the fact real estate is at a premium and Amsterdam flats tend to be tiny, guesthouse stays in people's homes are severely limited and the law also

prevents more than four people lodging in a private home at any one time. That said, **Bed and Breakfast Holland** provides an excellent resource for researching and finding those limited rooms that are available.

BEYOND AMSTERDAM

The NBTC's website lists more than 2,000 hotels throughout the Netherlands, with comprehensive information about each of them. Although this guide does not cover hotels outside Amsterdam, the information about booking and paying, hotel gradings, hostels and camping applies throughout the entire country.

The bar of Arena Hotel (see p223), a hostel near Oosterpark

DIRECTORY

INFORMATION

NBTC
Postbus 458, 2260 MG Leidschendam.
Tel 070 370 5705.
Fax 070 320 1654.
www.holland.com

GAY HOTELS AND INFORMATION

Golden Bear
Kerkstraat 37, 1017 GB Amsterdam. **Map** 1 C3.
Tel 624 4785.
www.goldenbear.nl

ITC
Prinsengracht 1051, 1017 JE Amsterdam. **Map** 5 A3.
Tel 623 0230. **Fax** 420 4369.

Pink Point
Westermarkt, 1016 DH Amsterdam. **Map** 1 B4.
Tel 428 1070.

Quentin
Leidsekade 89, 1017 PN, Amsterdam. **Map** 4 D1.
Tel 626 2187.
www.quentinhotels.com

Vrolijk
Paleisstraat 135, 1012 ZL Amsterdam. **Map** 7 B5.
Tel 623 5142. **Fax** 638 3807. **www**.vrolijk.nu

CHAIN HOTELS

Best Western
Tel 0800 022 1455.
www.bestwestern.com

NH Hoteles
Tel 0800 0115 0116.
www.nh-hotels.com

RESERVATIONS

Amsterdam Tourist Board (VVV) Offices
Centraal Station, Stationsplein 10, Platform 2B.
Map 8 D1. Leidseplein 1.

Map 4 E2. Schiphol Airport, Arrivals Hall 2.
www.amsterdamtourist.nl

NRC
Plantsoengracht 2, 1441 DE Purmerend. **Tel** (0299) 689 144. **Fax** (0299) 689 154. **www**.hotelres.nl

HOSTELS

Stayokay
Stadsdoelen (city centre).
Map 7 C4. **Tel** 624 6832.
Vondelpark. **Map** 4 D2.
Tel 589 8996.
www.stayokay.com

CAMPING

Amsterdamse Bos
Kleine Noorddijk 1, 1187 NZ Amstelveen.
Tel 641 6868.
Fax 640 2378.
www.camping amsterdamsebos.nl

Gaasper Camping
Loosdrechtdreef 7, 1108 AZ Amsterdam.
Tel 696 7326.
Fax 696 9369.
www.gaaspercamping.nl

Vliegenbos
Meeuwenlaan 138, 1022 AM, Amsterdam.
Map 2 F2.
Tel 636 8855.
Fax 632 2723.

Zeeburg
Zuider IJdijk 20, 1095 KN, Amsterdam.
Tel 694 4430.
Fax 694 6238.

STAYING IN PRIVATE HOMES

Bed & Breakfast Holland
Tel 615 7527.
www.bbholland.com

Amsterdam's Best: Hotels

The hotels recommended on these two pages possess an individual charm and character not found in most of their chain-hotel counterparts. All of these recommendations have a typically Dutch atmosphere, ranging from the simple and homely to the ornate, and some have an historical interest. Many of these hotels are impeccably restored 17th-century canal houses offering both canal and garden views, in addition to steep and narrow staircases. So whether you are after a reasonably priced B&B or looking for luxury, there is a huge choice available in Amsterdam.

Canal House
This atmospheric B&B has been restored to create an ambience of past grandeur. (See p218.)

Western Canal Ring

Pulitzer
This surprising, labyrinthine hotel was created by joining together 24 old canal houses and their gardens. (See p220.)

Central Canal Ring

HOTEL DE FILOSOOF

De Filosoof
Perhaps the city's most unusual hotel, "The Philosopher" has rooms named after the world's greatest thinkers, with thematic decor. (See p221.)

Museum Quarter

Ambassade
This classy B&B is an ideal choice for those who want to stay in a characterful, gabled canal house without forgoing comfort. (See p220.)

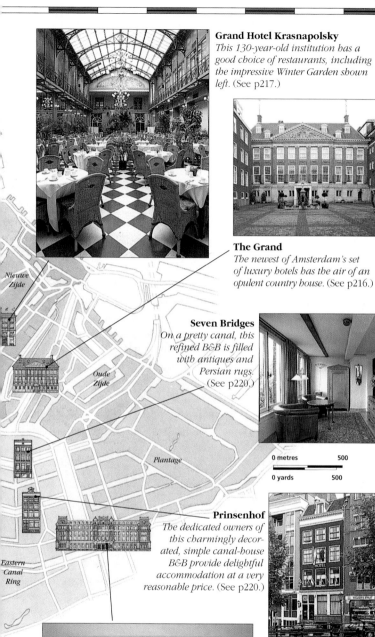

Grand Hotel Krasnapolsky
This 130-year-old institution has a good choice of restaurants, including the impressive Winter Garden shown left. (See p217.)

The Grand
The newest of Amsterdam's set of luxury hotels has the air of an opulent country house. (See p216.)

Seven Bridges
On a pretty canal, this refined B&B is filled with antiques and Persian rugs. (See p220.)

Nieuwe Zijde

Oude Zijde

Plantage

0 metres	500
0 yards	500

Prinsenhof
The dedicated owners of this charmingly decorated, simple canal-house B&B provide delightful accommodation at a very reasonable price. (See p220.)

Eastern Canal Ring

Intercontinental Amstel
Situated by the side of the Amstel, the city's number one hotel is serene, breathtakingly beautiful and utterly luxurious. (See p223.)

Choosing a Hotel

The hotels listed below have been selected across
a wide price range for their excellence of facilities,
location or character. The listings start with the central
areas and continue with hotels outside of the centre.
For map references, see the street finder maps on
pp280–87. For restaurant listings, see pp228–35.

PRICE CATEGORIES
The following prices are for a standard
double room per night, including
breakfast, tax and service.

€ under 100 euros
€€ 100–150 euros
€€€ 150–200 euros
€€€€ 200–250 euros
€€€€€ over 250 euros

OUDE ZIJDE

Amstel Botel   €

Van Riemsdijkweg (across the IJ), 1011 AE **Tel** *521 0350* **Fax** *639 1952* **Rooms** *175*   **Map** *8 E1*

Rooms on this big ship are on the small side, but they are clean and well equipped. The hotel is great for travellers
with teenagers: the lounge area has a pool table, juke-box and retro video games. The Amstel Botel will be moored
at this location until 2008–9. To get there, take the NDSM ferry from behind Centraal Station. **www.amstelbotel.nl**

Stayokay Stadsdoelen   €

Kloveniersburgwal 97, 1011 KB **Tel** *624 6832* **Fax** *639 1035* **Rooms** *13*   **Map** *7 D3*

Aimed firmly away from the backpack brigade, Stayokays focus on families and large groups, and offer packages
themed around nature or architecture. In a townhouse near Nieuwmarkt, spartan rooms accommodate eight to 20
people. There is a nice courtyard garden and a simple bar where evening meals are served. **www.stayokay.com**

MISC   €€

Kloveniersburgwal 20, 1012 CV **Tel** *330 6241* **Fax** *330 6242* **Rooms** *6*   **Map** *7 D3*

This funky, small hotel nestled among the cafés and bars of Nieuwmarkt is ideally situated for carousing (breakfast
is served until noon) and culture. The bright rooms are decorated individually by theme, such as "Afrika". The
owners are very helpful and will organize everything from a walking tour to a boat trip. **www.hotelmisc.nl**

Residence Le Coin   €€

Nieuwe Doelenstraat 5, 1012 CP **Tel** *524 6800* **Fax** *524 6801* **Rooms** *42*   **Map** *7 C4*

On a pleasant café-lined street near the university, this residence offers spacious apartment-style rooms. They are
furnished in a bright, modern style with big windows and equipped with kitchenettes, which makes Le Coin a
good bet for families and visitors on longer stays (there are special monthly rates). **www.lecoin.nl**

The Grand   €€€€€

Oudezijds Voorburgwal 197, 1012 EX **Tel** *555 3111* **Fax** *555 3222* **Rooms** *182*   **Map** *7 C3*

Amsterdam's former town hall abuts the Red Light District but couldn't be further away from the seediness close by.
Once inside the courtyard, guests are cocooned in luxury. Everything you expect from a deluxe hotel is here: marble
bathrooms, spacious rooms and discreet service. The on-site restaurant (Roux) is also excellent. **www.thegrand.nl**

Hotel de l'Europe   €€€€€

Nieuwe Doelenstraat 2–8, 1012 CP **Tel** *531 1777* **Fax** *531 1778* **Rooms** *100*   **Map** *7 C4*

A landmark hotel commanding fabulous views over the Amstel. There are top-of-the-range suites – including bridal
and a split-level penthouse – and these, as well as more workaday rooms, are luxuriously decorated with drapes and
chandeliers. Bathrooms are seriously opulent, featuring Bulgari toiletries. Service is attentive, too. **www.leurope.nl**

Radisson SAS   €€€€€

Rusland 17, 1012 CK **Tel** *623 1231* **Fax** *520 8200* **Rooms** *243*   **Map** *7 C4*

On a beautiful street between two atmospheric canals, this big hotel has a glorious atrium that can be enjoyed from
the rooms as an alternative "view". Rooms are large by Amsterdam standards, and furnishings are a mixture of
classic and funky. There is an in-house fitness room and conference facilities. **www.radissonsas.com**

NIEUWE ZIJDE

Avenue   €

Nieuwezijds Voorburgwal 33, 1012 RD **Tel** *530 9530* **Fax** *530 9599* **Rooms** *80*   **Map** *7 C1*

Great for exploring Nieuwe Zijde nightlife and, with two lifts, good for those with mobility problems. Avenue consists
of four East India Company spice warehouses spliced together – the rooms are good, but some residents complain of
lack of attention to detail (such as running out of breakfast food and coffee). **www.avenue-hotel.nl**

Key to Symbols *see back cover flap*

Singel Hotel €

Singel 13–17, 1012 VC **Tel** *626 3108* **Fax** *620 3777* **Rooms** *32* **Map** *7 B1*

One of the few budget choices in the city, the Singel is good for its proximity to the station and accessibility to canal walks. Once inside the attractive, 17th-century house, things are pretty basic. Rooms are all en suite with showers and, in the main, clean and tidy. Those at the front, however, can get a little noisy. **www.singelhotel.nl**

Winston Hotel €

Warmoesstraat 129, 1012 JA **Tel** *623 1380* **Fax** *020 639 2308* **Rooms** *69* **Map** *7 C2*

A youth-oriented place on the fringes of the Red Light District, the Winston occupies the space between hotel and hostel. The best rooms are the individually decorated "art rooms", though there are also cheaper, plain ones. The residents' bar is open round the clock and there is an on-site – and excellent – nightclub, too. **www.winston.nl**

Citadel €€

Nieuwezijds Voorburgwal 98–100, 1012 SG **Tel** *627 3882* **Fax** *627 4684* **Rooms** *38* **Map** *7 C1*

A reliable town-centre hotel halfway between the Jordaan and old quarter, the Citadel is ideal for urban explorers. It has been refurbished and though rooms are clean, they are on the plain side. Public spaces like the reception area and bar, however, are decorated in warm wood tones. Staff are helpful. **www.hotelcitadel.nl**

Hotel Sint Nicolaas €€

Spuistraat 1A, 1012 SP **Tel** *626 1384* **Fax** *623 0979* **Rooms** *24* **Map** *7 C1*

Located near Centraal Station (*see p79*), this family-run hotel has quirky touches (an outsized lift and odd-shaped rooms) that reflect its former life as a mattress factory. Although fairly basic, all rooms are neat and have en-suite facilities – some with baths. Free wireless Internet in every room is a welcome touch. **www.hotelnicolaas.nl**

Nova €€

Nieuwezijds Voorburgwal 276, 1012 RD **Tel** *623 0066* **Fax** *627 2026* **Rooms** *61* **Map** *7 B2*

A reliable city-centre standard located in an old townhouse. Rooms have up-to-date decor, with brick walls and blonde wood furniture; they are comfortable, though bathrooms are rather cramped. It is ideal for all the sights – some rooms have views of the Koninklijk Paleis (*see p74*) – and for exploring nearby nightlife. **www.novahotel.nl**

Hotel des Arts €€€

Rokin 154–156, 1012 LE **Tel** *620 1558* **Fax** *624 9995* **Rooms** *22* **Map** *7 B4*

This cosy, family-run place is ideal for shopping addicts, since it is just steps away from from the main consumer thoroughfare, Kalverstraat. There are 18 spacious rooms (pitched at groups and families) and a couple of smaller ones; although on the dark side, they all have glamorous touches such as chandeliers. **www.hoteldesarts.nl**

Ibis Amsterdam Centre €€€

Stationsplein 49, 1012 AB **Tel** *638 9999* **Fax** *620 0156* **Rooms** *187* **Map** *2 D3*

Ideal for late arrivals or early departures, this hotel is metres from Centraal Station (*see p79*). Although on the bland side, the rooms are air-conditioned and reasonably sized. They also come with a "15-minute satisfaction" pledge: if a problem is not solved within this time limit, then your stay is free. Pets are welcome. **www.ibishotel.com**

NH Barbizon Palace €€€

Prins Hendrikkade 59–72, 1012 AD **Tel** *556 4564* **Fax** *554 5500* **Rooms** *270* **Map** *8 D1*

The jewel in the NH crown, this hotel has sleek black-and-white decor in public spaces. Rooms, by contrast, are all dowdy beiges and browns and seem a little tired. Facilities are outstanding: excellent breakfasts, the Michelin-starred Restaurant Vermeer and a 14th-century chapel serving as one of the eight conference rooms. **www.nh-hotels.com**

Renaissance Amsterdam €€€

Kattengat 1, 1012 SZ **Tel** *621 2223* **Fax** *627 5245* **Rooms** *405* **Map** *7 C1*

A large hotel excellent for exploring the Jordaan. Rooms are a touch flowery, but they deliver chain-hotel luxuries like movies, interactive video and PlayStation. Good for business travellers: as well as being close to Centraal Station (*see p79*), its conference facilities are in the 17th-century domed Koepelkerk, next door. **www.marriott.com**

Rho Hotel €€€

Nes 5–23, 1012 KC **Tel** *620 7371* **Fax** *620 7826* **Rooms** *170* **Map** *7 B3*

Just metres from bustling Dam Square, though tucked down a backstreet bristling with interesting bars, restaurants and theatres, this hotel is well placed and good value. Its glory days as a gold merchants' office are visible in the beautiful Art Nouveau lobby. Though plain, the rooms are neat and tidy. **www.rhohotel.nl**

Swissotel Amsterdam €€€

Damrak 96–98, 1012 LP **Tel** *522 3000* **Fax** *522 3223* **Rooms** *109* **Map** *7 C2*

Rooms here have stylish decor in soothing pastel shades. All are soundproofed, so a good night's sleep is guaranteed. Book the suite for a treat: it overlooks the Dam, and the huge bathroom has a Jacuzzi. Being directly opposite the city's best department store, De Bijenkorf, makes this hotel an ideal base for shopaholics. **www.swissotel.com**

Grand Hotel Krasnapolsky €€€€

Dam 9, 1012 JS **Tel** *554 9111* **Fax** *622 8607* **Rooms** *468* **Map** *7 C2*

The location of this hotel – on Dam Square, overlooking the Koninklijk Paleis (*see p74*) – is great. Accommodation ranges from utter luxury in the Tower Suite to compact rooms at the back. Facilities are top-notch: restaurants, café, cocktail bar. The Winter Garden is where weekend brunches are consumed. **www.nh-hotels.com**

Die Port van Cleve

€€€€€

Nieuwezijds Voorburgwal 176–180, 1012 SJ **Tel** *624 4860* **Fax** *622 0240* **Rooms** *120*　　　　**Map** *7 B2*

Beer fans will be delighted to stay here, in the very building where Heineken began brewing in the 1870s. Non-drinkers will be equally satisfied with the hotel's big, luxurious rooms and suites. Gourmets will enjoy the renowned on-site steak restaurant, as well as the city's restaurant scene on the doorstep. **www.dieportvancleve.com**

Estherea

€€€€€

Singel 305, 1012 WJ **Tel** *624 5146* **Fax** *623 9001* **Rooms** *71*　　　　**Map** *7 A3*

An elegant, family-run hotel that has been in the same careful hands for more than 60 years. There are 71 rooms spread across six canal houses, all with an emphasis on opulent fabrics and luxury, from DVD players to marble bathrooms. Facilities include an intimate library and a lounge with watery views. **www.estherea.nl**

Hotel Amsterdam – Roode Leeuw

€€€€€

Damrak 93–94, 1012 LP **Tel** *555 0666* **Fax** *620 4716* **Rooms** *79*　　　　**Map** *7 C2*

Open since 1911, the privately owned Red Lion doesn't look much from the outside. Inside, though, rooms are warmly decorated and reasonably sized. Unusually for Amsterdam hotels, there are in-room tea and coffee facilities, and suites have espresso machines. The restaurant offers highly rated Dutch cooking. **www.hotelamsterdam.nl**

Sofitel

€€€€€

Nieuwezijds Voorburgwal 67, 1012 RE **Tel** *627 5900* **Fax** *623 8932* **Rooms** *148*　　　　**Map** *7 B1*

A good base for sightseeing, dining and shopping, the Sofitel is furnished with top-of-the-range luxuries: there is a sauna, a tiny gym, a restaurant, and the bar is modelled on the Orient Express. The staff are helpful, and the rooms themselves are smart, if somewhat staid, with lots of wood and opulent Regency stripes. **www.sofitel.com**

WESTERN CANAL RING

Belga

€

Hartenstraat 8, 1016 CB **Tel** *624 9080* **Fax** *623 6862* **Rooms** *10*　　　　**Map** *7 A3*

In the middle of a chic shopping street, yet miles from the designer wealth surrounding it, Belga is a straightforward, plain kind of lodging house, so do not expect four-star trimmings. Some rooms sleep five, making this a good destination for budget-savvy families. Staff are helpful and they will gladly organize a baby-sitter. **www.hotelbelga.nl**

Hotel Acacia

€

Lindengracht 252, 1015 KH **Tel** *622 1460* **Fax** *638 0748* **Rooms** *20*　　　　**Map** *1 B3*

It is back to basics at this functional, if a little care-worn, place in a quiet corner in the farthest reaches of the Jordaan. Rooms are small and completely frill-free, leading some guests to liken Acacia to a seaside B&B. They also rent out two houseboats on nearby Lijnsbaangracht. **www.hotelacacia.nl**

Hotel van Onna

€

Bloemgracht 102–108, 1015 TN **Tel** *626 5801* **Rooms** *41*　　　　**Map** *1 A4*

On the most scenic canal in Amsterdam, this hotel spread over three canal houses from the 17th to 20th centuries is a few minutes' walk from the Westerkerk (see p90) and Anne Frank's house (see p90). It is a non-smoking hotel; rooms are basically furnished and equipped, with reasonable rates for single travellers. **www.hotelvanonna.nl**

Shelter Jordan

€

Bloemstraat 179, 1016 LA **Tel** *624 4717* **Fax** *627 6137* **Rooms** *104*　　　　**Map** *1 A4*

The only hostel accommodation in this area, this Christian-run dorm – sleeping up to 20 – is not for the hedonistic backpacker brigade: drugs and alcohol are banned, for starters. It is clean and secure, however, and there is no curfew. All bed linen is provided, as is breakfast. There is also an on-site café. **www.shelter.nl**

Truelove Antiek and Guesthouse

€€

Prinsenstraat 4, 1015 DC **Tel/Fax** *320 2500* **Rooms** *2*　　　　**Map** *7 A1*

A dinky, two-roomed romantic bolt hole atop an antique shop (also the hotel's reception) at the heart of Amsterdam's most interesting shopping area. It is non-smoking, simple and stylish; although there is no breakfast (you are spoiled for choice nearby), there are considerate touches like wine, water and fresh flowers in the room. **www.truelove.be**

Canal House

€€

Keizersgracht 148, 1015 CX **Tel** *622 5182* **Fax** *624 1317* **Rooms** *26*　　　　**Map** *7 A1*

An elegant retreat for those who are seeking quiet refuge: under-12s are banned from this abundantly chandeliered hotel, leaving the grown-ups to be pampered. Rooms, in classical style with heavy wooden furniture, are TV-free, adding further to the serenity. Those without a canal view overlook the pretty inner garden. **www.canalhouse.com**

Hotel de Looier

€€

3e Looierdwarsstraat 75, 1016 VD **Tel** *625 1855* **Fax** *627 5320* **Rooms** *27*　　　　**Map** *4 D1*

In a previous life, the building was a diamond factory; now it is a comfortable hotel that is a good base for exploring the Jordaan's markets. The De Looier antiques market is directly opposite, and the Noordermarkt (see p92) a short stroll away. Although fairly characterless, rooms are en suite, spotless and have in-house movies. **www.hoteldelooier.com**

Key to Price Guide see p216　**Key to Symbols** see back cover flap

't Hotel

Leliegracht 18, 1015 DE **Tel** *422 2741* **Fax** *626 7873* **Rooms** *9*

Map *7 A2*

A plain name for a lovely hotel nesting on a beautiful Jordaan canal. Rooms are not full of luxuries, but they are very stylish, painted in neutral tones with 1920s-influenced furniture. They are also spacious and have enormous windows. Room number 8, at the very top, is on a split level and sleeps five. **www.thotel.nl**

Hotel Toren

Keizersgracht 164, 1015 CZ **Tel** *622 6352* **Fax** *626 9705* **Rooms** *96*

Map *7 A1*

A stylish place decorated in tasteful pastel hues and stripes, Hotel Toren boasts a fascinating history: it has been a merchant's house and a university, and it was also used to hide Jews during World War II. On the downside, standard rooms are small, so spend a little extra on a superior: you get extra legroom and a spa bath. **www.hoteltoren.nl**

The Dylan

Keizersgracht 384, 1016 GB **Tel** *530 2010* **Fax** *530 2030* **Rooms** *41*

Map *1 B5*

Staff here will make you feel like a superstar, attending to your every whim. For a dose of chromatherapy, book rooms by colour according to your mood: soothing green, for example. Every detail has been thought through, from the restaurant's East-meets-West menu to the arrangement of the cushions in the bar. **www.dylanamsterdam.com**

CENTRAL CANAL RING

Hotel Brouwer

Singel 83, 1012 VE **Tel** *624 6358* **Fax** *520 6264* **Rooms** *8*

Map *7 B1*

Recently renovated, this hotel has been in the same family's hands since 1917. The eight rooms, all named after Dutch artists, are individually decorated and well maintained, and the canal views are lovely. All rooms are en suite and no-smoking, and there is even a lift, making the Brouwer all-round great value. **www.hotelbrouwer.nl**

Hotel Leydschehof

Leidsegracht 14, 1016 CK **Tel/Fax** *638 2327* **Rooms** *7*

Map *7 A5*

On a genteel canal near the Leidseplein nightlife (*see p110*), this is ideal for relaxing after a fun night out. Run by the Piller family, the hotel has well-equipped en-suite rooms, with fridges and tea-making facilities a welcome touch. All are bright and simple, and overlook the garden. A simple, pleasing place to stay. **www.freewebs.com/leydschehof**

Agora

Singel 462, 1017 AW **Tel** *627 2200* **Fax** *627 2202* **Rooms** *16*

Map *7 A5*

In a lovely house from the 1730s, the Agora is a cosy hotel. Although lacking flourishes, it is a soothing place to stay: rooms without canal views overlook the garden at the back, and breakfast is served in the conservatory. Just steps from the flower market (*see p123*), this is ideal for flora fans. **www.hotelagora.nl**

Amsterdam Wiechmann

Prinsengracht 328–332, 1016 HX **Tel** *626 3321* **Fax** *626 8962* **Rooms** *40*

Map *1 B5*

A cosy little place ideal for exploring the Jordaan, Wiechmann combines its old-fashioned charm with modern touches like (free) WiFi Internet. The comfortable rooms have chintzy decor, and eccentric knick-knacks abound. The teapot-lined breakfast room has huge windows looking on to the canal. **www.hotelwiechmann.nl**

Imperial

Thorbeckeplein 9, 1017 CS **Tel** *622 0051* **Fax** *624 5836* **Rooms** *14*

Map *7 C5*

Though located on a pedestrianised square, this non-smoking hotel is far from quiet: Amsterdam's nightlife is directly outside. Not the best choice for light sleepers, since the revelry continues into the small hours. Rooms are en suite and individually decorated – from chintzy to dark woods. Some could do with a refurb. **www.imperial-hotel.com**

Nicolaas Witsen

Nicolaas Witsenstraat 4, 1017 ZH **Tel** *623 6143* **Fax** *620 5113* **Rooms** *29*

Map *5 A4*

One of the few hotels in the area between De Pijp and the Museum Quarter, this is a good bet for culture-seekers. It is perhaps a little overpriced for what you get: a basic, functional place providing plain and frill-free accommodation. The rooms on the ground floor can get a bit noisy. **www.hotelnicolaaswitsen.nl**

Best Western Eden

Amstel 144, 1017 AE **Tel** *530 7878* **Fax** *623 3267* **Rooms** *327*

Map *8 D5*

A chain standard situated on the Amstel, close to Rembrandtplein (*see p118*) and the sights. It is handy for travellers with mobility problems: most rooms are wheelchair accessible, and one has full disabled facilities. For individuality, pay extra for an "art room" designed by students from the Rietveld art school. **www.edenhotelgroup.com**

Dikker & Thijs Fenice Hotel

Prinsengracht 444, 1017 KE **Tel** *620 1212* **Fax** *625 8986* **Rooms** *42*

Map *4 E1*

Owned by a publisher, this hotel is proud of its literary connections and the authors who stay here. The 18th-century warehouse building is magnificent, and the decor is smart. Although just moments from Leidseplein (*see p110*), the atmosphere here is resolutely upmarket. All the sights are within walking distance. **www.dtfh.nl**

Houseboat Cecilia

Prinsengracht, near Westerkerk **Rooms** 2   **Map** 1 B5

Experience Amsterdam from a duck's eye view on this gorgeous houseboat near the Jordaan. Although near sights like Anne Frank's house (*see p90*) and the Westerkerk (*see p90*), you probably won't ever want to set foot on dry land once you are ensconced in the deluxe interior. Even the outside deck is heated. **www.houseboatinamsterdam.com**

Mercure Hotel Arthur Frommer

Noorderstraat 46, 1017 TV **Tel** 622 0328 **Fax** 620 3208 **Rooms** 90   **Map** 4 F2

Within walking distance of the sights, Rembrandtplein (*see p118*) and restaurant-lined Utrechtsestraat, this is one of the best placed hotels in Amsterdam. It is pleasantly arranged around a courtyard, and rooms look out on to quiet residential streets. Rooms are comfortable, smart and fairly spacious, as well as non-smoking. **www.mercure.com**

Ambassade Hotel

Herengracht 341, 1016 AZ **Tel** 555 0222 **Fax** 555 0277 **Rooms** 64   **Map** 7 A4

With its long literary associations, this is the bookworm's choice of lodgings: the library is lined with signed copies from the numerous authors who have stayed here. Arranged across ten buildings, rooms are furnished in an unfussy, classic way, and bathrooms, though small, are marbled. Staff are discreet and attentive. **www.ambassade-hotel.nl**

Hotel Pulitzer

Prinsengracht 315–331, 1016 GZ **Tel** 523 5235 **Fax** 627 6753 **Rooms** 230   **Map** 1 B5

Spread over 25 adjoining canal houses, this hotel is perfect for a luxurious splurge. Rooms are spacious and stylish, with marble bathrooms, and antiques pop up everywhere. The garden is a floral oasis in summer. In August, the Pulitzer hosts the classical music Grachtenfestival, which culminates on the canal outside. **www.pulitzer.nl**

EASTERN CANAL RING

Hotel de Munck

Achtergracht 3, 1017 WL **Tel** 623 6283 **Fax** 620 6647 **Rooms** 14   **Map** 5 B3

Near the Amstel, on the fringes of town, this sea captain's house has a pleasantly ramshackle air. Arranged pell-mell, bedrooms are homely and basic, if a touch tired. The breakfast room, however, is a kitsch treat: lined with pop memorabilia, its centrepiece is a jukebox that plays while you eat. **www.hoteldemunck.com**

Hotel Prinsenhof

Prinsengracht 810, 1017 JL **Tel** 623 1772 **Fax** 638 3368 **Rooms** 10   **Map** 5 A3

A small, no-frills hotel with only ten rooms, most of which share facilities, and all of which are clean and well cared for. Single rooms are pretty cramped. Close to the nightlife and restaurant hub, this is a good budget bet for those who will spend most of their stay exploring and just want a base for sleeping. **www.hotelprinsenhof.com**

Armada

Keizersgracht 713–715, 1017 DX **Tel** 623 2980 **Fax** 623 5829 **Rooms** 26   **Map** 5 A3

On a quiet part of Keizersgracht, just near Utrechtsestraat's great shops and restaurants and close to the bright lights of Rembrandtplein (*see p118*), this hotel has one major selling point: location. Rooms are being renovated and soon they will all have en-suite facilities. A good budget bet if you want to save your euros for shopping or clubbing.

Asterisk

Den Texstraat 16, 1017 ZA **Tel** 626 2396 **Fax** 638 2790 **Rooms** 40   **Map** 5 A4

Decorated in chintzy style from breakfast room to bedrooms (the cheapest have shared facilities), this hotel on a pleasant residential street near the museums is also good for exploring De Pijp. There is also a lift, which is a welcome touch, given the traditional, steep stairs. If you pay cash, breakfast is included in the price. **www.asteriskhotel.nl**

NH Schiller

Rembrandtplein 26–36, 1017 CV **Tel** 554 0700 **Fax** 554 4400 **Rooms** 92   **Map** 7 C5

Fun-seekers should look no further than this hotel, with its commanding view over Rembrandtplein (*see p118*). The rooms at the back are not so noisy, and all are decorated with standard-issue smart furnishings. Brasserie Schiller is very cosy, while the eponymous next-door bar has Art Deco fittings and attracts a media crowd. **www.nh-hotels.com**

Seven Bridges

Reguliersgracht 31, 1017 LK **Tel** 623 1329 **Rooms** 8   **Map** 5 A3

In a former merchant house dating back to the 1600s, Seven Bridges is one of the city's best-kept hotel secrets and a perfect hide-out for those seeking peace and quiet. There are just eight rooms, with either garden or canal views; each is furnished with antiques and breakfast is served in the room. **www.sevenbridgeshotel.nl**

Albus Grand

Vijzelstraat 49, 1017 HE **Tel** 530 6200 **Fax** 530 6299 **Rooms** 74   **Map** 4 F1

Recently renovated, the breakfast room of this very central hotel has now been transformed into a hip little café. Standard rooms are brighter, too, though still rather cramped; pay extra for superior or deluxe ones, which have slick fitted furnishings and chocolate hues. There are three apartments for long stays. **www.albusgrandhotel.com**

Key to Price Guide *see p216* **Key to Symbols** *see back cover flap*

Banks Mansion €€€€€

Herengracht 519–525, 1017 BV **Tel** *420 0055* **Fax** *420 0993* **Rooms** *51* **Map** *7 B5*

In an imposing former bank, this hotel is all-inclusive: everything, from the Internet to movies to the minibar, is free. This is not just a one-gimmick place, either. Rooms are lovely, with Frank Lloyd Wright-inspired decor, plasma TVs and bathrooms kitted out with oversized shower heads. There is even a pillow menu. **http://banksmansion.carlton.nl**

Hotel 717 €€€€€

Prinsengracht 717, 1017 JW **Tel** *427 0717* **Fax** *423 0717* **Rooms** *8* **Map** *5 A3*

Small and expensive, this is one of Amsterdam's luxurious secrets. It's popular with antique hunters from the nearby Spiegelkwartier. Each of the eight rooms has the best accoutrements: blankets from Wales, sheets from New York, and DVDs from Bang & Olufsen. Everything is sumptuous, with fresh flowers all over. **www.717hotel.nl**

MUSEUM QUARTER

Bellington €

PC Hooftstraat 78–80, 1071 CB **Tel** *671 6478* **Fax** *671 8637* **Rooms** *11* **Map** *4 D3*

Do not come here expecting luxury. The Bellington is a serviceable budget hotel providing just the basics. Though they are a little tired, rooms are clean, with TVs and minibars. Note that double rooms with shared bathrooms off-season work out cheaper than dorm beds in a hostel. **www.hotel-bellington.com**

Flying Pig Uptown Hostel €

Vossiusstraat 46, 1071 AJ **Tel** *400 4187* **Fax** *421 0802* **Rooms** *22* **Map** *4 D3*

A well-equipped place near the museums, this hostel offers both dorm beds and (rather pricey) twin rooms. The international backpacker crowd comes here as much for the scene as the accommodation, and enjoys cut-price beer in the bar. There is free Internet and free inline skates for nearby Vondelpark (see p128). **www.flyingpig.nl**

Hestia €

Roemer Visscherstraat 7, 1054 EV **Tel** *618 0801* **Fax** *685 1382* **Rooms** *18* **Map** *4 D2*

On an architecturally fascinating street between Leidseplein (see p110) and the museums, this small, private hotel is aimed at families and small groups. Rooms, sleeping up to five, offer nothing fancy but are spotlessly clean and have comfy beds. There is a small garden for guest use; room 15 has a balcony overlooking it. **www.hotel-hestia.nl**

Hotel Jupiter €

2e Helmersstraat 14, 1054 CJ **Tel** *618 7132* **Fax** *616 8838* **Rooms** *20* **Map** *4 D2*

This family-run, two-star place in a residential side street is just a few minutes' stroll from the park and museums and near numerous bars and restaurants on Overtoom. Rooms are smallish and functional, but they are clean, tidy and cosy. The cash-conscious can opt for triples or rooms with shared facilities. **www.jupiterhotel.nl**

Stayokay City Hostel Vondelpark €

Zandpad 5, 1054 GA **Tel** *589 8996* **Fax** *589 8955* **Rooms** *105* **Map** *4 D2*

The second Amsterdam outpost of a worthy organisation, this hostel on the edge of the Vondelpark (see p128) is ideal for nature lovers. Accommodation ranges from double rooms to 20-bed dorms, and it is all non-smoking. There is a TV room, and Brasserie Backpackers has a lovely terrace looking on to the park. **www.stayokay.com**

De Filosoof €€

Anna van der Vondelstraat 6, 1054 GZ **Tel** *683 3013* **Fax** *685 3750* **Rooms** *38* **Map** *3 C2*

A much-loved hotel on a street off the Vondelpark (see p128). Every room here is individually decorated according to a different philosopher or treatise. There is Passion, Wittgenstein or local boy Spinoza, for example. It is a favourite of brooding intellectuals, who make use of the lovely garden and, of course, the library. **www.hotelfilosoof.nl**

Owl €€

Roemer Visscherstraat 1, 1054 EV **Tel** *618 9484* **Fax** *618 9441* **Rooms** *34* **Map** *4 D2*

Close to Leidseplein (see p110), but on a quiet street ensuring a restful sleep, this enduring, family-run favourite is housed in an attractive villa. There is a bar and a relaxing conservatory overlooking a garden. Rooms are not spacious or particularly stylish, but they are well-looked after, as are guests, many of whom come back. **www.owl-hotel.nl**

Piet Hein €€

Vossiusstraat 52–53, 1071 AK **Tel** *662 7205* **Fax** *662 1526* **Rooms** *36* **Map** *4 D3*

A stylish hotel that has been refurbished in soothing caramel and cream tones. The rooms are pleasing on the eye and gentle on the wallet, and rather spacious for Amsterdam. The most popular ones overlook Vondelpark (see p128). There is a late-opening bar and relaxing lounge area, and the staff are helpful, too. **www.hotelpiethein.nl**

Smit €€

PC Hooftstraat 24–28, 1071 BX **Tel** *671 4785* **Fax** *662 9161* **Rooms** *63* **Map** *4 E3*

Compared to other hotels in the surrounding area, Smit charges somewhat over the odds. Rooms are tidy and equipped with everything you need, but the decor is stuck in the 1980s. On the plus side, staff are friendly and helpful, and rooms at the top are rewarded with views of the Rijksmuseum (see p130). **www.hotelsmit.com**

Amsterdam Marriott Hotel

€€€

Stadhouderskade 12, 1054 ES **Tel** *607 5555* **Fax** *607 5511* **Rooms** *392*

Map *4 D2*

With 11 floors, the Marriott is a bit of a red-bricked behemoth, but it does occupy an excellent position bordering the Vondelpark (*see p128*), with Leidseplein (*see p110*) lying nearby. Rooms are corporate smart, in country clubbish greens and browns. There are plenty of business facilities, including 11 conference rooms. **https://marriott.com**

Atlas Hotel

€€€

Van Eeghenstraat 64, 1071 GK **Tel** *676 6336* **Fax** *671 7633* **Rooms** *23*

Map *3 C3*

Tucked between consulates, this restful hotel – part of a small chain – is in a beautiful Art Nouveau villa behind Vondelpark (*see p128*); there are architectural delights, like ornate gables and stained glass, all over. Rooms are plainer, in warm colours and hung with attractive original paintings, with comfortable beds. **www.hotelatlas.nl**

Best Western Museum Hotel

€€€

PC Hooftstraat 2, 1071 BX **Tel** *662 1402* **Fax** *673 3918* **Rooms** *110*

Map *4 E2*

In a handsome corner building on Amsterdam's exclusive shopping thoroughfare, this hotel is, as the name suggests, also minutes from the big museums. Rooms are not luxurious, but they are well equipped and light; some are housed in an annexe in a separate building. It is currently being given a (timely) overhaul. **www.bestwestern.com**

Gresham Memphis

€€€

De Lairessestraat 87, 1071 NX **Tel** *673 3141* **Fax** *673 7312* **Rooms** *74*

Map *4 D4*

At the heart of the chic Oud Zuid residential area, this non-smoking hotel is popular with both package tourists and classical musicians playing at the nearby Concertgebouw (*see p128*). Public spaces are smart, but room decor, though cared for, does not quite match this standard. The bar offers food throughout the day. **www.gresham-hotels.com**

Vondel

€€€

Vondelstraat 26, 1054 GE **Tel** *612 0120* **Fax** *685 4321* **Rooms** *78*

Map *3 C3*

Near the museums and designer shops, this stylish non-smoking place is decorated throughout with art, and it appeals to a chic crowd. Rooms, named after poems by the hotel's namesake, are spacious and decorated in calming creamy tones. Best of all are the suites, nestling in the eaves, with splendid views over Amsterdam. **www.hotelvondel.nl**

The College Hotel

€€€€

Roelof Hartstraat 1, 1071 VE **Tel** *571 1511* **Fax** *571 1512* **Rooms** *40*

Map *4 E5*

Stay in this stylish boutique hotel and you will be looked after by students from Amsterdam's hotel and catering school, learning their craft in situ. Do not expect reduced prices, though: the emphasis is on indulgence, from decor through to dinner. The glamorous TCH suite is bigger than most city apartments. **www.thecollegehotel.com**

PLANTAGE

Hotel Adolesce

€

Nieuwe Keizersgracht 26, 1018 DR **Tel** *626 3959* **Fax** *627 4249* **Rooms** *10*

Map *8 F5*

At the upper end of the budget category, this hotel is similar to Fantasia, a few doors down. Its unfussy rooms all have their own sanitation and are geared towards family groups. Although the hotel does not provide breakfast, guests can help themselves all day long to drinks and snacks in the lounge. **www.adolesce.nl**

Luckytravellers Fantasia Hotel

€

Nieuwe Keizersgracht 16, 1018 DR **Tel** *623 8259* **Fax** *622 3913* **Rooms** *18*

Map *5 B3*

A simple hotel that is good for culture-seekers on a budget, the Fantasia is a few doors down from the Hermitage and minutes from Waterlooplein (*see p63*) and the Plantage, at the quiet end of a main canal. Rooms are nothing fancy, though: all but one are en suite and all have tea- and coffee-making facilities. **www.fantasia-hotel.com**

Rembrandt

€

Plantage Midden 17, 1918 DA **Tel** *627 2714* **Fax** *638 0293* **Rooms** *17*

Map *8 F5*

One of the few cheaper options in this area, this hotel is good for families intent on visiting nearby Artis zoo (*see p142*). Public spaces are covered in flamboyant murals that recall the hotel's namesake, and have dark, wooden furniture. The bedrooms, meanwhile, are brighter and more modern, and all are en suite. **www.hotelrembrandt.nl**

Bridge Hotel

€€

Amstel 107–111, 1018 EM **Tel** *623 7068* **Fax** *624 1565* **Rooms** *36*

Map *5 B3*

In a former stonemason's workshop, this hotel stands in splendid isolation right on the river bank, looking towards Rembrandtplein (*see p118*). All of the rooms are simple and bright, but those looking onto the water cost extra. There are apartments with kitchenettes for stays of three days or longer. **www.thebridgehotel.nl**

Ibis Stopera

€€

Valkenburgerstraat 68, 1011 LZ **Tel** *531 9135* **Fax** *531 9145* **Rooms** *207*

Map *8 E4*

One of two central branches of this useful chain, this hotel lies just behind the opera house on a busy thoroughfare. Nevertheless, it is ideally placed for discovering the old Jewish quarter and the Eastern Docklands. The air-conditioned rooms (with WiFi) deliver no surprises, but are none the worse for it. Pets are welcome. **www.ibishotel.com**

Key to Price Guide *see p216* **Key to Symbols** *see back cover flap*

Best Western Lancaster

Plantage Midden 48, 1018 DH **Tel** *535 6888* **Fax** *535 6889* **Rooms** *92*

Map *6 D2*

Although away from the sights, this hotel is just a short tram ride from Centraal Station (*see p79*). Rooms are bigger than in the centre; painted in earthy tones, with triples and quads, they are handy for families and groups. It is a good choice for businesspeople, too: all rooms have desks and there is free WiFi in the lobby. **www.edenhotelgroup.com**

InterContinental Amstel Amsterdam

Professor Tulpplein 1, 1018 GX **Tel** *622 6060* **Fax** *622 5808* **Rooms** *79*

Map *5 B4*

This imposing building overlooking the river has been the city's top hotel since 1867. This is the place where royalty and rock stars stay when in town (as hordes outside testify), and its prices reflect its status. The huge rooms are soundproof and have everything you can think of. Restaurant La Rive has a Michelin star. **www.ichotelsgroup.com**

FURTHER AFIELD

Between Art and Kitsch

Ruysdaelkade 75–II, 1072 AL **Tel/Fax** *679 0485* **Rooms** *2*

Map *4 E4*

A refreshing change from faceless corporate chains. The name of this B&B says it all: one room has pastiche Baroque decoration, the other features Art Deco touches, and there are fun trinkets scattered all over. On a pleasant canal, it is ideal for exploring the nearby museums and enjoying De Pijp. **www.between-art-and-kitsch.com**

Bicycle Hotel

Van Ostadestraat 123, 1072 SV **Tel** *679 3452* **Fax** *671 5213* **Rooms** *16*

Map *4 F5*

This cheapish, cheerful place is geared to pedal enthusiasts, though equally welcoming to pedestrians. They rent two-wheelers, there is a bike park and staff are happy to suggest cycle routes. After a hard day's cycling, guests retire to simple yet clean and comfy rooms or enjoy the wide range of restaurants in De Pijp. **www.bicyclehotel.com**

Cake Under My Pillow

Jacob van Campenstraat 66, 1072 BH **Tel** *751 0936* **Fax** *776 4604* **Rooms** *2*

Map *4 F4*

Run by – and located above – the city's most outrageous cake shop, this B&B is very gay-friendly. It is a brilliant base for exploring De Pijp and is just a 15-minute walk from the centre. Cosy rooms are decorated in flamboyant, kitsch style, and breakfast usually includes freshly baked treats from downstairs. **www.cakeundermypillow.nl**

Lloyd Hotel

Oostelijke Handelskade 34, 1019 BN **Tel** *561 3636* **Fax** *561 3600* **Rooms** *116*

This hotel and "cultural embassy" offers everything from one- to five-star accommodation, and all kinds of arts events. Formerly a borstal, the Lloyd (intentionally) retains an institutional feel, but two restaurants, an intimate bar and attentive staff add to an unusual experience in the up-and-coming Eastern Docklands. **www.lloydhotel.com**

Arena

's Gravesandestraat 51, 1092 AA **Tel** *850 2410* **Fax** *850 2415* **Rooms** *127*

Map *6 D4*

The restaurant, bar and nightclub are the stars of this former orphanage in a slightly out-of-the-way residential district, so the Arena is ideal for young trendies intent on socialising in situ. Unless you shell out top dollar for one of the extra-large rooms or suites (by leading local designers IDing), rooms may well disappoint. **www.hotelarena.nl**

Hotel V

Victorieplein 42, 1078 PH **Tel** *662 3233* **Fax** *676 6398* **Rooms** *24*

A trek away from the sights, the V is ideally located for those with business at the Amsterdam RAI (*see p151*) and seeking a break from corporate blandness. Hidden in a residential block, this boutique B&B has funky decor in all rooms. There are few extras, but the lounge, featuring an open fire, is warm and cosy. **www.hotelv.nl**

Hampshire Hotel Savoy Amsterdam

Ferdinand Bolstraat 194, 1072 LW **Tel** *644 7445* **Fax** *644 8989* **Rooms** *42*

Map *4 F5*

As good for travellers with business at RAI (*see p151*) as it is for epicures exploring De Pijp, the Savoy is a welcome addition to the area's (limited) hotel scene. Once inside the formidable red-brick building, things are bright, with good-sized rooms and bathrooms. The bar is in soothing shades of beige. **www.hampshirehotels.nl**

Amsterdam Hilton

Apollolaan 138, 1077 BG **Tel** *710 6000* **Fax** *710 6080* **Rooms** *271*

Map *3 C5*

Still famous after all these years for being the place where John Lennon and Yoko Ono had their bed-in, this luxury chain standard is now geared mainly towards the business market. Very close to Schiphol airport (*see p155*), it is also near the financial district and, naturally, it has the full complement of business amenities. **www.hilton.com**

Bilderberg Garden

Dijsselhofplantsoen 7, 1077 BJ **Tel** *570 5600* **Fax** *570 5654* **Rooms** *124*

Map *3 C5*

On a quiet canal in an upmarket residential area, this hotel (with a highly rated restaurant) feels deliciously isolated, yet it is just a short walk from Museumplein (*see p126–7*). Rooms are a little staid, but they are spacious and many have whirlpool baths. Extensive conference facilities make it popular with business travellers. **www.gardenhotel.nl**

RESTAURANTS, CAFES AND BARS

Although the Netherlands does not enjoy the gastronomic reputation of France or Italy, the chances of finding good food at a reasonable price in Amsterdam are high. Many cafés and bars serve tempting snacks, and some, known as *eetcafés*, provide full three-course menus at exceptionally good prices *(see pp236–7)*. In addition to the city's selection of Dutch restaurants, where portions are invariably generous, there are also hundreds of other places to try, offering a range of culinary delights from around the world. The following pages will help you locate the best quality food and most exciting cuisine in all price categories. Detailed reviews on each of the selected restaurants are provided on pages 228–35 and this introduction gives a few practical tips to help you enjoy eating out in Amsterdam.

A typically cosy, atmospheric restaurant, Amsterdam

WHERE TO EAT

Amsterdam is a small city, and most of the restaurants listed in this guide are fairly central. The highest concentrations of restaurants are along Van Baerlestraat in the Museum Quarter, in the Red Light District and along Spuistraat in the Nieuwe Zijde, on Regu-liersdwarsstraat and Utrecht-straat in the Eastern Canal Ring and in the Jordaan. Cheap meals can also be enjoyed in any of the city's *eetcafés*.

WHAT TO EAT

In the past, Dutch home cooking and snacks were traditionally offered in *eetcafés*, and Indonesian-based cuisine was the main cheap alternative. French food was served in more expensive restaurants. Today, there is a much greater choice of international cuisine available and many of the city's restaurants combine French cooking techniques with seasonal Dutch ingredients.

Since Indonesia was once a Dutch colony, Amsterdam is one of the best places in Europe to sample its diverse flavours. Much of the cooking may lean too heavily towards the Chinese style for purists, but it is possible to sample genuine Indonesian recipes. Japanese and Thai food is also popular and affordable. Italian cooking is another favourite and the standard is improving. Indian, Mexican and African food can also be found, but the quality is variable.

On the whole, vegetarians are very well catered for here. Vegan and vegetarian eateries are particularly prolific on the canalsides of the Jordaan area.

WHAT TO DRINK

Beer is the drink of preference in most Dutch cafés and bars, and all have a wide selection of local and imported brews *(see p48–9)*. Wine is widely available and nearly all restaurants in Amsterdam offer a good choice, with emphasis on French wines. Most Spanish and Italian restaurants also have an interesting range of their own local wines. A special symbol is awarded to

Amsterdam's famous floating Chinese restaurant, the Sea Palace *(see p235)*

those restaurants listed in this guide that offer an exceptionally good choice of wines.

Restaurants specializing in traditional cuisine tend to have the best selection of *jenevers* (Dutch gin) *(see p48–9)*.

HOW MUCH TO PAY

Dutch people like to know exactly how much they are going to pay for a meal, so almost all restaurants display a menu in the window. This gives the prices, which include VAT (BTW) and service. Prices vary markedly in the city and a meal at a luxurious restaurant can cost more than 80 per head. However, if you are on a budget, Amsterdam has a wide choice of places serving meals at under 45 per head. The cost of drinks is invariably extra and the mark-up levied by a restaurant, especially on cheap wine, can be high.

Enjoying attentive service – a feature of eating out in Amsterdam

OPENING TIMES

Since the Dutch don't view lunch as the main meal of the day, few restaurants are open during the day. However, many designer bars and brown cafés *(see pp236–7)* serve lunch from around noon to 2pm. In most restaurants, dinner is served from 6pm onwards, and last orders are often taken as early as 10pm. Nowadays, however, some kitchens are deciding to stay open longer. Some restaurants, particularly those in the central areas, now take orders until 11pm, and a few remain open considerably later. Traditionally, many do not open at all on a Monday,

Outdoor café life near the Waag in Nieuwmarkt

although this is also changing. For details of café and bar opening times, see *Light Meals and Snacks* on pages 236–7.

MAKING A RESERVATION

When visiting one of the city's more celebrated restaurants, it is always wise to book in advance. The listings on pages 228–35 indicate where booking is advisable.

Popular brown cafés and designer bars can also become crowded in the evening, but few of them take reservations.

READING THE MENU

The menus at many tourist restaurants are written in Dutch, French and English. However, as most waiters and waitresses in the city speak good English, and often another European language, it is rarely a problem ordering a meal anywhere in Amsterdam. For more details on what to order, see pages 226–7.

ETIQUETTE

Most restaurants in Amsterdam are relaxed, so smart casual or semi-formal dress is suitable almost everywhere. Although there is nothing to stop you dressing up for special occasions, nowhere insists on a tie. For details of eating out with children, see page 253.

SMOKING

In 2005 the Dutch government embarked upon an anti-smoking campaign. Cafés and restaurants are now required

to state their smoking policy on a sign at the door, which could be that there are some non-smoking areas, no non-smoking areas or separate areas just for smokers. By the end of 2008, it is expected that at least 75% of all cafés and restaurants will have to provide a non-smoking section.

DISABILITIES

Disabled visitors will be able to get into the majority of ground-floor restaurants in the city. However, toilets can be difficult to get to as access to them is often via steep stairs.

TIPPING

A service charge of 15 per cent is automatically included on bills in restaurants, cafés and bars. This rarely goes to the server, however, so most Amsterdammers leave a gratuity of about 10 per cent. This is left as change rather than included on a credit card payslip.

The picturesque terrace at the ever-popular De Jaren café *(see p228)*

The Flavours of Amsterdam

From its street-corner fish-stalls to its cafés and top-flight gourmet restaurants, eating out in Amsterdam can be full of surprises. Traditional Dutch cuisine may be simple, wholesome and hearty, but the variety of food on offer in the city is huge and influenced by culinary styles from across the globe. Holland was once a major colonial power and its trading ships brought back exotic ingredients, ideas and people from former colonies to settle. Dutch chefs branched out and tried new flavours, and as such, "fusion" food has long been a feature of Amsterdam's menus.

Edam cheese

Sampling pickled herring at one of Amsterdam's many fish-stalls

HOME-GROWN STAPLES

The typical Dutch menu offers good, solid fare. Plainly prepared fish or meat is served with well-cooked vegetables. Pork, hams and all kinds of sausages are popular. The North Sea provides plenty of fresh fish, especially cod, herring and mackerel, as well as its own variety of tiny brown shrimps. Leafy green vegetables, such as cabbage, endive (chicory) and curly kale make regular appearances, frequently mashed with the ubiquitous potato. Sauerkraut arrived from Germany long ago and is now considered a native dish, as are French fries dowsed in mayonnaise, which are a Belgian import. The world famous Gouda and Edam cheeses are sold at various stages of maturity, and with flavourings such as cloves, cumin or herbs.

THE MELTING POT

Amsterdam has long had a reputation for religious and political tolerance. Refugees who found a safe haven there brought along their own styles of cooking. In the 16th century, Jews fleeing persecution in Portugal and

Bami goreng (fried noodles with chicken and shrimp)

Fried tofu with sambal oelek (chilli sauce)

Steamed rice

Prawn crackers

Selection of typical *rijsttafel* dishes

Satay ayam (chicken satay)

Gado gado (vegetable salad with peanut sauce)

LOCAL DISHES AND SPECIALITIES

Brown shrimp

Dining out in Amsterdam is almost guaranteed to come up with some curious quirks. Cheese, ham and bread are standards at breakfast, but you may also find *ontbijtkoek* (gingerbread) and *hagelslag* (grains of chocolate) to sprinkle over bread. Ham and cheese are also lunchtime staples, often served in a bread roll with a glass of milk, though more adventurous sandwiches and salads are creeping in. Numerous pancake houses provide both sweet and savoury snacks throughout the day. The evening is the time when Amsterdam's eateries have the most to offer. The soups and mashed vegetables of Dutch farmhouse cooking sit alongside spicy Indonesian delights, as well as innovative cuisine from some of Amsterdam's fine chefs.

Erwtensoep *is a thick pea and smoked sausage soup, which is often served with rye bread and slices of ham.*

Baskets of wild mushrooms at an organic market

Antwerp were some of the first foreigners to make their home in the city. Today, Amsterdammers count as their own such Jewish specialities as *pekelvlees* (salt beef), pickled vegetables (often served as salad) and a variety of sticky cakes, now found mostly in the more old-fashioned tea-rooms.

The 20th century saw an influx of immigrants from Turkey and several North African countries. Large Arab and Turkish communities have become established in Amsterdam. As a result, restaurants with menus that feature Middle-Eastern style stuffed vegetables, succulent stews and couscous, are almost everywhere. *Falafel* (fried chickpea balls) are readily available from road-side take-aways and are now

one of the city's favourite late-night snacks. Ethiopians, Greeks, Thais, Italians and Japanese are among other waves of immigrants to make their culinary mark, and most recently traditional British fare has become popular.

Gouda on offer in an Amsterdam cheese shop

INDONESIAN LEGACY

The Dutch began colonizing Indonesia in the 17th century and ruled the south-east Asian archipelago right up until 1949. Indonesian cuisine has had a marked influence on eating habits in Holland. Ingredients once regarded as exotic have crept into Dutch dishes. It is now common-place to spice up apple pies and biscuits with cinnamon, which is sometimes even used to flavour vegetables. Coconut and chillis are very popular flavourings, too, and sampling a *rijsttafel* (see below) is considered one of the highlights of any trip to Amsterdam.

THE RIJSTTAFEL

Dutch colonialists in Indonesia often found that the modest local portions failed to satisfy their hunger. To match their larger appetites, they created the *rijsttafel* (literally "rice-table"). It consists of around 20 small spicy dishes, served up with a shared bowl of rice or noodles. Pork or chicken *satay* (mini kebabs with peanut sauce) and *kroepoek* (prawn crackers) usually arrive first. A selection of curried meat and vegetable dishes follows, with perhaps a plate of fried tofu and various salads, all more or less served together. A sweet treat, such as bananas fried in batter, rounds it all off.

Shrimp croquettes *are shrimps in a creamy sauce, coated in breadcrumbs and deep-fried until golden.*

Stamppot *is a hearty dish of curly kale, endive (chicory) and crispy bacon mixed with mashed potato.*

Nasi goreng, *an Indonesian-style dish of egg-fried rice with pork and mushrooms, is also popular for a* rijsttafel.

Choosing a Restaurant

The restaurants in this guide have been selected
across a wide range of price categories for their
good value, exceptional food and interesting locations.
The restaurants are listed area by area; entries are
alphabetical within each price category. Information
on cafés and bars can be found on pp236–7.

PRICE CATEGORIES
The following price ranges are for a
three-course meal for one, including
half a bottle of wine, plus all
unavoidable extra charges,
such as cover, service and tax.
€ under 30 euros
€€ 30–40 euros
€€€ 40–50 euros
€€€€ over 50 euros

OUDE ZIJDE

Bird
🚹   ♿   €

Zeedijk 72–74, 1011 HB **Tel** *620 1442*   **Map** *8 D2*

The best Thai eatery in town is spacious, with authentic decor and impeccable service from the mainly Thai staff.
Renowned for its sublime red- and green-curry sauces – which are combined with fish, beef, chicken, pork and tofu –
Bird is also great value for money. Alternatively, pop over to the tiny, typically Thai snack bar opposite. Closed lunch.

Café Bern
🖥️   ♿   🚹   €

Nieuwmarkt 9, 1011 JR **Tel** *622 0034*   **Map** *8 D3*

A stone's throw from the Red Light District, this cheap and cheerful brown bar/restaurant specializes in Swiss cheese
fondues, served alongside simple salads and desserts. It is particularly popular with locals (many of whom eat at the
bar), so advance reservations are recommended. A wide range of spirits and house wines is available. Closed lunch.

Kilimanjaro
🚹   🏮   €

Rapenburgerplein 6, 1011 VB **Tel** *622 3485*   **Map** *5 C1*

An absolute gem, this warm and friendly pan-African restaurant specializes in dishes from across the vast continent.
Additional delights include the Alligator cocktail, Mongozo beer (served in a bowl) and Ethiopian coffee, which
comes with popcorn. In warm weather, they also set up a charming outdoor terrace. Closed lunch; Mon.

De Jaren
🚹   🏮   ♿   €€

Nieuwe Doelenstraat 20–22, 1012 CP **Tel** *625 5771*   **Map** *7 C4*

This huge, high-ceilinged grand café serves simple soups and sandwiches on the ground floor, and heartier meat,
fish and vegetarian dishes in the first-floor restaurant (which also features a large salad bar). Both areas have
pleasant outdoor terraces. On the downside, when things can get busy (and they often do), service can be slow.

Éenvistwéévis
🚹   €€

Schippersgracht 6, 1011 TR **Tel** *623 2894*   **Map** *5 C1*

Located near Kilimanjaro (*see above*), this small, charming restaurant is a paradise for fish lovers. The chef transforms
the catch of the day – be it plaice, sea bass, oysters or tuna – into simple, no-frills dishes where the flavours are not
drowned in unnecessary sauces. A modest pavement terrace allows *al fresco* eating in summer. Closed lunch; Mon.

Hemelse Modder
♿   🚹   🏮   ♿   €€

Oude Waal 11, 1011 BZ **Tel** *624 3203*   **Map** *8 E2*

This spacious, modern and gay-friendly restaurant, on one of the city's oldest canals, offers international cuisine with
strong French and Italian influences, and an eclectic wine list. The *pièce de résistance*, however, is its charming
terrace at the back. It is wise to book outdoor tables in advance during the warmer months. Closed lunch; Mon.

Oriental City
🚹   €€

Oudezijds Voorburgwal 177, 1012 EV **Tel** *626 8352*   **Map** *7 C3*

Popular with both tourists and the local Chinese community, this huge, multifloored restaurant gets so busy, you may
have to wait for a table, especially at weekends. Arriving early or booking ahead might help. Its reputation is built on
its dim sum and Cantonese and Szechuan specialities. A window table allows views over the Red Light District.

In De Waag
🚹   🏮   ♿   €€€

Nieuwmarkt 4, 1012 CR **Tel** *422 7772*   **Map** *8 D3*

In De Waag is set in a castle-like building dating from 1488 (*see p60*). Above the restaurant, which is lit entirely by
candles, is where Rembrandt made sketches for *The Anatomy Lesson of Dr Tulp*, his first group portrait. On the menu
are eclectic (if a tad expensive) meat and fish dishes and vegetarian options. Desserts are also divine. Book ahead.

Blauw aan de Wal
🚹   🏮   ♿   €€€€

Oudezijds Achterburgwal 99, 1012 DD **Tel** *330 2257*   **Map** *8 D3*

One of the Red Light District's best-kept secrets is this stylish restaurant hidden at the end of a tiny alley. Refined
palates will enjoy the imaginative Mediterranean fusion delights and excellent wine list. Blauw's reputation means
that advance reservations are necessary (especially to eat on its peaceful terrace in summer). Closed lunch; Sun.

Key to Symbols *see back cover flap*

Café Roux (The Grand Hotel)

Oudezijds Voorburgwal 197, 1012 EX **Tel** 555 3560

€€€€

Map 7 C3

This informal Art Deco restaurant affords a unique opportunity to try dishes created by master chef Albert Roux at a reasonable price (especially the set menu). The wonderful French and British dishes are made using the best-quality local products. Wine selection is excellent. Breakfast is served 6.30–10.30am; English high tea, 3–5pm daily.

Vermeer (NH Barbizon Palace Hotel)

Prins Hendrikkade 59–72, 1012 AD **Tel** 556 4885

€€€€

Map 8 D1

Set within four adjoining 17th-century buildings, this Michelin-starred restaurant produces rich gastronomic delights from France. Start the adventure in the intimate cocktail lounge, where you can enjoy options such as seared duck liver or beef skirt with oyster, truffle, wakame and Japanese artichokes. Inspired wine list. Closed Sat lunch, Sun.

NIEUWE ZIJDE

Brasserie Harkema

Nes 67, 1012 KD **Tel** 428 2222

€

Map 7 B4

A classic Parisian brasserie with a stylish New York sensibility, Harkema serves *haute cuisine* at affordable prices. It is immensely popular, especially in the evenings, so it is wise to book ahead. Feast on delights such as sautéed venison steak on toast with fried chanterelle mushrooms, followed by chocolate tart with a Bastogne biscuit base.

Kantjil & De Tijger

Spuistraat 291–293, 1012 VS **Tel** 620 0994

€

Map 7 A4

Authentic Indonesian cuisine in a warm, modern interior. Opt for the *rijsttafel* (rice table), or dine early (4.30–6.45pm) and get a full meal in a *mangkok* (bowl) for just under 9 euros. This includes rice or noodles with a meat or vegetable dish, pickled cucumber, egg in coconut sauce and prawn/vegetarian crackers. Open for lunch Sat & Sun.

Keuken van 1870

Spuistraat 4, 1012 TS **Tel** 620 4018

€

Map 7 C1

Something of an Amsterdam institution, this former soup kitchen (dating from 1870) still maintains its policy of providing cheap meals – though its patrons these days are office workers, students and pensioners. The set daily changing menu of "homely Dutch cooking" (meat and veg dishes) costs just 7.50 euros. Closed lunch; Sun.

Tibet

Lange Niezel 24, 1012 GT **Tel** 624 1137

€

Map 8 D2

A marvellous find, and veritable haven, in the bowels of the bustling Red Light District – not least because it serves food until 1am. The menu offers an overwhelming choice of mostly Chinese Szechuan dishes, alongside staple Tibetan fare like *momo* (dumplings). Eclectic Tibetan decor, and relaxed, friendly, attentive service. Closed Tue.

Green Planet

Spuistraat 122, 1012 VA **Tel** 625 8280

€€

Map 7 B2

This bright vegetarian restaurant uses mostly organic ingredients in its imaginative fare – from soups to salads and pasta dishes. Quality food, however, takes time to prepare, so come armed with patience. The chef will oblige any special dietary needs. Try Green Planet's renowned vegan tofu-lemon cheesecake and chocolate cake. Closed Sun.

1e Klas

Stationsplein 15, 1012 AB **Tel** 625 0131

€€€

Map 8 D1

The former first-class waiting room on platform 2B of Centraal Station (see p79) is now a grand café/restaurant exuding Art Nouveau elegance throughout its stunning interior. On the menu, everything from standard fare, such as soup and salads, to first-class fare in the form of traditional French dishes. Breakfast is served from 8.30am.

Kapitein Zeppos

Gebed Zonder End 5, 1012 HS **Tel** 624 2057

€€€

Map 7 B4

Tucked down a tiny alley, lit by fairy-lights, this bar-restaurant (with Belgian ceramic-tile tables and eclectic ornaments) was once a coach stable, then a cigar factory. The kitchen turns out delicious French-Mediterranean cuisine, with Italian, Moroccan and Spanish influences. Ideal for a romantic evening. Occasional live music. Closed Mon.

De Compagnon

Guldehandsteeg 17, 1012 RA **Tel** 620 4225

€€€€

Map 8 D1

This small restaurant, hidden down a little alleyway, can be hard to find, but persistence will be rewarded. De Compagnon's Burgundian kitchen produces meat, fish and vegetarian dishes, made with mostly organic ingredients. It is the ideal place for intimate dinners: book a table by the window. Exceptional wine list. Closed Sat lunch, Sun.

Supperclub

Jonge Roelensteeg 21, 1012 PL **Tel** 344 6400

€€€€

Map 7 B3

Remove your shoes and recline on cushioned beds at this spacious restaurant-club. DJs spin upbeat lounge as you graze on culinary delights from the open kitchen – all spread out over five courses. Fine wines, video art, massage and offbeat performances complete this assault on the senses. There is also a lounge bar downstairs. Closed lunch.

WESTERN CANAL RING

De Bolhoed
Prinsengracht 60–62, 1015 DX **Tel** *626 1803*   **Map** *1 B3*

A charming vegetarian restaurant with a delightful canalside terrace, great for sunny afternoons and balmy evenings. Chefs whip up imaginative international dishes – the daily vegan dish is superb – from mostly organic ingredients. Plates overflow, but be sure to leave room for the delicious desserts. Service can be slow. Reservations recommended.

De Vliegende Schotel
Nieuwe Leliestraat 162, 1015 HE **Tel** *625 2041*   **Map** *1 B4*

Enormously popular with the artistic and alternative crowd, "The Flying Saucer" dishes up cheap and hearty organic vegetarian/vegan fare in two bright, canteen-style rooms (one is no-smoking). Check the blackboard for the daily specials and place your order at the counter with the friendly staff. No alcohol. The kitchen opens at 4pm daily.

Foodism
Oude Leliestraat 8, 1015 AW **Tel** *427 5103*   **Map** *7 A2*

Hidden down a small street in the Jordaan, five minutes' walk from the Dam, this bright and endearing restaurant serves anything from New York-style breakfasts to hearty soup/sandwiches for lunch and wild-basil pasta for dinner. Or simply pop in for a mid-afternoon coffee and cake. No alcohol. Opens 11.30am (12.30pm Sun).

Semhar
Marnixstraat 259–261, 1015 WH **Tel** *638 1634*   **Map** *1 A4*

The friendly Ethiopian owners of this spacious restaurant (ideal for groups) create sublime traditional dishes from their homeland and neighbouring Eritrea. Their *injera* (pancake) dishes are a must – especially for vegetarians. An absolute gem despite its location on a rather unattractive street (albeit on the edge of the Jordaan). Open from 4pm.

Spanjer & Van Twist
Leliegracht 60, 1015 DJ **Tel** *639 0109*   **Map** *7 A2*

Less than a minute's walk from the Anne Frank Huis (*see p90*), this split-level café-restaurant opens at 10am for breakfasts and has a seasonally changing menu of soups, sandwiches or pasta and curry dishes. It features a reading table and a charming canalside terrace. The kitchen shuts at 10.30pm, but light snacks are served until closing time.

Chez Georges
Herenstraat 3, 1015 BX **Tel** *626 3332*   **Map** *7 A1*

Small and seductive, this restaurant is a veritable tour de force of Burgundian cuisine. It is a must for gourmands, who will delight in owner/chef Georges' superb meat and fish dishes (opt for the five-course or seven-course menus). It is also great value for money, though the fine wines could push up the price. Book ahead. Closed lunch; Wed, Sun.

De Gouden Reael
Zandhoek 14, 1013 KT **Tel** *623 3883*   **Map** *1 C1*

This 1648 building used to be a herring warehouse and then a 19th-century *jenever* (Dutch gin) bar. Located in one of the most picturesque parts of Amsterdam, this low-key bar-restaurant is popular with lovers of French and Alsatian cuisine. A good wine list complements the food, and there are great waterfront views from the small terrace.

Werck
Prinsengracht 277, 1016 GW **Tel** *627 4079*   **Map** *1 B4*

Rustic lounge decor, stairways, a kitchen in a greenhouse, subtle nooks and crannies, a peaceful courtyard and upstairs terrace all give this restaurant its nice ambience. International food is well presented and of a reasonable quality, but service can be slow. Werck remains, however, well worth a visit. Closed Mon–Fri lunch in winter.

Lof
Haarlemmerstraat 62, 1013 ES **Tel** *620 2997*   **Map** *2 D3*

Despite its rather innocuous appearance, Lof is a firm favourite of many of the city's most discerning diners. The daily changing offerings revolve around seasonal fish, meat and game. There is no menu: the staff come to your table and simply describe what is on offer to you. For intimate, lingering dining, book the small backroom. Closed lunch; Mon.

Stout!
Haarlemmerstraat 73, 1013 EL **Tel** *616 3664*   **Map** *2 D3*

A hip, yet unpretentious, restaurant offering creative international fusion fare, with inspired combinations of flavours. The speciality dish (Plateau Stout; for a minimum of two people) allows you to sample ten small, varied dishes. Stout! is also renowned for its wine list; a wine-tasting event is held here every third Sunday of the month.

Toscanini
Lindengracht 75, 1015 KD **Tel** *623 2813*   **Map** *1 C3*

Despite its huge size, this Italian restaurant gets booked up quickly. Formerly a coach house, then a blacksmith's forge, the venue retains its original 19th-century glass roof. Chefs create authentic regional dishes in the open kitchen, while the wine list affords the chance to drink both classic and lesser-known wines from Italy. Closed lunch; Sun.

Key to Price Guide *see p228* **Key to Symbols** *see back cover flap*

Bordewijk

Noordermarkt 7, 1015 MV **Tel** *624 3899*

€€€€

Map *1 C3*

Renowned for its superb French international cuisine and for service that will make you feel truly pampered, Bordewijk is one of the best restaurants in town. The chef will come to your table in person to describe the day's menu. As it fills up, the acoustics can sometimes make the place quite loud. Book ahead. Closed lunch; Mon.

Christophe

Leliegracht 46, 1015 DH **Tel** *625 0807*

€€€€

Map *7 A2*

This canalside establishment, owned by one of the finest chefs in the Netherlands, makes for an exceptional and intimate dining experience. The inventive, pure, full-flavoured dishes have earned Jean-Christophe a well-deserved Michelin star every year for more than a decade. Closed lunch; Sun, Mon.

CENTRAL CANAL RING

Wagamama

Max Euweplein 10, 1017 MB **Tel** *528 7778*

€

Map *4 E2*

Fast food but relaxed service are the norm at this Japanese noodle restaurant with a designer canteen-style interior. Still, you could do worse for a snack, lunch or dinner within the touristic surroundings of the Leidseplein (*see p110*). Practically next door to the Paradiso music venue, this is one of Amsterdam's very few non-smoking restaurants.

Balthazar's Keuken

Elandsgracht 108, 1016 VA **Tel** *420 2114*

€€

Map *1 B5*

A clutter of pots and pans hangs from the open kitchen here. In fact, it is so cosy, you will feel as though you're eating at the home of owners Karin and Alain, not least because there is no menu: guests are simply given a weekly changing, three-course international meal. Closed lunch; Mon, Tue, Sat, Sun (on these days large groups can rent it).

Envy

Prinsengracht 381, 1016 HL **Tel** *344 6407*

€€

Map *1 B5*

The menu here consists of tiny Italian delicacies that can be chosen individually, at your leisure. The Envy chefs expertly combine flavours in an open kitchen by the tall window of this narrow, designer warehouse space. An absolute must for foodies, this is one of Amsterdam's finest offerings. Frequented by smart thirtysomethings. Closed lunch.

Los Pilones

Kerkstraat 63, 1017 GC **Tel** *320 4651*

€€

Map *7 A5*

A small and warm cantina run by two Mexican brothers who serve authentic dishes from their country. This is some of the best Mexican food in the whole of Amsterdam. Expect the occasional unusual combination such as enchiladas with a chocolate sauce. The *pièce de résistance* is their huge range of tequilas (around 35 brands). Closed lunch; Mon.

NOA

Leidsegracht 84, 1016 CR **Tel** *626 0802*

€€

Map *4 E1*

NOA (Noodles of Amsterdam) is a trendy canalside, New York-style lounge establishment. Relax on the comfy couches at the front with a cocktail, or dine in the restaurant at the back by the open kitchen. The food on offer is broadly fusion in style, subtly combining East and West.

Mayur

Korte Leidsedwarsstraat 203, 1017 RB **Tel** *623 2142*

€€€

Map *4 E2*

Authentic tandoori dishes cooked in a wood-fired clay oven are the speciality of this spacious restaurant just off the Leidseplein (*see p110*). Preparation of food is also given special attention: meats are marinated for 24 hours in yogurt and spices, resulting in dishes that are spicy but not eye-wateringly hot. Closed lunch.

Nomads

Rozengracht 133, 1016 LV **Tel** *344 6401*

€€€

Map *1 A5*

The ultimate treat for decadent diners is this first-floor restaurant inspired by Arabic nomad culture. Kick off your shoes and lounge on beds in a scene straight out of *Arabian Nights*, while Eastern food is served from bronze platters. DJs at weekends. Late-opening kitchen (11.30pm) and bar (1am weekdays; 3am weekends). Closed lunch; Mon.

Odeon

Singel 460, 1017 AW **Tel** *521 8555*

€€€

Map *7 A5*

Consisting of a plush, cosmopolitan restaurant, a cocktail bar, a brasserie and an upstairs club/theatre, Odeon takes up an entire canal house dating from 1662. The food served in the basement brasserie is disappointing and poor value for money; but the restaurant (closed Mon, Sun) offers competent international cuisine.

Proeverij 274

Prinsengracht 274, 1016 HH **Tel** *421 1848*

€€€

Map *1 B5*

Popular with both locals and visitors to the city, this warm and romantic two-floored restaurant serves classic international dishes using predominantly organic ingredients. Book the round table by the door for a delightful view over the canal. Groups of up to 25 people can be catered for in the downstairs basement. Closed lunch.

Blue Pepper
Nassaukade 366, 1054 AB **Tel** *489 7039*

€€€€

Map *4 D1*

Flawless and inspired contemporary Indonesian cuisine (with Chinese and Filipino influences), with extraordinary combinations of flavours. The *rÿsttafel* created by the Javanese chef is utterly unique. No wonder this small, chic restaurant is adored by foodies, despite the rather ordinary location. Impressive wine list. Closed lunch.

The Dylan
Keizersgracht 384, 1016 GB **Tel** *530 2010*

€€€€

Map *4 E1*

The intimate gourmet restaurant at this stunning boutique hotel offers international cuisine with an inspired choice of traditional and contemporary dishes. Service is attentive and the wine menu eclectic. Outdoor dining is on offer in the beautiful courtyard when the weather is good. A must for the discerning diner. Dinner only. Closed Sunday.

EASTERN CANAL RING

Bazar
Albert Cuypstraat 182, 1073 BL **Tel** *675 0544*

€

Map *5 A5*

A terrific Eastern-style restaurant within a former church located halfway up the bustling Albert Cuyp street market (*see p122*). On the menu is a mouth-watering choice of North African, Moroccan, Iranian and Turkish dishes for breakfast, lunch or dinner (during the week, it opens at 8am; 9am at weekends). Great for vegetarians.

Zushi
Amstel 20, 1017 AA **Tel** *330 6882*

€

Map *7 C5*

A large, bright, high-ceilinged modern sushi restaurant where you can take your sushi straight from the oval conveyor belt, while chefs in the middle of the belt prepare additional goodies. Each plate is colour-coded according to price. Wash the wasabi down with Japanese beers like Sapporo, Kirin or Asahi.

De Waaghals
Frans Halsstraat 29, 1072 BK **Tel** *679 9609*

€€

Map *4 F3*

A superb vegetarian restaurant that will leave even the most hardened of carnivores sated. Each month, the menu focuses on a different country, and organic produce is used wherever possible; even the beer is locally brewed and the wines organic. In summer, ask for a table in the charming garden at the back. Book ahead. Closed lunch, Mon.

Rose's Cantina
Reguliersdwarsstraat 38–40, 1017 BM **Tel** *625 9797*

€€

Map *7 B5*

A sprawling, long-established Mexican restaurant with a terrific atmosphere and delicious food (though a limited choice for vegetarians). Its success is due to a combination of friendly service, great value and classic menu: choose fillings for your taco, enchilada or quesadilla. Great cocktails, too. Small patio terrace in summer at rear. Closed lunch.

SSK
Falckstraat 3, 1017 VV **Tel** *330 1128*

€€

Map *5 A4*

You will feel like you are having dinner at a friend's house at SSK. Hostess/chef Hanneke van den Bergh creates a fixed three-course meal using produce she has bought fresh from the market and specialist shops. The cuisine is traditional Mediterranean… with a twist. Organic wines are carefully chosen to match the food. Closed lunch; Sun–Tue.

Vamos A Ver
Govert Flinckstraat 308, 1073 CJ **Tel** *673 6992*

€€

Map *5 A5*

The best Spanish restaurant in town is found in the neighbourhood of De Pijp. Although the interior might be a little tacky, the food served is no-nonsense, authentic Spanish fare – and it is outstanding. Service is very friendly, but do not come here if you're after a hip and trendy tapas bar. Closed lunch; Tue.

De Utrechtsedwarstafel
Utrechtsedwarsstraat 107, 1017 WD **Tel** *625 4189*

€€€

Map *5 A3*

This modern French-oriented restaurant is a must for indecisive diners: you do not choose the food itself but only the number of courses (three to five) and menu type ("simple" to "gastronomic"). The details are left to the owner of this establishment. Exclusive wines from all over the world are matched to your food. Closed Sun, Mon, Tue; Jan.

Garlic Queen
Reguliersdwarsstraat 27, 1017 BJ **Tel** *422 6426*

€€€

Map *7 B5*

A small, quaint restaurant with a dark interior located on Amsterdam's trendy gay street. Its novel speciality is – yes, garlic! Every dish contains it – from the starters to the desserts – yet it complements rather than overwhelms the flavours. Friendly service and a pleasant, relaxed ambience complete the experience. Closed lunch; Mon, Tue.

Le Zinc… et les Autres
Prinsengracht 999, 1017 KM **Tel** *622 9044*

€€€

Map *5 A3*

Creative and hearty French-international cuisine is on offer here. Le Zinc has a formal, classic interior complemented by wooden beams and rustic furniture, and is located over two floors of a beautifully restored warehouse. Other perks include an excellent wine list, a canalside terrace for balmy nights and no mobile phones. Closed lunch; Sun.

Key to Price Guide *see p228* **Key to Symbols** *see back cover flap*

Proeflokaal Janvier
Amstelveld 12, 1017 JD **Tel** *626 1199* **Map** *5 A3*

A hip, lounge-style restaurant housed within the white Amstelkerk (*see p119*). A choice of three- or four-course menus offers classic French dishes with a twist. The majority of wines on the list are also available by the glass. Proeflokaal Janvier also features one of the most peaceful terraces in town. Closed lunch; Mon.

Tempo Doeloe
Utrechtsestraat 75, 1017 VJ **Tel** *625 6718* **Map** *5 A3*

For authentic Indonesian food, ring the doorbell of Tempo Doeloe. Opt for the rice table (shared between two people), which includes 25 small dishes and two types of rice, or choose à la carte: spicy dishes are marked on the menu. Beware: hot means hot! Friendly service, superb wines and good vegetarian options. Book ahead. Closed lunch; Sun.

Van de Kaart
Prinsengracht 512, 1017 KH **Tel** *625 9232* **Map** *4 E2*

Do not be fooled by the smart, yet unremarkable, interior of this restaurant: a quick perusal of the exciting French-Mediterranean menu will provoke a much stronger reaction. Starters alone include delights such as salad niçoise with half a grilled lobster, poached quail eggs and potato confit. Smoking allowed only after dinner. Closed lunch; Sun.

Beddington's
Utrechtsedwarsstraat 141, 1017 WE **Tel** *620 7393* **Map** *5 B3*

One for discerning taste buds and those in search of slow-paced dining in sober, stylish surroundings. From the open kitchen, British owner/chef Jean Beddington produces seamless French and Asian fusion, with a sprinkling of British sensibility. Delightful desserts and friendly service; vegetarians are also well catered for. Closed lunch; Sun, Mon.

Gorgeous
Tweede van der Helststraat 16, 1072 PD **Tel** *379 1400* **Map** *5 A5*

A relatively new addition to Amsterdam, this small yet stylish, modern French restaurant offers a variety of adventurous "gastronomic tapas" (which live up to their name). Alternatively, choose from the (rather limited) à la carte menu. The small pavement terrace is conducive to people-watching on this bustling street. Closed lunch; Sun, Mon.

Segugio
Utrechtsestraat 96, 1017 VS **Tel** *330 1503* **Map** *5 A3*

The simple yet smart interior of this intimate, split-level restaurant belies the exquisite menu, offering classic and modern Italian dishes. Delicacies include gnocchi with wild boar, or fillet of sole with crab and Vernaccia wine; the risotto is also divine. Superb wine list. Closed lunch; Sun; Christmas/New Year.

MUSEUM QUARTER

Pompa
Willemsparkweg 6, 1017 HD **Tel** *662 6206* **Map** *4 D3*

In an area short of restaurants – let alone inexpensive ones – this tapas bar is a real find, especially after an evening at the nearby Concertgebouw (*see p128*), when most restaurants are filled to the brim. Split-level, warm and friendly, this eatery has a broad, value-for-money menu offering Mediterranean dishes and tapas; great salads, too.

Café Toussaint
Bosboom Toussaintstraat 26, 1054 AS **Tel** *685 0737* **Map** *4 D1*

This absolute gem is well worth the five-minute stroll from the busy Leidseplein (*see p110*) across to this quiet street. It is a small but charming café with an open kitchen where healthy international fare, such as sandwiches, soups and tapas (with plenty for vegetarians), is created. Cosy and romantic at night, with a peaceful terrace and no mobiles.

Pulpo
Willemsparkweg 87, 1071 GT **Tel** *676 0700* **Map** *4 D3*

Just east of the Vondelpark (*see p128*), near the Museumplein, is this popular, relaxed and unpretentious restaurant. The Mediterranean cuisine is occasionally imbued with subtle African and Middle Eastern hints, such as bass, roasted carrots, lemon cous-cous and saffron *labne* or a dessert of terrine of rice, dates and mango lime chutney. Closed Sun.

Vertigo
Vondelpark 3, 1071 AA **Tel** *612 3021* **Map** *4 D2*

Resembling a wine cellar, this spacious and comfortable international restaurant is within Amsterdam's historic Filmmuseum (*see p129*), at the top of the Vondelpark (*see p128*). Warm and candlelit in the winter, it has one of the city's most popular terraces in summer, when they also sell picnics that you can take into the park.

The College Hotel
Roelof Hartstraat 1, 1071 VE **Tel** *571 1511* **Map** *4 E5*

Head to this training hotel for catering students before (it is also open for breakfast) or after a day's shopping on nearby PC Hooftstraat. The renovated gymnasium of an 1895 school building is home to an elegant gourmet restaurant where classic Dutch dishes are given a contemporary twist. Closed Sun.

The Mansion €€€

Hobbemastraat 2, 1071 ZA **Tel** *616 6664*   **Map** *4 E2*

Begin on the three designer cocktail bars on the ground floor; then head up to the classically-styled restaurant, where Hong Kong chefs serve exquisite modern Chinese cuisine; finally, party into the small hours in the stylish basement club. Good value for money, though wines can push up the bill. Closed lunch; Mon.

Brasserie van Baerle €€€€

Van Baerlestraat 158, 1071 BG **Tel** *679 1532*   **Map** *4 E4*

This French-style brasserie is particularly popular with Dutch celebrities, especially for lunch and Sunday brunch (when it opens at 10am). Mouth-watering dishes include grilled sea bass with home-made crab mayonnaise and a roast-pepper dressing. Exceptional wine list and gorgeous garden terrace. Reservations recommended. Closed Sat lunch.

Le Garage €€€€

Ruysdaelstraat 54–56, 1071 XE **Tel** *679 71 76*   **Map** *4 E4*

A favourite haunt of Dutch celebs is this elegant bistro with red plush seating and mirrors. The food is French-international, and organic ingredients are used whenever possible. Le Garage is renowned for its three-course menu and superb wine list featuring classic and lesser-known wines from all over the world. Closed Sat & Sun lunch.

PLANTAGE

Plancius €€

Plantage Kerklaan 61, 1018 CX **Tel** *330 9469*   **Map** *6 D2*

A gay-friendly restaurant in a former fire station opposite the main entrance to Artis Zoo (see *p142*). Although the designer decor is stark, it is comfortable and friendly. The menu is French-oriented, with an accent on meat and fish, but there are also tempting vegetarian options. On Saturdays and Sundays they also serve breakfasts.

La Rive (Amstel Hotel) €€€€

Professor Tulpplein 1, 1018 GX **Tel** *520 3264*   **Map** *5 B4*

This Michelin-starred restaurant within the Amstel Hotel is one for connoisseurs. Outstanding cuisine from its modern French-Mediterranean kitchen is matched by an excellent wine list. Reserve the chef's table in the kitchen (four to eight people) for an unusual twist to your dining experience. Dress code is elegant. Closed Sat lunch, Sun.

FURTHER AFIELD

Amsterdam €

Watertorenplein 6, 1051 PA **Tel** *682 2666*

Within a former water-pumping house dating from 1897, this huge, industrial-style restaurant near the Westerpark serves simple, well-priced European food – from steak and fries to grilled wild-boar cutlets. There is a relaxing grass terrace at the back, which makes it great for families. The kitchen is open until 11.30pm on Friday and Saturday.

Gare de L'Est €€

Cruquiusweg 9, 1019 AT **Tel** *463 0620*

Within a former coffee house built in 1901 (resembling an old railway station), this unique, romantic restaurant is hugely popular with locals and those who have wandered through the redeveloped Eastern Docklands area, where Gare de L'Est is located. Reservations for the daily changing, four-course global dinners are a must.

Pacific Parc €€

Polonceaukade 23, 1014 DA **Tel** *488 7778*   **Map** *1 A1*

Part of a redeveloped gas factory, this spacious, funky place is great for hearty lunches or dinners that combine international ingredients with French cooking techniques. DJs take to the decks for post-dinner dancing (Wed–Sun), and there is live music, too. Other touches include an open fire in winter and a waterside terrace in summer.

Star Ferry €€

Piet Heinkade 1, 1019 BR **Tel** *788 2090*

Named after the Hong Kong ferry company, and located within the architecturally stunning Muziekgebouw aan 't IJ, this spacious, glass-walled café-restaurant specializes in Asian-influenced international cuisine. There are incredible views across the busy waterfront behind Centraal Station (see *p79*), but avoid the unshaded terrace on hot days.

Wilhelmina-Dok €€

Noordwal 1, 1021 PX **Tel** *632 3701*   **Map** *2 F2*

Take the ferry from behind Centraal Station across the River IJ to this spacious 1950s-style restaurant with waterfront terrace offering splendid views of Amsterdam's skyline. With its great-value Mediterranean food, reasonable wine list and extensive bar, it is ideal for groups and informal business lunches, and it can get packed when the sun is out.

Key to Price Guide see *p228* **Key to Symbols** see *back cover flap*

De Odessa
Veemkade 259, 1019 CZ **Tel** *419 3010*

Head to this enchanting Ukrainian fishing boat as the sun sets and enjoy cocktails on the deck, while snacking on oysters. De Odessa's international menu (predominantly fish and meat) is well presented and reasonable – but the draw is the experience itself. DJs play on the lounge-style deck below. Closed lunch in winter; Mon, Tue in winter.

Onassis
Westerdoksdijk 40, 1013 AE **Tel** *330 0456*　　　　　　　**Map** *2 D1*

This exquisite designer restaurant is the haunt of the city's chic and trendy crowd – especially for its huge waterside terrace in summer. The mouth-watering menu offers Italian-oriented cuisine, and you will be spoilt for choice whether you pop by for a quick lunch or a lingering dinner.

Sea Palace
Oosterdokskade 3, 1011 AD **Tel** *626 4777*　　　　　　　**Map** *8 F2*

This floating, pagoda-style Chinese restaurant is an impressive sight on a small dock, five minutes from Centraal Station (*see p79*) en route to the Muziekgebouw aan 't IJ. The huge menu offers Cantonese staples such as won ton soup, alongside more unusual Pekingese and Szechuan dishes.

Vakzuid
Olympisch Stadion 35, 1076 DE **Tel** *570 8400*

A spacious, modern establishment within the grandstand of the Olympic Stadium. From the large open-plan kitchen, chefs create subtle Asian-French fusion food with often surprising tastes and combinations. Vegetarian options are limited, though. There is also a large, cushioned terrace and a cocktail lounge. Closed Sat, Sun (bar open).

Visaandeschelde
Scheldeplein 4, 1078 GR **Tel** *675 1583*

This spacious, white-linen seafood restaurant opposite the RAI (*see p151*) is popular with well-heeled fish lovers. Creative dishes based on Mediterranean cuisine, with a nod to Japanese, use fresh fish from the market (pick your lobster from the tank). Signature dishes are *bouillabaisse* and *fruits de mer*. No mobiles. Closed Sat & Sun lunch.

Ciel Bleu (Okura Hotel)
Ferdinand Bolstraat 333, 1072 LH **Tel** *678 7450*　　　　　**Map** *4 F5*

A Michelin-starred French restaurant on the 23rd floor of the Okura Hotel renowned for its creative, innovative dishes, and terrific views of Amsterdam. A must for impressive business lunches and dinners – or dates. The adjacent cocktail bar opens at 6pm, half an hour before the restaurant. Closed lunch.

De Kas
Kamerlingh Onneslaan 3, 1097 DE **Tel** *462 4562*

An upmarket, organic Mediterranean restaurant set within a 1926 greenhouse (ingredients are picked fresh from the adjacent nursery or their own land elsewhere). Although popular for business lunches, De Kas becomes a romantic destination in the evening. Reserve the chef's table in the kitchen and the terrace in summer. Closed Sat lunch, Sun.

Fifteen
Jollemanhof 9, 1019 GW **Tel** *0900 343 8336*

British celebrity chef Jamie Oliver's open-plan restaurant is situated within a renovated, waterfront warehouse. Book ahead for the set four-course modern Italian tasting menu (with a vegetarian alternative), or just turn up and eat pasta, risotto and ravioli in the cheaper trattoria. Waiting staff and sommelier are very attentive. Closed lunch.

La Sirène (Le Méridien Apollo)
Apollolaan 2, 1077 BA **Tel** *570 5724*　　　　　　　**Map** *4 E5*

The display of shellfish as you enter the restaurant, the nautical interior and the surrounding canals combine to provide a unique experience in Amsterdam. The selection of seafood is mouth-watering, but the menu has a varied selection of dishes, including meat. Great service and a peaceful waterside terrace are other pluses. Sunday brunch.

Mangerie de Kersentuin (Garden Hotel)
Dijsselhofplantsoen 7, 1077 BJ **Tel** *570 5600*　　　　　**Map** *4 D5*

Experience the pure tastes of unpretentious French-Mediterranean cuisine within the enjoyable, informal atmosphere of this long-established restaurant. The menu changes frequently, the comprehensive wine list is well chosen, and there is a terrace for outdoor dining. No mobile phones. Closed Sat lunch, Sun.

Supperclub Cruise
Pier 4 (Behind Centraal Station), 1012 AB **Tel** *344 6403*　　　**Map** *2 E3*

Fancy dining on a 1960 ship, once used by the late Queen Juliana to entertain visiting dignitaries? On Fridays and Saturdays, fashionistas catch the sun on the top deck, sip champagne and cocktails in the bar below, then retire to dinner on the lower deck as the boat sails along the River IJ. Booking necessary. Board at 7.30pm.

Yamazato (Okura Hotel)
Ferdinand Bolstraat 333, 1072 LH **Tel** *678 8351*　　　　　**Map** *4 F5*

This Michelin-starred restaurant serves traditional Japanese specialities. For less adventurous palates, its sushi bar has more than 20 types of freshly prepared sushi and sashimi. Authenticity extends throughout – from the food to the tatami room, private-dining spaces and kimono-clad Japanese waiting staff. Also open 7.30–9.30am for breakfast.

Light Meals and Snacks

In addition to the normal assortment of burger joints, pizzerias and the like, most Dutch cafés and bars serve food ranging from simple bar snacks to a three-course meal. Those that offer lunch-time snacks and an evening meal are generally known as *eetcafés*. While the choice of dishes tends to be limited, the quality is generally high and prices are often very reasonable. Some *eetcafés* have started serving more adventurous dishes and generally offer a good vegetarian selection. However, café and bar kitchens close early and it is difficult to get a meal after 9pm. For more information on cafés and bars, including a selection of the top ten in Amsterdam, see pages 46–7.

BARS AND STREET STALLS

Almost all bars serve a range of snacks. The standard selection of nibbles includes olives, chunks of Dutch cheese served with mustard and *borrelnoten* (nuts with a savoury coating). More substantial tapas-like snacks include *bitterballen* (deep-fried meatballs), *vlammetjes* (deep-fried batter envelopes similar to meat and vegetable spring rolls) and *osseworst* (a spicy mince-beef sausage).

Given the maritime tradition of the Netherlands, it is worth trying the fish dishes available in bars and from stalls on the street, such as herring served with onion or gherkins. Pizza, sandwiches and hamburgers are also commonly available from stalls. However, the most popular snack from street stalls is french fries or *patat frites*, which are served with mayonnaise in a plastic tray or a paper cone *(see p226)*.

PANCAKE HOUSES

Pancakes *(pannenkoeken)* are a popular, value-for-money light meal in Amsterdam. The French-style *crêpe* is believed to have been adopted in the Netherlands during the Napoleonic occupation *(see pp30–31)* as a way of using up leftovers.

These days there is nothing penny-pinching about the wide range of sweet and savoury toppings available at most pancake houses in Amsterdam. It is not uncommon to find up to 70 varieties on offer and you can usually combine any of these to create the pancake of your choice. The best places

include **De Carrousel**, **Boerderij Meerzicht**, **The Pancake Bakery** and **Upstairs**. Portions may seem small, but they are deceptively filling. Pancakes and waffles served with syrup are also available as the staple snack at smoking coffeeshops *(see p49)*.

BROWN CAFÉS AND BARS

The term *eetcafés* is usually applied to traditional brown cafés *(see also p48)*. These often offer much better value and a more relaxed ambience than many small restaurants. Outstanding brown cafés include **De Prins**, **Het Molenpad**, **Café du Lac**, **Carel's**, **De Reiger** and **Blincker**, which have extensive and appealing menus. Not surprisingly, they often get crowded and it can be hard to find a free table.

The majority of basic *eetcafés* just offer filling home-made fare, such as sandwiches, soups, salads, omelettes and chips. The only unfamiliar dishes you are likely to come across are *uitsmijter* (a large open sandwich with roast beef or ham, topped with fried eggs) and *erwtensoep* (a thick pea soup with pork). Of the cheaper, more down-to-earth varieties of *eetcafés*, **De Doffer** and **Zongo's** both serve filling food that is excellent value. Zongo's has a menu that offers international food and each week invites a guest chef and De Doffer has the attraction of a billiard room. Both places attract a young, lively crowd and are popular with students. For the best french fries in the city, head to **Vleminckx Vlaamse Friteshuis**.

An increasing number of Amsterdam's cafés and bars are becoming more ambitious in the food they offer. **Café Cox**, located in De Stadsschouwburg *(see p111)*, is a perfect example of this approach. At smart *eetcafés*, the menu is rarely limited to a single style or national cuisine. A notable exception to this rule is **Van Puffelen**, which offers more formal French-style dishes. Meals are served in the back extension, and adjacent building, of this intimate brown café, which has an impressive 19th-century interior.

DESIGNER BARS

An extensive range of food is offered in some of the more up-market designer bars *(see p49)*. This type of bar is invariably more expensive than other types of cafés and bars in the city and in most cases the quality of the fare does not justify such inflated prices. **Café Schiller**, housed in a beautiful Art Deco building on Rembrandtplein, is an honourable exception. Amid portraits of 1930s cabaret stars painted by Frits Schiller, you can enjoy a value-for-money selection of snacks and meals in an evocative period bar. Both **Het Land van Walem** and **De Balie** also serve tasty food in a stylish setting. **Morlang**, next door to Het Land van Walem, is less chic, but the food definitely is better value, and the trendy **Caffé Esprit** is very popular with Kalverstraat shoppers.

SPECIALIST CAFÉS

If you feel like trying something different, sample the delicious food at the Flemish cultural centre **De Brakke Grond**, where international dishes with a Belgian twist are served in both the café and the restaurant. **De Zotte** also serves down-to-earth Flemish food and stocks a huge variety of Belgian beers. While the quality of the food may not be that exceptional, the portions certainly are large enough to soak up the strongest of beers.

DIRECTORY

PANCAKE HOUSES

Boerderij Meerzicht
Koenenkade 56.
Amsterdamse Bos.
Tel 679 2744.

De Carrousel
Tweede
Weteringplantsoen 1.
Map 4 F3.
Tel 625 8002.

The Pancake Bakery
Prinsengracht 191.
Map 1 B4.
Tel 625 1333.

Upstairs
Grimburgwal 2.
Map 7 B4.
Tel 626 5603.

BROWN CAFÉS AND BARS

Blincker
St Barberenstraat 7.
Map 7 B4.
Tel 627 1938.

Café Carel's
Frans Halsstraat 76.
Map 4 F4.
Tel 679 4836.

Café Cox
Marnixstraat 429.
Map 4 D1.
Tel 523 7850.

Café du Lac
Haarlemmerstraat 118.
Map 1 C3.
Tel 624 4265.

De Doffer
Runstraat 12–14.
Map 4 E1.
Tel 622 6686.

't Doktertje
Rozenboomsteeg 4.
Map 7 B4.
Tel 626 4427.

Molenpad
Prinsengracht 653.
Map 4 E1.
Tel 625 9680.

Pieper
Prinsengracht 424.
Map 4 E1.
Tel 626 4775.

De Prins
Prinsengracht 124.
Map 1 B4.
Tel 624 9382.

Van Puffelen
Prinsengracht 375–377.
Map 1 B4.
Tel 624 6270.

De Reiger
Nieuwe Leliestraat 34.
Map 1 B4.
Tel 624 7426.

De Tuin
2e Tuindwarsstraat 13
(near Westerstraat).
Map 1 B3.
Tel 624 4559.

Vleminckx Vlaamse Friteshuis
Voetboogstraat 33.
Map 7 B4.
Tel 624 6075.

Zongo's
Keizersgracht 335.
Map 1 B5.
Tel 428 2609.

PROEFLOKALEN AND MODERN TASTING BARS

De Drie Fleschjes
Gravenstraat 18.
Map 7 B2.
Tel 624 8443.

In De Wildeman
Kolksteeg 3.
Map 7 C1.
Tel 638 2348.

L&B Limited
Korte Leidsedwarsstraat
82–84. **Map** 4 E2.
Tel 625 2387.

Mulliner's Wijnlokaal
Lijnbaansgracht 266–267.
Map 4 E2.
Tel 627 9782.

GRAND CAFÉS AND DESIGNER BARS

De Balie
Kleine Gartmanplantsoen
10. **Map** 4 E2.
Tel 553 5131.

Café Americain
American Hotel,
Leidsekade 97. **Map** 4 E2.
Tel 556 3000.

Caffè Esprit
Spui 10.
Map 7 B4.
Tel 622 1967.

Café Luxembourg
Spui 22–24.
Map 7 B4.
Tel 620 6264.

Café Schiller
Rembrandtplein 26.
Map 7 C5.
Tel 624 9846.

De Jaren
Nieuwe Doelenstraat
20–22.
Map 7 C4.
Tel 625 5771.

De Kroon
Rembrandtplein 17.
Map 7 C5.
Tel 625 2011.

Het Land van Walem
Keizersgracht 449.
Map 7 A5.
Tel 625 3544.

Morlang
Keizersgracht 451.
Map 7 A5.
Tel 625 2681.

Vertigo
Nederlands
Filmmuseum,
Vondelpark 3
Map 4 D2.
Tel 612 3021.

SMOKING COFFEESHOPS

The Bulldog
Leidseplein 15.
Map 4 E2.
Tel 625 6278.

Caffe Chocolata
Spuistraat 51.
Map 7 B1.
Tel 622 6241.

Global Chillage
Kerkstraat 51.
Map 4 E1.
Tel 777 9777.

The Grasshopper
Nieuwezijds
Voorburgwal 59.
Map 7 A4.
Tel 624 6753.

Rusland
Rusland 16.
Map 7 C4.
Tel 627 9468.

Siberië
Brouwersgracht 11.
Map 1 C3.
Tel 623 5909.

COFFEESHOPS AND SALONS DE THÉ

Arnold Cornelis
Elandsgracht 78.
Map 1 B5.
Tel 625 8585.

Backstage
Utrechtsedwarsstraat 67.
Map 5 A3.
Tel 622 3638.

Bagels & Beans
Ferdinand Bolstraat 70.
Map 4 F4.
Tel 672 1610.

Coffee Company
Haarlemmerdÿk 62.
Map 1 C2.
Tel 626 3776.

Flores
Brouwersgracht 139.
Map 1 B2.
Tel 330 4649.

Metz & Co
Leidsestraat 34–36.
Map 4 F1.
Tel 520 7020.

Pompadour
Huidenstraat 12.
Map 7 A4.
Tel 623 9554.

SPECIALIST CAFÉS

De Brakke Grond
Nes 43.
Map 7 B3.
Tel 626 0044.

De Zotte
Raamstraat 29.
Map 4 E1.
Tel 626 8694.

SHOPS AND MARKETS

Amsterdam has a huge range of shops and markets, so if you are present-hunting, you will find no shortage of ideas. Most of the large clothing and department stores are to be found in the Nieuwe Zijde, especially along Kalverstraat (see p72), but there are many other shopping areas to discover. The narrow streets which cross the Canal Ring, such as Herenstraat and Hartenstraat, contain a diverse array of specialist shops selling everything from ethnic fabrics and beads to unusual games and handmade dolls. The best luxury fashion is to be found on the classy PC Hooftstraat and Van Baerlestraat. However, if you are looking for a bargain, take time to explore the street markets and numerous second-hand shops. Here you can pick up recent fashion items and worn leather jackets cheaply.

Atrium of the Magna Plaza in the former Postkantoor

OPENING HOURS

Shops are usually open from 9am or 10am to 6pm Tuesday to Saturday and from 1pm to 6pm on Monday (see p257). Many shops are now also open on Sundays. In the city centre, shops stay open until 9pm on Thursdays. However, legislation does allow shopkeepers in the city centre to remain open between 7am and 10pm seven days a week. Retailers are most likely to take advantage of this law in the run up to Sinterklaas (see p53) and during Christmas.

HOW TO PAY

Cash is the most popular method of payment, so if you intend to use a credit card, ask if they are accepted before buying. Although cards are becoming more widely accepted, department stores often require purchases to be paid for at a special till, and smaller shops may only accept them for non-sale items and goods

costing more than €45. Travellers' cheques are accepted in most shops and, if you have a bank account in the Netherlands, direct debits are popular. Some tourist shops take foreign currency, but offer a poor rate of exchange.

VAT EXEMPTION

Most Dutch goods are subject to value added tax (BTW) of either 19 per cent for clothes and other goods, or 6 per cent for books. Non-EU residents are entitled to a refund, subject to certain conditions. Shops which stock the relevant forms will have a sign saying "Tax free for tourists". On leaving the country, present your goods, receipt and the form at customs who will refund you 10 per cent of the purchase price of your goods. Refunds are only made on purchases above €137.

SALES

Sales take place mainly in January and July but smaller shops and boutiques may offer discount items at any time. *Uitverkoop* describes anything from a closing-down sale to a stock-clearance sale, while *korting* merely indicates that discounts are being offered.

Towards the end of a sale, further discounts, which will be calculated at the till, are often subtracted from the marked-down price. Beware

of clothes rails marked, for example, *VA 40* or *Vanaf 40* as this sign means "From 40" – the items cost €40 or more, rather than exactly €40.

DEPARTMENT STORES AND MALLS

Perhaps Amsterdam's best-known department store is **De Bijenkorf** on Dam square, often described as the Dutch Harrods. It has a huge perfumery, and stocks a wide range of men's and women's clothing, plus toys, soft furnishings and household goods. At Christmas it devotes a whole floor to decorations. Both **Maison de Bonneterie** and **Metz & Co** are more exclusive. Among the less expensive stores, **Hema** is very popular for household goods, children's clothes and underwear. Also popular for basic items is **Vroom & Dreesmann**. The only shopping malls in central Amsterdam are the Kalvertoren (Kalverstraat, near Singel) and Magna Plaza, which is housed in the old Postkantoor building (see p78). The impressive, vaulted interior of this former head post office now contains a huge assortment of upmarket boutiques and shops.

Stoeltie Diamonds (see p242)

MARKETS

Amsterdammers' love of street trading is most graphically illustrated on 30 April during Queen's Day (see p50), when Amsterdam turns into the biggest flea market in the world, as local people crowd the city to sell off all their unwanted junk. Such is the crush of eager bargain-hunters that the entire city centre is closed to traffic during the festivities.

As Amsterdam still resembles a collection of small villages, every district has its own local market. The best-known of these, because of its size, is the Albert Cuypmarkt (see p122) in the Pijp district, which sells a wide assortment of food, both Dutch and ethnic. This market is also good for cheap clothes and reasonably priced flowers.

Apart from the local markets, Amsterdam has a wide range of specialist markets. Seasonal flowers are on sale at the Bloemenmarkt (see p123). Another market popular with tourists is Waterlooplein flea market (see p63). Despite the crowds, vigilant collectors can still seek out the odd bargain among the bric-a-brac; there is also a selection of new and second-hand clothes for sale.

Browsers will be fascinated by the hundreds of stalls at the Looier Kunst Antiekcentrum (see p113), which sell anything from antique dolls to egg cups. Every Wednesday and Saturday on the Nieuwezijds Voorburgwal there is a specialist market for stamp and coin collectors. On Fridays there is a second-hand bookmarket on Spui. Gourmets should head for the Noordermarkt (see p92), which holds an organic food market on Saturdays. The best prices, however, are to be found about 25 km (16 miles) northwest of Amsterdam in the port town of

MEXX, a smart boutique on PC Hooftstraat (see p126)

Beverwijk, where the **Beverwijkse Bazaar**, open weekends, is one of Europe's largest indoor flea markets. Next door the market continues with a cross-section of Oriental merchandise, including rugs, carpets, pottery, crafts and food.

Smoked fish on display at the Albert Cuypmarkt

SPECIALIST SHOPS

Dotted throughout Amsterdam are dozens of small specialist shops. One of the more unusual is **Condomerie Het Gulden Vlies**, located in a former squat, which sells condoms from all over the world. Equally unusual is **Christmas**

Palace, which sells festive adornments all year round, and **Party House**, which has a vast collection of paper decorations. **Capsicum Natuurstoffen** has a huge selection of exotic silks and linens, while **Coppenhagen 1001 Kralen** has more than 1,000 different types of beads. It is also worth making time to explore **Joe's Vliegerwinkel** for its wide range of kites, **Simon Levelt** for tea and coffee, or **Hooy & Co.** for an array of wonderful-smelling herbs.

BOOKS, NEWSPAPERS AND MAGAZINES

As books are subject to value added tax in the Netherlands, you may find them slightly more expensive than at home. English-language books are generally available, particularly at **The American Book Center** and **Waterstone's**. Holiday reading can be picked up very cheaply at second-hand book-shops, such as **De Slegte**. Collectors of comics should not miss a visit to **Lambiek**. Amsterdam now has two English-language newspapers; the *Amsterdam Weekly* and the *Amsterdam Times*. Most city-centre newsagents stock foreign papers. *Het Financieel Dagblad* has a daily business update in English and publishes a weekly English-language edition. *Day by Day* is a useful listings magazine (see p256).

A selection of seasonal flowers, including sunflowers, roses and lilies

What to Buy in Amsterdam

Traditional wooden clogs

Amsterdam has hundreds of tourist shops selling souvenirs, but those looking for something different will find a better selection of genuine Dutch items in one of the city's specialist shops or even at an ordinary supermarket. Authentic Delftware is only found at a handful of licensed dealers, but there are still many jewellers selling anything from uncut stones to second-hand diamond rings. Dutch cheese, chocolate and locally produced beers and *jenevers* offer a flavour of the city, while a bunch of flowers is always appreciated.

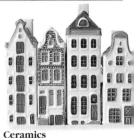

Ceramics
Finely detailed model canal houses can be be bought singly or by the row.

Droste chocolate pastilles

Sweet and salty varieties of drop liquorice

Dutch Sweets
Handmade Belgian chocolates and Droste pastilles are both delicious, but salty liquorice is an acquired taste.

Handmade Belgian chocolates

Flowers
Bulbs and cut flowers are a colourful reminder of the city and, due to greenhouse production, many blooms are available all year round.

Tulip bulbs

A bunch of fresh tulips

Gouda Cheese
There are many types of Gouda of different maturity (see p242). Any shop will be happy to let you try a slice before making a purchase.

Two popular brands of beer

Beer in Amsterdam
A huge variety of imported, bottled beers are sold in Amsterdam as well as many local brews (see p242).

Sturdy stone flagons of *jonge* and *oude jenever* (see pp48–9) – also available in flavoured varieties

Dutch windmill prints

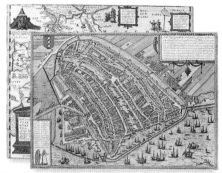

Old Maps and Prints

Historically famous for cartography, Amsterdam has a good selection of new and old maps, and many second-hand bookshops stock etchings.

Reproductions of old maps of Amsterdam and Russia

Diamond brooch

Chain-link, diamond-encrusted bracelet

Diamonds

Diamond-cutting was first established in Amsterdam during the 16th century. The city is still one of the major diamond centres.

Different coloured brilliant-cut diamonds

ROYAL DELFT

In response to the demand for Chinese design, more than 30 factories sprang up in Delft in the 17th century, producing distinctive blue-and-white ceramics *(see p195)*. Today, only De Porceleyne Fles still makes real Delftware. Items from this factory are sold with a certificate of authenticity.

Polychrome jug painted in colours used on 17th-century majolica

Pynaker tobacco jar influenced by Japanese Imari ware

Plate painted in traditional Delft blue

Painter's initials

Year code – DB means 1982

Trademark since 1876

Item number

Genuine De Porceleyne Fles marks

Delft-blue vase

17th-century plate made for rich family

Decorative 17th-century fireplace tile

Antique Delft

Old Delftware is highly sought after and expensive, but Delft fireplace tiles can be picked up more cheaply.

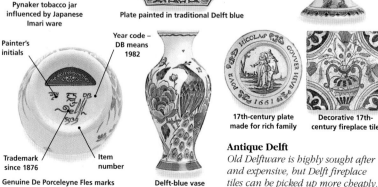

Where to Shop in Amsterdam

The Netherlands is justly famous for its flowers, beer and cheese. A wide choice of these indigenous products is available in Amsterdam, which has also long been regarded as the world centre for diamonds. Owing to the large numbers of overseas settlers living in Amsterdam and the cosmopolitan outlook of its residents, it is easy to find a selection of foreign goods in the city. These range from Indonesian beads to French designer wear.

FASHION AND CLOTHES

Van Baerlestraat and PC Hooftstraat contain numerous designer boutiques such as **MEXX**, offering top names like Katharine Hamnet and the leading French and Italian designer labels. The smart set from the Canal Ring haunt the stylish **The People of the Labyrinths** and **Pauw** for their timeless clothes and accessories.

Boutiques in the Nieuwe Zijde offer less pricey items. The French designer **Agnès B** has her own shop along Rokin selling classic designer wear. If leather's your thing, try **Robin & Rik** on Runstraat for handmade leather clothes and accessories. Along Kalverstraat, **Sissy Boy** specializes in refined classic suits as well as eye-catching designs.

Fanatics of second-hand clothes will find well-priced and stylish selections at shops such as **Zipper**. For the widest choice of fashionable boots and shoes, **Dr Adams** is almost a Dutch institution.

ANTIQUES AND FURNISHINGS

While you can pick up the odd bargain on Waterlooplein (see p63) and at the Noordermarkt (see p92), the best place for antiques is around Spiegelgracht. A wide selection of shops sells everything from 17th-century tiles to icons. The **EH Ariëns Kappers** has a comprehensive collection of old prints, maps and graphic art. It is also interesting to visit an auction house. Both **Sotheby's** and **Christie's** have branches in Amsterdam. Looier Kunst en Antiekcentrum (see p113), has a potpourri of odds and ends, while **Fanous Ramadan** has a colourful collection of Arabic lampshades, pottery and furniture. **De Looier Kunst en Antiekcentrum** (see p113) is a good place for antiques.

FLOWERS AND BULBS

No Dutch person would dream of visiting a friend without a bunch of flowers, so Amsterdam is crowded with flower shops. Worth visiting are **Madelief**, for a vast assortment of colourful domestic blooms, and **Gerda's Bloemen en Planten**, for its stock of tropical flowers.

Cut flowers are cheapest at Albert Cuypmarkt (see p122), but Bloemenmarkt (see p123) has a better selection, as well as hundreds of bulbs and tubers. It also sells potted plants, but due to customs regulations, these usually can't be exported.

DIAMONDS

Amsterdam has a long tradition of cutting and polishing diamonds (see p32). It is still possible to purchase loose stones and diamonds in a new setting at one of the city's many diamond-cutting centres, such as **Gassan Diamonds** or Coster Diamonds (see p128). The city is also well stocked with jewellers, several specializing in diamonds. The best second-hand jewellery can be found in the fascinating antique shops around Spiegelgracht.

CHEESE

You can buy a good selection of cheese at street markets and specialist shops such as **Wout Arxhoek**, or at supermarkets such as **Albert Heijn**. Instead of buying the red-wax-covered Edam, try one of the many varieties of Gouda. Mature Gouda (overjarige kaas) has a rich, salty taste and crumbly texture, while young Gouda (meikaas) is fresh and curdy. This cheese is also sold with cummin (leidsekaas) or cloves (nagelkaas) (see p226).

CHOCOLATES

Verkade and Droste are the best-known makes of chocolate in the Netherlands. For a treat, visit **Pompadour**, for its delicious hand-made chocolates, or a branch of the up-market Belgian chocolate specialist, **Leonidas**.

BEERS AND SPIRITS

The Dutch are knowledgeable beer drinkers. Along with brand-name lagers like Heineken, Grolsch and Amstel, there is also a huge range of bottled beers on offer. Local specialities include Zatte, a rare, bottle-fermented beer and Wieckse Witte, a white beer. Specialist shops like **De Bierkoning** offer the widest choice and best advice.

The Dutch spirit jenever, the "father" of gin, is often sold in stone bottles and flavoured with herbs or fruit (see p48).

POTTERY AND GLASSWARE

Blue-and-white pottery is stocked by most shops, but only items with a certificate are real Delftware. **Rinascimento** sells the real thing from De Porceleyne Fles, one of the original Delft potteries.

The Jordaan is the best place to hunt for modern pottery, while **Glasgalerie Kuhler** has a stunning range of modern glass, and **Het Klei Kollektief** offers an ever-changing choice of bright ceramics.

POSTERS AND PRINTS

The best places to find good reproductions of paintings are in museum shops. **Art Unlimited** offers an excellent selection of the less famous Dutch scenes.

A range of old etchings can be found at **Hoogkamp Old Prints** and among the stalls at the Oudemanshuispoort (see p61).

DIRECTORY

DEPARTMENT STORES

De Bijenkorf
Dam 1.
Map 7 B2.
Tel 0900 0919.

Hema
Kalvertoren, Kalverstraat.
Map 7 B4.
Tel 422 8988.
Nieuwendijk 174–176.
Map 7 B2.
Tel 623 4176.

Maison de Bonneterie
Rokin 140–142.
Map 7 B4.
Tel 531 3400.

Metz & Co
Leidsestraat 34-36.
Map 7 A5.
Tel 520 7020.

Vroom & Dreesmann
Kalverstraat 201.
Map 7 B5.
Tel 0900 235 8363.

MARKETS OUTSIDE THE CITY

De Beverwijkse Bazaar
Montageweg 35
Beverwijk
Tel 0251 262666.

SPECIALIST SHOPS

Capsicum Natuurstoffen
Oude Hoogstraat 1.
Map 7 C3.
Tel 623 1016.

Christmas Palace
Singel 508.
Map 7 B5.
Tel 421 0155.

Condomerie Het Gulden Vlies
Warmoesstraat 141.
Map 7 C2.
Tel 627 4174.

Coppenhagen 1001 Kralen
Rozengracht 54.
Map 1 B4.
Tel 624 3681.

Jacob Hooy & Co
Kloveniersburgwal 12.
Map 8 D3.
Tel 624 3041.

Joe's Vliegerwinkel
Nieuwe Hoogstraat 19.
Map 8 D3.
Tel 625 0139.

Party House
Rozengracht 92b.
Map 1 B4.
Tel 624 7851.

Simon Levelt
Prinsengracht 180.
Map 1 B4.
Tel 624 0823.

BOOKS, NEWSPAPERS AND MAGAZINES

The American Book Center
Kalverstraat 185.
Map 7 B5.
Tel 625 5537.

Lambiek
Kerkstraat 78.
Map 7 A5.
Tel 626 7543.

De Slegte
Kalverstraat 48–52.
Map 7 B3.
Tel 622 5933.

Waterstone's Bookseller
Kalverstraat 152.
Map 7 B4. **Tel** 638 3821.

FASHION AND CLOTHES

Agnès B
Rokin 126.
Map 7 B4.
Tel 627 1465.

Dr Adams
Oude Doelenstraat 5–7.
Map 7 C3.
Tel 622 3734.

MEXX
PC Hooftstraat 118–120.
Map 4 D3.
Tel 675 0171.

Pauw
Leidsestraat 16.
Map 7 A5.
Tel 626 5698.

The People of the Labyrinths
Van Baerlestraat 44.
Map 4 D3.
Tel 664 0779.

Robin & Rik
Runstraat 30. **Map** 7 B4.
Tel 627 8924.

Sissy Boy
Kalverstraat 210.
Map 7 B4.
Tel 626 0088.

Zipper
Huidenstraat 7.
Map 7 A4.
Tel 623 7302.

ANTIQUES AND FURNISHINGS

Christie's
Cornelis Schuytstraat 57.
Map 3 C4.
Tel 575 5255.

EH Ariëns Kappers
Nieuwe Spiegelstraat 32.
Map 4 F2.
Tel 623 5356.

Fanous Ramadan
Runstraat 33.
Map 4 E1.
Tel 423 2350.

Kitsch Kitchen
Rozengracht 8–12.
Map 1 B4.
Tel 428 4969.

De Looier
Elandsgracht 109.
Map 1 A5.
Tel 624 9035.

Sotheby's
De Boelelaan 30.
Map 7 B4.
Tel 550 2200.

FLOWERS AND BULBS

Gerda's Bloemen en Planten
Runstraat 16.
Map 4 E1.
Tel 624 2912.

Madelief
Haarlemmerdijk 93.
Map 1 C2.
Tel 625 3239.

DIAMONDS

Gassan Diamonds
Nieuwe Uilenburgerstraat
173–175. **Map** 8 E4.
Tel 622 5333.

CHEESE

Albert Heijn
Nieuwezijds Voorburgwal
226. **Map** 7 B2.
Tel 421 8344.
Many other branches.

Wout Arxhoek
Damstraat 19. **Map** 7 C3.
Tel 622 9118.

CHOCOLATES

Leonidas
Damstraat 15. **Map** 7 B3.
Tel 625 3497.

Pompadour
Huidenstraat 12. **Map** 7
A4. **Tel** 623 9554.

BEERS AND SPIRITS

De Bierkoning
Paleisstraat 125.
Map 7 B3.
Tel 625 2336.

POTTERY AND GLASSWARE

Fleur de Lys
Beethovenstraat 41.
Map 4 D5. **Tel** 662 1737.

Galleria d'Arte Rinascimento
Prinsengracht 170.
Map 1 B4.
Tel 622 7509.

Glasgalerie Kuhler
Prinsengracht 134.
Map 1 B4.
Tel 638 0230.

Het Kleikollektief
Hartenstraat 19.
Map 7 A3.
Tel 622 5727.

POSTERS AND PRINTS

Art Unlimited
Keizersgracht 510.
Map 7 A5. **Tel** 624 8419.

Hoogkamp Old Prints
Spiegelgracht 27.
Map 4 F2. **Tel** 625 8852.

ENTERTAINMENT IN AMSTERDAM

Amsterdam offers a diverse array of world-class entertainment. A variety of performances are staged in hundreds of venues throughout the city, ranging from the century-old Concertgebouw *(see p128)* to the 17th-century IJsbreker café on the Amstel *(see p248)*. The Dutch passion for American jazz draws many international greats such as BB King and Pharoah Sanders to annual events such as the Blues Festival and Drum Rhythm Festival *(see p50)*. The city's most popular events take place in the summer, and include the Holland Festival *(see p51)* and the Amsterdam Roots Festival *(see p51)*. There is a huge choice of multilingual plays and films throughout the year. There is also plenty of free entertainment to be enjoyed from the multitude of street performers and live bands in late-night bars and cafés.

ENTERTAINMENT INFORMATION

One of the most useful sources of entertainment information is *Uitkrant,* a free listings magazine *(see p256)*. It is printed monthly and available, as are a variety of other Dutch-language listings, from theatres, cafés and bars, libraries and tourist offices. Although written in Dutch, it is easy to follow and offers the most comprehensive daily listings of what's going on.

The **Amsterdam Tourist Board** *(see also p256)* publishes an English-language listings magazine every two weeks called *Day by Day*. It can be picked up for a nominal price at Tourist Board offices and some newsagents, or free

Late-night bar in the Red Light District

issues can be found in selected hotels and restaurants. *Amsterdam Weekly* is a free English-language listings magazine. For music listings look out for the *Pop & Jazz Uitlijst* published by the **AUB** (Amsterdam Uitburo). Daily newspapers including *De Volkskrant, Het Parool, NRC Handelsblad* and *De Telegraaf* publish a selection of listings on Wednesdays, although they are mainly excerpts from *Uitkrant.*

BOOKING TICKETS

Amsterdam's major classical music, opera and dance performances, such as those by the Dutch National Ballet, are likely to be sold out weeks ahead of time. It is advisable to book tickets in advance to ensure the day, time and seats of your choice. For most other events, it is possible to buy tickets on the day. The AUB has a last-minute window (noon–7:30pm daily) selling tickets for same-day shows.

The main reservations office for entertainment and all cultural activities is the AUB, which is located next to the Stadsschouwburg *(see p111)* in Leidseplein. You can make reservations, pick up tickets in advance (a booking fee is charged) and obtain information in person or over the telephone. You can also make bookings at the venue itself, or through Tourist Board offices. Tickets to major rock concerts can be obtained at the Tourist Board, AUB and at some of the large record shops in the city centre. Although some of the most popular club

The Stopera complex, home to the Dutch national opera and ballet companies

The Neo-Classical-style pediment of the Concertgebouw *(see p128)*

dates need to be booked in advance, entrance to clubs like the Paradiso and De Melkweg *(see pp110–11)* can usually be bought at the door. Going to the cinema is very popular with Amsterdammers, so it is advisable to book tickets in the afternoon for evening performances during a film's opening week. Most multi-screen cinemas provide a Dutch-speaking automated booking service. All booking offices are usually open from Monday to Saturday, between 9am and 6pm, or later. Credit cards are usually not accepted and it is important to collect reserved tickets at least an hour before the show starts, or the tickets may be resold.

Theatre sign on Nes *(see p74)*

REDUCED-PRICE TICKETS

Entry to some performances can be obtained at bargain prices for holders of the Cultureel Jongeren Passport (CJP). Valid for one year, it is available to anyone under the age of 26 for €15. Some hotels include reduced-price entry to certain events as part of their package deals – check details with your travel agent. Some cinemas offer a 30 per cent discount from Monday to Thursday. Several venues, such as the Concertgebouw *(see p128)* and the Westerkerk *(see p90)*, have free lunchtime concerts throughout the year.

FACILITIES FOR THE DISABLED

Most major theatres, cinemas and concert halls in Amsterdam have unrestricted wheelchair access, and assistance is always available. A number of the city's smaller venues, however, are housed in old buildings not designed with the disabled in mind. Venues like De Kleine Komedie *(see p246)* will make special arrangements if they are notified beforehand. Cinemas also provide facilities for the hard of hearing and visually impaired. Always telephone the box office a couple of days before your visit and specify what you require.

OPEN-AIR ENTERTAINMENT

Since Amsterdammers are avid supporters of theatre and of all sorts of music, there are plenty of open-air venues operating throughout the summer. In the heart of the city, the Vondelpark

open-air theatre *(see p128)* stages a wide variety of free concerts and theatre performances. The restored turn-of-the-century Nederlands Filmmuseum *(see p129)* is housed in a pavilion in the park. During the summer, free screenings and documentaries are shown, as well as silent films that are sometimes accompanied by live music.

The Prinsengracht classical music concert *(see p51)* is performed in August on a group of canal barges. On the outskirts of the city, the scenic Amsterdamse Bos *(see p155)* is the setting for productions of Shakespeare, Chekhov and other classical dramatists, staged in the open-air theatre. In the south, Amstelpark *(see p154)* is the venue for De Parade at the end of July *(see p246)*. Amsterdammers also enjoy rowing on the Amstel, where rowing clubs operate from a boathouse near Amstelpark.

USEFUL ADDRESSES

AUB/Last-Minute Ticket Office
Leidseplein 26. **Map** 4 E2.
Tel 0900 0191.
www.uitburo.nl

Amsterdam Tourist Board
Centraal Station, Platform 2.
Map 2 E3.
Tel 0900 400 4040.
Stationsplein 10. **Map** 8 D1.
Tel 0900 400 4040.
Leidseplein 1. **Map** 4 E2.
Tel 0900 400 4040.
www.visitamsterdam.nl
www.amsterdamtourist.nl

Customers enjoying café life in the popular Thorbeckeplein

Theatre, Dance and Film

Theatre and dance are important aspects of cultural life in Amsterdam, and performances take place throughout the year in dozens of venues all over the city. Experimental theatre can be found in one of the oldest streets in the city, along the Nes (see p74). Theatres on the Nes, such as De Brakke Grond, are also popular venues for radical theatre productions. The city's main locations for dance include the Felix Meritis, Meervaart, Muziektheater, Stadsschouwburg and the Dutch Dance Laboratory, for experimental productions. The Dutch love cinema and, though Amsterdam has only a few large cinema complexes, there is a surprising number of venues that show a variety of films, from first-run, mainstream and art, to foreign-language, revival and gay.

THEATRE AND CABARET

Amsterdam has more than 50 theatre venues and boasts a number of English-speaking companies. The Toneelgroep Amsterdam is the resident theatre company at the **Stadsschouwburg**, and the **Felix Meritis** (see p113), **Westergasfabriek** and **Bellevue** are important venues for many touring theatre companies.

Experimental theatre can be found at a range of locations throughout Amsterdam, including the **Westergasfabriek**. The **Theatercompagnie** is a small company that specializes in translating and staging the classics, as well as promoting works by young playwrights. The Orkater musical theatre company often holds performances at Stadsschouwburg and the Theater Bellevue.

The annual Holland Festival (see p51) in June offers a prestigious series of opera, theatre and dance performances. It features international talent such as Peter Brook, Peter Zadek and John Jesurum. The International Theatre School Festival presents innovative performances at **De Brakke Grond**, **Frascati** and other venues on the Nes (see p74) at the end of June. The **Tropentheater** has a packed programme of lively productions from developing countries. Downriver from the Muziektheater, near the smart Amstel Inter-Continental (see p223), the **Koninklijk Theater Carré** plays host to long-running international musicals such as Les Misérables and Cyrano. The **Koninklijk Theater Carré** is often the setting for elegant premières attended by members of the Dutch royal family. Closer to the Muziektheater and also facing the Amstel is the charming 17th-century **De Kleine Komedie**. It can seat an audience of up to 500 and offers a perfect setting for cabaret. It also features stand-up comedy and occasionally has English-language theatre productions. Although De Kleine Komedie is closed throughout the summer, such is its reputation throughout Europe, that bookings must be made at least three months in advance. Stand-up comedy (in English) also can be found at the **Leidseplein Theater. Panama** is one of the latest venues to offer cabaret shows.

Summer outdoor theatre can be seen at the **Vondelpark** open-air theatre (see p128) and at the Amsterdamse Bos (see p155), a woodland park on the edge of town. Here, a pathway lined with Classical Greek statuary leads to a 1,800-seat amphitheatre, the venue for performances of Shakespeare and Chekhov plays. In the south of Amsterdam, the Amstelpark (see p154) is the venue for De Parade, a tent city erected each summer in late July and early August where international dance, theatre and circus acts perform before a rapturous audience. Merry-making often carries on into the early morning hours.

DANCE

The Netherlands possesses two world-class ballet companies, the Dutch National Ballet and the Nederlands Dans Theater (NDT). The Dutch National Ballet is housed in the 1,600-seat **Muziektheater** (see p63), which provides magnificent views along the Amstel river, and is renowned for its classical and modern repertoire.

The NDT regularly performs in venues throughout the city. Ballets from the Czech artistic director, Jiri Kylian, form the majority of the programming. In addition to the core company, the NDT also has two other companies, NDT2 and NDT3. NDT2 is a younger company made up of dancers aged 18–21 who perform the work of established choreographers such as Hans van Manen. It also performs the works of younger choreographers such as Lionel Hoche and Paul Lightfoot. NDT3 is composed of former members of the original Nederlands Dans Theater. These highly experienced dancers, who are all over the age of 40, perform shows of unparalleled technical expertise and control.

Dance is often performed at Stadsschouwburg and at the Felix Meritis, Amsterdam's 18th-century concert hall and one of its earliest performance venues. Westergasfabriek, the former gasworks, also holds dance performances.

Amsterdam is a laboratory for experimental dance, and many innovative performances can be seen throughout the city. They are not confined to any one venue though, so it is best to check the entertainment listings, such as Uitkrant (see p256), for full details. Experimental dance can be enjoyed regularly at top venues like the Stadsschouwburg and the **De Meervaart**. Companies to look out for include Introdans, who combine jazz with flamenco alongside other varieties of ethnic dance, and Opus One, who mix jazz, classical ballet and tap. Needless to say, the Nederlands Dans Theater's repertoire also includes experimental dance routines.

The Holland Festival in June *(see p51)* is used as the principal platform for premières of shows by top choreographers from both the Nederlands Dans Theater and the Dutch National Ballet. The International Theatre School Festival, also in June, focuses increasingly on dance, with performances taking place in the historic street of Nes *(see p74)*, which is one of the very oldest parts of the city.

FILM

Amsterdammers love the cinema, and there are more than 45 venues in the city. All films are screened in the original language with subtitles. Movie lovers should not miss the plush Art Deco Tuschinski Theater *(see p123)*. Built between 1918 and 1921, this cinema features a luxurious foyer, stained-glass windows, tables, sofas and lamps. First-run films often open at the Tuschinski, and this is often the place to catch public appearances by film stars.

It is easy to find out which films are showing where, as each cinema has a listing at its entrance, and details are also posted in bars and cafés.

Programmes change on a Thursday, and most new film listings, carried in the daily newspapers, are printed on the Wednesday. *De Filmkrant* is a free monthly film magazine that carries complete listings; these are written in Dutch but very easy to understand. It is also possible to check online at www.film ladder.nl.

Ticket prices vary from €7 to €10, depending on whether it is a matinée or an evening screening, although some longer films can command a slightly higher admission price.

Some of the larger cinema complexes carry afternoon matinées during the week and these usually begin at 2pm. At the weekend the schedule varies. Some of the cinemas, such as the mainstream **City** and the arthouse **Kriterion**, often schedule several showings of children's films at the weekend. For adults, the Kriterion offers a great selection of arthouse and mainstream films, with late-night screenings of cult and erotic movies.

Evening shows usually begin at either 6:30pm or 7pm, and there is a second showing at 9pm or 9:30pm, although a few cinemas also have an 8pm screening. Be prepared for the intermission, known as the "pauze". This is a 15-minute obligatory break that is usually scheduled to coincide exactly with the most exciting scene of the film.

If you suddenly get the urge to see a film and don't particularly mind what it is, check out Leidseplein *(see p110)*, one of the biggest gathering areas in the city, where cinemas, cafés, restaurants and bars abound.

One first-run and mainstream cinema that can be found within a two-minute walk of Leidseplein is the high-profile, seven-screen, 2,094-seat **City** complex.

The Movies near Harlemmerpoort *(see p93)* specializes in films with a psychological connection. The theatre also houses a pleasant pub and restaurant. For arthouse films there is also the **Cinecenter**, situated on a side street just off the main square across from De Melkweg *(see p110)*; and for a real treat, **Filmtheater de Uitkijk**, which is a short walk along Leidsestraat to Prinsengracht. This small, venerable 158-seat venue specializes in movie classics and, best of all, refuses to indulge in the dreaded "pauze". Dating from 1913, De Uitkijk is Amsterdam's oldest operational cinema. The Filmmuseum *(see p129)* also shows films in its Cinerama complex.

DIRECTORY

THEATRE AND CABARET

De Brakke Grond
Vlaams Cultureel
Centrum, Nes 45.
Map 7 C3.
Tel 626 6866.
www.brakkegrond.nl

De Kleine Komedie
Amstel 56–58. **Map** 5 B3.
Tel 624 0534.
www.dekleinekomedie.nl

Felix Meritis
Keizersgracht 324.
Map 1 B5. **Tel** 623 2321.
www.felix.meritis.nl

Frascati
Nes 63. **Map** 7 B4.
Tel 626 6866.
www.nestheaters.nl

KIT/Tropentheater
Linnaeusstraat 2.
Map 6 E3. **Tel** 568 8500.
www.kit.nl

**Koninklijk
Theater Carré**
Amstel 115–125. **Map**
5 B3. **Tel** 0900 252 5255.
www.theatercarre.nl

Leidseplein Theater
Leidseplein 12. **Map** 4 E2.
Tel 423 0101.
www.boomchicago.nl

Panama
Oostelijke Handelskade 4.
Tel 311 8686.
www.panama.nl

Stadsschouwburg
Leidseplein 26. **Map** 4 E2.
Tel 624 2311.
www.stadsschouwburg.nl

Theater Bellevue
Leidsekade 90. **Map** 4 D1.
Tel 530 5301.
www.theaterbellevue.nl

Theatercompagnie
Kloveniersburgwal 50.
Map 7 C3. **Tel** 520 5320.
www.theatercompagnie.nl

Westergasfabriek
Haarlemmerweg 8–10.
Map 1 A1. **Tel** 586 0710.
www.westergasfabriek.com

DANCE

De Meervaart
Meer en Vaart 300. **Tel** 410
7777. www.meervart.nl

Het Muziektheater
Amstel 3. **Map** 7 C5.
Tel 625 5455.
www.muziektheater.nl

See also venues under
Theatre & Cabaret

FILM

Cinecenter
Lijnbaansgracht 236.
Map 4 E2. **Tel** 623 6615.

City Theater
Kleine Gartmanplantsoen
15–19. **Map** 4 E2.
Tel 0900 1458.

**Filmtheater de
Uitkijk**
Prinsengracht 452.
Map 4 E2. **Tel** 623 7460.

Kriterion
Roetersstraat 170
Map 5 C3. **Tel** 623 1708

The Movies
Haarlemmerdijk 161.
Map 1 B2. **Tel** 638 6016.

Classical Music and Opera

Amsterdam is a city with a long and rich tradition in classical music and opera. The principal orchestral venues house some of the world's finest musical events. The city has also acquired a reputation as a centre for early music and organ recitals, with performances in traditional settings such as the English Reformed Church or the Oude Kerk. In summer, concerts can be enjoyed as you relax in one of the city's beautiful parks.

ORCHESTRAL, CHAMBER AND CHORAL MUSIC

Amsterdam's music centre-piece is the **Concertgebouw** *(see p268)*, renowned for its acoustics and home to the celebrated Royal Concert-gebouw Orchestra. International orchestras and soloists come here regularly, and each summer it hosts Robeco Groep concerts, which are famous for showcasing young talent. Early music is also performed here, often by the world-famous Amsterdam Baroque Orchestra and the Orchestra of the Eighteenth Century.

The **Beurs van Berlage** *(see p79)* was originally the city's stock and commodities exch-ange and is now the resi-dence of the Netherlands Phil-harmonic Orchestra. Many of the country's better orchestras and chamber choirs perform here. The **RAI** *(see p151)* is principally a convention centre, but is often the setting for classical music and opera events. The **KIT/Tropentheater** *(see pp152–3)* often features traditional music from developing countries. Modern classical music, opera and choirs can also be heard at De Melkweg *(see pp110–11)* and the Paradiso *(see p251)*.

Though **Cristofori's** main business is buying, restoring and selling grand pianos, it also organizes orchestral, chamber and choral concerts. Many performers are internationally renowned artists who can often be called upon to talk about their work before or after a performance.

The **Muziekgebouw aan the IJ**, a 15-minute walk from Centraal Station, is Amster-dam's new grand location for innovative modern music concerts, festivals and multi-media events.

MUSIC IN CHURCHES

Churches in Amsterdam offer concerts throughout the year. The city prides itself on its 42 historic church organs, and those in the **Oude Kerk** *(see pp68–9)* and the **Nieuwe Kerk** *(see pp76–7)* are particularly magnificent.

Carillon concerts are often held in the Oude Kerk and at lunch time on Tuesdays in the **Westerkerk** *(see p90)*. The 17th-century **English Reformed Church** holds concerts that range from Baroque to modern. In the summer, free lunch-time concerts are given by new ensembles and young musicians. The **Thomaskerk**, built a few decades ago, holds a free lunch-time concert every other Tuesday (except in July and August). Concerts are also held in the **Waalse Kerk** and **Noorderkerk** *(see p92)*.

OPERA

Built in 1988, the **Muziek-theater** houses the Stadhuis (town hall) and the Dutch National Opera. Its nickname, the Stopera, is a combination of both names *(see p63)*. It is one of Europe's most up-to-date theatres and features an internationally famous reper-toire, as well as lesser-known and some experimental works. Opera can also be seen at the Stadsschouwburg *(see p111)* on Leidseplein. More exper-imental opera is performed at nightclubs such as the Paradiso and De Melkweg *(see p251)*. Also, check the Holland Festival listings for world premières *(see p51)*.

OPEN-AIR CONCERTS

The Prinsengracht concert *(see p51)* takes place in late August. Musicians perform on barges on the canal in front of the Pulitzer Hotel *(see p220)*. In summer, concerts also take place in the Vondel-park open-air theatre and the Amsterdamse Bos *(see p155)*, and at various other parks.

DIRECTORY

ORCHESTRAL, CHAMBER AND CHORAL MUSIC

Beurs van Berlage
Damrak 243. **Map** 7 C2.
Tel 521 7575.
www.berlage.com

Concertgebouw
Concertgebouwplein 2–6.
Map 4 D4. **Tel** 671 8345.
www.concertgebouw.nl

Cristofori
Prinsengracht 583 (near Molenpad). **Map** 4 E1.
Tel 626 8485.
www.cristofori.nl

KIT/Tropentheater
Linnaeusstraat 2.
Map 6 E3. **Tel** 568 8500.
www.tropenmuseum.nl

Muziekgebouw aan 't IJ
Piet Heinkade 1.
Tel 788 2000.
www.muziekgebouw.nl

RAI
Europaplein 8.
Tel 549 1212.
www.rai.nl

MUSIC IN CHURCHES

English Reformed Church
Begijnhof 48. **Map** 7 B4.
Tel 624 9665.

Nieuwe Kerk
Dam. **Map** 7 B2.
Tel 638 6909.

Oude Kerk
Oudekerksplein 23.
Map 7 C2. **Tel** 625 8284.

Thomaskerk
Prinses Irenestraat 36.
Tel 673 8171.

Waalse Kerk
Oudezijds Achterburgwal 159. **Map** 7 C3.
Tel 623 2074.

Westerkerk
Prinsengracht 281.
Map 1 B4. **Tel** 624 7766.
www.westerker.nl

OPERA

Muziektheater
Amstel 3. **Map** 7 C5.
Tel 625 5455.
www.muziektheater.nl

Pop, Rock and Nightclubs

Amsterdam is bursting with live music. From the omnipresent street entertainers to a whole variety of music venues and nightclubs, as well as countless music cafés, it is hard to avoid the city's rock and pop and club scene. Concerts and clubs tend to be cheap and relaxed, with few venues having a strict door policy or dress code. Local bands and musicians are encouraged, and many venues receive subsidies from the local council, so tickets, with the exception of the big-name concerts, rarely cost more than 8. Some of the best bands can be enjoyed for the price of a drink. Fierce competition means that venues and clubs come and go. For the latest information and gig guides, consult the free *Pop & Jazz Uitlijst*, available from cafés and libraries as well as the AUB ticket service and Tourist Board offices *(see p245)*. Both AUB and tourist offices sell advance tickets for major concerts. The free magazine *Uitkrant* and English-language *Day by Day* also carry concert listings *(see p244)*.

POP AND ROCK

Many big names tend to by-pass Amsterdam and head for Rotterdam's Ahoy and Utrecht's Vredenburg stadiums instead. However, mainstream pop and rock concerts are held at the RAI *(see p151)*, Amsterdam Arena (home to Ajax football club) and the **Heineken Music Hall**. Middle-of-the-road artists tend to play in large theatres, such as the Theater Carré *(see p145)* and the Theater Bellevue *(see p247)*. The Marcanti Plaza and Escape nightclubs *(see p251)* host a variety of hot dance and soul acts.

For most Amsterdammers, rock and pop are synonymous with two venues – **Paradiso** and **De Melkweg**. Paradiso, housed in a converted church just off Leidseplein, is more prestigious. De Melkweg is housed in a former dairy, hence the name, the "Milky Way" *(see pp110–11)*.

Both the Paradiso and De Melkweg offer an extremely varied and entertaining programme: rock, pop, dance, rap and world music. The standards range from chart-toppers and cult heroes to local hopefuls trying their luck at one of the regular talent nights. Big-name bands which come to play in Amsterdam invariably turn up at one of these two places.

The brown café **Fifth Element** opts for guitar rock and attracts a mainly student crowd, while followers of rock'n'roll should visit the **Cruise-Inn**. The **Arena** is part of the well-known hotel *(see p223)*, where tourists and locals cram in to dance to the latest music played by live DJs. **The Waterhole**, located near Leidseplein, features live rock nightly.

Blues music alternates with rock at the loud and crowded **Maloe Melo**. Smoky, sweaty and beer-soaked, this place may not seem particularly inviting, but the atmosphere is convivial. From May to September, free concerts are held every Sunday afternoon in the Vondelpark open-air theatre *(see pp128–9)*, often featuring some of the country's top pop acts. The Drum Rhythm Festival *(see p50)*, held annually at the end of May, is a high-spirited celebration of the sheer diversity of popular music. Cutting edge musicians from around the world come to Amsterdam for a weekend extravaganza featuring drum-and-bass, asian underground, jungle, hiphop, R&B, soul, triphop, world music and more. Every Saturday afternoon, the **Grand Café de Plantage** hosts a live radio programme which plays pop, jazz and world music.

JAZZ

There may well be more jazz venues in Amsterdam than anywhere else in the world. The relaxing rhythms of jazz music are perfectly suited to the mood of the brown cafés and bars *(see pp46–9)*.

The city's jazz flagship is the **Bimhuis**, a venue that takes its music seriously. Commonly known as the "Bim", it is the best venue in Amsterdam for contemporary jazz and has an international reputation. In late 2005, Bimhuis moved next to the Muziekgebouw, Piet Heinkade 1.

Café-restaurant **Casablanca**, in the Red Light District on the Zeedijk, offers live jazz three or four times a week (always on Friday, Saturday and Sunday). More traditional than the Bimhuis, the music here is played by both veterans and newcomers alike.

The many jazz cafés dotted around the city are very popular. Most of them are small brown cafés where local bands perform. Late opening and free entry boost their appeal, although drinks cost a little above average. Most cafés hold weekly jam sessions, when anyone can take the stage.

Around Leidseplein are the **Alto Jazz Café** and the **Bourbon Street**. Alto is best on Wednesday evenings when Hans Dulfer, the so-called "father" of the Amsterdam jazz scene, is in residence. His daughter Candy is a regular attraction at the **De Heeren van Aemstel**. **De Engelbewaarder** has popular jam sessions on Sunday afternoons. The Vondelpark *(see pp128–9)* is also a popular jazz venue in the summer, when free open-air concerts are held here.

The Dutch passion for jazz turns to frenzy in the summer, when there is a festival held in almost every town. In July, the North Sea Jazz Festival *(see p51)*, held in Rotterdam, attracts some of the biggest names in the world of jazz.

WORLD MUSIC AND FOLK

In the Netherlands the world-music scene has been heavily influenced by its many immigrant communities. The West Indian, Indonesian, Maghreb, West African, Surinamese and Turkish traditions are thriving, and are actively encouraged by the city's authorities. A high-brow programme of ethnic, classical and popular concerts is on offer at the Soeterijn theatre *(see p246)*. Groups from around the world appear there on a regular basis, with a strong emphasis on Asian music.

The **Akhnaton** is a multi-cultural centre. Its main strengths are Caribbean, African and Arabic music. In addition, there are regular performances by reggae, rap, and salsa artists. These styles are also features of the dance nights.

De Melkweg, and to a lesser extent the Paradiso and Panama, also schedule world music – De Melkweg hosts a colourful Amsterdam Roots Festival *(see p51)* in June. **De Badcuyp**, in the lively Pijp neighbourhood, swings with salsa, tango, African music and dance options. The venue often holds free workshops high-lighting Cuban dance and salsa traditions.

The indigenous folk music of the Netherlands is an acquired taste. It sounds like a mix of traditional German folk music, French *chanson* and old sea shanties. Large cafés around Rembrandtplein, including **Jantjes Verjaardag** and **Hof van Holland**, provide folk music for tourist consumption. For a more authentic experience, head for the Jordaan. In bars like **De Twee Zwaantjes** and **Café Nol** regulars sometimes burst into joyous song.

Many of Amsterdam's Irish pubs feature live music. Some of the best include **Mulligan's, The Blarney Stone** and the huge and extremely popular **O'Donnells**, where you can hear authentic fiddle playing almost every weekend.

CLUBS AND DISCOS

Amsterdam is well-known for its lively nightclub scene. There is little pretension here, and the mood is relaxed and carefree. Most clubs open at 11pm but don't really get going before 1am. They usually close at 4am during the week, and 5am on Friday and Saturday nights. Entrance prices are relatively low and drinks are reasonably priced. Few clubs enforce a strict dress code, but they do reserve the right to refuse admission. It is an established custom to tip the doormen on the way out.

Amsterdam was one of the very first cities to embrace house music during the late 1980s. It still dominates most clubs, but there is now more variety on offer. DJs and music vary from one night to the next, so check listings for details.

More is presented as the successor of the exclusive Roxy which, before it burned down, was where the beautiful people of Amsterdam gathered to rub shoulders with which-ever stars were in town. More has a members-only policy, though it often only applies during busy times.

Even harder to get into is **Jimmy Woo**, famous for its tough door policy. Inside it's Hong-Kong hip, with plenty of black leather and a great sound system. The **Wester-gasfabriek**, to the north of the Jordaan, is a huge former gasworks. The two-year renovation programme is nearing completion, and the Westergasfabriek is now a collection of music and dance spaces.

Amsterdam's students have established their own club, called **Dansen Bij Jansen**. The two sweaty dance floors in this rambling club are always packed at weekends. You will need a student card to get in, but provided you look the part there should not be a problem.

The leading non-house club in town is **The Sugar Factory**, with its varied and enjoyable menu of soul, funk and jazz-dance. The **Odeon** has been recently renovated. Here, you can party your way up from the brasserie in the basement to the dance palace on the first floor.

The city's two biggest dance halls are **Escape** and the **Kingdom**, which attract a predominantly young crowd who usually come from out of town each weekend. The discos around Leidseplein are basically just extended bars with only small dance floors, catering for tourists and attracting a much wider age range of people. On the whole, mainstream and chart music tend to be played.

GAY AND LESBIAN CLUBS

Clubbing is at the heart of Amsterdam's gay scene. The techno sounds and camp floor shows at many venues attract a trendy clientele. Crowds are often mixed and most gay clubs will rarely turn away women or straight men.

Exit, in Reguliersdwars-straat, is a slick bar with three levels and a balcony for viewing the dance scene below. Practically next door, **ARC** is a combination of bar and Grand café. Drop in for a drink during the day or join the dance crowd later. Up the road, the designer café **Reality**, also in the Reguliersdwarsstraat, offers disco with different styles of music.

On Friday nights, the gay community centre, **COC Amsterdam**, organizes a popular mixed disco (Saturday is ladies' night). **De Trut** is housed in the basement of a famous former squat and packs in a mixed crowd on Sunday nights. The decor is seedy, but the dance floor is big and the drinks are cheap.

The newest lesbian disco is **You II**, with music from the Top 40. Details of other events are available from the **Gay and Lesbian Switchboard** and the Pink Point kiosk. **Gayforcing** organizes gay and lesbian bridge afternoons. The decor is imaginative and the atmos-phere friendly. **Saarein II** is frequented by lesbians and gays and offers a friendly, relaxed atmosphere.

DIRECTORY

POP AND ROCK

Arena
's-Gravesandestraat 51.
Map 6 D4.
Tel 850 2400.

Cruise-Inn
Zuiderzeeweg 29
(Amsterdam-Noord).
Tel 692 7188.

Escape
Rembrandtplein 11–15.
Map 7 B5.
Tel 622 1111.

Fifth Element
Reguliersdwarsstraat 41.
Map 7 B5.
Tel 626 5435.

Heineken Music Hall
Arena Boulevard 590.
Tel 0900 687 424255.

Maloe Melo
Lijnbaansgracht 163.
Map 4 D1.
Tel 420 4592.

De Melkweg
Lijnbaansgracht 234a.
Map 4 E2.
Tel 531 8181.
www.melkweg.nl

Paradiso
Weteringschans 6–8.
Map 4 E2.
Tel 626 4521.
www.paradiso.nl

The Waterhole
Korte Leidsedwarsstraaat
49. **Map** 4 E2.
Tel 620 8904.

Winston International
Warmoesstraat 123–9.
Map 7 C2.
Tel 623 1380.

JAZZ

Alto Jazz Café
Korte Leidsedwarsstraat
115.
Map 4 E2.
Tel 626 3249.
www.jazz-cafe-alto.nl

Bimhuis
Piet Heinkade 3.
Tel 788 2188.
www.bimhuis.nl

Bourbon Street
Leidsekruisstraat 6–8.
Map 4 E2.
Tel 623 3440.

Brix
Wolvenstraat 16.
Map 7 A3.
Tel 639 0351.

Casablanca
Zeedijk 24/26.
Map 8 D2.
Tel 625 5685.

De Engelbewaarder
Kloveniersburgwal 59.
Map 8 D3.
Tel 625 3772.

Grand Café de Plantage
Plantage Kerklaan 36.
Map 5 C2.
Tel 638 3646.

De Heeren van Aemstel
Thorbeckeplein 5.
Map 7 C5.
Tel 620 2173.

WORLD MUSIC AND FOLK

Akhnaton
Nieuwezijds Kolk 25.
Map 7 C1.
Tel 624 3396.

De Badcuyp
Sweelinckstraat 10.
Map 5 A5.
Tel 675 9669.
www.badcuyp.nl

The Blarney Stone
Nieuwendijk 29.
Map 7 C1.
Tel 623 3830.

Café Nol
Westerstraat 109.
Map 1 B3.
Tel 624 5380.

Hof van Holland
Rembrandtplein 5.
Map 7 C5.
Tel 623 4650.

Jantjes Verjaardag
Reguliersdwarsstraat
108–114.
Map 6 F4.
Tel 627 2710.

Mulligan's
Amstel 100.
Map 7 C5.
Tel 622 1330.

O' Donnell's
Ferdinand Bolstraat 5.
Map 4 F5.
Tel 676 7786.

De Twee Zwaantjes
Prinsengracht 114.
Map 1 C3.
Tel 625 2729.

CLUBS AND DISCOS

Dansen Bij Jansen
Handboogstraat 11.
Map 7 B4.
Tel 620 1779.

Escape Theater
Rembrandtplein 11.
Map 7 C5.
Tel 622 1111.

Jimmy Woo
Korte Leidsedwarsstraat
18. **Map** 4 E2.
Tel 626 3150.

Kingdom
Jan van Galenstraat 6–8.
Map 1 C1.
Tel 488 9888.

The Ministry
Regulierdwardsstraat 12.
Map 7 B5.
Tel 623 3981.

More
Rozengracht 133.
Map 1 A5.
Tel 344 6402.

Odeon
Singel 460.
Map 7 C5.
Tel 521 8555.

Sinners
Wagenstraat 3–7.
Tel 620 1375.

Sugar Factory
Lijnbaansgracht 238.
Map 4 E2.
Tel 627 0008.

GAY AND LESBIAN CLUBS

ARC
Reguliersdwarsstraat 44.
Map 7 B5.
Tel 689 7070.

COC Amsterdam
Rozenstraat 14.
Map 1 B5.
Tel 626 3087.

Exit
Reguliersdwarsstraat 42.
Map 7 B5.
Tel 625 8788.

Gayforcing
Gay & lesbian bridge club.
Tel 624 4163.

Gay and Lesbian Switchboard
Tel 623 6565.
www.switchboard.nl

Reality
Reguliersdwarsstraat 129.
Map 7 C5.
Tel 639 3012.

Saarein II
Elandsstraat 119.
Map 1 B5.
Tel 623 4901.

De Trut
Bilderdijkstraat 165.
Map 3 C1.

You II
Amstel 178.
Map 7 C5.
Tel 421 0900.

CHILDREN'S AMSTERDAM

As a lively, cultural city, Amsterdam can be a fascinating place to visit with children. Its network of canals is fun to explore and many of the squares are alive with street musicians and performers. The city's many parks offer a wide range of outdoor activities and the streets are lined with tempting shops, restaurants, cafés and food stalls. Even in summer, there is no guarantee of good weather, but you can always find something to do on wet days. Some theatres and museums are geared for children and there is nearly always an English-language film showing that is suitable for children.

PRACTICAL ADVICE

If you are visiting Amsterdam with a very young child, a baby sling or pouch is essential. While the city centre is small enough to be covered on foot, manoeuvring a heavy pushchair around the cobbled streets can be tough going. Negotiating one of the city's notoriously steep flights of stairs or getting on a crowded tram or canal boat with a pushchair is virtually impossible, and they are actually banned in some of the museums.

For sightseeing, it is worth taking a boat trip. Details of the options available are given on pages 276–7. Most of the operators offer discounts to children under 12 and allow toddlers to travel free. Trams are another entertaining and efficient way to get around (see p272), although they tend to be crowded at peak periods. Like all other forms of public transport in the city, children under four go for free and under-12s travel at half-price.

Children are welcome at the majority of hotels in Amsterdam (see p212). Some of the bigger ones even provide babysitting facilities. If your hotel does not offer this, Babysit Centrale Kriterion provides reliable, cheap child care. The service is 24-hour, but bookings must be made 9–11am and 4:30–8pm.

BABYSITTING SERVICE

Babysit Centrale Kriterion
Roetersstraat 170.
Tel 624 5848.
www.kriterionoppas.org

THEATRES AND MUSEUMS

Many theatres, such as the **Circus Elleboog** and **De Krakeling**, hold children's shows on Wednesdays or Sundays and the Vondelpark (see p128) stages weekly open-air shows in summer.

Seasonal attractions include the Christmas circus at the Koninklijk Theater Carré (see p145). The Amsterdam Tourist Board's monthly publication, *Uitkrant*, contains a complete listing, which is easy to understand, despite being written in Dutch (see p256).

A number of Amsterdam's museums have sections which are geared for children. Nemo (see p150) is one of the best for older children, with its wide range of hands-on exhibits and buttons to press. Adventurous 6- to 12-year-olds will like the exhibitions at Tropenmuseum Junior (see pp152–3), which brings to life the cultures and traditions of the developing world. Would-be pirates love climbing aboard the *Amsterdam*, a full size replica of an 18th-century East Indiaman moored outside the Nederlands Scheepvaart Museum (see pp146–7).

Rangda witch from Bali at the Kindermuseum

The waxworks at Madame Tussauds Scenerama (see p74) are also worth a visit, although small children may be upset by a few of the more gruesome exhibits. The **Ajax Museum** and World of Ajax Tour are popular with football fans. Most of Amsterdam's museums offer substantial discounts to children and toddlers under four normally get in free.

CHILDREN'S THEATRES AND MUSEUMS

Ajax Museum
Arena Boulevard 1.
Tel 311 1336.
www.amsterdamarena.nl.

Circus Elleboog
Passeerdersgracht 32. **Map** 4 E1.
Tel 626 9370.

De Krakeling
Nieuwe Passeerdersstraat 1. **Map** 4 D1. **Tel** 624 5123.

Crocodiles basking in the Reptile House of Artis zoo *(see pp142–3)*

The full-size replica of the *Amsterdam*, outside the Scheepvaart Museum

ZOOS AND CITY FARMS

Artis zoo *(see pp142–3)* incorporates both covered and open-air animal pens, along with a Planetarium and the Geologisch Museum. Cheaper, but less extensive, animal-viewing options in and around the city include the animal enclosure in the Amsterdamse Bos *(see p155),* donkeys and llamas in the Vondelpark *(see p128)* and free-roaming Highland cattle in the Amstelpark *(see p154).*

SPORTS AND RECREATION

Amsterdam's parks provide a whole range of activities for children. The Vondelpark *(see p128)* has well-maintained playgrounds, free puppet shows and face-painting sessions at the Milk Bar in summer. The Amstelpark *(see p154)* and Amsterdamse Bos *(see p155)* also have a range of activities. The Electrische Museumtramlijn *(see p155)* runs regular round trips to and from the Amsterdamse Bos in vintage trams. You can also camp in designated sites in this park *(see p213).* On a rainy day, head to **TunFun**, an indoor recreation centre for children aged up to 12.

There are a number of indoor swimming pools around Amsterdam. The best is **Miranda Bad**, a tropical paradise with water chutes, a beach and a wave machine. Indoor pools tend to close in the summer and are replaced by open-air pools, like the municipal one in Twiske, a

rural park north of the IJ. The seaside, which is only a short train ride away, has miles of clean, sandy coastline.

Perhaps the most fun can be had simply exploring Amsterdam's network of canals by hiring canal bikes *(see p277).* When the canals are frozen during a hard winter, your children will enjoy the thrill of skating around the city.

RECREATION CENTRES

Miranda Bad
De Mirandalaan 9. **Tel** *546 4444.*

TunFun
Mr Visserplein 7. **Map** 8 E4.
Tel *689 4300.*

EATING OUT

Children may not be welcome in some of the more expensive restaurants, but most places are tolerant. Many cafés and cheaper restaurants offer a

children's menu such as chicken, chips and *appelmoes* (apple purée). At the **Kinderkookkafé** the food is cooked and served by children. Advance dinner reservations (at least a month) are essential, both for eating and for kids who want to cook. Between 10am and 5pm, however, no booking is required.

Amsterdam also has a good selection of pancake houses *(see p236).* Other treats include *poffertjes,* which are tiny pancakes loaded with butter and icing sugar.

CHILDREN'S CAFÉS

Kinderkookkafé
Kattenlaantje, Vondelpark 6 (path at Overtoom 333). **Map** 3 B3.
Tel *625 3257.* ☐ *10am–8:30pm daily.* **www**.kinderkookkafe.nl

SHOPPING

Alongside an assortment of large toyshops, there are also a few small shops that sell traditional wooden and handcrafted toys. Look out for the exquisite dolls'-house furniture at **De Kleine Nicolaas**.

For something out of the ordinary in the way of children's clothes, go to **Oilily**.

SHOPS FOR CHILDREN

De Kleine Nicolaas
Cornelis Schuytstraat 19. **Map** 3 C1.
Tel *676 9661.*

Oilily
PC Hooftstraat 131–133. **Map** 4 D3.
Tel *672 3361.*

Children resting weary legs after a hard day's play *(see p225)*

SURVIVAL
GUIDE

PRACTICAL INFORMATION

Amsterdam is a cosmopolitan city and visitors should find its citizens, who are often multilingual, helpful and friendly. The official networks for helping tourists, whether with information about sights or medical attention, are efficient and straightforward. Telephones, parking meters and cash dispensers may seem familiar to European visitors,

Exploring the city on foot

but other tourists will need to follow instructions closely. One of the particular pleasures of visiting the city is to enjoy the relatively car-free environment. Trams, water transport, bicycles and pedestrians are all given a much higher priority in the centre than motor vehicles. Indeed, the ideal ways to explore are on foot *(see pp270–71)*, or by bicycle *(see pp274–5)*.

The Tourist Board office on Stationsplein, opposite Centraal Station

TOURIST INFORMATION

Very few cities are as well-equipped to help the visitor as Amsterdam, and in general the Netherlands has a comprehensive network of tourist inform-ation centres. The state-run **Amsterdam Tourist Board**

The logo of the Amsterdam Tourist Board

(VVV) is still widely known by its former name VVV, which is pronounced "fay-fay-fay".

Be wary if you use accom-modation agencies unrelated to the Tourist Board: the accommodation they offer can often be unnecessarily expensive or of poor quality.

THE AMSTERDAM TOURIST BOARD (VVV)

There are three Tourist Board offices in Amster-dam, and almost 450 through-out the Netherlands. The multi-lingual staff provide useful

information on sights, entertainment, events, transport, walks and tours. They will also change money and book hotels, plays, shows, excur-sions, and concerts (all for a small fee). Most Tourist Board leaflets and maps are also avail-able from news-agents and museums. If you are seeking information before you travel, the **NBTC** (Netherlands Board of Tourism and Conventions) produces its own brochures, maps and useful leaflets.

ENTERTAINMENT

Posters and listings in the city's bars and cafés are an immediate guide to entertainment in Amsterdam *(see p244)*. *Amsterdam Weekly* has good listings, as does the Dutch-language *Uitkrant*. Both are free. The Amsterdam Tourist Board produces the

monthly *Day by Day*, which has a useful calender section.

The Tourist Board also produce a number of free English language leaflets providing details of festivals and cultural highlights.

AUB Uitburo *(see p244)* gives information on and sells advance tickets for the city's theatres and concerts, for a small fee. AUB also publish a leaflet listing venues for non-classical music. Libraries and theatres supply entertainment freesheet listings and display cinema programmes.

I AMSTERDAM CARD

This pass entitles the holder to free public transport, free canal trip and free access to almost all of Amsterdam's museums, as well as discounts at some restaurants and attractions. It is available from VVV offices, the GVB and major hotels: valid for 24 (€33), 48 (€43) or 72 hours (€53).

Some of the best of Amsterdam listings, in both English and Dutch

◁ **Illuminated bridge with pretty gabled houses on Herengracht**

Museum entrance tickets

MUSEUM CARD

The very successful Museum Card *(Museumkaart)* costs €25 and provides admission to more than 400 museums throughout the Netherlands. This includes almost all of Amsterdam's museums though it does not cover their special exhibitions. Valid for a year, and with separate cards for adults and under 18s, you will recoup the cost after about three visits. The card can be bought from Tourist Board and NBTC offices and all the participating museums.

DISABLED VISITORS

For such a forward-looking city, Amsterdam sometimes displays a certain disregard for the needs of disabled people, although there is information available *(see p212)*. While museums, galleries, cinemas, theatres and now even churches often have wheelchair access and adapted toilets, getting around from venue to venue can be a real problem. Cobbled streets make life very difficult for wheelchair users, and public toilets with easy access are virtually non-existent.

Sign for disabled parking

OPENING TIMES

Opening times for retailers in Amsterdam vary enormously, but each shop has its hours of business posted on the door *(see p238)*. Shops in the centre of town may be open between 7am and 10pm all week, including Sundays *(see p238)*. Popular opening hours are 11am to 5pm from Monday to Saturday. In Amsterdam, Thursday is *koopavond* or shopping night, when the shops close at about 9pm. Banks open from 9 or 10am to 4 or 5pm, though many in the centre stay open till 7pm on Thursday. Many of the state-run museums are closed on Monday, and open from 10am to 5pm, Tuesday to Saturday and from 1 to 5pm on Sunday. Most of the museums also adopt these Sunday hours for all national holidays *(see p53)*, apart from New Year's Day, when they are always closed.

Shoppers on Kalverstraat

LANGUAGE AND ETIQUETTE

People whose mother tongue is English will not have a language problem in Amsterdam. Nearly all Dutch people speak some English, but it's appreciated if you can handle a few niceties, such as saying *Dag* (Good day) before asking a Dutch person whether they speak English. This guide has a phrase book on pages 311–12. The Dutch are quite liberal in many ways, but they retain a few conventions. Expect your hand to be shaken a lot, and if you are out with a crowd, introduce yourself, or people may think you standoffish. When eating out, the Dutch tend to pay for their own share of the bill.

DIRECTORY

TOURIST INFORMATION

AUB Uitburo
Leidseplein 26.
Map 4 E2.
Tel 0900 0191.
www.uitlijn.nl

Amsterdam Tourist Board (VVV) Offices
www.visitamsterdam.nl
www.amsterdamtourist.nl

Centraal Station
Platform 2 and in front of station, Stationsplein 10.
Map 8 D1.
Tel 551 2525.

Leidseplein
Leidseplein 1.
Map 4 E2.
Tel 551 2525.

Schiphol Airport
Arrivals Hall 2.

NETHERLANDS BOARD OF TOURISM AND CONVENTIONS (NBTC) OFFICES WORLDWIDE

PO Box 458,
Leidschendam 2260 MG .
Tel 070 3705 705.
www.nbtc.nl

Canada
14 Glenmount Court, Whitby, Ontario L1 N5 M8.
Tel (1) 905-666 5960.
Fax (1) 905-666 5391.
www.holland.com

UK
PO Box 30783,
London WC2B 6DH.
Tel 0906 871 7777
or 020 7539 7950.
Fax 020 7539 7953.

USA
355 Lexington Avenue, 19th floor, New York, NY 10017.
Tel (1) 212-557 3500.
Fax (1) 212-370 9507.

Personal Security and Health

After a recent clean-up by the authorities, Amsterdam is now one of the safest cities in Europe. It does have a reputation for crime, most of which is drugs-related, but tourists should not be affected by this provided they act sensibly. It is a good idea, however, to take out travel insurance which should cover any loss of money or personal items. For those who do find themselves in trouble on holiday, the city has efficient emergency services and facilities ranging from an **HIV Positive Line** to a **Legal Advice Centre**.

Policeman on wheels

Members of the armed Dutch police force

Damrak leading to Centraal Station: a place to be wary of pickpockets

PERSONAL PROPERTY

While Amsterdam is safer than most American and European cities, theft is still a cause for concern. Pickpockets work crowded tourist areas and on the trams, especially in summer, so take precautions: don't put wallets and money in back pockets, leave handbags exposed or flash cash about.

Bicycle and car theft, particularly of foreign vehicles, is also a problem. Muggings are fairly rare, but it is best to avoid parks and poorly lit places at night. Women would also be wise not to frequent bars and cafés late at night. Finally, don't take photographs of prostitutes in the Red Light District, as it causes serious offence.

If you are the victim of theft or assault, report it to the nearest police station. You are anyway obliged to report any personal injury. In serious cases or emergencies, phone the **Emergency Services**.

MEDICAL TREATMENT AND INSURANCE

All EU members can receive medical and dental treatment in the Netherlands at a reduced charge. Before travelling, British visitors should obtain the European Health Insurance Card (EHIC) – the form is available from post offices – and seek a refund for any non-private treatment from the DoH on their return home. You will never be turned away by a doctor even if you do not have an EHIC, but you may have to pay more for treatment. It is also a good idea to take out private insurance, which should cover the cost of repatriation in an emergency.

Minor problems can be dealt with by a chemist *(drogist)*, who stocks non-prescription drugs. For a medicine on prescription, go to a pharmacy *(apotheek)*, open from 8:30am to 5:30pm Monday to Friday. Details of pharmacies open

Fire engine

Ambulance

Police car

outside normal hours are posted in all pharmacy windows and in the afternoon newspaper *Het Parool*. The **Central Medical Service** *(Centrale Doktersdienst)* will direct you to the nearest pharmacy open outside normal hours, and can also refer you to a duty GP or supply the name of a dentist.

Minor accidents are treated in hospital outpatient clinics, open 24 hours a day; the VVV *(see p256)* can advise on these. In an emergency, go to a hospital with a casualty unit, or call an ambulance.

MOSQUITOES

Attracted by the canals, mosquitoes can be a real irritant. Residents and regular summer visitors deal with them in various ways. Burning coils,

A selection of anti-mosquito preparations

ultra-violet tubes, mosquito nets, repellent sprays and anti-histamine creams and tablets are available from large pharmacies or supermarkets.

DRUGS

Though soft drugs have not been legalized in the Netherlands, the police tend to ignore the possession of small amounts of cannabis. They also tolerate the sale of small amounts in designated "smoking" coffeeshops *(see p49)*. Hard drugs are a different matter. The Zeedijk area has been cleaned up but is still best avoided late at night, and anyone caught with hard drugs will certainly be prosecuted. Never try to take drugs out of the country: penalties are stiff.

Hash Museum sign *(see p61)*

LOST PROPERTY

To help with any insurance claim, you must report lost or stolen property as soon as possible, preferably to a police station in the vicinity of the loss. They hold recovered items for a day or so before sending them to the main police lost-property office. If you lose your passport, you must also tell your consulate *(see p265)*. For items lost on public transport, try **Centraal Station** or the GVB head office *(see p273)*.

DIRECTORY

PHARMACIES

Dam
Damstraat 2.
Map 7 C3.
Tel 624 4331.

Jordaan
Westerstraat 180.
Map 1 B3.
Tel 624 9252.

Koek, Schaeffer & Van Tijen
Vijzelgracht 19.
Map 4 F3.
Tel 623 5949.

Medicijnman
Utrechtsestraat 86.
Map 5 A3.
Tel 624 4333.

Het Witte Kruis
Rozengracht 57.
Map 1 A5.
Tel 623 1051.

HOSPITALS

Academisch Medisch Centrum
Meibergdreef 9.
Tel 566 9111.

Sint Andreas Lucas Ziekenhuis
Jan Tooropstraat 164.
Tel 510 8911.

Onze Lieve Vrouwe Gasthuis (with casualty unit)
1e Oosterparkstraat 279.
Map 6 D4.
Tel 599 9111.

VU Medisch Centrum
De Boelelaan 1117.
Tel 444 4444.
24-hour first aid:
Tel 444 3636.

EMERGENCY SERVICES

Ambulance, Fire & Police
Tel 112.

HELPLINES

AIDS SOA Helpline
Tel 0900 204 2040.
◯ 2–10pm Mon–Fri.

Central Medical Service
Tel 592 3434.

Legal Advice Centre Amsterdam

Rechtshulp, Spuistraat 10.
Map 7 B1.
Tel 520 5100 (call in normal office hours for appointment).

Servicepunt HIV Vereniging (Assoc.)
Tel 689 2577.
◯ 2–10pm Mon–Fri.

SOS Crisis Helpline
Tel 675 7575.
◯ 24 hours a day.

SEXUAL ABUSE

Advies-en Steunpunt Huiselijk Geweld
(Advice and Support Centre for Domestic Violence)
Tel 611 6022.
◯ 24 hours a day
(for women who have suffered sexual violence and/or ill treatment).

POLICE

Tel 0900 8844.

Main Police Stations

Lijnbaansgracht 219.
Map 4 E2.

Beursstraat 33.
Map 7 C2.

Nieuwezijds Voorburgwal 104. **Map** 7 A4.

LOST PROPERTY

Centraal Station
NS Lost Property Information, Stationsplein 15.
Map 8 D1. **Tel** 0900 321 2100. ◯ 9am–5pm Mon–Fri. After five days, items found on trains are sent to a central depot. When claimed, items will be sent to your hotel or home address abroad.

GVB
Arlandaweg 100
(near Sloterdijk Station).
Tel 0900 8011.
◯ 9am–4pm Mon–Fri.

Police
Stephensonstraat 18.
Tel 559 3005.
◯ noon–3:30pm Mon–Fri.

Banking and Local Currency

Amsterdammers are strangely partial to cash transactions and, surprisingly, credit cards are not as universally acceptable in the Netherlands as in many other countries. The larger hotels, shops and most restaurants will, however, accept the major credit cards. Many will also take travellers' cheques as payment.

Amsterdam has an excellent foreign exchange network, and transactions are virtually hassle-free for visitors, particularly English speakers. Most currencies can be exchanged at the airport or ferry terminal. There is no limit to the amount of currency you can bring into the country.

ABN-AMRO automatic cash dispenser

GWK exchange counter at Schiphol Airport

TRAVELLERS' CHEQUES

Travellers' cheques are still a good way to carry the bulk of your money. They are useful for paying hotel bills, but remember that if you use them in a restaurant, for example, the management is not obliged to pay you the change if the cheque is larger than the bill.

Choose a name that is well known, like American Express, and they can be changed for cash in most Dutch banks, and are accepted in many retail outlets.

CHANGING MONEY

You can change currency in banks *(see p257)*, **American Express** offices and **Postbank** offices. These will all charge a small commission for the service. The independent bureaux de change charge an exorbitant commission and give a poor exchange rate, but the official

ones, **GWK** *(grenswissel-kantoren)*, are fair.

If you arrive by ferry, don't change any money on the boat, where you can still pay for things in sterling. The recommended thing to do is to wait until you can visit the GWK just after disembarkation. This stays open both for day and night arrivals. Avoid changing your money in hotels, as their charges tend to be very high.

CREDIT CARDS

Most credit cards can be used to obtain money. The exchange rate is slightly better than for currency. Bank automatic cash dispensers most commonly accept Access, American Express, Mastercard, Diner's Club, Banknet, and Visa. Few banks will advance you cash against credit cards. Some restaurants require a minimum purchase to use a credit card. Check you have some cash just in case.

DIRECTORY

BANKS AND CASH DISPENSERS

ABN-AMRO
Dam 2. **Map** 7 B2. *Tel* 0900 0024.

Postbank
Singel 250–256.
Map 7 A2. *Tel* 561 1611.

Rabobank
Dam 16. **Map** 7 B3. *Tel* 777 8899.

AMERICAN EXPRESS

Tel 504 8504.

GWK

Tel 0900 0566 (general number).
Centraal Station. **Map** 8 D1.
⏰ 9am–10pm daily.
Dam 23–25. **Map** 7 B3.
⏰ 9:15am–7pm Mon–Sat,
10:15am–5:45pm Sun.
Damrak 86. **Map** 7 C1.
⏰ 10am–10pm daily.
Leidseplein 1–3. **Map** 4 E2.
⏰ 8:30am–10pm daily.
Schiphol Airport Station.
⏰ 7am–10pm daily.
Amstel Station.
⏰ 8am–8pm Mon–Fri, 8:15am–7:30pm Sat, 10am–5pm Sun.

LOST OR STOLEN CARDS AND CHEQUES

American Express
Tel 0800 622 0100.

American Express Travellers' Cheques
Tel 0800 022 0100.

Diner's Club
Tel 654 5511.

MasterCard
Tel 0800 0225821.

Visa
Tel 660 0611.

THE EURO

Twelve countries have replaced their traditional currencies, such as the Dutch guilder, with the euro. The Netherlands, Austria, Belgium, Finland, France, Germany, Greece, Ireland, Italy, Luxembourg, Portugal and Spain are all members of the European Union and chose to join the new currency. The euro was introduced on 1 January 1999, but only for banking purposes. Notes and coins came into circulation on 1 January 2002.

Each country using the euro produces their own coins, which have one common European side, but these, like the notes which are all uniform in design, can also be used anywhere inside any of the participating member states.

Bank Notes

Euro bank notes have seven denominations. The 5-euro note (grey in colour) is the smallest, followed by the 10-euro note (pink), 20-euro note (blue), 50-euro note (orange), 100-euro note (green), 200-euro note (yellow) and 500-euro note (purple). All notes show the 12 stars of the European Union.

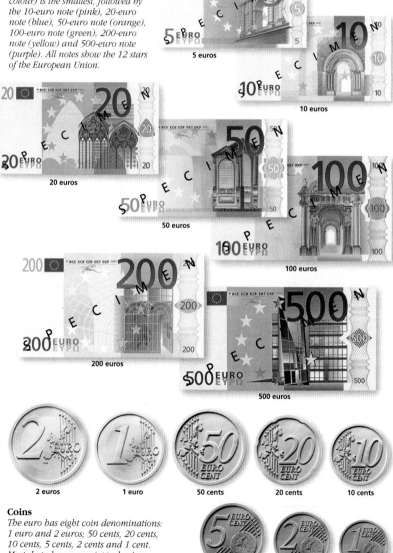

5 euros

10 euros

20 euros

50 euros

100 euros

200 euros

500 euros

2 euros

1 euro

50 cents

20 cents

10 cents

Coins

The euro has eight coin denominations: 1 euro and 2 euros; 50 cents, 20 cents, 10 cents, 5 cents, 2 cents and 1 cent. Most shops have now stopped using the 1- and 2-cent coins and purchases are rounded up or down.

5 cents

2 cents

1 cent

Communications

KPN telephone booth at station

Before 1989, telephone and postal services in the Netherlands were part of the same state-run company, PTT. This has now been separated into two companies – KPN Telecom and PTT Post. Both services are among the most forward-looking and efficient in Europe. For some years, Telfort public telephones have also been appearing beside the KPN telephone boxes, but these are mostly found at train stations.

USING THE TELEPHONE

Public telephones can be found on streets all over the city, at train stations, in post offices, and in cafés and bars. The city's green-trimmed glass booth pay-phones take phone-cards; some also take credit cards. Phonecards can be bought at post offices, supermarkets, newsagents and train stations. Instructions for using the telephones are

KPN telecoms logo

in English and Dutch. When you phone popular numbers such as airports, you may encounter an electronic voice which tells you, *"er zijn nog een (one)/twee (two) wachtenden voor u"*, "there are one/two people in the queue before you". Most hotels have IDD (International Direct Dialling) units, but be aware that the telephone costs on your bill are likely to be inflated.

Storefront of a telephone shop

USING A CARD PHONE

1 Lift the receiver.

2 Insert phone- or credit card. Wait for dialling tone – a low hum.

3 Dial the number. The ringing tone in the Netherlands comprises long medium-pitch tones. The engaged tone is slightly faster. Instructions are also in English.

4 Replace the receiver at the end of the call and withdraw card.

REACHING THE RIGHT NUMBER

- Internal directory enquiries, dial 118 or visit www.detelefoongids.com
- Local operator, dial 0900 8008. International operator, dial 0900 8418 Mon–Fri.
- To phone the USA or Canada, dial 001 followed by the number.
- To phone the UK, dial 0044 followed by the number, omitting the 0 from the area code.
- To phone Australia, dial 0061 followed by the number.
- To phone New Zealand, dial 0064 followed by the number.
- To phone the Irish Republic, dial 00353 followed by the number.

ELECTRONIC COMMUNICATIONS

Faster than a letter and cheaper than a phone call, sending and receiving electronic mail is easy and convenient once you have set up a free email account (go to www.hotmail.com for example, and follow the instructions).

There are many internet cafés in Amsterdam where, for a modest fee, you can check your email account in comfort. They offer a variety of refreshments ranging from alcohol and coffee to light snacks. Most are close to the

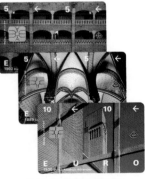

Colourful selection of Dutch pictorial phonecards

24-hour internet access at the Europe-wide chain easyInternetcafé

main attractions and so are easily accessible to visitors. Opening hours vary, but some are open until late at night.

Also worth a look is the website www.amsterdam.nl. Financed by Amsterdam city council, it offers a wealth of well-designed information about the city in Dutch and English, as well as access to councillors, commercial services and hundreds of local home pages.

POSTAL SERVICES

Amsterdam's numerous post offices are distinguished by the TPG logo. In addition to offering the usual postal services – stamps, telegrams, poste restante – they will also change currency and travellers' cheques, and have telephone, telex and fax services. Larger post offices may have photocopying facilities and sell commemorative stationery and stamps. Smaller ones may only offer basic services.

SENDING A LETTER

When you want to post letters going abroad or outside Amsterdam, use the *overige bestemmingen* slot in any of the red post boxes to be found throughout the city. A sign on the post box will indicate when mail is collected.

Letters up to 20 g can be sent anywhere in Europe – not just within the EU – for a universal flat rate, while destinations further afield cost slightly more. Postal charges have been increasing at intervals since privatization. It is worth sending important documents by insured or registered mail. There are often long queues for stamps

(postzegels) at post offices and it can be quicker to purchase them at tobacconists or souvenir shops. Most post offices are open Monday to Friday only, from 9am–5pm.

POSTE RESTANTE

If you're not sure where you'll be staying, you can have your mail sent to **poste restante**, addressed to the Central Post Office. The service is free but you will need some form of photo identification, such as a passport or driving licence when you come to collect your mail.

DIRECTORY

Postal Information and Lost Mail Enquiries
(phone enquiries only).
Tel 058 2333 333.
www.tpgpost.nl
🕐 8am–8pm Mon–Fri, 9am–4pm Sat.

Main Post Office
Hoofdpostkantoor TPG Post, Singel 250–256, 1012 SJ.
Map 7 A2.
Tel 0900 767 8562.
🕐 9am–6pm Mon–Fri, 10am–1:30pm Sat.
Poste restante 🕐 9am–6pm Mon–Fri, 10am–1:30pm Sat.

easyInternetcafé
Damrak 33.
Map 7 C1.
🕐 9am–10pm daily.

Internet Café Freeworld
Nieuwendijk 30.
Map 7 C2.
Tel 620 0902.
🕐 9:30am–1am Sun–Thu, 9:30am–3am Fri & Sat.

Internet City
Nieuwendijk 76.
Map 7 B2.
Tel 620 1292.
🕐 10am–midnight daily.

Monkeytail Internet Café
Staalstraat 28.
Map 8 D4.
Tel 771 9758.
🕐 noon–8pm daily.

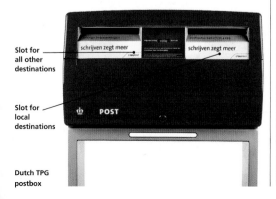

Slot for all other destinations

schrijven zegt meer   schrijven zegt meer

Slot for local destinations

⚓ POST

Dutch TPG postbox

Additional Information

Pre-packed tulip bulbs in Bloemenmarkt

VISAS AND CUSTOMS

For a stay lasting up to three months, Australian, EU, New Zealand and US nationals need only a valid pass-

Diamond brilliants

port. EU nationals over 17 years of age are entitled to import limitless goods for personal use, except for tobacco and alcohol on which duty has already been paid. The limits are: 800 cigarettes; 400 small cigars; 200 cigars; 1 kg of tobacco; 10 litres of spirits; 20 litres of fortified wine; 90 litres of wine; 110 litres of beer. Bulbs can be brought into the UK, but the US requires an inoculation certificate. Non-EU members buying diamonds can reclaim VAT on returning home. Phone the free **Customs Information** line for details.

Cats and dogs may be brought in, providing they have a certificate of inoculation against rabies.

DUTY-FREE GOODS

Citizens of non-EU countries must abide by the following restrictions: 200 cigarettes or 50 cigars or 250 g of tobacco; 1 litre of spirits

or 2 litres of fortified wine or 2 litres of non-sparkling wine; 50 g of perfume; 500 g of coffee; 100 g of tea; other goods or gifts to the value of 56. Duty-Free goods are no longer available to EU citizens.

Bulbs must have a certificate of inspection from the Plant Protection Service if being taken to the USA or Canada.

TOILETS

Amsterdam is short on public conveniences, and visitors resort to using hotels, museums and cafés. A few cafés and bars will charge up to 25c. The large stores also expect 15c as do station toilets have attendants who will

TOILET

Sign for public conveniences

insist on a tip. Parents will also have to pay 15c for baby-changing rooms in large shops. The only café with toilets for disabled people is 't Nieuwe Café, located in Dam square.

Browsing among the bottles in the duty-free shop at Schiphol Airport

CONVERSION TABLE

Imperial to Metric
1 inch = 2.54 centimetres
1 foot = 30 centimetres
1 mile = 1.6 kilometres
1 ounce = 28 grams
1 pound = 454 grams
1 pint = 0.6 litres
1 gallon = 4.6 litres

Metric to Imperial
1 centimetre = 0.4 inches
1 metre = 3 feet, 3 inches
1 kilometre = 0.6 miles
1 gram = 0.04 ounces
1 kilogram = 2.2 pounds
1 litre = 1.8 pints

TIME

Like all its neighbouring countries, the Netherlands is on Central European Time, which is 1 hour ahead of Greenwich Mean Time. Sydney is 10 hours ahead in winter (8 in summer); Moscow 3 hours ahead; Johannesburg is 2 hours ahead; while New York is 6 hours behind and Los Angeles 9 hours behind.

Standard continental plug

ELECTRICITY

The voltage in the Netherlands is 220, 50-cycle AC, and compatible with British equipment, but since the Dutch use two-pin continental plugs you will need an adaptor.

American visitors need to convert their equipment or buy a transformer. Dutch wall sockets require a larger plug than those used in the USA.

TELEVISION

The nine main channels of Dutch TV serve standard European and US fare, but all hotels and homes have cable TV, with 30 or so channels available, including British, French, German, Belgian and Italian stations, such as BBC1,

BBC2 and BBC World; NBC Superchannel, offering largely American programming and international news; CNN; and the Euroversion of MTV, with pop and rock videos 24 hours a day. All British and American shows are subtitled on the Dutch and Belgian channels, but are dubbed on the French, Italian and German channels.

RADIO

In the Netherlands, news is broadcast on Dutch Radio 1 (98.9MHz), pop music on Radio 3 (96.8MHz) and classical music on Radio 4 (94.3MHz). It is also possible to pick up BBC Radio 4 on 198kHzAM and the World Service on 648kHzAM. Stations of all kinds are often opening in the city, aimed especially at youth.

NEWSPAPERS

Most foreign daily and Sunday newspapers reach the city centre by lunch time on publication day. The widest variety is sold at **Athenaeum Nieuwscentrum** and **Waterstones** in Kalverstraat, and includes the *Wall St Journal, International Herald Tribune*, the *Guardian* and other quality newspapers.

EMBASSIES AND CONSULATES

Most embassies are located in Den Haag *(see pp186–7)*, which is a 45-minute train ride from Centraal Station to

A selection of newspapers available

the Central Station of The Hague. Some countries, however, also have special consular facilities situated in Amsterdam. These include the UK, USA, France, Germany and Italy.

For a comprehensive list of offices in the city, consult the main Amsterdam telephone directory under *Consulaat*.

DIRECTORY

EMBASSIES AND CONSULATES

Australia
Carnegielaan 4, 2517 KH Den Haag.
Tel *(070) 310 8200.*
www.australian-embassy.nl ⬜ *8:30am–5pm Mon–Fri.*

Canada
Sophialaan 7, 2514 JP Den Haag.
www.canada.nl
⬜ *9am–5:30pm Mon–Fri.*

Ireland
Dr Kuyperstraat 9, 2514 BA Den Haag.
Tel *(070) 363 0993.*
www.irishembassy.nl
⬜ *10am–12:30pm, 2:30–5pm Mon–Fri.*

New Zealand
Carnegielaan 10, 2517 KH Den Haag. **Tel** *(070) 346 9324.* **www.** immigration.govt.nz
⬜ *9:15am–12:30pm, 2:30–5:30pm Mon–Fri.*

South Africa
Wassenaarseweg 40, 2596 CJ Den Haag.
Tel *(070) 392 4501.*
www.zuidafrika.nl
⬜ *9am–noon Mon–Fri, 2–4pm Mon–Fri: phone only.*

UK Consulate
Koningslaan 44. **Map** 3 B4.
General enquiries: **Tel** *676 4343.* ⬜ *8:30am–1:30pm Mon–Fri.*

Visa enquiries: **Tel** *676 4343.* ⬜ *By appt only.*

UK Embassy
Lange Voorhout 10, 2514 ED Den Haag.
Tel *(070) 427 0427.*
www.britain.nl

US Consulate
Museumplein 19
Map 4 E3.
Tel *5755309.*
http://netherlands.usembassy.gov
⬜ *8:30am–11:30am.*

US Embassy
Lange Voorhout 102, 2514 EJ Den Haag.
Tel *(070) 310 2209.*
http://netherlands.usembassy.gov

RELIGIOUS SERVICES

Anglican
Episcopal Christ Church
Groenburgwal 42.
Map 5 A2.
Tel *624 8877.*
www.christchurch.nl
Services in English: 10 & 11:45am Sun.

Dutch Reformed Church
Oude Kerk *(see pp68–9)*, Oudekerksplein 1.
Map 7 C2.
Tel *664 3655.*
⬜ *11am–5pm Mon–Sat, 1–5pm Sun. Service: 11am Sun.*
Westerkerk *(see p90)*, Prinsengracht 281.
Map 1 B4. **Tel** *624 7766.*
⬜ *Apr–Sep: 11am–3pm Mon–Fri; Aug–Sep: 11am–3pm Sat. Service: 10:30am Sun.*

English Reformed Presbyterian Church
Begijnhof 48 *(see p75)*.
Map 1 C5. **Tel** *624 9665.*
www.ercadam.nl
⬜ *During services only; in English: 10:30am Sun. Service in Dutch: 7pm Sun.*

Jewish
Orthodox Community Amsterdam
PO Box 7967, 1008 AD, Van der Boechorststraat 26.
Tel *646 0046.*
⬜ *9am–5pm Mon–Fri (phone first).*
Liberal Jewish Community Amsterdam
Jacob Soetendorpstraat 8.
Tel *540 0122.*
Services: 8pm Fri, 10am Sat.

Muslim
Stichting Islamitisch Centrum Amsterdam,
Tweede Van Swindenstraat 208. **Map** 6 F3.
Tel *668 5000.*

Quaker
Religieus Genootschap der Vrienden
Vossiusstraat 20. **Map** 4 D3. **Tel** *0570 655 229.*
Meeting: 10:30am Sun.

Roman Catholic
St John & St Ursula
Begijnhof 30. **Map** 1 C5.
Tel *622 1918.*
⬜ *1pm–6:30pm Mon, 9:30am–6:30pm Tue–Fri, 9–6pm Sat–Sun. Services: 9am & 5pm Mon–Fri, 9am Sat, 10am Sun. Service in French: 11:15pm Sun.*

CUSTOMS INFORMATION

Tel *0800 0143 (freephone).*
www.douane.nl

NEWSAGENTS

Athenaeum Nieuwscentrum
Spui 14–16. **Map** 7 B4.
Tel *624 2972.*

Waterstone's
Kalverstraat 152.
Map 7 B3. **Tel** *638 3821*

GETTING TO AMSTERDAM

One of Europe's most popular tourist destinations, Amsterdam, as you would expect of a modern cosmopolitan city of this size, is easily accessible by plane, coach, car, ferry and train. Of course, since the autumn of 1994, travellers from the UK have also been able to reach Amsterdam via the Channel Tunnel. Naturally, each method has its own benefits and disadvantages, and the choice will largely depend on various factors, in particular whether time, money or comfort is the priority. Whichever method of transport you choose in the end, it is always worth making a few enquiries to find the best deal to suit your requirements. Not only is there an ever-increasing selection of "packages" and special-interest holidays on offer, but prices can fluctuate widely depending on the time of year you travel, and new operators and ventures are emerging all the time.

Clear directions from the departures board at Schiphol

BY AIR

There is an immense choice of flights to Amsterdam from the UK and the Republic of Ireland, with seven carriers operating direct flights. These include the national airlines **Aer Lingus, British Airways** and **KLM**. Cheap trips are advertised in the national newspapers, in listings magazines, on the Internet and are also available through discount agencies. Smaller operators, such as **Easyjet**, can be less expensive than the national airlines. Flights are very quick – under an hour from London, for example.

There are dozens of inclusive package deals. Organized through a reliable agency, these can be far cheaper than booking a ferry or flight and separate accommodation.

USING AMSTERDAM AIRPORT SCHIPHOL

All the airport signs at Schiphol are colour-coded: yellow ones indicate the transfer desks and gates, green ones the amenities such as coffee bars, restaurants, shops, children's play area and well-equipped baby rooms. For business people and those in transit, there is an amazing range of facilities from business centre and conference rooms to sauna and golf and fitness centres.

A4 to Amsterdam

A4 to Rotterdam

AIRPORT COMPLEX

DEPARTURE LEVEL

Gates F
Bar
Lounge
Gates G
Duty-free shops
Gates E
Lounge
Bar
Gates D
Duty-free shops
Gates C/B
Gates E/F

Gates E/F/G
Train tickets
Airport information
Gates D
Airline desks

Shopping plaza
Airport information
Hotel reservation
Car rental
Taxis
Meeting point
To trains
Main exit
Gates C/B
Holland Tourist Information

ARRIVAL LEVEL

KEY

☐	Public access
☐	Check-in
☐	Passengers only
▨	Customs
☐	Passport control
☐	Baggage reclaim
☐	No access

Planes on runway at Amsterdam Airport Schiphol

LONG-DISTANCE FLIGHTS

Amsterdam is a popular staging post for overseas visitors to Europe. You can fly from many US cities to Schiphol, and operators running non-stop services on scheduled flights include the Dutch company **Martinair**, **Delta**, **United Airlines** and **Northwest Airlines**/KLM. These last two also offer free or reduced-price connecting flights. Other operators fly via the major European capital cities, such as Paris and Rome, but London is probably the cheapest trans-Atlantic destination, with uniquely varied connections. Fare prices vary according to

Signs showing departure gates

season, with APEX the cheapest year-round option. The leader in the field of charter flights from the USA is Martinair which offers mid-range prices on non-stop flights from a number of cities.

Cheaper still are the fares of the "seat consolidators", who buy up unsold seats from the major carriers and sell them off at a huge reduction. For bargain flights, check out the free weeklies and travel sections of newspapers. Several companies offer excellent-value package tours. KLM has the widest range of options, but as always, it's well worth shopping around. The cheapest route for visitors from Australia and New Zealand is also a London stop-over, as scheduled flights direct to Amsterdam are expensive. **STA Travel**, which has offices in Australia, New Zealand and the USA, is a source of expert advice for independent travellers.

ARRIVING AT SCHIPHOL

Amsterdam airport Schiphol has maintained its single terminal status and remains one of the world's most modern, efficient, clean and user-friendly airports. In the welcoming arrivals hall, you will find a tourist information desk, a post office, a bureau de change desk and left-luggage facilities. All signs are posted both in Dutch and in English, helping to diminish the feeling of

disorientation when arriving in a foreign country. Between the arrivals hall and the railway station are also dozens of high street shops as well as a fully stocked grocery.

There are two main ways of getting into the centre of Amsterdam, 18 km (11 miles) to the northeast.

Taxis are plentiful at the rank outside the arrivals hall, but the rule that cabbies stopping here are obliged to wear ties and jackets seems hardly enough justification for the high taxi fares. The best method for getting to Amsterdam centre is by rail.

Transfer desk at Schiphol

FROM SCHIPHOL BY RAIL

For the Schiphol airport rail service, just walk into the shopping plaza, buy a ticket to Amsterdam's Centraal Station and catch the next train. Trolleys, which are free of charge, can be taken right on to the platform.

Trains run four to seven times an hour between 6am and midnight, after which they run hourly. The journey takes about 20 minutes, and the fare is cheaper than the bus. There are also rail connections from Schiphol to the majority of stations in the Netherlands.

Travel poster from the 1950s advertising KLM's European flights

Railway platform at Schiphol Plaza – destination Amsterdam

Beware of pickpockets at Amsterdam's Centraal Station

BY FERRY

The Dutch railways, Nederlands Spoorwegen, in conjunction with **Stena Line** and **One Railway**, operate a boat-train service called the Dutch Flyer, which runs from London to Amsterdam via Harwich and the Hook of Holland. The total journey time is about 7 hours 30 minutes. **P&O** operate an overnight service from Hull to Zeebrugge or Rotterdam and this is a 10-hour journey.

DFDS Seaways run an overnight service from Newcastle to IJmuiden (the ticket does not include the journey from IJmuiden to Amsterdam).

The logo of Dutch Railways

BY TRAIN

Eurostar runs from London via the Channel Tunnel; passengers for Amsterdam must change at Brussels. Journey time is about 7 hours. All trains arrive at Centraal Station, including those from Schiphol Airport. The station has all the amenities of a big terminus. However, it's very crowded and a magnet for pickpockets and drug-pushers. Head for Stationsplein by the main entrance, following signs to the Amsterdam Tourist Board (VVV) (see p256). Avoid the rear entrance which can be the haunt of prostitutes. On Stationsplein, beware of hotel touts. The tram stops are only a few yards from the entrance, and the bus stops are further across the square on the left.

Most tram and bus routes start here (see pp272–3). The Tourist Board office is the white pavilion building found on your left, and the GVB municipal transport authority office is located in the same building. Students and those under 26 can benefit from considerable discount rail travel both to and within the Netherlands. The Interrail pass allows up to 1 month and the Eurodomino 3–8 days of unlimited travel in the Netherlands. For more information contact **Rail Europe**. You don't even have to be a student to qualify for some of the deals.

Centraal Station is being extensively reorganized and work will continue until 2011. Parts of the station will be closed off and tram and bus stops might be moved.

BY BUS AND COACH

Long-distance bus or coach travel can be a cheap, if sometimes tiresome, option for those visiting Amsterdam. **National Express** offer a service through the Channel Tunnel and sometimes by ferry from Dover to Calais. They run three daily services in summer from London to Amstel Station (there is a metro connection to Centraal Station), and at least one service a day in winter.

With all the various transport permutations available to UK–Amsterdam travellers, it's worth spending the time searching out the one that best suits your needs of schedule, money or comfort.

Comfortable travel by coach

BY CAR

In Europe only the Irish have to cross the sea to get to Amsterdam. An ever-expanding motorway system makes it easy to reach the Netherlands from most of western, central and southern Europe. A valid driver's licence

Cars parked on Afsluitdijk, between the North Sea and IJsselmeer

Taking the car and bicycles

is sufficient for driving in the Netherlands, although many car-hire firms and the motoring organization **ANWB** (Royal Dutch Touring Club) favour an international one. To take your own car into the Netherlands you will need proof of registration, valid insurance documents, a road safety certificate from the country of origin and an international

identification disc. Major roads (marked N) are well-maintained, but Dutch motorways (labelled A) have narrow lanes, traffic lights and sometimes no hard shoulder. European routes are labelled E.

There are four levels of speed limit: 100 km/h (60 mph) or 120 km/h (75 mph) on motorways, 80 km/h (50 mph) outside cities and 50 km/h (30 mph) in urban areas. From the A10 ring road, the S-routes (marked by blue signs) take you to the centre of Amsterdam.

The ANWB provides a break-down service for members of foreign motoring organizations. A non-member can pay for the ANWB's services, or become a temporary ANWB member.

If you have a breakdown on a major road or motorway, use the yellow telephone pillars.

DRIVING IN AMSTERDAM

Be careful of cyclists and trams when driving in the city. Trams take precedence and cyclists need ample space. Take care when turning, and allow cyclists priority. Much of the city centre is one-way, and when driving in the canal area, remember that the water should be to your left. Main roads with priority are marked by a white diamond with a yellow centre; otherwise priority is from the right.

The blue signs guiding you to city centres

DIRECTORY

AIRLINES IN BRITAIN AND IRELAND

Aer Lingus
London
Tel 0870 876 5000.
Dublin
Tel 0818 365 000.
www.aerlingus.ie

British Airways
Tel 0870 850 9850.
www.britishairways.com

British Midland
Tel 0870 607 0555.
www.flybmi.com

KLM
Tel 0870 507 4074.
www.klm.com

AIRLINES IN USA

British Airways
Tel (800) Airways.

Delta
Tel (800) 241 4141.
www.delta.com

Martinair (charter)
Tel (800) 627 8462.
www.martinairusa.com

Northwest Airlines
Tel (800) 447 4747.
www.nwa.com

United Airlines
Tel (800) 538 2929.
www.united.com

STA TRAVEL

www.statravel.com
Australia
Tel 1300 733 035.
New Zealand
Tel 0508 782 872.
UK
Tel 0870 630 026.
USA
Tel 800 781 4040.

SCHIPHOL AIRPORT

www.schiphol.com

Information Service
Tel 0900 7244 7465.

AIRLINE OFFICES

Aer Lingus
Tel 517 4747.

British Airways
Tel 346 9559.

British Midland
Tel 346 9211.

Delta
Tel 201 3536.

Easyjet
Tel 244 2366 or 0235 684 880. www.easyjet.com

KLM
Tel 474 7747.

Northwest Airlines
Tel 474 7747.

Transavia
Tel 020 736 4997. (UK)
Tel 0900 0737. (NL)
www.transavia.com

United Airlines
Tel 201 3708.

FERRY OPERATORS

DFDS Seaways
Tel 08702 520 524.
www.dfdsseaways.nl

P&O Ferries
Tel 0870 600 9955.
www.ponsf.com

Stena Line
Tel 08705 707 070.
www.stenaline.com

RAIL INFORMATION

Eurostar
Tel 08705 186 186.
www.eurostar.com

One Railway/ Stena Line
Dutch Flyer
Tel 08705 455 455.
www.dutchflyer.com

Rail Europe
Tel 08702 302 008.
www.raileurope.co.uk

BRITISH COACH INFORMATION

National Express
Tel 08705 808 080.
www.nationalexpress.com

BREAKDOWN

Royal Dutch Touring Club (ANWB)
24-hour emergency service
Tel 08 000 888.

GETTING AROUND AMSTERDAM

The best way to see Amsterdam is on foot. Almost everything of interest is within comfortable walking distance. The city's layout is quite simple, with its concentric canals *(grachten)* and interlocking roads, but it can seem confusing at first. The *Street Finder (see pp278–91)* will help you negotiate the maze of narrow streets. The simplest way to orientate yourself is to remember that, starting from the Singel, the main canals are arranged in the alphabetical sequence of Herengracht, Keizersgracht, Prinsengracht and Singel. Houses are numbered starting at Centraal Station and finishing, with the high numbers, at the Amstel. Amsterdam is not a city to drive around and there are limited and expensive facilities for motorists.

Street sign indicating district

Pedestrian crossing, Dam square

WALKING

Before embarking on a walk around the city, make sure that you are wearing sensible shoes – the brick-cobbled streets can be tiring as well as hazardous. Another problem is dog mess, so look down before looking up to admire canalside architecture.

Some people may not be used to trams and bicycles, so remember to look both ways when crossing tram routes (trams can be almost silent), and keep off the cycle paths.

Many pedestrian crossings are regulated by lights. Those without lights only indicate what is thought to be a suitable place to cross the road, and cars are not required to stop for you.

WALKING TOURS

The canal walk on pages 94–105 takes in some of the city's grandest canals. The Guided Walk along the Historic Waterfront *(see pp160–61)*

explores Amsterdam's trading history. For a tour of the tranquil Jordaan and the Western Islands, see pages 158–9.

Walks organized by **Yellow Bike Tour** pass many of the important buildings and monuments around the Canal Ring and in the Jordaan. **Amsterdam City Walks** organizes guided walks, which are conducted in English, that focus on the history and archaeology of Amsterdam – they also take in the Red Light District. Guided tours from **Mee in Mokum** also take you around the historic parts of the city. **Archivisie** covers the heart of the city, including examples of Amsterdam School architecture *(see p97)* and medieval areas.

CARS IN AMSTERDAM

Although the city is ill-suited to motor traffic, provision is

The penalty for illegal parking

made for those who visit as part of a motoring holiday. However, parking is difficult, clamping prevalent and theft rife, so it is wise to follow some simple rules.

If you're staying in a hotel, book with a secure parking facility and leave your car there while in the city. If you are coming from outside, park on the outskirts of the city in a "P&R" (park and ride) and use the excellent public transport into the centre. If you do drive into town, use a car park rather than a meter or roadside space. Finally, if you do park in a public

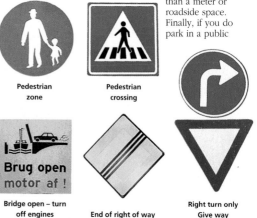

Pedestrian
zone

Pedestrian
crossing

Right turn only
Give way

Bridge open – turn
off engines

End of right of way

place, remember to remove your car radio and all other valuables.

Parking space is at a premium in the city, especially on the streets, and meters on main canal banks are least free in office hours. Most meters are limited to two hours. They take coins and/or parking cards. Avoid out-of-order meters as you could get fined or clamped. If you use a car park, first put money in the ticket machine, which can be some way from the parking place.

Illegally parked cars get clamped and you will be fined. If you have a credit card, phone the **Stadstoezicht** and a Pay-and-Go car will arrive. You pay on the spot and the clamp is removed. To pay with cash, go to the nearest Stadstoezicht service centre within 24 hours, otherwise your car will be towed away incurring additional charges.

There are now several 24-hour covered car parks, such as **Muziektheater-Parking** and **Byzantium**. Uncovered car parks are free from midnight to early morning. All city car

Press green button for ticket
Insert coins
Take ticket

A pay-and-display ticket machine

parks are denoted by a white P on a square blue background. A one-day parking pass costs around €26 from all Stadstoezicht centres and parking meters.

The reorganization around Centraal Station (until 2011) may cause delays and diversions.

CAR RENTAL

You must be aged 21 or over to hire a car and possess a licence and passport. Some companies also insist on at least one year's driving experience. Most of the major agencies have offices in the city, and at Schiphol Airport, but local Dutch firms are significantly cheaper. All outlets require a substantial deposit.

TAXIS

The best ways to find a cab are to pick one up at a taxi rank or phone **TCA Taxicentrale**, which runs a 24-hour service. You will find that the response is fast, apart from Friday and Saturday nights. Rates are quite high, so give only a small tip, unless your driver has been particularly helpful.

Taxi drivers waiting patiently for a fare

DIRECTORY

Travelling by Public Transport

Amsterdam's integrated public transport system, for which Centraal Station is the focal point, is efficient and inexpensive. The **OVR** gives information on all public transport within the city and the rest of the Netherlands, but does not make reservations. The cheapest way to travel in Amsterdam is to buy a *strippenkaart* from the **GVB**, Tourist Board offices, newsagents, and post offices. Also good value is the All Amsterdam Transport Pass, available at Canalbus kiosks.

Watch out for trams

at the front and pay the driver. This is difficult in the rush hour, as trams can get very crowded. If you have a young child or heavy suitcase, keep one foot on the bottom step when you board, to hold the door open. The new white and blue trams are more convenient to use with a low entrance towards the rear.

Tram stops will generally be announced, but if you're not sure where to get off, ask for guidance. Press a button inside the tram to open the doors, and remember that many stops are in the middle of the road, so take care when you get off.

One of Amsterdam's modern white and blue trams

TRAMS

Amsterdam's tram lines, whose routes are shown on a free transport map, obtainable from the GVB, are the most common form of transport in the city. Trams start operating at 6am on weekdays and slightly later at weekends. They finish just after midnight, when night buses take over. Blue boards at the tram and bus stops give the name of the stop and the route numbers it serves. Maps in the shelters are helpful and show the routes. You can get on and off by any but the front door. On trams with a conductor, use the rear door only to board and offer your ticket for stamping. When there is no conductor use the stamping machines inside. If you need to buy a ticket, you can board

BUSES

Like the trams, the majority of Amsterdam's buses set out from Centraal Station, but they soon branch out from the city centre and largely complement the tram network.

No. 35 bus serving the north of the city from Centraal Station

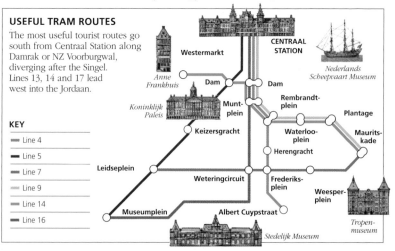

USEFUL TRAM ROUTES

The most useful tourist routes go south from Centraal Station along Damrak or NZ Voorburgwal, diverging after the Singel. Lines 13, 14 and 17 lead west into the Jordaan.

KEY

━━ Line 4
━━ Line 5
━━ Line 7
━━ Line 9
━━ Line 14
━━ Line 16

CENTRAAL STATION

Westermarkt

Anne Frankhuis

Koninklijk Paleis

Dam

Munt-plein

Keizersgracht

Leidseplein

Weteringcircuit

Museumplein

Albert Cuypstraat

Stedelijk Museum

Dam

Rembrandt-plein

Waterloo-plein

Herengracht

Frederiks-plein

Nederlands Scheepvaart Museum

Plantage

Maurits-kade

Weesper-plein

Tropen-museum

USING THE STRIPPENKAART

Time indicator   Insert *strippen-kaart* here

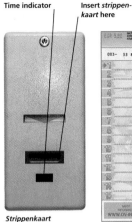

1 Starting from the top, fold top strip back and stamp the second one for one person travelling in central Amsterdam for up to one hour. The stamp indicates time and date of travel and zone in which you have boarded.

2 For a second person travelling in the centre, stamp here as well, to validate two more strips.

3 For a subsequent journey which crosses into two zones, such as a visit from Dam square to the Olympic Quarter *(see p154)*, validate the next three strips by stamping the *strippenkaart* here.

Strippenkaart
stamping machine

They have the same stops and ticketing system as the trams, but you must board by the front door. A small bus "de Opstapper" leaves every 10 minutes from Centraal Station (Mon–Sat) along Prinsengracht to Waterlooplein and back. It runs close to many sights, museums and shopping areas. Normal public transport tickets can be used on this.

Night-bus stops feature a black square with a special number on it, running from 71 to 79. Buses run all night but the service is infrequent, so be prepared for a long wait or take a taxi.

METRO

Amsterdam's underground system comprises only four lines, three terminating at Centraal Station. Mainly used by commuters, it is of little use to tourists as it only covers four stations in the centre, all on the eastern side – Amsterdam CS, Nieuwmarkt, Waterlooplein and Weesperplein. The Metro runs for around half an hour longer than trams on weekdays, and the ticketing system is the same. Take care at night when stations are popular with drugdealers.

Sign for Metro station

Checking a train timetable

TRAINS

The Dutch national railway company, Nederlandse Spoorwegen, runs a busy network, which is considered one of the best in the world. It is reliable, clean and reasonably priced. The OVR (Openbaar Vervoer Reisinformatie) office gives a mass of information on rail trips for tourists, plus details of special fares, such as family rovers, which allow you to stop off en route to your destination. It does not, however, sell tickets, which are sold at the ticket office. Information and bookings for rail travel abroad is available from the **Nederlandse Spoorwegen Internationaal** office, which is located in the hall of Centraal Station.

TRAM AND BUS TICKETS

The *strippenkaart* (ticket strip), available in multiples of 15 units, allows you to travel all over the Netherlands. Each unit, or strip, relates to the number of zones you travel through. From the top, count the number of strips/zones required for your journey then fold them back and stamp the next one in the machine. Any number of people can travel on a single *strippenkaart*, providing it has enough unused strips left.

Tickets for one hour's unlimited travel can be purchased on board, but cost more. The *dagkaart* (day ticket), extendable for up to 9 days, and a season ticket are both on sale from the GVB.

Three-day dagkaart

2007 will see the introduction of the OV Chipkaart. This will work like a rechargeable telephone card, with each trip being deducted from the credit available.

DIRECTORY

GVB (Gemeente Vervoer Bedrijf)
Stationsplein 14. **Map** 2 E3.
Tel 0900 8011.
Tel 0900 9292 (national public transport enquiries).
◻ 7am–9pm Mon–Fri, 8am–9pm, Sat, Sun & public hols.
www.gvb.nl

Nederlandse Spoorwegen Internationaal
Centraal Station. **Map** 2 E3.
Tel 0900 9296.
◻ 6:30am–9pm daily.
www.ns.nl

OVR (Openbaar Vervoer Reisinformatie)
Tel 0900 9292.
◻ 6am–midnight Mon–Fri, 7am–midnight Sat, Sun & public hols (for information on all public transport in the Netherlands).
www.9292ov.nl

Getting Around by Bicycle

Promoting the pleasures of biking

The bicycle is the ideal form of transport in Amsterdam. More than half a million people cycle to school or work, and use a bicycle to do the shopping or go out in the evening. The city's traffic system is biased in favour of bicycles, with an excellent network of integrated cycle lanes (*fietspaden*), dedicated traffic lights and road signs, and special routes linking different parts of the city. More and more tourists are adopting this way of exploring Amsterdam and its environs. You can bring your own bicycle, hire one for just a day or join a cycle tour.

Bicycle safety helmet

Cycle tour crossing Nieuwe Herengracht

RULES OF THE ROAD

Amsterdam's traffic can appear to be chaotic at first, so above all remember always to ride on the right. Be aware that motorists, tram drivers and other cyclists will not necessarily recognize you as an inexperienced tourist.

Motorists and other cyclists have priority when entering your road from the right, unless otherwise stated. Trams have priority, if only because they are bigger and can't be steered, so don't argue with them. Always keep a wary ear open for their distinctive rattle and stay clear. If you are not sure who has right of way – or anything else err on the side of caution. You will need to be patient with pedestrians who are clearly tourists and unfamiliar with the local rules of the road. Dutch cyclists are naturally an-archic and often ride through red lights, but don't try to follow their example. Many novices dismount at busy junctions and cross on foot, to be on the safe side.

The part of the road with tramlines should be used only by trams, buses, taxis and emergency services. If you have to move inside the tracks to pass a stationary vehicle, do so at an angle, otherwise your front wheel may get stuck. Also watch out for people emerging from parked cars, and foreign coaches whose drivers may be unsympathetic to cyclists. You may cycle two abreast, but only if you do not block traffic. Don't carry passengers on your bike, or ride on foot-paths or pavements – even though the Amsterdammers do.

You are legally obliged to have reflector bands on both wheels and a large reflector at the back, as well as lights. Don't try to copy the Amsterdammers, who tend not to use lights at night. And, although the locals don't bother, it is a wise precaution to wear a helmet.

For a puncture or mechanical problem, head for one of the many bicycle shops (*fietsen-makers*) found around the city.

Crossing tramlines at a safe angle

BUYING A BICYCLE

Be careful when buying a bicycle. A cheap one for sale on the street will almost certainly have been stolen, and an expensive one from a specialist shop will probably end up being stolen. On the other hand, it's worth buying a second-hand bargain if you are staying for a few weeks and plan to do a fair amount of cycling. There are quite a number of reputable second-hand dealers in Amsterdam, and you'll find that some hire companies also sell bicycles.

Traffic lights for bicycles

Bicycles allowed

No entry except to bicycles and mopeds

HIRING A BICYCLE

Bicycle hire shops abound in Amsterdam. All require a deposit and your passport. Rental costs start at around five euros a day with deposits varying from €20 to €100. Tandems are more expensive.

The brakes on some Dutch bikes are worked by back-pedalling. This can take some practice to master, so if you think you'll find it difficult, insist on a cycle with handlebar brakes.

A selection of bicycles for hire

BICYCLE SECURITY

Bicycle theft is rife, so it's essential to secure your cycle even when parking for just a few minutes. Fasten both front wheel and frame to a post or railings with a metal U-shaped lock. Hire shops are happy to advise on security matters, and will normally provide a lock in the rental price.

A metal U-lock

Transporting a bike long-distance

TAKING YOUR OWN BICYCLE

Taking a bicycle on the ferry to the Netherlands is free. When you book your ferry ticket, inform the clerk of your plans. If you're travelling to one of the British ferry ports by train, you will need to book the bicycle on British Rail. On your arrival in the Netherlands, if you want the cycle to go with you by train, buy a ticket for it. To take your bicycle by air, you must make a cargo booking with the airline at least a week in advance. It will have to be included in your 20-kg (44-lb) luggage allowance, and you must pay any excess. Remove the wheels and fold down the handlebars ready for transportation.

BICYCLE TOURS

Guided bicycle tours are increasingly popular as a way of discovering the city and its environs at a sedate pace. The price of the tours usually includes bicycle hire. **Yellow Bike** organizes tours in the city, and you can book tours at their office or at an Amsterdam Tourist Board office *(see p256)* from April to October.

If you want to go it alone, the Tourist Board also provides maps with routes, cycle lanes and refreshment stops. Arena Hotel *(see p223)* produces an excellent folder with suggestions and maps for cycle trips around and outside the city. City tours usually take about 3 hours, country trips rather longer at around 7 hours.

MacBike's multilingual cycle guide for energetic visitors

DIRECTORY

BICYCLE HIRE

Bike City
Bloemgracht 70. **Map** 1 A4.
Tel 626 3721.
www.bikecity.nl

Bulldog
Oudezijds Voorburgwal 216. **Map** 7 C3.
Tel 421 7068.

Damstraat Rent-a-Bike
Damstraat 20-22. **Map** 7 C3. **Tel** 625 5029.
www.bikes.nl

Holland Rent-a-Bike
Damrak 247. **Map** 7 C2.
Tel 622 3207.

MacBike
Centraal Station, Stationsplein 12.
Map 8 D1.
Tel 620 0985.
www.macbike.nl

Marnixstraat 220.
Map 4 D1.
Tel 626 6964.

Mr Visserplein 2.
Map 8 E4.
Tel 620 0985.

Rent A Bike Frederic
Brouwersgracht 78.
Map 1 B2.
Tel 624 5509.

Rijwielshop Amstel
Amstelstation, Julianaplein 1.
Tel 692 3584.

Wielertaxi
Tel 06 282 47550.
www.wielertaxi.nl

BICYCLE TOURS

Cycletours Holland
Buiksloterweg 7A.
Map 2 F2. **Tel** 521 8490.
www.cycletours.com
(countrywide trips, no city tours)

Yellow Bike
Nieuwezijds Kolk 29.
Map 7 C1. **Tel** 620 6940.
www.yellowbike.nl

SECOND-HAND BICYCLES

Groeno
2e H De Grootstraat 12.
Map 1 A4.
Tel 684 4270.

John's Fiets Inn
Spinozastraat 2.
Map 5 C4.
Tel 428 4385.

MacBike
See under Bicycle Hire.

Zijwind
Scheldestraat 11.
Tel 673 7026.

Getting Around by Canal

Amsterdam has evolved around its network of canals, earning it the name "Venice of the North". Though the canals were built for moving goods rather than people, today they provide a marvellous means of viewing the city's splendid sights, as well as its everyday life. Canal boats offer a huge variety of tours to satisfy the most diverse requirements, and are usually featured in tourist brochures. Boat trips are particularly well-suited to those without the time to explore on foot or by tram, or to the elderly and families with children, who are not able to walk long distances.

A brightly decorated row boat

Embarkation point for P. Kooij

CANAL TOURS

There are many operators in Amsterdam offering canal tours with foreign-language commentaries. Boats depart from a number of embarkation points, mainly from opposite Centraal Station along Prins Hendrikkade, the Damrak and along the Rokin. Many *rond-vaartboten* (tour boats) have glass tops, some of which can be opened in fine weather. It is not always necessary to book seats for tours, but it is wise to do so for lunch time, evening and dinner cruises, especially during the peak tourist season.

Night cruises can feature cheese-and-wine refreshments, a stop at a pub or a romantic candlelit dinner. **Lovers** offers a comprehensive selection of such cruises in addition to its daytime trips. Beside city-centre tours, **Artis Express** operates a special service from Centraal Station to Artis *(see pp142–3)*, the Scheepvaart Museum *(see pp146–7)*, Tropenmuseum *(see pp152–3)* and the Hortus Botanicus *(see p142)*. On hot days, try **P. Kooij**, as it has the most open-topped boats.

Brochures and ticket for canal cruises

CANALBUS

The Canalbus service runs every 30 mins along three routes, with 14 stops located near the major museums, shopping areas and other attractions. You can embark or alight at any of the stops along the routes. It is claimed that the canalbus is the first boat of its kind in Europe to run on gas.

A day ticket can be purchased, and the canalbus is also available on Saturday evenings for one-and-a-half-hour jazz cruises which start from outside the Rijksmuseum at 8pm and 10pm, from April to November. It is generally advisable to reserve a place on these beforehand at a **Canalbus** kiosk, as they are very popular and can get fully booked very quickly, especially in summer.

You can also purchase from the Canalbus kiosks the All Amsterdam Transport Pass, which, among other things, entitles you to a free round trip of the canals. Passes can last for one, two or three days.

Canal tour on the Oude Schans, showing the Montelbaanstoren in the background

The Museum Boat on Singelgracht

MUSEUM BOAT

Amsterdam's **Museum Boat** takes in, and stops near, all the major city sights. Tours start every 30 minutes daily, between 10am and 5pm, from opposite Centraal Station. You can buy an ordinary ticket, which gives unlimited use for one day, or a day-ticket and a discount on the museum admission prices. Both can be bought at at the Centraal Station embarkation stage or any landing points. Details of landing stages are on the transport map on the inside back cover of this guide.

Polished interior of a water taxi

WATER TAXIS

Water taxis are more convenient than canal boats for sightseeing. They are also expensive – for an 8-seater, the tariff is around €85 for the first 30 minutes and €70 per half hour thereafter. There are also special "walk-in" same-day rates, with up to four people

paying €15 per person for the first half hour. After that period, the normal rate is charged. Food, drink and guides can also be booked in advance. If you want to use one of these boats you will need to book in advance from **Water Taxi**.

Sightseeing by canal bike

CANAL BIKES

The keep-fit way to see the city is by canal bike. These are really two- or four-seater pedal-boats. Propelling them requires considerable energy, but when you've had enough, you can stop for a drink. You can pick up or leave a pedal-boat at any of the canal-bike moorings in the city: Prinsengracht at the Westerkerk, Keizersgracht near Leidsestraat, Leidseplein between the Marriott and American hotels, and along the Singelgracht just outside the Rijksmuseum. These locations operate 10am–6pm daily (9:30pm in July and August, 5:30pm in winter). There is a €50 deposit.

Between November and March only the Singelgracht mooring is open. At weekends, Prinsengracht and Leidseplein are also usually open. Rain shields are provided at no extra cost in wet weather, along with a route-planning map of the city.

Canal taxi logo

DIRECTORY

CANAL TRIPS

Amsterdam Canal Cruises
Nicolaas Witsenkade 1a,
opposite Heineken Brouwerij.
Map 4 F2. **Tel** 626 5636.
www.amsterdamcanalcruises.nl

Artis Express
opposite Centraal Station, next the
tram stop No. 1. **Map** 8 D1.
Tel 530 1090.
www.lovers.nl

The Best of Holland
Damrak 34. **Map** 8 D1.
Tel 623 1539 or 420 4000.
www.thebestofholland.nl

Canalbus & Canal Bike
Weteringschans 24
Map 4 E2.
Tel 623 9886.
www.canal.nl

Holland International
Prins Hendrikkade 33a,
opposite Centraal Station.
Map 8 D1.
Tel 622 7788.
www.thatsholland.com

Lindbergh
Damrak 26. **Map** 8 D1.
Tel 622 2766.
www.lindbergh.nl

Lovers
Opposite Prins Hendrikkade
25–27, **Map** 8 D1.
Tel 530 1090.
www.lovers.nl

Meyers
Jetty 4-5, Damrak.
Map 8 D1.
Tel 623 4208.

Museum Boat
Stationsplein 8. **Map** 8 D1.
Tel 530 1090.
www.lovers.nl

P. Kooij
Opposite Rokin 125.
Map 7 B4.
Tel 623 3810.
www.rederijkooij.nl

Water Taxi
Stationsplein 8. **Map** 8 D1.
Tel 535 6363.
www.water-taxi.nl

STREET FINDER

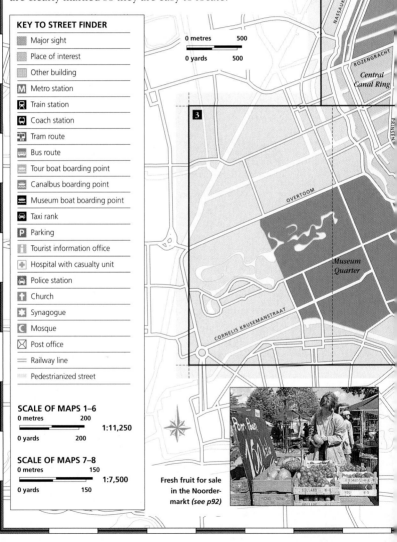

The page grid superimposed on the *Area by Area* map below shows which parts of Amsterdam are covered in this *Street Finder*. The map references given for all sights, hotels, restaurants, shopping and entertainment venues described in this guide refer to the maps in this section. A complete index of the street names and places of interest marked on the maps follows on pages 288–91. The key, set out below, indicates the scales of the maps and shows what other features are marked on them, including transport terminals, emergency services and information centres. All the major sights are clearly marked so they are easy to locate.

KEY TO STREET FINDER

	Major sight
	Place of interest
	Other building
M	Metro station
	Train station
	Coach station
	Tram route
	Bus route
	Tour boat boarding point
	Canalbus boarding point
	Museum boat boarding point
	Taxi rank
P	Parking
	Tourist information office
	Hospital with casualty unit
	Police station
	Church
	Synagogue
C	Mosque
⊠	Post office
=	Railway line
	Pedestrianized street

SCALE OF MAPS 1–6

0 metres   200

0 yards   200

1:11,250

SCALE OF MAPS 7–8

0 metres   150

0 yards   150

1:7,500

0 metres   500

0 yards   500

Fresh fruit for sale in the Noordermarkt *(see p92)*

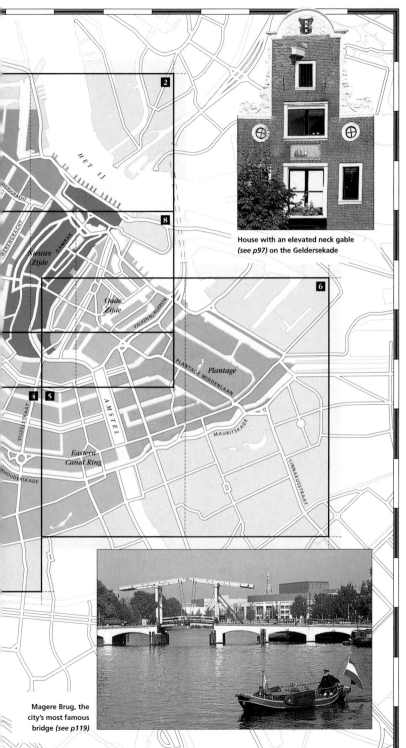

House with an elevated neck gable *(see p97)* **on the Geldersekade**

HET IJ

WESTGRACHT

JERENGRACHT

DAMRAK

Nieuwe
Zijde

Oude
Zijde

VALKENBURGERSTR

PLANTAGE MIDDENLAAN

Plantage

AMSTEL

VIJZELSTRAAT

MAURITSKADE

LINNAEUSSTRAAT

Eastern
Canal Ring

HOUDERSKADE

**Magere Brug, the
city's most famous
bridge** *(see p119)*

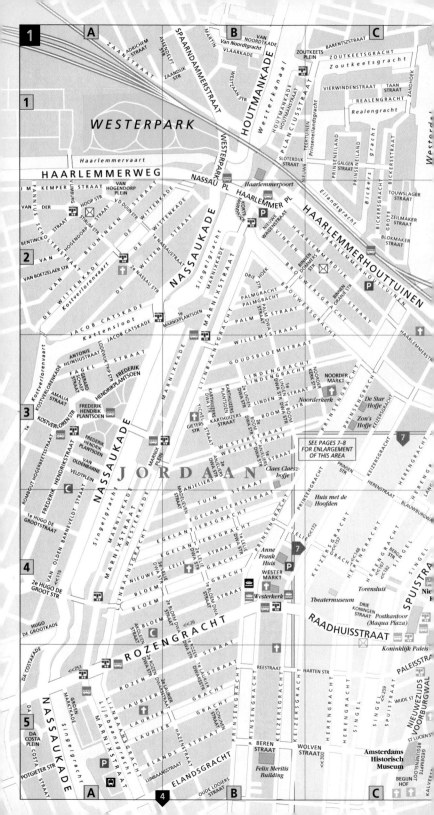

Grid references (top):
1 | A | B | C

1

Labels and streets:

ZAANDIJK STR
ADRICIEM STRAAT
ZAANSTRAAT
ASSENDELFT STR
SPAARNDAMMERSTRAAT
MARTIN
Van Noordtgracht
VAN NOORDTKADE
VLAARKADE
WESTZAAN STR
HOUTMANKADE
ZOUTKEETS PLEIN
BARENTSZSTRAAT
ZOUTKEETSGRACHT
Zoutkeetsgracht
VIERWINDENSTRAAT
TAAN STRAAT
ZANDHOEK
REALENGRACHT
Realengracht

1

WESTERPARK

Westerkanaal
HOUTMANKADE
Houtmankade
PLANCIUSSTRAAT
Prinseneilandgracht
PRINSENEILAND
PRINSENEILAND
GALGEN STRAAT
PRINSENEILAND

Haarlemmervaart

HAARLEMMERWEG
WESTERPARK
NASSAU PL
Haarlemmerpoort
HAARLEMMER PL
SLOTERDIJK STRAAT
NIEUWE
TEERTUINEN
BICKERS GRACHT
Bickersgracht
BICKERSSTRAAT
Westerdo
TOUWSLAGER STRAAT

J M
FANNIUS
VAN DER
KEMPER
STRAAT
LIMBURG
STIRUM STR
VAN HOGENDORP PLEIN
HOOP STR
VD DUIJN STR
DE WITTENKADE
WITTENKADE
Westerkanaal
MORTEL
Ellandsgracht
BICKERSGRACHT
GROTE
ZEILMAKER STRAAT

VAN
BENTINCK
SCHOLTENSTRAAT
VAN HOGENDORP STR
DE BEUNINGEN
STRAAT
1e NASSAUSTRAAT
HAARLEMMER PL
NIEUWE WAGENSTRAAT
HAARLEMMERDIJK
HAARLEMMERHOUTTUINEN
VINKEN
BLOKMAKER STRAAT

VAN BOETZELAER STR
DE WITTENKADE
2e NASSAU STR
Singelgracht
MARNIXKADE
DRIE HOEK
BROUWERS STR
BINNEN DOMMERS STR
HAARLEMMERHOUTTUINEN
BINNEN ORANJE STR

2

VAN WITTENKADE
Kostverlorenvaart
MARNIXSTRAAT
PALMGRACHT
PALMGRACHT
BROUWERSGRACHT
PALM STRAAT
PALM DWA STR

JACOB CATSKADE
Kattensloot
JACOB CATSKADE
MARNIXPLANTSOEN
WILLEMSSTRAAT
HAARLEMMERST

ANTONIE HEINSIUSTRAAT
Kostverlorenvaart
LODEWIJK TRIP STR
FREDERIK
HENDRIKPLANTSOEN
GOUDSBLOEMSTRAAT
LINDENGRACHT
LINDENGRACHT
NOORDER KERK STR
NOORDER MARKT
De Star Hofje
PRINSENGRACHT

3

1e KOSTVERLORENVAART
AMALIA STRAAT
FAGEL
GERARD SCHAEP
STRAAT
FREDERIK
HENDRIKSTRAAT
1e LINDEN DWA STR
KARTHUIZERS PLANTSOEN
LINDEN DWA STR
1e BOOM DWA STR
BOOM STR
Noorderkerk
KEIZERSGRACHT
Zon's Hofje

FREDERIK HENDRIK PLANTSOEN
MARNIX
PLEIN
TICHEL STR
GIETERS STR
KARTHUIZERS STRAAT
LINDEN STRAAT
BOOM DWA STR
WESTERSTRAAT
2e ANJELIERS DWA STR
SEE PAGES 7–8
FOR ENLARGEMENT
OF THIS AREA

NASSAUKADE
ROMBOUT HOGERBEETSSTRAAT
FREDERIK HENDRIKSTRAAT
VAN OLDENBARNE VELDTPLEIN
J O R D A A N
WESTERSTRAAT
1e ANJELIERS DWA STR
Claes Claeszhofje
PRINSENGRACHT
PRINSEN STR
KEIZERSGRACHT
HERENSTRAAT
HERENGR
7

1e HUGO DE GROOTSTRAAT
VAN OLDEN BARNEVELDT STRAAT
Singelgracht
MARNIXSTRAAT
2e ANJELIERS STRAAT
TUIN STRAAT
MAGDELEN STRAAT
Huis met de Hoofden
HERENSTRAAT
BLAUWBURGWA

4

2e HUGO DE GROOT STR
WESTERKADE
LINBAANSGRACHT
EGELANTIERSSTRAAT
EGELANTIERSGRACHT
EGELANTIERSGRACHT
1e LELIE DWA STR
2e LELIE DWA STR
LELIE STRAAT
PRINSENGRACHT
LELIE GRACHT
Anne Frank Huis
7
KEIZERSGRACHT
HERENGRACHT
BERGSTR
SINGEL

HUGO DE GROOTKADE
MARNIXSTRAAT
NIEUWE DWA STR
BLOEM STRAAT
1e BLOEM DWA STR
WESTER MARKT
Westerkerk
Torensluis
Nic

2e BLOEM DWA STR
AKELEIEN STRAAT
BLOEM
2e ROZEN DWA STR
1e ROZEN DWA STR
Theatermuseum
DRIE KONINGEN STRAAT
Postkantoor
(Maqua Plaza)
SPUISTRA

DA COSTAKADE
ROZENGRACHT
RAADHUISSTRAAT
Koninklijk Paleis

ROZEN STRAAT
2e JAURIER DWASTRAAT
1e LAURIER DWASTR
REESTRAAT
HARTEN STR
HERENGRACHT
HERENGRACHT
PALEISSTRA
NIEUWEZIJDS VOORBURGWAL

5

DA COSTA PLEIN
NASSAUKADE
GROEN MARKTKADE
Singelgracht
MARNIXSTRAAT
LINBAANSGRACHT
LAURIER GRACHT
KONINGEN STRAAT
HAZENSTRAAT
LAURIER STRAAT
PRINSENGRACHT
KEIZERSGRACHT
WOLVEN STR
SINGEL
SPUISTRAAT
WIJDE ST
ST LUCIEN ST

POTGIETER STRAAT
DA COSTA STR
ELANDSGRACHT
LINBAANSGRACHT
ELANDSGRACHT
BEREN STRAAT
Felix Meritis Building
OUDE LOOIERS STRAAT
Amsterdams Historisch Museum
GEDEMPTE BEGIJNENSLOOT
BEGIJN HOF

Grid references (bottom):
A | B | C
4

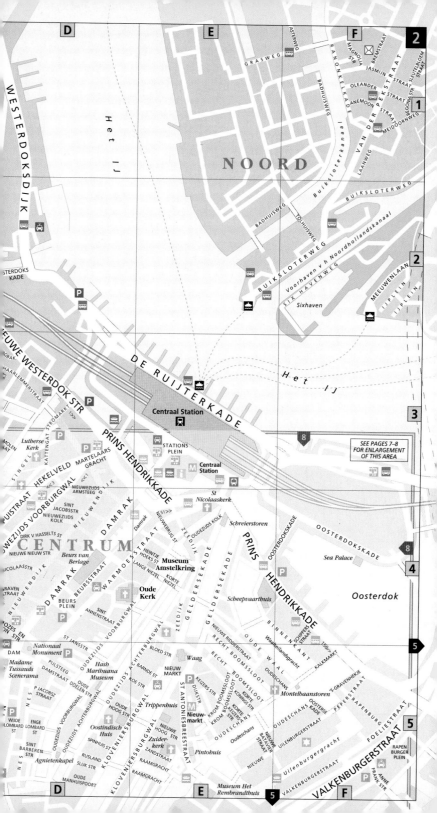

SEE PAGES 7–8 FOR ENLARGEMENT OF THIS AREA

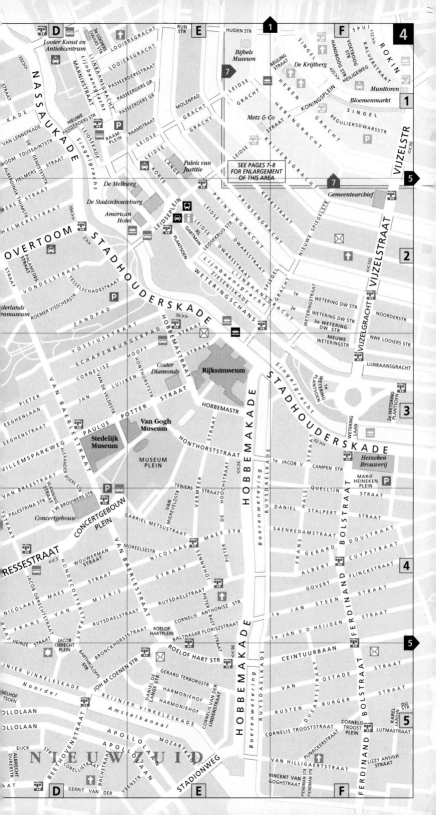

D 4

Looier Kunst en Antiekcentrum

E
RUN STR

HUIDEN STR
1

F
SPUI 112>>
ROKIN
4

LOOIERS DWARSSTR

LOOIERSGRACHT

Bijbels Museum

7

BEULING STRAAT

De Krijtberg

Handboog STR

Voetboog STR

HEILIGEWEG

Kalverstraat

MARNIXSTRAAT

LIJNBAANSGR

PASSEERDERSSTRAAT

PASSEERDERS GR

PASSEERDERS GR

NIEUWE PASSEERDERS STR

RAAM-
PLEIN

Singelgracht

MOLENPAD

HEREN

KONINGSPLEIN

Munttoren

Bloemenmarkt

1

Metz & Co

REGULIERSDWARSSTR

VAN LENNEPKADE

KADE

P

LEIDSE

KORTE

LEIDSE

RAAMSTRAAT

RAAMSTRAAT

GRACHT

GRACHT

HERENGRACHT

SINGEL

VIJZELSTR <<39

BOOM TOUSSAINTSTR

HELMERS STRAAT

ALBRECHT THMSTR

Paleis van Justitie

KEIZERSGRACHT

SEE PAGES 7–8 FOR ENLARGEMENT OF THIS AREA

LEIDSE

GRACHT

KERKSTRAAT

5

De Melkweg

De Stadsschouwburg

American Hotel

LEIDSEPLEIN

Gemeentearchief

7

OVERTOOM

STADHOUDERSKADE

PALAMEDES STRAAT

VONDELSTRAAT

TESSELSCHADESTRAAT

LEIDSE

GARTMAN

PLANTSOEN

LEIDSE DWARSSTRAAT

KL LEIDSEKRUIS STR

LIJNBAANSGRACHT

PRINSENGRACHT

PRINSENGRACHT

LEIDSE DWARSSTRAAT

SPIEGEL

NIEUWE SPIEGELSTR

<<102
2

derlands mmuseum

ROEMER VISSCHERSTR

ZANDPAD

P

VOSSIUSSTRAAT

39>>

HOBBEMASTRAAT

STRAAT

ZIESENISKADE

WETERINGSCHANS

WETERINGSTRAAT

WETERING DW STR

3e WETERING DW STR

NIEUWE WETERINGSTR

NOORDERSTR

NWE LOOIERS STR

LIJNBAANSGRACHT

VIJZELGRACHT

VIJZELSTRAAT

SCHAPENBURGERPAD

HOOFT

STRAAT

Coster Diamonds

Rijksmuseum

STADHOUDERSKADE

1e WETERING PLANTSOEN

CORNELISZ

HONTHORSTSTR

VAN DE VELDESTR

PIETER

JAN

PAULUS POTTER STRAAT

HOBBEMASTR

HOBBEMASTR

Singelgracht PLANTSOEN

WETERING LAAN

2e WETERING PLANTSOEN

3

EEGHENLAAN

EEGHENSTRAAT

Stedelijk Museum

Van Gogh Museum

STRAAT

HONTHORSTSTRAAT

HOBBEMAKADE

VILLEMSPARKWEG

ALEXANDER BOERS STR

MUSEUM PLEIN

VERMEER

STRAATWEG

1e JACOB V CAMPEN STR

Heineken Brouwerij

MARIE HEINEKEN PLEIN

P

VAN BREESTRAAT

P

TENIERS

Boerenwetering

RUYSDAELKADE

QUELLIJN STRAAT

RESSESTRAAT

WANING STRAAT

PALESTRINA STRAAT

JW BROUWERS STR

Concertgebouw

CONCERTGEBOUW PLEIN

GABRIEL METSUSTRAAT

VAN MIEREVELDSTR

VAN

DE HOOCHSTRAAT

PIETER

DANIEL

STALPERT

STRAAT

SAENREDAMSTRAAT

FRANS

GERARD

DOUSTRAAT

HALS

4

NICOLAAS MAES STRAAT

VAN

FRANS

VAN

JACOB OBRECHTSTR

MAES

WOUWERMAN STRAAT

MOREELSESTR

NICOLAAS

VAN BAERLESTRAAT

JOHANNES

PIETER

ALBERT

GOVERT

CUYPSTRAAT

FLINCKSTRAAT

MIERIS

STRAAT

RUYSDAELSTRAAT

STRAAT

1e JAN STEEN STRAAT

STRAAT

HEINZE STRAAT

JACOB OBRECHT PLEIN

BARTHOLS STR

BRONCKHORSTSTRAAT

RUYSDAELSTRAAT

CORNELIS ANTHONISZ STR

BALTHASAR FLORISZSTRAAT

PIETER AERTSZSTRAAT

1e JAN V D HEIJDEN STRAAT

STRAAT

NICOLAAS

FRANS

JNIER VINKELESKADE

ROELOF HARTPLEIN

ROELOF HART STR

<<98

CEINTUURBAAN

STRAAT

5

ELHOF TSOEN

Noorder

JOH M COENEN STR

GERARD TERBORGSTR

VAN

OLLOLAAN

OLLOLAAN

REIJNIER VINKELESKADE

DANIEL DE LANGE STR

HARMONIEHOF

HARMONIEHOF

CORNELIS VAN DER LINDENSTRAAT

OSTADE

RUSTEN

BURGER

DUSARTSTRAAT

STRAAT

STRAAT

DH STR

KAREL JARDIN

Amstelkanaal

MOZARTKADE

CORNELIS TROOSTSTRAAT

CORNELIS TROOST PLEIN

LUTMASTRAAT

LIZZY ANSIGH STRAAT

EIJCK STR

ALBRECHT DÜRERSTR

N I E U W Z U I D

BEETHOVENSTRAAT

CORELLISTRAAT

APOLLO LAAN

APOLLO LAAN

BACHSTR

VEENSTR

STADIONWEG

VAN HILLIGAERTSTRAAT

PIJNACKERSTRAAT

PIENEMAN STR

PIENEMAN STR

VINCENT VAN GOGHSTRAAT

FERDINAND BOLSTRAAT

HOBBEMAKADE

STADHOUDERSKADE

D GERRIT VAN DER

E

F

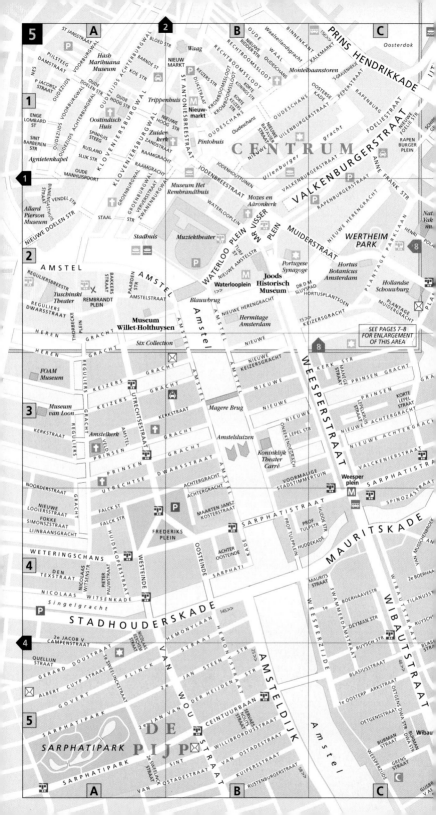

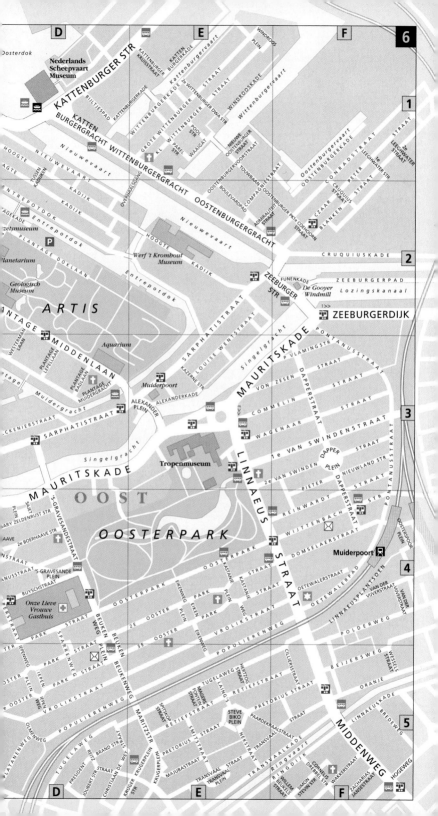

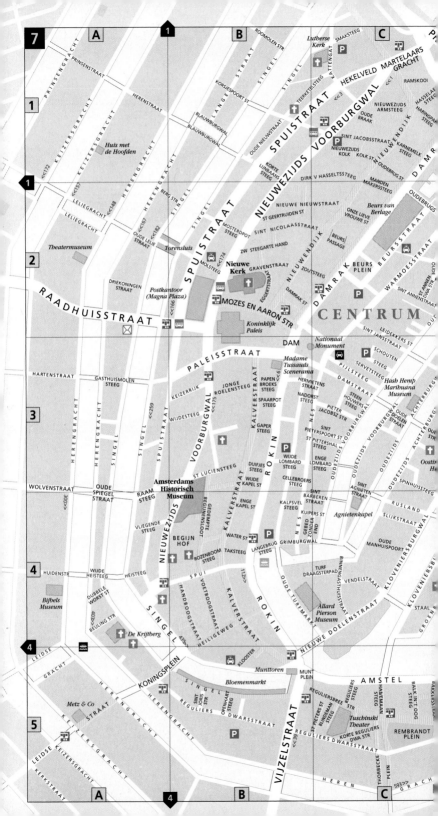

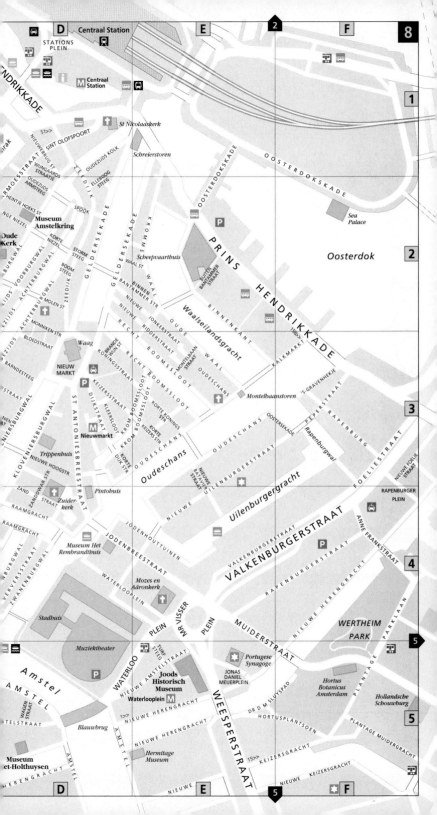

Street Finder Index

General Index

Acknowledgments

Dorling Kindersley would like to thank the following people whose help and assistance contributed to the preparation of this book.

Main Contributor

Robin Pascoe has lived in Amsterdam since the 1980s. She is a freelance journalist and writes for various Dutch newspapers. She also works for the Dutch national news agency ANP, the international development news agency IPS, and the BBC.

Christopher Catling has been visiting the Netherlands for two decades, since writing his first guide for business travellers in 1984. He has since written a further four guides to Amsterdam and the Netherlands. Besides this guide, he has contributed to four *Dorling Kindersley Travel Guides:* Florence and Tuscany, Venice and the Veneto, Great Britain and Italy.

Additional Photography

Steve Gorton, Ian O'Leary, Tony Souter, Clive Streeter, Gerard van Vuuren

Additional Illustrations

Arcana (Graham Bell), Richard Bonson, Stephen Conlin, Roy Flooks, Mick Gillah, Kevin Goold, Stephen Gyapay, Chris Orr, Ian Henderson, Philip Winton, John Woodcock

Editorial and Design

MANAGING EDITORS Vivien Crump, Helen Partington
MANAGING ART EDITOR Steve Knowlden
SENIOR EDITOR Peter Casterton
DEPUTY EDITORIAL DIRECTOR Douglas Amrine
DEPUTY ART DIRECTOR Gaye Allen
PRODUCTION David Proffit
PICTURE RESEARCH Lorna Ainger
DTP DESIGNER Siri Lowe
Johan Blom, Susan Churchill, Lucinda Cooke, Seán O'Connell, Martin Cropper, Karlien van Dam, Russell Davies, Gadi Farfour, Anthea Forlee, Fay Franklin, Robin Gauldie, Annette Jacobs, Gail Jones, Nancy Jones, David Lindsey, Sam Merrell, Rebecca Milner, Marianne Petrou, Caroline Radula-Scott, Sands Publishing Solutions, Simon Ryder, Debbie Scholes, Sadie Smith
Hotel listings: Kim Renfrew
Restaurant listings: Pip Farquharson

Fact checkers

Iris Maher, Gerard van Vuuren

Index

Hilary Bird

Cartography

Jane Hanson, Phil Rose, Jennifer Skelley
(Lovell Johns Limited)
MAP CO-ORDINATORS Michael Ellis, David Pugh

Special Assistance

Greet Tuinman, Charlotte van Beurden, Poppy

Photography Permissions

Dorling Kindersley would like to thank the following for their kind permission to photograph at their establishments: Airborne Museum, Arnhem; Allard Pierson Museum; Amstelkring Museum; Amsterdams Historisch Museum/Willet-Holthuysen Museum; Artis Zoo; Aviodrome; Beurs van Berlage; Boerhaave Museum, Leiden; Carré Theater; Concertgebouw; Coster Diamonds; Domkerk, Utrecht; Electrische Museumtramlijn; Europoort, Rotterdam; Filmmuseum; Frankendael; Anne Frankhuis; Grote Kerk, Alkmaar; Grote Kerk, Edam; Hash Marihuana Museum; Heineken Museum; Hollandse Schouwburg; Hortus Botanicus, Leiden; Joods Historisch Museum; Justitie Hall; Koninklijk Paleis; Krijtberg; Kröller-Müller Museum and National Park, Otterlo; Nederlands Scheepvaart Museum; Madurodam, Den Haag; Maritime Museum, Rotterdam; Monnickendam; Nieuwe Kerk; Nieuwe Kerk and Oude Kerk, Delft; Oude Kerk; Paleis Het Loo, Apeldoorn; Peace Palace, Den Haag; Portugese Synagoge; Prince William V Gallery, Den Haag; Prinsenhof, Leiden; Prison Gate Museum, Den Haag; RAI International Exhibition Centre; Rijksmuseum; Rijksmuseum, Utrecht; Rijksmuseum van Oudheden, Leiden; Rijksmuseum van SpeelklokTot Pierement, Utrecht; St Bavo, Haarlem; St Nicolaaskerk; SAS Hotel; Scheveningen Sea Life Centre; Sint Janskerk, Gouda; Stadhuis-Muziektheater; Stedelijk Museum; Stedelijk Molenmuseum, Leiden; Technologie Museum; Teylers Museum, Haarlem; Theater Museum; Tropenmuseum; Vakbonds Museum; Van Gogh Museum; Van Loon Museum; Verzetsmuseum; Werf 't Kromhout Museum; Westerkerk; Westfries Museum, Hoorn; Zuiderzee Museum.

27clb, 30cl, 31t, 31cb, 32cl, 33cr, 40cl, 81t, 81tr, 81cr, 81br, 82b, 83t, 83b, 90b, 94, 120cl, 120c, 120bl, 121cr; ANP PHOTO: 37tc, 37crb, 37bl.

B&U INTERNATIONAL PICTURE SERVICE: 37tl, 51cr, 53b, 101bl, 105br, 180cl, 203t; BRIDGEMAN ART LIBRARY: Christie's London *The Groote Market Haarlem with the Church of St Bavo* Gerrit Berckheyde c.1668 176t; Giraudon/ Musée Crozatier Le Puy-en-Velay France *King Louis XIV* 27br; Kremlin Museums Moscow 30bl; Private Collection *Self-Portrait Kazimir Malevich* 137cr; Stapleton Collection Delft tile 19th century 192tl; BUREAU MOMUMENTEN & ARCHEOLOGIE (BMA): 117cr.

CAMERA PRESS: Karsh of Ottawa 137tr; JEAN-LOUP CHARMET: Musée de l'Armée 28br; COLORSPORT: 36cla; CORBIS: Dave Bartruff 226cl; Owen Franken 227c.

JAN DERWIG: 99tr, 151b, 224b, 266cl, 267cr; DRENTS MUSEUM, ASSEN: 20bl.

MARY EVANS PICTURE LIBRARY: 9c, 21cra, 21bc, 23bl, 25br, 26bl, 27br, 29bl, 31br, 32cb, 32bc, 33bl, 35crb 55c, 163c; Louis Raemaehois 34bc; Jean Veber 33br; EYE UBIQUITOUS: T RAFFERTY 263br. THE FLIGHT COLLECTION: Ian Loasby 155br; FOTO NATURA: Fred Hazelhoff 205cb.

GAUGUIN RESTAURANT: 224cl; GEMEENTEARCHIEF, AMSTERDAM: 21tl, 23ca, 23cb, 24tl, 24bc, 31cr, 99tl, 99cl, 100clb, 101br, 102bl, 103tr, 103cr, 104tr, 105tr, 105cr; GEMEENTEARCHIEF, KAMPEN: 23tl; GVB: 272cl.

FRANS HALS MUSEUM, HAARLEM: 27tl, 30–31c, 178t, 178bl, 178br, 179tl, 179tr, 179bl, 179br; VANESSA HAMILTON: 97tl, 101cr, 104cl; ROBERT HARDING PICTURE LIBRARY: 58tr; Peter Scholey 116t; Adam Woolfitt 11br; HERMITAGE AMSTERDAM: Maurice Boyer 145br; HOLLANDSE HOOGTE: Adrie Mouthaan 150tr; Co de Kruijf 11br; Emile Luider 10cl; Peter Hilz 11tr; HULTON-DEUTSCH COLLECTION: 40t.

ICONOGRAFISCH BUREAU: 103tl; THE IMAGE BANK: Bernard van Berg 52cr; Fotoworld 50b; ING GROUP: 37cra; INTERNATIONAL FLOWER BULB CENTRE: 26bc, 180bc, 181tl, 181cla, 181cl, 181clb, 181bl; INTERNATIONAL INSTITUTE OF SOCIAL HISTORY: 34tl. JAMES DAVIS TRAVEL PHOTOGRAPHY: 225tr; COLLECTION JEWISH HISTORICAL MUSEUM, AMSTERDAM: *Mahzor*, Illuminated Manuscript on Parchment, Cologne area, c. 1250 64crb; Liselore Kamping 65br; *Charlotte Salomon, Self-Portrait* (1940) © Stitching Charlotte Salomon 64cl; *Hanukah Lamp* Peter Robol II, silver, Amsterdam (1753) on loan from NIHS, Amsterdam 65tl.

KONINKLIJKE TPG POST BV: 262tl, 262ca, 262cb; NPK Industrial Design 263b; KPN: 262br; KRÖLLER-MÜLLER MUSEUM: 204tl; MAURITSHUIS, DEN HAAG: 188t, 188c,

188bl, 189t, 189cr, 189br, 189bl, 193tl; MGM CINEMAS BV: 35cr; MUNICIPAL MUSEUM DE LAKENHAL, LEIDEN: 184b; MUSEUM BOIJMANS VAN BEUNINGEN, ROTTERDAM: 200–1 all; MUSEUM HET SCHIP: 151tr; MUSEUM HUIS LAMBERT VAN MEERTEN, COLLECTION RBK: 195t. NATIONAAL FIETSMUSEUM VELORAMA, NIJMEGEN: 33tl, 274tr; NETHERLANDS ARCHITECTURE INSTITUTE ARCHIVE: 98cl; Isaac Gosschalk 105cl; De Klerk 35t, 97cra; NEMO SCIENCE AND TECHNOLOGY CENTER: 150b. PICTURE BOX: Lee Auteur 156; © PHOTO RMN, PARIS: 8–9; PRENTENKABINET DER RIJKSUNIVERSITEIT, LEIDEN: 32br.

RANGE PICTURES: 28tr; REGIOPOLITIE AMSTERDAM-AMSTELLAND: 258br; MUSEUM HET REMBRANDTHUIS: 59b; RETROGRAPH ARCHIVE LTD: 267bl; Martin Breese 32tl; RIJKSMUSEUM-FOUNDATION, AMSTERDAM: 26tl, 28tl, 30cla, 40c, 42b, 130cl, 130b, 131t, 131cl, 131br, 132t, 132b, 133t, 133b; RIJKSMUSEUM PALEIS HET LOO, APELDOORN: E Boeijinga 206tr, 207tl, R Mulder 206cl; AAW Meine Jansen 206bl; R Mulder 206clb; ROYAL PALACE, AMSTERDAM: Erik Hemsmerg 27tr, 39cr, 70, 74t. SCHEEPVART MUSEUM: 19b, 28cr, 29c, 146tl, 146ca, 146cb, 147c; SCIENCE PHOTO LIBRARY/Earth Satellite Corporation: 12cl; HARRY SMITH HORTICULTURAL COLLECTION: 36b; SPAARNESTAD FOTOARCHIEF: 35c, 97tr, 99cb; STEDELIJK MUSEUM, ALKMAAR: 34c; STEDELIJK MUSEUM, AMSTERDAM: 136tr, 137tl, 137tc; © ABC/Mondriaan Estate/Holtzmann Trust, licenced by ILP 1995 *Composition in Red, Black, Blue, Yellow and Grey* Piet Mondriaan 1920 136br; © ADAGP Paris and DACS London 1995 *Portrait of Artist with Seven Fingers* Marc Chagall 1912–13 136cl; © DACS London 1995 *Red Blue Chair* Gerrit Rietveld 1918 136bl; © DACS London 1995 *Steltman Chair* Gerrit Rietveld 1963 40bl; © Jasper Johns/DACS London/VAGA New York 1995 *Untitled* Jasper Johns 1965 137cb; STEDELIJK MUSEUM DE LAKENHAL, LEIDEN: 104br; TONY STONE IMAGES: 173cl, 268bl; Kim Blaxland 181tr; David Hanson 208–9; John Lamb 2–3; Manfred Mehlig 162–3; Rohan 100t. TROPENMUSEUM: 152tr, 152ca, 152cl, 153tc, 153cl, 153br; HANS TULLENERS: 99tl, 100cr, 102c. UNIVERSITEITSBIBLIOTHEEK VAN AMSTERDAM: 96tr; VINCENT VAN GOGH (FOUNDATION), VAN GOGH MUSEUM, AMSTERDAM: 40br, 134t, 134c, 134bl, 134br, 135t, 135cr, 135crb; VZA AMBULANCE SERVICE AMSTERDAM: Ron Sitek 258cb. WESTERN AUSTRALIAN MARITIME MUSEUM: 28ca; WORLD PICTURES: 95cr. ZEFA: CPA 52b; Steenmans 53c. ZUIDERZEEMUSEUM: 171bc.

Front Endpaper: All special photography except ROYAL PALACE AMSTERDAM Erik Hemsmerg trc. JACKET: Front: DK IMAGES: Max Alexander clb; MASTERFILE: Brian Reinhart main. Back: DK IMAGES: cla, tl; Neil Setchfield clb; Tony Souter bl. Spine: DK IMAGES: Steve Gorton b; MASTERFILE: Bryan Reinhart t.

All other images © Dorling Kindersley.
For further information see: www.dkimages.com

SPECIAL EDITIONS OF DK TRAVEL GUIDES

DK Travel Guides can be purchased in bulk quantities at discounted prices for use in promotions or as premiums. We are also able to offer special editions and personalized jackets, corporate imprints, and excerpts from all of our books, tailored specifically to meet your own needs.

To find out more, please contact:
(in the United States) **SpecialSales@dk.com**
(in the UK) **Sarah.Burgess@dk.com**
(in Canada) DK Special Sales at **general@tourmaline.ca**
(in Australia) **business.development@pearson.com.au**

Phrase Book

In Emergency

Help!	**Help!**	Help
Stop!	**Stop!**	Stop
Call a doctor	**Haal een dokter**	Haal uhn **dok**-tur
Call an ambulance	**Bel een ambulance**	Bell uhn ahm-bew-**luhns**-uh
Call the police	**Roep de politie**	Roop duh poe-**leet**-see
Call the fire brigade	**Roep de brandweer**	Roop duh **brahnt**-vheer
Where is the nearest telephone?	**Waar is de dichtstbijzijnde telefoon?**	Vhaar iss duh **dikhst**-baiy-zaiyn-duh tay-luh-**foan**
Where is the nearest hospital?	**Waar is het dichtstbijzijnde ziekenhuis?**	Vhaar iss het **dikhst**-baiy-zaiyn-duh **zee**-kuh-houws

Communication Essentials

Yes	**Ja**	Yaa
No	**Nee**	Nay
Please	**Alstublieft**	Ahls-tew-**bleeft**
Thank you	**Dank u**	Dahnk-ew
Excuse me	**Pardon**	Pahr-**don**
Hello	**Hallo**	Hallo
Goodbye	**Dag**	Dahgh
Good night	**Slaap lekker**	Slaap **lek**-kah
morning	**Morgen**	**Mor**-ghuh
afternoon	**Middag**	**Mid**-dahgh
evening	**Avond**	**Ah**-vohnd
yesterday	**Gisteren**	**Ghis**-tern
today	**Vandaag**	Vahn-**daagh**
tomorrow	**Morgen**	**Mor**-ghuh
here	**Hier**	Heer
there	**Daar**	Daar
What?	**Wat?**	Vhat
When?	**Wanneer?**	Vhan-**eer**
Why?	**Waarom?**	Vhaar-**om**
Where?	**Waar?**	Vhaar
How?	**Hoe?**	Hoo

Useful Phrases

How are you?	**Hoe gaat het ermee?**	Hoo ghaat het er-**may**
Very well, thank you	**Heel goed, dank u**	Hayl ghoot, dahnk ew
How do you do?	**Hoe maakt u het?**	Hoo maakt ew het
See you soon	**Tot ziens**	Tot zeens
That's fine	**Prima**	**Pree**-mah
Where is/are?	**Waar is/zijn...**	Vhaar iss/zayn...
How far is it to...?	**Hoe ver is het naar...?**	Hoo vehr iss het naar...
How do I get to ...?	**Hoe kom ik naar...?**	Hoo kom ik naar...
Do you speak English?	**Spreekt u engels?**	Spraykt ew **eng**-uhls
I don't understand	**Ik snap het niet**	Ik snahp het neet
Could you speak slowly?	**Kunt u langzamer praten?**	Kuhnt ew **lahng**-zahmer praa-tuh
I'm sorry	**Sorry**	Sorry

Useful Words

big	**groot**	ghroaht
small	**klein**	klaiyn
hot	**warm**	vharm
cold	**koud**	khowt
good	**goed**	ghoot
bad	**slecht**	slekht
enough	**genoeg**	ghuh-**noohkh**
well	**goed**	ghoot
open	**open**	open
closed	**gesloten**	ghuh-**slow**-tuh
left	**links**	links
right	**rechts**	rekhts
straight on	**rechtdoor**	rehkht dohr
near	**dichtbij**	dikht baiy
far	**ver weg**	vehr vhekh
up	**omhoog**	om-**hoakh**
down	**naar beneden**	naar buh-**nay**-duh
early	**vroeg**	vroohkh
late	**laat**	laat
entrance	**ingang**	**in**-ghahng
exit	**uitgang**	**ouht**-ghang
toilet	**wc**	vhay say
occupied	**bezet**	buh-**zett**
free (unoccupied)	**vrij**	vraiy
free (no charge)	**gratis**	**ghraah**-tiss

Making a Telephone Call

I'd like to place a long distance call	**Ik wil graag interlokaal telefoneren**	Ik vhil ghraakh **inter**-loh-kaahl tay-luh-foe-**neh**-ruh
I'd like to call collect	**Ik wil 'collect call' bellen**	Ik vhil 'collect call' **bel**-luh
I'll try again later	**Ik probeer het later nog wel eens**	Ik pro-**beer** het laater nokh vhel ayns
Can I leave a message?	**Kunt u een boodschap doorgeven?**	Kuhnt ew uhn **boat**-skhahp **dohr**-ghay-vuh
Could you speak up a little please?	**Wilt u wat harder praten?**	Vhilt ew vhat **hahr**-der **praah**-tuh
Local call	**Lokaal gesprek**	Low-**kaahl** ghuh-**sprek**

Shopping

How much does this cost?	**Hoeveel kost dit?**	Hoo-**vayl** kost dit
I would like	**Ik wil graag**	Ik vhil ghraakh
Do you have...?	**Heeft u...?**	Hayft ew...
I'm just looking	**Ik kijk alleen even**	Ik kaiyk alleyn **ay**-vuh
Do you take credit cards?	**Neemt u credit cards aan?**	Naymt ew credit cards aan
Do you take traveller's cheques?	**Neemt u reischeques aan?**	Naymt ew wat **raiys**-sheks aan
What time do you open?	**Hoe laat gaat u open?**	Hoo laat ghaat ew opuh
What time do you close?	**Hoe laat gaat u dicht?**	Hoo laat ghaat ew dikht
This one	**Deze**	**Day**-zuh
That one	**Die**	Dee
expensive	**duur**	dewr
cheap	**goedkoop**	ghoot-**koap**
size	**maat**	maat
white	**wit**	vhit
black	**zwart**	zvhahrt
red	**rood**	roat
yellow	**geel**	ghayl
green	**groen**	ghroon
blue	**blauw**	blah-ew

Types of Shops

antique shop	**antiekwinkel**	ahn-**teek**-vhin-kul
bakery	**bakker**	**bah**-ker
bank	**bank**	bahnk
bookshop	**boekwinkel**	**book**-vhin-kul
butcher	**slager**	slaakh-er
cake shop	**banketbakkerij**	bahnk-**et**-bahk-er-aiy
cheese shop	**kaaswinkel**	**kaas**-vhin-kul
chip shop	**patatzaak**	pah-**taht**-zaak
chemist (dispensing)	**apotheek**	ah-poe-**taiyk**
delicatessen	**delicatessen**	daylee-kah-**tes**-suh
department store	**warenhuis**	**vhaar**-uh-houws
fishmonger	**viswinkel**	**viss**-vhin-kul
greengrocer	**groenteboer**	**ghroon**-tuh-boor
hairdresser	**kapper**	**kah**-per
market	**markt**	mahrkt
newsagent	**krantenwinkel**	**krahn**-tuh-vhin-kul
post office	**postkantoor**	**pohst**-kahn-tor
shoe shop	**schoenenwinkel**	**sghoo**-nuh-vhin-kul
supermarket	**supermarkt**	**sew**-per-mahrkt
tobacconist	**sigarenwinkel**	see-**ghaa**-ruh-vhin-kul
travel agent	**reisburo**	**raiys**-bew-roa

Sightseeing

art gallery	**galerie**	ghaller-ee
bus station	**busstation**	**buhs**-stah-shown
bus ticket	**strippenkaart**	**strip**-puh-kaahrt
cathedral	**kathedraal**	kah-tuh-**draal**
church	**kerk**	kehrk
closed on public holidays	**op feestdagen gesloten**	op **fayst**-daa-ghuh ghuh-**slow**-tuh
day return	**dagretour**	**dahgh**-ruh-tour
garden	**tuin**	touwn
library	**bibliotheek**	bee-bee-yo-**tayk**
museum	**museum**	mew-**zay**-uhm
railway station	**station**	stah-**shown**
return ticket	**retourtje**	ruh-**tour**-tyuh
single journey	**enkeltje**	**eng**-kuhl-tyuh
tourist information	**VVV**	fay fay fay
town hall	**stadhuis**	staht-**houws**
train	**trein**	traiyn

B O O K

Staying in a Hotel

Do you have a vacant room?	Zijn er nog kamers vrij?	Zaiyn er nokh **kaa-mers** vray
double room with double bed	een twee persoonskamer met een twee persoonsbed	uhn **tvhay**-per **soans**-kaa-mer met uhn tvhay-per-**soans** beht
twin room	een kamer met een lits-jumeaux	uhn **kaa-mer** met uhn lee-zjoo-**moh**
single room	eenpersoons-kamer	ayn-per-soans-kaa-mer
room with a bath	kamer met bad	**kaa-mer** met baht
shower	douche	doosh
porter	kruier	**krouw**-yuh
I have a reservation	Ik heb gereserveerd	Ik hehp ghuh-ray-sehr-**veert**

Eating Out

Have you got a table?	Is er een tafel vrij?	Iss ehr uhn **tah**-fuhl vraiy
I want to reserve a table	Ik wil een tafel reserveren	Ik vhil uhn **tah**-fuhl ray-sehr-**veer**-uh
The bill, please	Mag ik afrekenen	Mukh ik **ahf**-ray-kuh-nuh
I am a vegetarian	Ik ben vegetariër	Ik ben fay-ghuh-**taahr**-ee-er
waitress/waiter	meneer/merrouw	Sehr-**veer**-ster/**oh**-ber
menu	de kaart	duh kaahrt
cover charge	het couvert	het koo-**vehr**
wine list	de wijnkaart	duh **vhaiyn**-kaart
glass	het glas	het ghlahss
bottle	de fles	duh fless
knife	het mes	het mess
fork	de vork	duh fork
spoon	de lepel	duh **lay**-pul
breakfast	het ontbijt	het ont-**baiyt**
lunch	de lunch	duh lernsh
dinner	het diner	het dee-**nay**
main course	het hoofdgerecht	het **hoaft**-ghuh-rekht
starter, first course	het voorgerecht	het **vohr**-ghuh-rekht
dessert	het nagerecht	het **naa**-ghuh-rekht
dish of the day	het dagmenu	het **dahgh**-munh-ew
bar	het cafe	het kaa-**fay**
café	het eetcafe	het **ayt**-kaa-**fay**
rare	rare	'rare'
medium	medium	'medium'
well done	doorbakken	dohr-**bah**-kuh

Menu Decoder

aardappels	**aard**-uppuhls	potatoes
azijn	aah-**zaiyn**	vinegar
biefstuk	**beef**-stuhk	steak
bier, pils	beer, pilss	beer
boter	boater	butter
brood/broodje	broat/**broat**-yuh	bread/roll
cake, taart, gebak	'cake', taahrt, ghuh-**bahk**	cake, pastry
carbonade	kahr-bow-**naa**-duh	pork chop
chocola	show-coa-**laa**	chocolate
citroen	see-**troon**	lemon
cocktail	cocktail	cocktail
droog	droakh	dry
eend	aynt	duck
ei	aiy	egg
garnalen	ghahr-**naah**-luh	prawns
gebakken	ghuh-**bah**-ken	fried
gegrild	ghuh-**ghrillt**	grilled
gekookt	ghuh-**koakt**	boiled
gepocheerd	ghuh-posh-**eert**	poached
gerookt	ghuh-**roakt**	smoked
geroosterd brood	ghuh-roas-tert broat	toast
groenten	**ghroon**-tuh	vegetables
ham	hahm	ham
haring	**haa**-ring	herring
hutspot	huht-spot	hot pot
ijs	aiyss	ice, ice cream
jenever	yuh-**nay**-vhur	gin
kaas	kaas	cheese
kabeljauw	kah-buhl-**youw**	cod
kip	kip	chicken
knoflook	**knoff**-loak	garlic
koffie	coffee	coffee
kool, rode of witte	coal, **roe**-duh off **vhit**-uh	cabbage, red or white
kreeft	krayft	lobster
kroket	crow-**ket**	ragout in bread-crumbs, deep fried
lamsvlees	lahms-flayss	lamb

lekkerbekje	lek-kah-bek-yuh	fried fillet of haddock
mineraalwater	meener-**aahl**-vhaater	mineral water
mosterd	**moss**-tehrt	mustard
niet scherp	neet skehrp	mild
olie	**oh**-lee	oil
paling	**paa**-ling	eel
pannenkoek	**pah**-nuh-kook	pancake
patat frites	pah-**taht** freet	chips
peper	**pay**-per	pepper
poffertjes	**poffer**-tyuhs	tiny buckwheat pancakes
rijst	raiyst	rice
rijsttafel	**raiys**-tah-ful	Indonesian meal
rode wijn	**roe**-duh vhaiyn	red wine
rookworst	**roak**-vhorst	smoked sausage
rundvlees	**ruhnt**-flayss	beef
saus	souwss	sauce
schaaldieren	**skaahl**-deeh-ruh	shellfish
scherp	skehrp	hot (spicy)
schol	sghol	plaice
soep	soup	soup
stamppot	**stahm**-pot	sausage stew
suiker	**souw**-ker	sugar
thee	tay	tea
tosti	**toss**-tee	cheese on toast
uien	**ouw**-yuh	onions
uitsmijter	**ouht**-smaiy-ter	fried egg on bread with ham
varkensvlees	**vahr**-kuhns-flayss	pork
vers fruit	fehrss frouwt	fresh fruit
verse jus	**vehr**-suh zjhew	fresh orange juice
vis	fiss	fish/seafood
vlees	flayss	meat
water	**vhaa**-ter	water
witte wijn	**vhih**-tuh vhaiyn	white wine
worst	vhorst	sausage
zout	zouwt	salt

Numbers

1	een	ayn
2	twee	tvhay
3	drie	dree
4	vier	feer
5	vijf	faiyf
6	zes	zess
7	zeven	**zay**-vuh
8	acht	ahkht
9	negen	**nay**-guh
10	tien	teen
11	elf	elf
12	twaalf	tvhaalf
13	dertien	**dehr**-teen
14	veertien	**feer**-teen
15	vijftien	**faiyf**-teen
16	zestien	**zess**-teen
17	zeventien	**zayvuh**-teen
18	achttien	**ahkh**-teen
19	negentien	**nay**-ghuh-teen
20	twintig	**tvhin**-tukh
21	eenentwintig	**aynuh**-tvhin-tukh
30	dertig	**dehr**-tukh
40	veertig	**feer**-tukh
50	vijftig	**faiyf**-tukh
60	zestig	**zess**-tukh
70	zeventig	**zay**-vuh-tukh
80	tachtig	**tahkh**-tukh
90	negentig	**nayguh**-tukh
100	honderd	**hohn**-durt
1000	duizend	**douw**-zuhnt
1,000,000	miljoen	mill-**yoon**

Time

one minute	een minuut	uhn meen-**ewt**
one hour	een uur	uhn ewr
half an hour	een half uur	uhn hahlf ewr
half past one	half twee	hahlf tvhay
a day	een dag	uhn dahgh
a week	een week	uhn vhayk
a month	een maand	uhn maant
a year	een jaar	uhn jaar
Monday	maandag	**maan**-dahgh
Tuesday	dinsdag	**dins**-dahgh
Wednesday	woensdag	**vhoons**-dahgh
Thursday	donderdag	**donder**-dahgh
Friday	vrijdag	**vraiy**-dahgh
Saturday	zaterdag	**zaater**-dahgh
Sunday	zondag	**zon**-dahgh

FOR PEACE OF MIND ABROAD
we've got it covered **wherever you are**

For an **instant quote** on quality worldwide travel insurance visit **www.dk.com/travel-insurance** or call:

UK 0800 258 5363
USA 1 800 749 4922 (Toll Free)
Spain 900 997 149
Australia 1300 669 999
New Zealand 0800 55 99 11
Canada www.dk.com/travel-insurance
Worldwide +44 870 894 0001

Cover provided to residents of over 46 countries for virtually every type of trip: Single, Annual Multi-Trip and Long Stay

Please quote our ref: Eyewitness Travel Guides

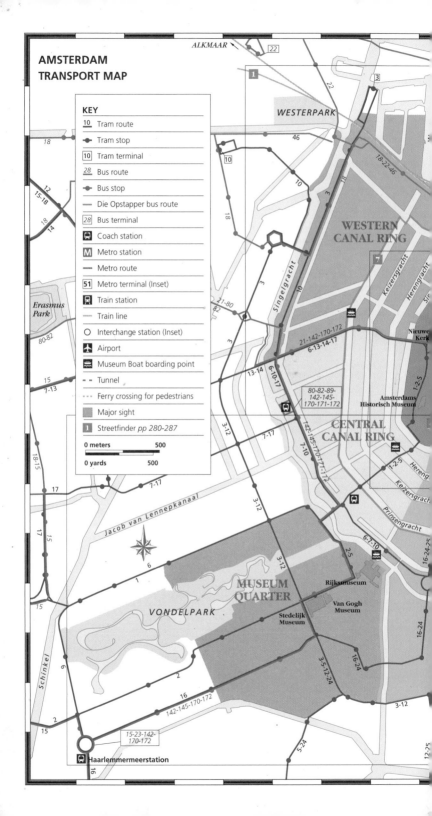

AMSTERDAM
TRANSPORT MAP

KEY

10	Tram route
•	Tram stop
10	Tram terminal
28	Bus route
•	Bus stop
—	Die Opstapper bus route
28	Bus terminal
🚌	Coach station
M	Metro station
—	Metro route
51	Metro terminal (Inset)
🚆	Train station
—	Train line
O	Interchange station (Inset)
✈	Airport
🚢	Museum Boat boarding point
– –	Tunnel
⋯	Ferry crossing for pedestrians
▨	Major sight
1	Streetfinder pp 280–287

0 meters	500
0 yards	500

ALKMAAR

WESTERPARK

WESTERN
CANAL RING

Singelgracht

Keizersgracht

Herengracht

Nieuwe
Kerk

Amsterdams
Historisch Museum

CENTRAL
CANAL RING

Herengracht

Keizersgracht

Prinsengracht

Erasmus
Park

Jacob van Lennepkanaal

MUSEUM
QUARTER

VONDELPARK

Rijksmuseum

Van Gogh
Museum

Stedelijk
Museum

Schinkel

Haarlemmermeerstation